Unlikely Angel

WOMEN COMPOSERS

The short, readable books in the Women Composers series introduce significant women composers to students and general readers and provide a convenient reference for performers and scholars.

Series books treat the broadest range of women composers, combining concise biographical information with a comprehensive survey of works.

A list of books in the series appears at the end of this book.

Unlikely Angel

THE SONGS OF
DOLLY PARTON

LYDIA R. HAMESSLEY

Foreword by Steve Buckingham

**UNIVERSITY OF
ILLINOIS PRESS**
Urbana, Chicago, and Springfield

Lyrics by Dolly Parton reproduced by permission of Velvet Apple Music.

Publication supported by grants from the AMS 75 PAYS Endowment of the American Musicological Society and the Judith McCulloh Endowment for American Music.

Library of Congress Cataloging-in-Publication Data
Names: Hamessley, Lydia, author.
Title: Unlikely angel: the songs of Dolly Parton / Lydia R.
    Hamessley; foreword by Steve Buckingham.
Description: Urbana: University of Illinois Press, 2020. | Series:
    Women composers | Includes bibliographical references
    and index.
Identifiers: LCCN 2020020804 (print) | LCCN 2020020805
    (ebook) | ISBN 9780252043529 (cloth) | ISBN 9780252085420
    (paperback) | ISBN 9780252052408 (ebook)
Subjects: LCSH: Parton, Dolly—Criticism and interpretation. |
    Country music—History and criticism.
Classification: LCC ML420.P28 H36 2020 (print) | LCC ML420.
    P28 (ebook) | DDC 782.42164092 [B]—dc23
LC record available at https://lccn.loc.gov/2020020804
LC ebook record available at https://lccn.loc.gov/
    2020020805

For Sam

"The music in my heart I bore,
Long after it was heard no more."
The Solitary Reaper, *William Wordsworth*

Contents

Foreword

A ccording to *All Music Guide* I have produced twenty albums with Dolly Parton. More important to me is the fact that Dolly and I have been friends since 1989. When Professor Lydia Hamessley contacted me about a book she was writing on Dolly I was initially a bit skeptical. Over the decades I have been asked to do countless interviews for newspapers, documentaries, magazines and books about Dolly. I did do some but declined most.

However, Professor Hamessley explained that she wanted to concentrate on Dolly Parton the songwriter, musician and artist. This certainly struck a note with me since most articles about Dolly deal with her appearance, larger than life personality and, very often, rumors. I was extremely interested to relate some of my musical experiences and a fascinating journey with one of the most incredibly talented artists in the world.

After several phone conversations with Professor Hamessley, I spoke to Dolly about this book and she wholeheartedly embraced the project saying, "We should do anything we can to help her with this." Professor Hamessley submitted a list of questions that were impressive in their thoroughness. Typically, Dolly gave the questions much thought and then, in one evening, recorded all of her responses. I'm sure the readers of this book will find some of Dolly's answers to be fascinating.

Over the decades Dolly and I sometimes talked about how the "cartoon" she had created (her word, not mine) often overshadowed her talent as a songwriter and musician. We always strove to put the music first. This was especially true in

1999 and 2000 when we recorded the albums *The Grass Is Blue* and *Little Sparrow*. Both projects featured sparse, acoustic-based Bluegrass/Mountain music where there was "no place to hide" as a vocalist. I assembled "God's Bluegrass Band," as Dolly called the musicians surrounding her. Simply put, they were the best in the business and everyone rose to the occasion. For both albums all the tracks were recorded in less than two days each. The spontaneity and talent on display were electrifying as Dolly's vocals pushed the musicians and their playing drove her. Critics were overwhelmingly positive in their reviews and both albums won Grammys: *The Grass Is Blue* for Best Bluegrass Album and "Shine" from the *Little Sparrow* album for Best Female Country Vocal Performance. Her music took precedence over the image.

Professor Lydia Hamessley has worked for many years to capture behind-the-scenes stories describing Dolly's influences, songwriting and musicality. I believe her amazingly detailed and researched book will open many eyes to one of the most iconic artists in history.

Make no mistake, Dolly Parton is a phenomenally gifted songwriter who never runs out of ideas. Just ask her peers. And don't let the long fingernails fool you! She is extremely adept on guitar, banjo, dulcimer and autoharp. She has a great rhythm or "lick" with her right hand. Just ask the world class musicians who have played with her. As a singer, she has never failed to astound all of us who have worked with her. Just ask another gifted vocalist such as Alison Krauss.

Finally, Dolly IS one of the kindest and most considerate people in a tough, demanding and often cynical business. Just ask me.

Steve Buckingham
Nashville, Tennessee /
Virginia Beach, Virginia

Preface and Acknowledgments

"Who doesn't love Dolly Parton? Someone
without a soul, that's who."

My first memories of Dolly Parton are from my childhood.[1] My parents always watched *The Porter Wagoner Show*, and although I did not pay much attention to the program, I noticed Dolly. She was the "girl singer" with the big wigs and flashy clothes. In the mid-1970s, I loved the song "Jolene," and, in the 1980s, I got to know Dolly better through her delightful performances in *9 to 5* and *Steel Magnolias*. Later, in the 1990s, it was impossible not to know the song "I Will Always Love You." When I eventually discovered that Dolly wrote the song, I immediately sought out her recording and was dumbstruck at how poignant and heartbreakingly beautiful it was. On a visit to the Country Music Hall of Fame, I saw one of her polyester pantsuits on a Dolly-proportioned mannequin and was astonished at how small she was. *White Limozeen* was the first Dolly album I bought, and when she released *The Grass Is Blue* I was thrilled. In 2016, I could not resist having my picture taken with a life-size cardboard Dolly at a welcome stop as I entered Tennessee on IH-81 on my way to Dollywood.

When Laurie Matheson, director of the University of Illinois Press, invited me to write a book on Dolly, I asked my friend and fellow musicologist Suzanne Cusick for her advice, and she said, "If I'd been asked to write a book on Dolly, I'd jump on that like a duck on a June bug." So I began my deeply rewarding, in-depth exploration of Dolly's music. When I told students in my country

FIGURE O.I. The author with Dolly Parton cardboard image at I-81 Welcome Center (Bristol/Sullivan County, Tennessee, July 17, 2016).

music history course that I was writing this book, one of them asked, "Does that mean you have to listen to all of Dolly's albums?" I expect they viewed such a project as an endless, tedious succession of term papers, rather than the enjoyable adventure it has been. My reply to the student: "It means I *get* to listen to all of her albums." And attend her concerts, watch her films, read her books, visit Dollywood, and read and listen to countless interviews with Dolly.

Two of Dolly's comments have been foundational for my work and analyses of her songs. First, "I can't stop writing songs. That's what I mean—I am so serious. If people really knew how serious I was about my music."[2] Second, when Dolly set out on her solo career she asserted, "I'm saying a lot more in my songs than a lot of people may know. Even the simplest of my songs, I've got really deep feelings inside of them."[3]

In her reflection on being a Dolly fan, classicist Helen Morales grapples with the "anxiety that attaches to confessing the objects of our admiration. It is exposing. It leaves you open to criticism.... Your admiration for a celebrity can invite mockery.... However, being a fan of Dolly Parton has enriched my life. I don't see why I should be ashamed to admit that."[4] My life, too, has been enriched by my decade-long immersion in Dolly's music. I chose the title of the book, *Unlikely Angel*, to highlight a beautiful and little-known song of Dolly's, to recognize the way that many of her fans think of her, and to capture the improbability of Dolly's success given her humble beginnings. It is also an acknowledgment of the gift she and this project have been in my life.

I start, then, by thanking Dolly Parton for her generosity in answering a long list of questions I submitted to her. She provided a thoughtful and wonderfully detailed account of her family history and earliest musical memories. My work greatly benefited by her openness in speaking about her process as a songwriter and the beautiful way she tells her story. Dolly's remarks about her connection to her mountain heritage and the power of her music were astute and incisive. I am grateful for the time she spent to record her answers on cassette tape so that I could hear her remarks—a lovely bonus! Her enthusiasm and support for this project have made a world of difference, and I cannot thank her enough.

Dolly was made aware of my project by Steve Buckingham, one of her producers and dear friends. Initially, I had contacted Steve for an interview about the albums he produced with her, and his insights and stories about his work with Dolly were invaluable. Soon thereafter, he got in touch with Dolly and made it possible for me to submit my questions to her. Steve also paved the way for many other tasks, in particular helping me make contacts regarding lyrics and photo permissions, which Dolly graciously granted. Steve and I have shared many more conversations about Dolly's music, and my students have enjoyed and learned from his visits to Hamilton College. I am very grateful for his tremendous generosity and keen interest in the book.

I am profoundly grateful to Laurie Matheson for her confidence in me as well as her patience, unflagging encouragement, and gentle guidance throughout the whole process. I thank Julie Laut, also of the University of Illinois Press, for her help in shaping the final manuscript as well as Nancy Albright for her excellent copyediting. I also thank the anonymous readers of the manuscript for their suggestions, and, in particular, Ellen Wright for her comments and encouragement. I attended two Writing Retreats sponsored by the Performance/History Working Group of the Central New York Humanities Corridor. Thanks to all the participants, organizers Mary Simonson and Christian DuComb, and the two facilitators, Amy Holzapfel and Elise Morrison, for their helpful feedback.

I am grateful to Hamilton College and the Dean of Faculty for travel and research support and the Interlibrary Loan staff and Reference Librarians at Burke Library, especially Lynn Mayo, Kristin Strohmeyer, and Alexandra Wohnsen, who tracked down many elusive items, often on their own time. Anne Debraggio, Director of the Kirkland Town Library, was a help as well. Thanks go to Jason Davis, editor, *The Mountain Press*, Sevier County, Tennessee, for sharing an article that was otherwise unavailable.

I am grateful for my supportive colleagues in the Music Department: Heather Buchman, Ryan Carter, Rob Hopkins, Rob Kolb, Mike Woods, and the late Sam Pellman who helped along the way. I am also thankful for the opportunities I have had to present my work on Dolly at various conferences: Feminist Theory and Music, the Society for American Music, and the American Musicological Society. I have benefited by conversations with many colleagues. Stephanie Vander Wel and I have enjoyed many happy hours discussing women in country music. Ron Pen has always sent his good cheer and wisdom my way when we have talked about Dolly and Appalachian music. Francis Whately and I shared a commitment to focusing on Dolly's music and her songwriting craft in our work.

My friends have supported my work by listening to my never-ending litany of Dolly stories, sending me news articles about her that I might have missed, attending my talks on Dolly, and making sure I have Dolly souvenirs: John Adams, Sheila Kay Adams, Jan Bailey, Jay Bloom, Katheryn Doran, Emily Eastwood, Ella Gant, Aimee Germain, Susan Jarosi, Petie Kristoph, Laura Lingo, Miriam Moore, Jim Mueller, Quincy Newell, Margo Okazawa-Rey, Deborah Pokinski, Frank Sciacca, Miriam Simmons, Kathryn Stenstrom, Pavitra Sundar, and Liz Wood. Others rolled up their sleeves and generously read segments of the book along the way. I cannot thank them enough for their time and help; they each made a lasting difference in the final outcome: Suzanne Cusick, Rachel Hamessley, Rob Hopkins, Daryl Hultberg, Amber Mueller, and Nancy Rabinowitz. In particular, I thank Marianne Janack for our weekly writing sessions early in the project; Peter Rabinowitz for offering beneficial feedback on early drafts of the full manuscript and encouraging me to keep plugging; Martha Mockus for her incisive reading of much later drafts with a keen eye for ideas I could explore further; Rosalind Miles and Robin Cross for their hospitality and great conversations about writing around their kitchen table at Wit's End in Wormley, England.

My family has been a wonderful support: my niece Jordan Hamessley, her husband Matt London, and their daughter Eleanor Rose London. My sister, Rachel Hamessley, and I share a way of thinking about music, even as we travel in different musical worlds, and I have been buoyed by her excitement about this project. My father Scotty Hamessley always encouraged me to aim high, and I have enjoyed his partner Geraldine Brown's enthusiasm for my work. My late mother, Mary Lou Hamessley, who first taught me about writing, is often in my thoughts as I parse sentences and search for just the right word.

Three people have made significant, indelible contributions to the project. Kristina Berg was a sustaining presence. The wisdom she shared with me infuses much of the book as well as my life. Heather Buchman was always on call to lend her "good ears" when I needed them, especially (but not only) when it came to hearing and understanding some of the trickier complexities in Dolly's music. Mary Volk has, to a great extent, been a partner with me in this endeavor, and I owe her many thanks. She read and commented extensively on at least three versions of the full manuscript, and she was always happy to listen to me talk about Dolly and her music. Her insatiable curiosity led us to many avenues of thought that I later developed and included in the book. She and I were together in the audience in St. Paul, Minnesota when Dolly made an impromptu appearance to introduce a staged reading of her musical, *Dolly Parton's Smoky Mountain Christmas Carol.* It was terrific to share that experience with someone else equally bowled over by Dolly's powerful presence.

Finally, I want to acknowledge Sam Pellman. Sam hired me over thirty years ago at Hamilton College, and he was the best mentor, colleague, and friend one could hope for. He was my personal IT support guy, a whiz at helping me figure out obscure musical moments and instruments in Dolly's music, and a wonderfully zany goofball who always made me smile. In many ways I owe my career to Sam. He believed in this book from the beginning, and I wish he had lived to see it published.

Unlikely Angel

Introduction

Hello, I'm Dolly

"Music was a freedom."

In the spring of 1964, Dolly Parton traveled to New York City with her high school senior class.[1] That January the hit musical *Hello, Dolly!* had opened on Broadway, three days before Dolly's eighteenth birthday, and Manhattan was plastered with billboards shouting "Hello, Dolly!" Dolly recalled, "It was all over the cabs, and the signs, and I said, 'They must have been waitin' for me!'"[2] Just three years later, Dolly's first solo album was released. It was titled *Hello, I'm Dolly*.

Although Dolly had previously contributed six songs to a tribute album, *Hits Made Famous by Country Queens* (1963), and recorded several singles, *Hello, I'm Dolly* was her introduction to a wider audience. Two of the album's songs were hits: "Dumb Blonde," by Curly Putman, and Dolly's own "Something Fishy." Dolly's photo on the album cover is a closeup of her face. Here is a self-assured young woman dressed conservatively in a muted orange turtleneck and white jacket. Her soon-to-be notorious figure is not pictured. Wearing very little makeup and sporting a hairdo that would not have seemed extravagant at the time, Dolly looks directly at us with the confident, pleasant look of someone who would walk right up to a stranger and introduce herself: "Hello, I'm Dolly." On the album's back cover, Dolly's producer, Fred Foster, wrote a fanciful introduction to Dolly, describing her as a reincarnated soul who takes in her new surroundings with a wisdom beyond her twenty-one years: "All the same things put together made something

FIGURE I.2. *Hello, I'm Dolly* album front cover, 1967.

different this time." She is "untouched somehow by all this new aroundness . . . not quite aloof, not quite yielding . . . just observing, just enjoying." His most compelling remark—Dolly is "a different breeze a-blowin'."[3]

What was so different about Dolly? It was not that she was a woman singer in the male-dominated country music industry. Kitty Wells, Loretta Lynn, and Tammy Wynette were also on the scene, and Patsy Cline's presence was still felt. And it was not yet her exaggerated image that has come to define her. No—the difference was that Dolly was a prolific and serious songwriter. Wells, Wynette, and Cline wrote very few to none of their own songs, and Lynn wrote significantly fewer than Dolly. For her debut album, Dolly had written ten of its twelve songs, and three were already hits by other artists when it was released. Here was a young woman who was writing and singing her own stories. That was different.

Since she said, "Hello, I'm Dolly," I call her Dolly, regardless of which role (real-world person, songwriter, businesswoman, singer, actress, character in a song) she is inhabiting.[4] Dolly is the persona she presents to the world, suggesting it is the "real" Dolly Parton as well. As she explained, "it's not like the image is separate from me."[5] Using her first name also reflects the personal connection her fans feel with her.

In talking with people while writing this book, I witnessed how widely admired she is. Faces light up at the mention of her name, and people rave about her, often breaking into song—usually "Jolene" or "9 to 5." They repeat some of Dolly's pithiest witticisms, laughing as if hearing her wisecracks for the first time. Some know a little about her philanthropy, primarily her literacy program for children, the Imagination Library. A few still remember her days on *The Porter Wagoner Show* in the late 1960s and early 1970s. Dolly's fans, as well as casual tourists (and myself), make pilgrimages to her hometown of Sevierville to have their picture taken with her statue at the courthouse. Many more visit Dollywood to experience her evanescent presence there, and everyone is tickled to learn I "had" to visit her theme park—three times—as part of my research. A few of us even follow sketchy directions into the mountains beyond Dollywood looking for her Locust Ridge home located thirteen miles away—about a 30-minute drive.[6] Many are curious about Dolly's personal life, which they know little about aside from her impoverished Appalachian upbringing.

What always surprises people the most is the extent to which Dolly is a songwriter. "She has written over 3,000 songs?" "And over 450 have been recorded?" Jaws drop at those figures. Many folks are still astonished to learn Dolly wrote "I Will Always Love You" and that her 1974 recording of the song was a #1 hit on *Billboard's* Hot Country Songs chart.[7] Known, or at least recognized, by millions of people, Dolly is a cultural icon. But aside from die-hard Dolly fans and aficionados, most have only a passing knowledge of Dolly as a deeply skilled, sensitive songwriter, and few realize the scope of her catalogue of songs.

It is no wonder Dolly's identity and work as a songwriter is unknown to many people. While she has always attracted extensive media attention, very little focus has been on her songwriting. Writing about Dolly ranges from journalistic articles in women's magazines too numerous to count—with their stories of her "elusive" husband Carl Dean and her figure, hair, and makeup—to sophisticated academic work that treats Dolly's image as a text itself. Some writers do consider Dolly's song lyrics, but usually pay little attention to the music even though Dolly consistently says she wants to be known as a songwriter first, and that writing songs is central to her identity and sense of well-being: "I am first and foremost a songwriter. I've been writing since I was seven—serious songs. Love and my family and writing about those days keeps me sane in an insane world."[8]

As a young songwriter in Nashville, Dolly knew she needed to stand out, and she suggests in numerous interviews that her exaggerated look was her way to do that. It began as a humorous gimmick intended to get attention that she hoped to turn to her songwriting. The first part of her plan succeeded. Unfortunately, though, her appearance has more often eclipsed the fact that she is a productive and gifted songwriter. As Dolly said, "People know I write songs, but I doubt they know how serious I am about it."[9] I believe the time is ripe, even overdue, to turn our attention to Dolly's songs. Her professional songwriting career has reached its 60-year mark, including 46 solo studio albums and 13 studio albums with Porter Wagoner. Many of her songs are known and loved by listeners who are not aware Dolly was their composer. Yet her body of work remains unexamined.

My approach is to focus on Dolly's songs, not image. Dolly's mountain music heritage and its deep influence on her music resonates with my own interests as a clawhammer banjo player and scholar of Southern Appalachian music, and this element of her musical practice is a continuous thread throughout my analyses. Dolly covers a lot of ground in her songs: love, heartbreak, death, inspiration, social injustices, poverty. In each case, from the light-hearted to the tragic, Dolly writes music on which her stories ride (to adapt a phrase of Paul Green's). I want to shine a light on the range and depth of her songs from my perspective as a musicologist, foregrounding the nuances of Dolly's music—her vocabulary of melody, harmony, and form.

I do not suggest Dolly thought consciously about all the elements I analyze in her music. She has an instinctive and emotional, not theoretical, approach to songwriting. But musical analysis identifies and clarifies her intuitive musical choices, explains their effects, and reveals Dolly's distinctive compositional voice, which touches millions of people. I once said to a class of non–music majors, I have the best job in the world: I get to listen to wonderful music and share it with them, teaching them about it so they can understand and enjoy it more deeply. That is my aim for this book. I am writing for anyone who wants to know more about Dolly's music, regardless of musical background.

This book is not a biography. Information about Dolly's life is available in numerous biographies, articles, documentaries, interviews, and her autobiography, all of which chronicle the details of her childhood, family, and career. I do, however, incorporate select details of Dolly's biography and Dolly's own comments about her life throughout the book in conjunction with my analyses of the songs—when this information illuminates our understanding of a song, provides insight into Dolly's use of a particular type of lyric or melody, or clarifies her approach to a subject or situation. Nonetheless, some may find it helpful to have a concise overview of her career, so I have provided a timeline of notable events, albums, and awards which readers may consult in Appendix B.

My most challenging task in writing about Dolly's songs was how to deal with her extensive catalogue. I illustrate her body of work through representative examples that I hope will lead readers to explore songs I do not include. One might expect I will move through her artistic work chronologically, starting with her early country songs and then her pop crossover songs, her return to country, her bluegrass phase, and into the present. Dolly's career could be traced through such a chronology. But, of course, a life is not a linear trajectory. Each of the stages, perhaps a better word is *facets*, of Dolly's musical life is a blend of styles. A mountain-type ballad appears on a country music album; a folksy song about the beauty of God's creation nestles in an album of pop crossover hits; a sexy disco number with electronic sound effects is followed by an acoustic guitar lead-in to a country song about busking for spare change. Dolly's musical work is variegated and folds back on itself, with all the melodic, harmonic, textual, and thematic overlaps that image brings. To present her body of work chronologically would miss a lot of these overlaps and nuances that characterize her songwriting. It is this connection between and among songs from across all facets of her musical life that I want to highlight, so I examine her songs by topic. Some I consider in detail, others are mentioned as songs orbiting a particular melodic or lyrical trope.

In the first section, I examine Dolly's songs from several foundational perspectives. After a sketch of her musical life in Chapter One, I examine Dolly's process as a composer in Chapter Two, foregrounding "Coat of Many Colors." In Chapter Three, I demonstrate that much of Dolly's music reveals a deep connection to her Appalachian heritage. As she often says, "my first and true love is that old mountain music. It's natural to me. I personally think I sing it better than anything else that I sing."[10] Not all of her songs contain elements of mountain music, but a large number do. I consider Dolly's mountain music heritage from her childhood, her concept album *My Tennessee Mountain Home*, elements of mountain music in her songs, and her bluegrass trilogy of albums. In Chapter Four, I extend my study of Dolly's mountain music heritage by considering two questions. How have critics characterized Dolly's songs and her voice as distinctively Appalachian? And how has Dolly understood her musical heritage in relation to her work as a songwriter?

In the second section, I study Dolly's songs by their subject. She once described her songs in this way: "We are all made up of the same things . . . a heart, a soul, and feelings. We want to be important and noticed, to be pleased and satisfied. We all have mothers and daddies and family problems. A lot of songs I write about, talk about just ordinary things. And I think the basic simplicity of my music attracts a lot of people. It's simple, yet it says a lot."[11] My list of topics may seem ordinary, but within each chapter I reveal connections between songs, cultural tropes, and Dolly's life experiences and beliefs that are far from simple.

I begin, in Chapter Five, with Dolly's songs about love, which include some of her most well-known hits, "I Will Always Love You" and "Jolene." I juxtapose her fairy-tale love songs with the pragmatic way Dolly has shaped her personal life, and I view her songs in the context of Dolly's wide-ranging ideas about love and independence. Chapter Six considers her songs about women's lives and struggles, and I place them in relief with Dolly's comments on feminism, trash identity, and her hypersexualized image. In Chapter Seven, I turn to Dolly's dark, tragic songs and explore their models. I offer a respite from all that gloom and anguish with a look at her uplifting, spiritual, and inspirational songs in Chapter Eight where I examine Dolly's complex relationship to faith and the way she conveys ecstasy in her music. The book's final chapter offers concluding remarks and acknowledges that Dolly's work is not finished.

This organizational principle means some songs appear in multiple chapters in the book. I want to demonstrate how intertwined her music is by encountering and reencountering Dolly's melodies, lyrics, and ideas in a variety of contexts as different stories and elements of the same song emerge—and families of tunes and lyrics materialize. Dolly is gifted at transforming specific feelings and circumstances into songs that lend themselves to multiple readings. Accordingly, there are various perspectives from which to interpret her songs, resulting in a non-singular reading of them.

I strongly recommend listening to the songs when they are presented in the text. Recordings of them, as well as their full lyrics, are readily available, and my discussion relies on readers hearing Dolly sing them. (All the songs mentioned in the book, along with their albums and dates, may be found in Appendix A.) As an aid to understanding some of the songs I analyze in depth, I occasionally provide a listening outline as a guide. In a small number of my analyses, I also include musical examples, which are useful as graphs even for those who do not read music. The versions of the songs I discuss are those from the albums on which they were first released, unless I note otherwise. Subsequent performances of Dolly's will differ from the original version and are also of interest. But her legacy will be left in her studio recordings, which I treat as the prototype.

Dolly is a master of language—in her lyrics and in conversation. So I draw on Dolly's own comments throughout my analyses, and I quote her liberally. I want readers to hear her voice directly because much of her meaning is linked to the way she speaks. Inevitably, there are ambiguities and contradictions in what Dolly says about her life and her songs. She has been interviewed thousands of times, and she has had a lot to say about her process and journey. While most threads remain constant, some of her ideas and stories shift depending on the date and context of her comments. When stories deviate, as with, for example, Dolly's backstory for "Coat of Many Colors," these variations are often the fissures that reveal a deeper truth about a song or an event—when the surface details change and one can ascertain what remains consistent throughout the telling. It is as if Dolly's memories and ideas are held in a deck of cards. Often there are multiple cards for the same story, and her genius is that she plays the appropriate card at the right time and place.

Dolly consistently quips that although she looks completely artificial, she is real on the inside, where it counts. She sings this paradox in "Backwoods Barbie": "Don't let these false eyelashes lead you to believe/That I'm as shallow as I look, 'cause I run true and deep." I would put her dichotomy this way: Dolly has a core set of values that guides her life and informs her songwriting, and these beliefs are genuine regardless of how she fashions her appearance. I start with the premise that Dolly's songs are the primary way she expresses her core beliefs, and my analyses reveal the web of resonances between Dolly's songs and her ideas. Her songs illuminate what she is most moved by. They reveal what she values in relationships, what she thinks about situations and systems of injustice, and the nature of her spiritual life as expressed in both sacred and secular realms.

Because Dolly so thoroughly blurs the distinction between her artificial persona and her real-world identity, people often assume her songs are autobiographical. Some songs are drawn from Dolly's personal experiences, as she says about "Yellow Roses": "There's some truth in that song too. In a way, it was kind of based on a true story about someone I knew that loved yellow roses and they had given me a yellow rose and the relationship had gone sour. That song is sad, ain't it?"[12] But Dolly explains she is also frequently inspired by other people's stories: "A lot of these songs were not about me or about Carl. It was about relationships in general. I wrote a lot about people, friends, family that have gone through things that I know they don't express it, or know how to, or couldn't get away with it. So I write for them. So I drew a lot of inspiration for some of these songs from . . . other folks as well."[13]

In this extended quote, Dolly discusses her emotional responses to different stories that inspire her songs. Whether personal to her or not, she embodies the feelings:

> I'm one of those people that gets so involved in what I'm writing because I feel it. Everything is very personal to me and I write about everything I feel. Or sometimes I write about something I've seen other people go through, people that I care deeply about. So I feel their sorrow too. A lot of times when I write, boy, I'll just be sitting there with tears rolling down my face. I get caught up in the emotion of it myself. So sometimes things will just start coming, almost like it's just channeling through me, and it's almost like I'm watching the movie or hearing the song myself. And it hits me and oh, I'll just be writing and a-crying and a-singing [laughs]. There was another song I wrote called "There's No Good Way of Saying Good-bye," and oh, I just slung snot all over that [laughs]. I love to write, because it's almost like going on an emotional journey every time I do it, whether I'm writing happy or sad. If I'm writing happy songs, I get really happy and really joyful with it, and if I'm writing a sad one, I just get down.[14]

Here, Dolly not only describes her process and the way she feels when writing songs, but she gets caught up in reliving those experiences, and her rising excitement is palpable. She begins with straightforward statements and then shifts from her dispassionate description to reenact the process. At the end, when she says her songwriting takes her on an emotional journey, it is clear she just relived that journey through her story about the process. What she reveals through the rhythm of her language here, as well as her hilariously graphic comment about the results of her crying, is a case in point of why I often choose to quote her.

Dolly is often viewed by others in a variety of dualities: she is not only a savvy businesswoman and superstar, she is also a mountain girl at heart. She is a country singer who made it big in the pop world. She writes uplifting, happy songs that are almost too cheery and answers them with devastating songs about dead children or suicide. She embodies what one critic called her "trademark blend of fragility and strength."[15] But Dolly has adopted three winged avatars for herself: the sparrow for vulnerability, the eagle for strength, and, most important, the butterfly for love and transcendent freedom. Dolly draws on these creatures in a number of her songs, and each has a signature song: "Little Sparrow," "Eagle When She Flies," in which she contrasts the eagle with the sparrow, and "Love Is Like a Butterfly." The butterfly and the eagle are prominently on display at

FIGURE 1.2. Dollywood sign at Dollywood (Pigeon Forge, Tennessee, July 13, 2018). Photo: Lydia Hamessley.

FIGURE 1.3. Eagle statue near Wild Eagle rollercoaster at Dollywood (Pigeon Forge, Tennessee, July 14, 2018). Photo: Lydia Hamessley.

Dollywood. The butterfly forms the *W* in the logo for Dollywood, which is also home to an eagle sanctuary and the magnificent Wild Eagle rollercoaster that soars twenty-one stories above the park.

Dolly said she put wings on her dreams to become a star—without wings, she says, you only have wishes. As a child, Dolly wanted the freedom to follow her dream of being a star: "I was always fascinated by things that flew, especially hummingbirds and butterflies. Maybe it was because I envied the freedom they had. To me, a hummingbird seemed to have the power to buzz right out of the holler, right across Locust Ridge and out into the real world."[16] Dolly's life has been marked by this same desire for the freedom to have a career writing and performing her own songs. Her choices—about the kind of marriage she wanted, to move on beyond Porter Wagoner, to transition into pop music, to create Dollywood—have all been ways of securing the financial and artistic freedom she needed to create music on her own terms.

Dolly buzzed out of the mountains of Locust Ridge for the "real world" of Nashville when she was eighteen, not long after that high school trip to New York City. She was convinced, against all odds, that she would be a successful songwriter and singer. By the time she released her first studio album, *Hello, I'm Dolly*, people were taking note of the mountain girl with insights that, in Fred Foster's words, seemed "too much for one young life."[17] Dolly's confidence paid off, and she has been a songwriter all her life. As she once remarked, "If somebody said to me, 'You can only do one thing in show business for the rest of your whole life. What will it be?' I would say, 'I'll write songs.' To me, it's like putting something in the world today that wasn't there yesterday that will still be there tomorrow. That's my favorite thing I do."[18] This musical passion is a constant thread of her identity whether personal or professional.

Dolly's songwriting has given her opportunities to move far beyond Nashville. She has traveled the world as an internationally recognized star and entertainer, an actress, a businesswoman, and a philanthropist. As she said, "It was my songs, and my singing, that brought me out of the Smoky Mountains, that really built the bridge into all of the other worlds that I've been in and live in. It was all built with songs. It was all built with the songs I write."[19] Her songs—and the artistic control she took over her musical life—allowed her to chart a course into pathways that would not have otherwise been possible.

Dolly's confidence in and dedication to her songwriting, along with her self-assured public persona, might lead us to believe she is certain of her standing as an artist. But occasionally she reveals a need for affirmation as she did in a 2018 interview with these self-effacing remarks: "It touches me to no end that I'm an inspiration. It makes you feel like you've done something right 'cause you don't really know in your life how you're gonna be seen or remembered. And I look back and then I still see that my music *seems* to be important."[20] The subtle hesitation Dolly expresses here—despite her numerous awards, international fame, and immense fortune—is likely because the image she created for herself has overshadowed her songwriting talent for many people. But through my immersion in Dolly's music, I have come to know and admire a gifted composer.

Chapter 1

"In the Good Old Days (When Times Were Bad)"

Dolly's Musical Life

"I'm a balance of the good things and the bad
things in my life, and I like that."

Dolly is a realist.[1] Yes, the woman who looks artificial has a firm grasp of reality. In her song "In the Good Old Days (When Times Were Bad)," Dolly describes the hard times of her childhood: failing crops, hunger, overwork, sickness, bitter cold without adequate shelter, and shame about one's appearance and clothes. But her memories are tinged with sweetness in the chorus:

> No amount of money could buy from me the memories that I have of then
> No amount of money could pay me to go back and live through it again
> In the good old days when times were bad

Of course, Dolly is being ironic in her use of "good old days." Nothing in her catalogue of privations is good; this is a perfunctory phrase we use about our past, often forgetting the problems and pain of an earlier time. But Dolly does not forget. Instead, she uses her songs to remember and take control of her experiences, both the good and the bad.

In this song, Dolly sets her childhood memories to a bluesy, lilting melody with a triple meter feel that propels each line into the next with an air of

FIGURE 1.1. *In the Good Old Days (When Times Were Bad)* album back cover (detail), 1969. "Part of the Partons. That's me standing in front of my dad. This is a picture taken in the good old days when times were bad. But times got even worse because there were four more children to be born, making a total of twelve—six boys and six girls."

inevitability. One hardship leads to another, and Dolly reinforces this litany by linking them through the use of internal rhymes: "we'd get up before *sun-up* to get the work *done up*," "we've got up *before* and found ice on *the floor*," and "I couldn't *enjoy then*, having a *boyfriend*."[2] Throughout the song, Dolly weaves her refrain, "in the good old days when times were bad," that becomes more poignant with each iteration.

Perhaps, it is the "badness" of these days that allows Dolly to suggest they were "good." As she said, "Life was good in its way at home. It was bad in its own way, but also good. Naturally after you're grown and after you're successful you always tend to glorify a situation. And then the hard times don't seem to matter. It's the good that you remember, and the bad makes you a better person and makes you appreciate the good that comes later on. It's the balance of the good and the bad that makes your life have meanin'. . . . There was always love and security in my family. That was so important."[3]

Although "In the Good Old Days (When Times Were Bad)" was about her impoverished childhood—"we've gone to bed hungry many nights in the past"—its sentiments are applicable to the many periods of Dolly's career in which she has struggled yet thrived. Dolly often remarks that even during her best days there were difficulties, and during her worst days there were successes. She remembers and honors these hard times and reshapes them into songs about poverty, loneliness, betrayal, heartbreak, abandonment, and abuse. But Dolly also writes uplifting songs of optimism and joy. As John Rockwell notes, "For someone who was raised in poverty and has struggled her way to the top of country music, Miss Parton seems possessed of a wonderfully sunny disposition. 'I'm able to put the hurting things into my songs,' she says, 'and then it don't hurt me any more. I get the world to share my hurt. It's better than a psychiatrist.'"[4]

Throughout the different phases of her career, Dolly was unswerving in her desire for fame and wealth, to overcome the limitations of her upbringing, and to become a star: "I dreamed of singin' and I dreamed of bein' famous and loved. It was like a fantasy life."[5] But despite her dreams of flying away, she did not want to leave her home behind completely: "I try to always remember where I came from, who I am and why I wanted to do this to start with. It was not to get away from my family. It was not because I wasn't proud of my home that I wanted to leave it. I just wanted to take the Smoky Mountains wherever I went."[6] When asked in 1978 about her aspirations for stardom, she agreed that was her goal, but that she saw it as something far in the future. "When I feel like I have accomplished the things that I want to accomplish, then maybe I will personally think of myself as a superstar. I want to be somebody that extremely shines. A star shines, of course, but I want to be really radiant."[7] Along her way toward radiance, Dolly has never forgotten what it was like to go to bed hungry even after she had her white limozeen.

Childhood: 1946–1964

Dolly was born on January 19, 1946, in Sevier County, Tennessee. The doctor who delivered her was paid with a sack of corn meal. Her parents, Avie Lee (née Owens) and Robert Lee Parton, had twelve children; Dolly was the fourth. The family grew most of what they ate, and tobacco was their cash crop, bringing in about $2,000 a year.[8] Dolly's mother was a devout Christian, the daughter of a Pentecostal preacher, Jake Owens. The family regularly attended his worship services filled with fire and brimstone sermons and altar calls accompanied by the impassioned singing of the congregation. Dolly was immersed in southern gospel music with 19th-century songs like "In the Sweet By and By" and "Power in the Blood," traditional folk hymns like "Wayfaring Stranger," and time-honored hymns such as "Amazing Grace" and "Farther Along." Dolly's mother, Avie Lee, also sang to her children at home: old ballads—Appalachian story songs of love, death, and betrayal—like "Barbara Allen" and "Two Little Babes." She also sang parlor songs and folk songs like "Little Rosewood Casket" and "In the Pines" that were first recorded in the 1920s.[9]

Dolly's childhood was filled with wonder at glittering butterflies, hummingbirds, and the allure of quartz that sparkled in the sunlight, but it was also filled with hardship: kids sleeping four to a bed, including the ones who peed in the bed (often the only source of warmth as long as one did not move the covers). There was the tedium of biscuits and gravy each morning, the patched-together clothing, and the rough treatment from bullies. Dolly wrote a number of songs early in her career that provide glimpses of her childhood poverty. Some, like "My Tennessee Mountain Home," "Better Part of Life," and "Tennessee Home-sick Blues," are idealistic, focusing on a loving family, the pleasures of nature, and the "simple things in life" without dwelling on harsh economic conditions. Others depict the poverty of her mountain life more overtly. In "Greatest Days of All," Dolly pulls no punches regarding the family's living conditions:

> A dirt dobber built its nest on my only Sunday dress
> And the roof leaked in my shoes and when they dried they were too small
> And the rats chewed a great big hole in my only winter coat
> And at night I'd hear them gnaw the paper off my bedroom wall

"Paradise Road" is equally blunt in its portrayal of poverty. The first line sets the scene: "I grew up dirty and I grew up poor." It continues with lyrics about being hungry, ragged, and cold, lines written by someone who grew up with too many kids in a small house without electricity and running water (unless you ran to get it, as Dolly often jokes) and who coped with inadequate clothing and insufficient food. According to Dolly biographer Alanna Nash: "If anyone has suspected Parton of exaggerating the severity of her childhood, in truth the poverty that she endured in the hollers . . . was worse than she ever let on."[10] But through the good and the bad, music remained a constant presence.

Dolly grew up in a family and community that was immersed in music; she remembered everyone playing musical instruments. Dolly's mother and her siblings played and sang at church and for funerals, and "they would sing if there was some kind of a shindig or some kind of a community gathering going on." The music-making possibilities seemed endless as people used household items for instruments: "spoons, . . . paper in a comb, and we'd use pots and pans, washtubs, bucket lids for drums, shake dried beans in a jar or in a can for percussion. So it was nothing for us to make music. Everybody knew a way to do that, and make it sound good. Even the little kids could get in on all of that. Music was a fun time for us. Music kind of passed the time, but it also healed a lot of hurt, and it also was just part of our nature."[11]

Dolly's family recalled that she sang at a very young age: her father said, "she was singing almost before she could talk," and her grandfather remembered

Dolly singing "ever since she quit cryin'."[12] Dolly began writing songs when she was five, and when she was around six she built a makeshift instrument out of an old mandolin body, minus its neck, and some discarded strings. Her mother's brothers took note of Dolly's musical interest. Uncle Louis gave her a Martin guitar when she was about seven, and Uncle Bill taught her chords and encouraged her talent. Dolly recalled:

> I would whang away at my old mandolin with the piano strings. I started getting pretty good with it, within its limitations, and people started to notice. Of course, that was exactly what I wanted. I was never one to shy away from attention. Finally, my Uncle Louis began to see that I was really serious about wanting to learn, so he taught me guitar. He gave me an old Martin guitar, and I learned the basic chords pretty quick. This was like manna from heaven to me. At last I could play along with the songs I heard in my head. Mama's family were all very musical, and I used to worry the heck out of all of them to "teach me that lick" or "play this with me."[13]

Beyond playing for her own pleasure, Dolly wanted to perform for others, and she entertained her siblings, and even the livestock, by putting on shows from the cabin's front porch:

> Sometimes I would take a tobacco stake and stick it in the cracks between the boards on the front porch. A tin can on top of the tobacco stake turned it into a microphone, and the porch became my stage. I used to perform for anybody or anything I could get to watch. The younger kids left in my care would become the unwilling audience for my latest show. A two-year-old's attention span is not very long. So there I would be in the middle of my act, thinking I was really something, and my audience would start crawling away. I was so desperate to perform that on more than one occasion I sang for the chickens and the pigs and ducks.[14]

Dolly was soon singing in church and small, local venues. When she was ten, Uncle Bill got her a spot on a Knoxville television and radio show, *The Cas Walker Farm and Home Hour*, for which she was paid $5 a show, as much as her father earned for a full day's work in the sawmill. During the school year, she made the 75-mile round trip on weekends, driven there by various relatives, and during the summer she did the show daily and lived with her Aunt Estelle (Dolly's mother's sister) in Knoxville. Dolly's account of this time emphasizes both the good and the bad. Resentful of her minor fame, the children at school teased and mocked her, once locking her in a dark coat closet.[15]

When Dolly was thirteen, Uncle Bill arranged for her to cut a demo record, "Puppy Love," a rockabilly style, bubblegum pop tune Dolly had cowritten with him two years earlier.[16] She recalled hearing herself for the first time on the radio singing it: "I thought, well, I've made it now. Of course, I hadn't."[17] During her youth, Dolly and Uncle Bill traveled back and forth to Nashville, visiting record companies and producers. Their car had a door wired shut with a coat hanger and a mismatched fender; it was their home away from home. They slept in it and cleaned up in gas station bathrooms. One of Uncle Bill's goals was to get Dolly on the Grand Ole Opry, and in 1959 she appeared there after sweet-talking another performer into giving up his slot. Although she was technically too young to be on the show, she was introduced by Johnny Cash. Another objective was to sell some of the songs she and Uncle Bill had cowritten, and in 1962 they signed with Tree Publishing. That same year, Dolly cut a demo of two songs with Mercury Records, but they did not amount to much. As Dolly remarked, "It is one thing to have a record company take a chance on an unknown and finance a record. It is quite another to get radio stations to play it."[18]

Back at home, Dolly's classmates' derision continued through high school. On the night of graduation, when each student stood to report their plans, Dolly confidently declared that she was going to Nashville to be a famous songwriter and singer. The students laughed at her, and Dolly was baffled because she truly believed she would be a star. Undaunted by their scorn and her embarrassment, Dolly left for Nashville the day after graduation. She boarded the bus with her guitar and three paper bags full of her dirty laundry. She says she cried all the way to Nashville, homesick already, but determined to follow her dreams.

Early Years in Nashville: 1964–1967

Once in Nashville, Dolly found what little money she had ran out well before she became a star. While peddling her songs to publishers and performers, she lived on her own, often surviving on "ketchup soup" and sneak eating her way through grocery stores before buying a pack of gum as payment. She earned money through babysitting and met her future husband Carl Dean outside the Wishy Washy Laundromat. Dolly began to get work singing on early morning radio shows, and eventually she and Uncle Bill signed publishing and recording deals with Combine Publishing and Monument Records for $50 a week. Dolly recalls, "they was rough times there for a while; we tryin' to pay rent, send money home out of that $50, and eat. For two weeks once I lived on mustard and horse relish."[19] Dolly's oldest sister Willadeene described the tough life of this time in Nashville:

> She did demo tapes, worked at odd jobs and baby-sat. She pounded the streets, knocking on the doors of the vast, complex music business. She and Uncle Bill traveled to shows all over Tennessee and in the surrounding states in his old car. They never knew if the car was going to get there or back or break down on the road. Many times Dolly came home from shows wrapped in a quilt because the car had no heater and cold air poured in through the holes in the floorboard. They always packed sandwiches, a thermos of coffee and fruit jars filled with tea, because they couldn't afford to buy anything at a restaurant.[20]

All this hard work finally paid off for Dolly and Uncle Bill when their cowritten song, "Put It Off until Tomorrow (You've Hurt Me Enough for Today)," was recorded by Bill Phillips, went to #6 on the country chart, and won the BMI Song of the Year for 1966. Dolly sang backup harmony (uncredited) on this recording. The interest in her as the mystery girl singer helped Dolly and Uncle Bill convince the producers at Monument to let Dolly record country songs on her own. Up to this point, Monument had only allowed her to sing "pop-oriented, rockabilly" music,[21] believing her voice was too distinctive for country music. But once Dolly was set loose with country songs, her career took flight.

When she was just 20, her 1966 single, "Dumb Blonde" (#24 on the country chart), written by Curly Putman, introduced Dolly to the wider country music industry with a refrain that seemed to epitomize Dolly herself: "Just because I'm blonde don't think I'm dumb/ 'Cause this dumb blonde ain't nobody's fool." Before long, one of Dolly's originals, "Something Fishy," charted at #17. It was a sassy, classic country song about a woman's witty response to her man's infidelity. He claims he has been fishing, although he always comes home empty-handed. In her threat to leave him she sings, "Some night when you come home and discover that I'm gone/You can bet there's something fishy going on." Dolly recorded both songs on her debut album, *Hello, I'm Dolly*, along with "Put It Off until Tomorrow (You've Hurt Me Enough for Today)." Also included were two songs she wrote that had been recorded by other country artists: "I'm in No Condition" recorded by Hank Williams Jr, and "Fuel to the Flame," which was recorded by Skeeter Davis and charted at #11.

Through these songs, Dolly introduced listeners to a range of perspectives that she would consistently return to in her music: a woman filled with sexual desire who struggles with temptation ("Fuel"), a lover who can only cope with abandonment through self-denial ("Put It Off"), a wounded but resilient woman who perseveres even in heartbreak ("I'm in No Condition"), a clever woman who humorously turns the tables on her man ("Something Fishy"), and a woman who is no man's fool despite her outward appearance ("Dumb Blonde"). Dolly's facility in moving between vulnerability, wit, and strength shines through the entire album, and *Hello, I'm Dolly* laid the groundwork for many of her later songs.

The Country Years: 1967–1976

Dolly's early successes came to the attention of Porter Wagoner, the host of a popular syndicated country music television show that ran from 1960–1981. When Porter invited Dolly to meet with him, she assumed he wanted to buy one of her songs. Instead he offered her the job of his new "girl singer" since the current singer, Norma Jean Beasler, was leaving the show. Suddenly, in 1967, Dolly had regular exposure on national television, and she was making $60,000 a year. Nevertheless, Dolly maintains, "Porter did not discover me, as my Uncle Bill had spent many years heading me in the right direction . . . and brought me to the attention of Fred Foster, Monument Records, and Combine Publishing."[22] Dolly typically sang her own songs on the show as a featured soloist. She and Porter soon began singing together, becoming one of the most popular country duos of the 1960s and 1970s. Porter attributed their success to a familial similarity in their voices: "Our harmony is so close it's almost like blood kin. Brother and sister, you know, can harmonize better than a great tenor and a great lead singer gettin' together. . . . Dolly and I sound nearly like brother and sister."[23]

During her time on Porter's show, Dolly recorded around 150 of her own songs. She released thirteen solo albums, which included some of her most well-known and popular songs ("Jolene," "Coat of Many Colors," "Touch Your Woman," "My Tennessee Mountain Home," and "I Will Always Love You," among dozens of others). The songs ranged from honky-tonk and classic country to folk and mountain-style songs to light country pop. During this time, Porter and Dolly recorded eleven duo albums, which included about 50 of Dolly's original songs, and Dolly said her years on the show "were some of the best songwriting years of my life."[24]

Dolly's enormously productive years with Porter came at a high price. She enjoyed the process of taking her songs from their inception to the final recording:

"There's nothing sweeter than takin' songs that I've written, and just hearin''em on the guitar, and then takin''em in the studio and hearin' arrangements and hearin' it all come to life. Oh, it's so excitin'!"[25] But Dolly and Porter differed on many musical fronts, and she was often frustrated with the musical arrangements that he favored as her producer. She explained, "a big part of my ideas were written in the songs, the arrangement ideas and all," but Porter had his own approach that Dolly said "just took away the joy of recordin' the song at all."[26] Dolly said they had "dueling dreams."[27] Porter did not take her seriously, and his authoritarian approach combined with Dolly's strong will led to many fights. As Dolly became more successful, the tension grew.

One member of Dolly's band recalled how difficult those days were for Dolly. "It almost kills her to have to record something not the way she wants to record it," and "if it wasn't the way she wanted to do it, she was miserable." He believed this was a big part of why Dolly split with Porter.[28] Eventually, this situation, combined with her songwriting successes of these years, particularly her #1 hit "Jolene," drove Dolly to make a break from Porter, and she left the show in 1974. Decades later, she commented, "I'm a songwriter, and I *ain't* your girl singer forever. I was out to be a solo artist. And I had my own band, I wanted to have my own show, I wanted to have my own life, and I don't want to just be the girl singer in somebody else's group. And that's when I wrote 'I Will Always Love You.'"[29] The song was Dolly's farewell to Porter and "the special, although painfully heart-wrenching, time we spent together."[30] Ever the optimist, Dolly credited those hard times with Porter as also being some of her best years: "I have . . . come to understand that even though it was the hardest and worst period of my life, those seven years were the most prosperous, productive, and growth-filled ones as well. When I think back on it all now, it is the good I remember."[31]

Although Dolly was no longer on Porter's show or performing with him, Porter produced three more of her solo albums, and they released two more duo albums.[32] They finally parted ways in 1976, and Dolly's success continued. She had top-charted hits with "The Bargain Store" and "The Seeker," and her 1976 album *All I Can Do* was nominated for a Grammy for Best Country Vocal Performance by a Female. After the break with Porter, Dolly toured with her own band, The Traveling Family Band, which included some of her brothers, sisters, and a cousin; her Uncle Louis was their manager. But she was not happy because she felt their music tied her too strongly to her past. After Dolly replaced Uncle Lewis with a new manager, Don Warden, she remained unhappy with her family band and made the personally difficult decision to disband the group. She also took some much-needed time off for her vocal health and reflection, though she was still uncertain of her next move.

When Dolly left Porter and set out on her own, she had the freedom she desired. But she soon learned that these new good days also brought hard times. As she explained: "When I left to try and expand, when I was one of the *big* country women, I wasn't makin' any money. I couldn't even clothe my band and pay for my bus. I was making $3,000 a night, and that was with all my expenses coming out of that. I'd be clearing a couple of hundred dollars a show if I was lucky. . . . I thought, 'Well, shit, this is the music business—why not think of the business end of the business?'"[33] At about this time, her friend Mac Davis suggested that Dolly needed a change and introduced her to his manager, Sandy Gallin of Katz, Gallin and Cleary, a Los Angeles firm. She signed with them in 1976, and Gallin continued as her manager for the next twenty-five years. Thus, the stage was set for Dolly's next chapter, her crossover into the pop world.

The Pop Crossover Years: 1976–1986

With her move toward a mainstream pop sound, Dolly released her first self-produced album, *New Harvest . . . First Gathering* in 1977. At the time, Dolly said, "it will always be my special album, because it was the first time in my whole life I got to do something totally on my own."[34] The album, which included some covers of R&B and pop songs, was not well received by some critics who believed that Dolly had sold out to pop, despite the fact that her song, "Light of a Clear Blue Morning," went to #11 on the country chart and another, "Applejack," featured country legends such as Kitty Wells, Chet Atkins, and Ernest Tubb. In response to critics, her record company, RCA, took out ads in the music trade magazines that included a quote from Dolly, "Any time you make a change, you gotta pay the price. A lot of country people feel I'm leaving the country, that I'm not proud of Nashville, which is the biggest lie there is. I don't want to leave the country, but to take the whole country with me wherever I go. There are really no limits now."[35] But a decade later she suggested a different reason for her departure from Nashville: "I got run out of town because I couldn't make a living with songs like 'Coat of Many Colors' and all that other stuff I really loved."[36] Dolly had competing desires: she loved singing her folk-styled music and songs that grew out of her mountain roots, and she wanted to be the radiant superstar she had always dreamed about. So she chose to focus on pop styles and downplay the music of her heart for a time to gain a wider following.

Her next album, *Here You Come Again*, also from 1977, was the one that fully landed her in the pop world. Dolly said it "was the first thing that I did after I made the change and it was not exactly what I had in mind. But it proved to be the smartest thing." Dolly did not write the title song and was hesitant to "be identified with it, because it's so smooth and pop-sounding . . . [even though] it was the biggest country record I ever had."[37] The song was #1 on the country chart for five weeks and #3 on the Hot 100 chart. The album went Gold in 1977 and Platinum in 1978, and Dolly won a Grammy for Best Country Vocal Performance by a Female for the album. However, Dolly wrote fewer than half the songs on the album, and at the time she was candid about her goal:

> I wouldn't want to get labeled with this slick production because my own songs are a lot more gutsy and a lot more soulful . . . We were purposely trying to get a single and an album that would cross over. . . . Evidently my own songs, as they were, didn't quite hack it, so we purposely included songs that were recognized by the pop world. But once I crack that market, my own songs *will* be accepted. And when I get to where I want to go—which is a long way from here—I'll still be going back and doing the old traditional songs and preserving them that way.[38]

With this deliberate move to broaden her musical reach, the debate continued about whether Dolly had abandoned country music and her longtime fans.

Although Dolly's next album, *Heartbreaker* (1978), was certified Gold, it was panned by *Rolling Stone*, and this quote from that harsh review is representative of the wider critical response to many of her crossover albums. "When a singer with as much integrity as Parton apparently had makes a dramatic shift in style, you generally assume that the change was artistically necessary, even if the results aren't very encouraging. But *Heartbreaker*, like its immediate predecessors, doesn't even seem like an honest failure: it's flat-out, commercial schmaltz aimed straight at the *Johnny Carson Show*."[39] To her critics, Dolly said that she loved country music, but that she liked "other music as well" and that she did not want to "get left behind." She remarked that she felt like "I'm fighting a battle when I didn't start a war. I'm just doing what I want to do, because my music is me, however it sounds."[40] She frequently stated her crossover presence was actually bringing attention to country music. But the Nashville community felt betrayed, and many critics and fans believed that Dolly had sold out to a slick pop sound that did not suit her.

In a 1980 interview in *Rolling Stone* with Chet Flippo, Dolly spoke candidly about her foray into pop: "I went all out and tried to find good management, which I did, and to record stuff that I don't particularly even like and am not even particularly proud of, other than the fact that it worked. But, the thing is, it got me where I wanted to be." After admitting she did not like her last few albums, Dolly elaborated on her desire for artistic control, which she linked to the number of her own songs she recorded:

> The main thing is, now I've got the freedom to do my music without havin' to worry about whether I'll make money or not.... From here on out, I'll be involved in producing my own records. I wrote about half of the songs on the *Nine to Five* album. I wrote *all* of the songs for the one that will follow that. You know, people thought I had sold out: what's this piece of shit that Dolly's done now? Or what's this and that? I'm very aware of all that stuff. The reviews of the last four or five albums were not good, but I still knew that I was tryin' to accomplish the right thing. Now I've got their attention; now I have to prove myself. Every day I feel like I'm just startin' my career.... I never intended to lose my country audience. I knew that I had to get myself into a position to do what I thought I should be doin' for country music. I think I have now. For what few people I may have lost, I feel like I've gained thousands more.[41]

Dolly seemed to have backed herself into a corner. She intended her crossover albums to get her wider attention and financial security so she could record her own "gutsy" and "soulful" songs. But with each new pop album, Dolly was recording fewer and fewer of her own songs. Her album *Dolly, Dolly, Dolly* (1980) contained no Dolly originals.

Dolly's reliance on other songwriters for material in these albums was likely one reason why they were not artistic successes; as she said, she was trying to "crack the market" with other people's songs so she could then record her own material. Dolly has always been at her best when performing her own songs or other country songs that she feels a connection with. While Dolly always put on the glamour and glitz, much of her appeal is in her homespun, mountain-girl strength combined with innocence and vulnerability she projects through her compositions and her performance style. These qualities were not suited to the heavily orchestrated pop arrangements and synthesized disco dance beats she was now recording. And she could not compete with contemporary singers like Barbra Streisand, Donna Summer, or Madonna, who sang in these styles more successfully.

Nonetheless, by the early 1980s, Dolly had positioned herself as a superstar; she had made a lot of money and had everyone's attention. So she was now free to develop her own artistic vision moving forward, and that meant, as she said, returning to country and proving herself. Her concept album *9 to 5 and Odd Jobs*

(1980) was a shift back toward country, though still somewhat pop-inflected, and her next album, *Heartbreak Express* (1982), had a stronger country feeling. By 1986, she had hosted two of her own television series and appeared in three films (*9 to 5*, *The Best Little Whorehouse in Texas*, and *Rhinestone*), writing songs for each of them. She had a huge crossover hit with Kenny Rogers on the Bee Gees' "Islands in the Stream" and was the first woman to receive a Grammy for Best Country Song without a male cowriter for "9 to 5" (which was #1 on the country and Hot 100 charts). She was named Entertainer of the Year by the Country Music Association, and she was inducted into the Nashville Songwriters Hall of Fame.

But these good days for Dolly were marred by days of physical and emotional pain. In 1979, Porter sued Dolly for breach of contract.[42] They settled out of court, but it took a major financial and emotional toll on her. That same year she suffered from severe vocal problems brought about by overwork and performing in venues with substandard sound systems. The following four years saw personal upheavals and health issues, and Dolly spiraled into an emotional state that gave her an understanding of "how people could let themselves become dependent on drugs and alcohol. I understood how a person could consider suicide."[43] Dolly later wrote about these turbulent days, about how close she had come to losing everything and how resilient she ultimately was:

> My face was everywhere. My boobs were everywhere. My name was a household word. . . . One doesn't have an experience like that without changing in some way. I will always be a little more fragile after that. . . . Meanwhile, I had let my band go. I had not worked in many months. I had not sung. I had not written. I had not played a guitar. Many people had given up on me. They thought I had lost my drive. It's okay to think that about Dolly Parton, but you better not stand in the road in front of her. I was about to come roaring back.[44]

The Return to Country: 1987–1999

In 1987, Dolly appeared with Emmylou Harris and Linda Ronstadt on an album, *Trio*, that looked back to a traditional country, folk, and even old-time sound. Dolly recalled, "every time we'd get together . . . we'd start singing a bunch of old songs nobody knew but us, old Smoky Mountain Appalachian songs. And we just sounded so good."[45] Most of the album featured traditional songs, and Dolly contributed "Wildflowers" to the project, a song she said told her story.[46] The lyrics recall Dolly's so-called departure from country, even as the musical style with autoharp and fiddle suggests a return to her country and Appalachian roots:

> Just a wild mountain rose, needing freedom to grow
> So I ran fearing not where I'd go
> When a flower grows wild, it can always survive
> Wildflowers don't care where they grow

As Ken Tucker wrote, "at precisely the moment when Parton had probably transcended the country-artist label, she chose to remind her public of it."[47]

In a twist of circumstances, it was at this time that RCA, the label she had been with since 1967, decided not to renew her contract. So Dolly signed with Columbia, and her first album on that label, *Rainbow* (1987), was widely panned by critics. It was also her last concentrated effort to record an exclusively pop album. With very weak chart placement, the album suffered from its overproduced sound and thick arrangements of primarily pop and country pop songs that were not a good fit for Dolly. Moreover, she contributed only two songs to the recording. It is possible to listen through the lush orchestration of her song "More than I Can Say" to hear what Dolly likely heard and would rather have recorded when she wrote it. A love song filled with images of nature and set to a gentle melody with modal touches, "More than I Can Say" has a charm better suited to a lighter, more folklike or country arrangement, though Dolly's performance is convincing and passionate. These albums, *Trio* and *Rainbow*, released only nine months apart, represent two distinct sides of Dolly's music from this time. Their vastly different reception makes it clear listeners preferred the traditional music and arrangements of *Trio*—which went Platinum and was awarded a Grammy for Best Country Performance by a Duo or Group—over the slick pop sounds of *Rainbow*.

Dolly also preferred a more traditional sound. When her next studio album, *White Limozeen* (1989), was released, she admitted that "for quite a while my heart wasn't totally in a lot of the music I was doing" and that many people she had been working with had "no feel for country music. . . . I think I'm really in a good place to do well, and make the kind of contribution to country music I always wanted to."[48] The album, which was certified Gold, included Dolly's "Yellow Roses," a country weeper, which reached #1 on the country chart. Dolly said the title song, "White Limozeen" (cowritten with Mac Davis), was her own rags to riches story.[49] In it, Dolly's Daisy Mae alter-ego arrives in Hollywood looking for fame and fortune. But she remains unchanged, still a country girl at heart. Thus, *White Limozeen* attested to Dolly's core country identity.

Her next two solo albums, *Eagle When She Flies* (1991) and *Slow Dancing with the Moon* (1993), went Platinum, with more country-inflected Dolly originals than her earlier pop crossover albums. For instance, "More Where That Came From" is a rousing Cajun-inspired number that features fiddle accompaniment to a folklike mostly pentatonic tune and Dolly's yodel-like vocal riffs. In 1995, her album *Something Special* peaked at #10 on the country chart and included Dolly's sassy Western swing song, "Speakin' of the Devil." But Dolly was unhappy with the lack of play her songs were getting on country radio. Dolly may have come roaring back to country, but country was moving down the road ahead of her to a new generation of stars such as Reba McEntire and George Strait in the late 1980s and Shania Twain and Garth Brooks in the 1990s. She recalled one song she wrote and recorded in an attempt to garner radio attention. "Romeo," from *Slow Dancing with the Moon*, included guest artists Mary Chapin Carpenter, Billy Ray Cyrus, Kathy Mattea, Pam Tillis, and Tanya Tucker, among others. Dolly explained this choice and her frustration:

> I was trying to get played on the radio, when we did "Romeo" [#27 *Billboard*, 1993]. Very commercial, but it still didn't do it. Still a piece of shit. I mean, the song was cute. I'm serious. But it was not a cute song for me.... But I was perfectly trying to get the young country audience.... But that didn't do it either. ... So I tried to do "More Where That Came From" [#58 *Billboard*, 1993], which is a great song, one of my better-written songs, but I purposely was trying to do that Cajun beat to where they'd dance to it. Didn't do it either. Now I'm doin' this [*Treasures*], and I don't know if it'll do it either.[50]

As Paul Kingsbury noted, Dolly "seems absolutely determined to keep making music, in spite of the '90s youth movement in Nashville that has been sweeping all her peers aside."[51]

The way Dolly kept making music was through recordings that looked to the past. *Honky Tonk Angels* (1993) was a collaboration with Loretta Lynn and Tammy Wynette, and *Heartsongs: Live from Home* (1994) included mountain-inflected Dolly originals and traditional ballads and songs. *Treasures* (1996) was a collection of country and pop covers from the 1960s, 1970s, and 1980s, songs that would be "fresh and new for some of the new country listeners," but that would also appeal to an older audience.[52] Dolly made it clear at the time that she was casting about for a way to have a viable radio presence. "I've had an album out every year for several years, but I ain't had no hits. So I'm just trying to fit into this new country. If I were trying to make a living at this, I'd starve to death, like some of my good friends are. I'm proud of the new country [acts].

Some of them are real good, . . . but it would be nice to get a balance, where some of the old folks could still make a living."[53] She later quipped, "I think of country radio like a great lover. You were great to me, you bought me a lot of nice things and then you dumped my ass for younger women."[54]

Her next album, *Hungry Again* (1998), had a country flavor (and a whiff of bluegrass) and included only Dolly originals—the first to do so in over twenty years (excluding the soundtrack for *Straight Talk* [1992] and *Something Special* [1995], which had one cowritten song). Then 1999 saw the release of *Trio II*, a followup to her recording with Harris and Ronstadt. This album, like its predecessor, garnered critical acclaim for its early country and roots flavor. Perhaps as if to welcome her home to country, Dolly was inducted into the Country Music Hall of Fame this same year.

During the leaner years of the late 1980s and early 1990s, at least with regard to her presence on the radio, Dolly worked on other projects, including major roles in two films (*Steel Magnolias* and *Straight Talk*). But she never stopped being "hungry as a songwriter and a singer. I still want to be part of the mainstream. For me, it's not about the money, it's about the art."[55] Dolly wanted to be musically active and relevant. Money was a means to an end—it was what gave her the security and freedom to create music on her own terms:

> I wanted to get rich enough to where I could afford to be poor, you see—and now I can afford to live simple, and do what I want to. Money in itself is no big deal, you see; its real value is that having it takes the pressure off, and you can do your real work. So now, I can be totally true. And when I write seriously, I can still write from my memories and from the stuff that's in my body. I can still write like I'm hungry, because I *am* hungry—hungry for the true thing that comes from me as a writer and a singer.[56]

Not content with being a legend, Dolly refashioned her career yet again, and this time she had both the celebrity and the financial freedom to follow her musical desires all the way back to her Appalachian roots.

The Bluegrass and Return to Roots Years: 1999–present

Looking back on her experiences of the previous decade, Dolly remarked: "When the new country came along, any artist over thirty-five was thought to be a has-been. And, Lord, I've been around for so long that people looked at me like a legend. But I wasn't near done. I felt like I was better than I ever was.

I feel like I'm just now seasoned enough to know how to be in this business. And I thought, 'Well, hell, I'm not going down with the rest of them old farts. I'm gonna find some new ways of doing it.' And that's exactly what I did."[57]

Dolly called this new phase of her career "my bluegrass thing."[58] In 1999, she released the first of three albums that explicitly turned to bluegrass, old-time music, and the sounds of her Appalachian heritage. *The Grass Is Blue* (1999), *Little Sparrow* (2001), and *Halos & Horns* (2002) were critically acclaimed, and they are, according to one writer, "nothing short of a songwriting bonanza and a career reinvention. Embracing her Smoky Mountain roots . . . she is writing and singing with a fire and conviction you might expect from a new artist with something to prove."[59] These albums showcased a variety of traditional acoustic styles: up-tempo fiddle tunes and banjo-driven songs, gospel numbers, gothic ballads, and bluegrass standards. Dolly also covered several rock songs in shimmering bluegrass arrangements. She contributed a number of gems herself; some were newly written or newly recorded by Dolly and others were acoustic/traditional revisions of some of her earlier songs.

Dolly remarked that she enjoyed this music the most, the music of her Appalachian roots: "the biggest part of these songs I used to sing as a kid growing up."[60] She explained her tie to mountain music went back to her ancestors who "came from the Gloucester area of England. It also seems that other Partons may have gone to Scotland. . . . Make no mistake: the music of that area of the Old World is in my blood. . . . I grew up in the Smoky Mountains listening to these ancient ballads that had crossed oceans and valleys to become an important basis for American folk, bluegrass, and country music."[61] Steve Buckingham, the producer of the first two of these albums, observed that other musicians recognized Dolly's affinity for this style of music: "I can remember people like old friends Linda Ronstadt and Emmylou Harris coming by the studio in Nashville, when we were working on *The Grass Is Blue* or *Little Sparrow*, and just going crazy over it, saying 'Dolly, this is what you should be doing.' That type of thing. And everybody loved it. The musicians, the critics, other singers. They all loved it."[62] The albums not only revitalized Dolly's career, but they helped reestablish her strong mountain identity.

Recorded on Dolly's own label, Blue Eye Records, these albums also represented Dolly's newfound independence from pressures of record companies and radio that would limit song lengths. With this independence came a greater sense of artistic fulfillment since she was able to "record the stuff I really want to." No longer driven by the need for money, fame, or radio play, Dolly said,

"I'm not catering to that anymore. And I'm happier than I've ever been doing it like that."[63] As she found greater artistic rewards in these bluegrass projects, Dolly reflected on her earlier pop ventures:

> I've been guilty of trying to do these things that are commercial, but it just doesn't work if I do things that aren't from my heart. My true soul is music; that's the thing that brought me out of the Smoky Mountain. None of that other matters to me as much as my true gift. It never means the same to me and it's evident to people that are really into real stuff; they know that I wasn't feeling it. We've all got to make a living, too; I make no apologies for stuff that I've done. But what I truly love is stuff like this, that comes from my God-given gift.[64]

Dolly did not stray far from her gift for traditional mountain music with her album *Those Were the Days* (2005), a collection of folk and pop hits from the 1960s and 1970s done in a bluegrass-inflected style. It included several guest artists from both the folk and bluegrass scenes. In 2008, she released *Backwoods Barbie*, a collection more country than mountain, though Dolly was still trading in Appalachian imagery and sounds with her modernized "signature blend of ancient modal melodies and optimistic pop confections."[65] The title song was featured in the Broadway musical version of the film, *9 to 5: The Musical* (2009), for which she wrote all the music.

With *Backwoods Barbie*, Dolly set out to "tailor-make" songs that would "get some play on the radio and let people know I'm dead serious about my music." To do this, she chose to "go back and do some of the types of things I did in my early career when I did have success."[66] This approach paid off; the album reached #2 on the country chart, and two songs, Dolly's "Better Get to Livin'" and "Jesus and Gravity" (written by Betsy Ulmer and Craig Wiseman), did well—thanks, in part, to Dolly's performance of the latter on *American Idol*.

Dolly continued to look to her earlier styles in two subsequent albums. In 2011, she released four other songs from *9 to 5: The Musical* on her *Better Day* album, which included only Dolly originals (one cowritten with Mac Davis) and was also more country than mountain in style. Three years later, her Smoky Mountain–inspired *Blue Smoke* (2014) featured a blend of country sounds with acoustic bluegrass instruments and included a version of a traditional murder ballad, "Banks of the Ohio," as well as her song "Home" (cowritten with Kent Wells).

With "Home," Dolly directly references her story of leaving home at a young age, as she had in a number of songs, most of which were written in the earlier part of her career: "My Blue Ridge Mountain Boy," "Will He Be Waiting for

Me," "The Greatest Days of All," "Take Me Back," "Tennessee Homesick Blues," and "White Limozeen." Moreover, Dolly revisits the setting of her childhood home—the place of grinding hardships of mountain life that she had recalled in "In the Good Old Days (When Times Were Bad)." But in "Home"—a song from much later in her career—Dolly sings from the perspective of a successful, though weary, artist who now views home through more forgiving and wistful eyes rather than as a place of hard times and poverty. Focusing not on the bad old days of her youth, but on the solace of home to relieve her burdens, Dolly sings a litany of rustic elements as the banjo weaves in and out of the band: the fishing hole, crickets and katydids, front porch swing, whippoorwills, muscadine wine, sweet tea, and ginseng. Of course, music is present in her memories as she recalls church bells and singing the songs of her childhood. Near the end of the song she even names the popular folk tune "Shady Grove," set in relief to her nod to Hank Williams's classic "I'm So Lonesome I Could Cry," borrowing his title line to explain why she needs to return home.

Dolly's next album, *Pure and Simple* (2016), was filled with love songs inspired by her 50th wedding anniversary, and again, all were written by Dolly. The album went to #1 on the country chart, a spot she had not held since 1991 with *Eagle When She Flies*. The *Pure and Simple* tour that accompanied the album's release did not feature a stage full of instrumentalists and backup singers as previous tours had; instead, there were only four musicians on stage, including Dolly, all of whom played a variety of instruments and sang. The ethos of the show was one of returning home—the stage outfitted only with a gauzy curtained backdrop of purple twilight dotted with white lights. Whether stars or fireflies, the lights were accompanied by the sound of cicadas as audiences awaited Dolly's appearance on what felt like her front porch.

Throughout her life, Dolly was always striving for stardom and musical autonomy, and each of these goals brought about a struggle. Her childhood successes and dreams alienated her from her schoolmates, and she was homesick and hungry during her early days in Nashville. Her desire for musical autonomy made her productive years with Porter Wagoner difficult. Striking out on her own, Dolly discovered that musical autonomy came with a high price tag, so she embarked on a new path in pop music to become a star with the means to mount the kind of career she desired. But she found that her goals were again at odds. In order to have the fame and financial freedom to write and record only what she wanted to, there was a time she had to relinquish musical control and record songs that were not "from her heart." Ultimately, through several refashionings of her career, she reached the point where her two goals, stardom and musical autonomy, coexisted easily.

Dolly often jokes about having a lot of money, and her classic remark—"it takes a lot of money to look this cheap"—obviously plays with the idea of a poor girl who made it rich. Perhaps she uses this wisecrack, possibly more than any of her other pithy one-liners, as a way to manage the tension inherent in her public persona of the poor mountain girl who went pop and struck gold. From her earliest fantasies about becoming a star, Dolly was driven to earn money to provide for her family and later for her community. She said that her crossover into pop music was a "smart move" that guaranteed she would not "go hungry. I can pay my hospital bills and help my family when I need to. What more can you ask for? Well, you can ask to be able to do music for the sake of the art."[67] Here again, financial security and artistic control were at odds. So when she quips, "I'll never have too much money,"[68] her comment is not rooted in greed but rather in a desire that she and those around her never again live in the kind of poverty she knew as a child. The memory, and even fear, of living in poverty does not fade.

Looking back on the realization of her dreams, Dolly commented, "I've been very fortunate and have made some good choices and good investments. And I'm not having to do any of it for the money now. That's a good feeling, but the thing is, that just goes to show you how passionate I am about the music. I have to write and sing. See, that was my first love, and I have to do that forever, however I have to do it."[69] One could say that Dolly made most of her career and life choices for the music she truly wanted to make, as she wrote in "The Sacrifice":

> Well, I've sacrificed time with family and friends
> Gave up vacations for work without end
> Twenty-four seven, three sixty-five
> But I was willing to make the sacrifice

"I've always suffered pain for my music," Dolly confessed, "and my music stops me suffering pain."[70] Her passion was always for the music of her heart, and her best music is her own, whether an original country song or a rendition of the kind of music she would have heard as a child in the Smoky Mountains.

"Coat of Many Colors"

Dolly's Songwriting Workshop

"All of those little pieces of your past, they're
all important. That's why I'm so thankful
I can write songs. I can capture all those
memories in my songs and keep those
memories alive."

Songwriting always came easily to Dolly.[1] Her father recalled "she was
writing songs before she knew how to hold a pencil."[2] Dolly described
her childhood fascination with rhyme, rhythm, and the everyday sounds
she made into music:

> Since I have been able to form words, I have been able to rhyme them. I could
> catch on to anything that had a rhythm and make a song to go with it. I would
> take the two notes of a bobwhite in the darkness and make that the start of a
> song. I would latch on to the rhythm my mother made snapping beans, and before
> I knew it, I'd be tapping on a pot with a spoon and singing. I don't know what
> some of this sounded like to my family, but in my head it was beautiful music.[3]

Dolly wrote her first song when she was around five. "Little Tiny Tassletop" was
about her doll made from a corn cob, dressed in corn husks with corn silk for
hair, with two brown eyes burned into the cob with a hot poker:

> Little tiny tassletop
> I love you an awful lot

Corn silk hair and big brown eyes
How you make me smile

Little tiny tassletop
You're the only friend I've got
Hope you never go away
I want you to stay

Dolly's mother was impressed with her rhyming ability and kept this song tucked away for years. Dolly has since sung it, always in a little girl voice, on television shows for children and in interviews about her early songwriting. She often concludes the song with a giggle, saying "Well, what did you expect? I was just a little kid!" or "I told you it was corny!"

In addition to rhymes, Dolly loved creating musical sounds, and she was inventive about making instruments to inspire and accompany her melodies. When she was about six, she would play around with a dilapidated piano in an old church, as noted in Chapter One. Dolly recalled: "I found an old wooden mallet in the smokehouse. I had wrapped a rag around it to soften the blow, and I would beat on those strings in that old piano. And I would get that old droning sound, and it made a really good sound, and I would just make up melodies with that." She also remembers "rigging up an old mandolin that the neck was gone. I had an uncle that had a sawmill up the road, and I had him build a board underneath it. And I had stretched some strings over that. I don't know if they were the bass guitar strings or something I had cut off the piano." Dolly would "bang on" these strings with a stick or, less often, strum with her thumb to create drones, like she did with the old piano: "So I would just make my melodies around sounds. And so anything that I could rig up to make a little different sound in addition to the other instruments, I would just do that."[4] Dolly most enjoyed creating drones, and these sounds were the sonic underpinning over which she spun her melodies.

Dolly's songwriting began in earnest when she got her first "little baby Martin" guitar when she was about seven or eight: "that's when I started to write some serious songs."[5] At around the age of eight or nine, Dolly wrote "Life Doesn't Mean Much to Me" after overhearing her mom and aunts talking about young men who had been killed in war. It is a sophisticated lyric for a child of that age with its rich imagery, consistent rhyme scheme, and refrain. She called it "a pretty deep song for a kid. . . . I don't ever remember thinking like a child."[6]

He's gone from my world
Left this country girl

To fight in a war 'cross the sea
The telegram said
He's been pronounced dead
Life doesn't mean much to me

What good is life
Without him by my side
Just lay me beside where he sleeps
My soldier boy's gone
Left me all alone
Now life doesn't mean much to me

Goodbye one and all
The river has called
I'll be with him eternally
Life doesn't mean much to me

Dolly's storytelling gift is evident here. She drops the listener immediately into the scene, lays out the emotional response to the soldier's death and, in a characteristically Dolly move, surprises the listener with a sudden and stunning conclusion. Looking back on the song, Dolly said, "I guess I'd hear them talk about people drowning themselves and heartbroken girls and all that. But at any rate those were serious songs at the time. And I was serious about it even though I did write some fun ones as well."[7]

From these charming and humble beginnings, Dolly estimates she has written over 3,000 songs, and over 450 of them have been recorded. Her songwriting has been recognized with numerous awards, including her induction into the Nashville Songwriters Hall of Fame in 1986 and the Songwriters Hall of Fame in 2001. Dolly consistently asserts that songwriting is her first priority and being a songwriter is her primary identity. In this chapter, I explore Dolly's approach to songwriting: what inspires her, what is her process? I also use her iconic song "Coat of Many Colors" as a touchstone through which to explore the way she shapes and reshapes pivotal stories of her life through her songs. Although not all of Dolly's songs are autobiographical, they are often informed by her life and the people and situations she observes. She turns memory into song.

"Coat of Many Colors"

Whenever pressed to choose her favorite song, Dolly always names "Coat of Many Colors," which is about a true story from her life. As a young child, she lacked a suitable coat for the winter, so her mother sewed one out of scraps given by neighbors. To make the homemade garment special for Dolly, she told Dolly the Bible story of Joseph and his coat of many colors. Dolly ran off to school, proud to show it off. But Dolly's classmates made fun of her, teasing her about her coat made of rags.

Many years later, in 1969, she composed the song about this incident. With its folklike melody and simple three-chord harmonic structure, the song's first-person account of these events draws listeners in to an intimate story of childlike innocence, pain, and grace. Dolly did not record the song immediately, and in the intervening time Porter Wagoner recorded it on two occasions in 1969, with Dolly apparently singing backup.[8] Dolly's recording was released in 1971 on her album *Coat of Many Colors*; the song went to #4 on the country chart, and it appears on many of her compilation and greatest hits albums. No live concert of Dolly's would be complete without it. Dolly also published the lyrics as a children's book in 1996. In 2016, she released a new version of the book as well as a made-for-television movie, *Dolly Parton's Coat of Many Colors*, seen by over 15 million viewers.[9] Dolly read the lyrics of the song as a bonus track on her 2017 children's album, *I Believe In You*. The song's melody hovers behind Dolly's voice, its music box timbre suggesting childlike innocence. In 2011, "Coat of Many Colors" was inducted into the National Recording Registry of the Library of Congress, whose purpose is "to maintain and preserve sound recordings and collections of sound recordings that are culturally, historically, or aesthetically significant."[10] The song was added to the Grammy Hall of Fame in 2019.

Why does "Coat of Many Colors" have such wide-ranging popularity, and why is it "culturally, historically, or aesthetically significant"? To begin with, the song is Dolly's version of a story from her life, which audiences value, believing that autobiographical songs are more powerful and emotionally honest. More-over, the song is primarily from the perspective of a child, which simultaneously takes listeners back to their own memories and arouses their empathy. That a mother plays such a pivotal role in the song, both as the giver of a precious gift and as the source of a deep reservoir of love, heightens the poignancy of the story. Listeners can also place themselves in the scenario as the teased child or the loving parent.

The aesthetic significance of "Coat of Many Colors" is not only measured by its compelling "true" story that allows us into Dolly's "real" life, but also its pliability which makes it an allegory. Most listeners can relate to the pain and embarrassment of being teased as a child, even if they have never lived in poverty. Dolly reports that the song is taught in schools to address bullying. "Sometimes they simply sing the song and discuss it. Other times, the children make their own coats with construction paper, each square representing something in their lives. It really touches my heart to think that the song is being used to teach respect and tolerance. I'm proud that in a small way my little song has helped so many people."[11]

Through "Coat of Many Colors" we discover why composing is essential for her. Dolly's songs constitute a memory palace—a place to store her memories in lyrics and melodies that evoke people, feelings, places, and events, bringing them to life whenever she sings one of her songs. Of course, not every song is based on Dolly's life. She is often inspired by other people's lives and experiences, and she writes some songs without calling on specific memories or events. But, a big part of Dolly's songwriting is to keep memories alive, and she points to "Coat of Many Colors" as one example: "Whenever I sing that I just see my whole childhood."[12] The song—like a teddy bear, a blanket, or the multicolored coat itself—is a transitional object that links the child to its mother. For the three minutes Dolly inhabits the song, she is that little girl, as well as the adult who, decades after she wore the coat, conjures up her mother's love, re-creating their bond and extending it into the present.

Dolly's Songwriting Process

Dolly believes "it has to be born of you to be a great songwriter. I think you have to have that gift and that burning desire."[13] Three principles define the way Dolly views her songwriting. First it is a *serious* endeavor. "I've often been misunderstood, and it has taken 40 years for people to realize how serious I am about the music. . . . My heart is in my music. I write every day. I will do that till the day I die, whether anybody buys them or hears those songs till after I'm dead. I'm dead serious about the music."[14] Second, Dolly describes her approach to songwriting as instinctive: "So many times when I write, stuff just comes to me; I have no choice in the matter."[15] Finally, she claims her creativity is a "God-given gift,"[16] her songwriting talent comes from God, and she is serious about her stewardship of that spiritual gift.

Those closest to her have seen her in action as a serious, instinctive, and gifted writer. Emmylou Harris once observed: "I've watched Dolly writing one song while she's singing another. I've never seen anyone so spontaneously creative. . . . With Dolly, it's like the songs come out whole. I don't think she questions anything in her creative process. She's inspired, but at the same time, she's a craftsman—she'll retain that strict country format and simplicity, but the songs are very complex, not these formula products."[17] Porter Wagoner recalled, "She is one of the most creative people I have ever met—and I've met some great ones, from Hank Williams on. She has the ability to put herself into a situation and write about it."[18] Producer Steve Buckingham commented: "There's a lot going on in that mind that I don't think most people really think about—what goes into that thought process, that creative process. It's complex, but it's a natural flow. It's organic. It's not over thought. She thinks a lot, believe me, about life and the universe. And obviously her music is the center of her life even though she has all these other things going. The music's the center. And spirituality is center."[19]

Dolly's approach to her songwriting is a mixture of compulsion, ecstasy, and craft. Composing melodies and rhymes seems effortless for her, and she has new song ideas every day. When Dolly was little she wrote constantly; it was "like a compulsion."[20] She also describes her writing in terms of a reflex action that "burns" in her, and she keeps a notebook, tape recorder, or guitar close at hand for the moments of inspiration when the songs come freely. What Dolly jots down are the lyrics and perhaps the chords, but not the melody since she does not read or write music. Sometimes just strumming a few chords or hearing someone's story will spur on more songs. Dolly composes everywhere—"on a plane, in the tub or on the bus"—and the lyrics and music flow simultaneously. Dolly explains, "writing's just as natural to me as getting up and cooking breakfast."[21]

Not all of her songwriting occurs in these short, breezy bursts. Dolly also likes to get away to her mountain home or lake house to spend weeks at a stretch working intensely in a reverie of songwriting. She prefers to write in solitude, usually in the very early hours of the morning, because, as she explains, "that's my time with God."[22] However, Dolly does have a special working relationship with her lifelong friend Judy Ogle, who is often part of the songwriting process.

> I sit with my guitar, and she writes everything down. Sometimes I'll ask her, "Put down all the words you can think of that rhyme with this or that," or whatever. I tend to forget to eat (if you can believe that) when I'm writing, and Judy always keeps me from hurting myself. Just about the time my blood sugar gets low, she'll be there with a bowl of Jell-O. Writing is an intensely personal thing, best done alone. Being with Judy is better. It's like being alone but with somebody, if that makes any sense.[23]

Dolly says she often loses track of time during these private, intense songwriting sessions, during which she might produce as many as twenty songs.

In these spells of songwriting, Dolly enters a trancelike mental state. For example, to write the songs for *Hungry Again*, Dolly returned to her mountain home to spend two weeks in a retreat mode, clearing a space for this focused state of mind: "I fasted and prayed for many days before the inspiration finally came."[24] During these concentrated intervals, the external world falls away. Dolly said,

> I get moods, great moods. . . . I just really get involved in what I'm doin' and I just can't stop. I've stayed up as long as three days before, or at least two days, and into the third day, before I could really make my mind stop enough to rest. . . . I get excited when I get inspired, because I can't wait to see what I come up with. . . . I just think, "I wish this was day after tomorrow, so I'd have all these on tape, and I know what all I came up with."[25]

When she is "on a wild streak" like this—binges that last two or three days—Dolly is in a private ecstasy of songwriting, a bookend to the public ecstasy of performance she feels on stage and in the studio when she shares her songs in their finished form, as I discuss in Chapter Eight. For Dolly, these writing sessions are simultaneously intellectual, "like mind exercises,"[26] and an "emotional journey," buoying her spirits when she writes uplifting songs and bringing her down when she writes depressing ones.[27] Dolly believes her songwriting is a "way of channeling my feelings and my thoughts. Not just mine, but the things I see, the people I care about. My head would explode if I didn't get some of that stuff out."[28] "I couldn't live without my writing. I put all the feelings, my very soul, into my writing. I tell the world in my songs things I wouldn't even tell my husband."[29] Because of this visceral and immersive approach Dolly remembers details about her songwriting sessions: "where I was and what I felt with every song I ever wrote. Even with the thousands of songs I've written, I almost remember what time of year it was, what time of day it was, if I was inside or outside, if I was on the porch, if I was in the car. You just remember those things when you allow yourself to feel that deeply."[30]

Dolly says the joy and thrill of writing songs comes from creating "something that was never in the world before"[31] and it is "a way to escape reality."[32] The following description of her songwriting process for "Down from Dover" illuminates the free-associative state she enters when creating these imaginary scenarios:

> I was on the bus one day with Porter and we were riding through Dover, Tennessee. . . . I just saw this crawling shadow across this field—it wasn't clover, but it rhymed with Dover and we were in Dover [laughs]—but whatever was in that field, the shadow swept across it. And I sang, "And the sun behind the cloud just cast a crawling shadow over the fields of clover." That was the first thought that

came to my mind, and then I thought, "Time is running out for me and I wish that he would hurry down from Dover." It was like little word triggers. All of a sudden, I thought, "This is great and it's a pretty tune. What'll I write about? Who would live in Dover? Some simple girl would live in Dover, because it was like a simple, country town."... And the next thing I knew I was writing about this pregnant girl. Anyhow, it just came and boy, once I got into it, it was one line after another. I love to stay in there when I'm writing the story [laughs]. I don't want to get out until I'm through with that movie.[33]

Inspired by a landscape and the name of a town, Dolly followed her thoughts from rhymes and word play to a melody and on to a scenario that easily unfolded cinematically. The result is one of her most compelling ballads. Thus, Dolly does not write what she calls "formula songs,"[34] adhering to the expectations of the marketplace or the recording industry. She trusts and follows her own instincts.

But as much as Dolly's songwriting is reflexive and instinctive, done during these intense sessions of artistic flow, she also approaches her songwriting with an artisan's sense of craft and design. As she remarked, "I look at my publishing company and my body of work as my workshop." She frequently revisits lyrics and melodies, revising songs for later recordings and reworking previous material into new songs. Sometimes she does this intentionally; other times the same melodic or lyric line emerges more organically as she describes:

> Sometimes I don't realize that I've stolen so much from myself until I think, "oh my lord, that sounds too much like so and so," and I thought, "oh well, it's mine. I'm not gonna sue myself." [laughs] When you write as many songs as I do, you're bound to repeat yourself with melodies, even sometimes with lines. I realize that I've put a line that's very similar to something else I had. And then sometimes I intentionally will do it if I think it's a song that somebody else might not hear. And I think, "well, what the hey, you know if they do hear it, it's still mine."[35]

Buckingham has seen Dolly in action in her workshop: "It's rare that you bring up a song of hers that she doesn't remember.... I mean, she'll remember everything. If not, she'll get the words from her office. Then she'll sit there and maybe rework the lyrics. It's fascinating to watch her work."[36]

A cluster of Dolly's songs from 1968 to 1970 demonstrates her workshop approach to songwriting (see Example 2.1). Dolly opens each of these songs with a similar melodic gesture: an active, stepwise descent from the 5th to the 1st scale degree in the first half of the line. The second half is a prolongation of the 2nd or 1st scale degree prior to the cadence on the tonic chord (the melody may or may not end with a fully closed cadence on the 1st scale degree; when it ends

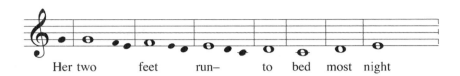

Her two   feet   run–   to   bed   most   night

We'd get   sun–   get   done work fields sun down

Ma– len–   hours   run   mea– –len– go play day

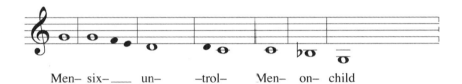

Men– six–___ un–   –trol–   Men– on– child

When o–   green   clov–   watch set end day

I   –self   beau–   song___ climb top cloud sky

EXAMPLE 2.1:

"Jeannie's Afraid of the Dark," 1968

"In the Good Old Days (When Times Were Bad)," 1969

"Malena," 1969

"Mendy Never Sleeps," 1970

"Everything's Beautiful (In Its Own Way)," 1965

"I Can," 1968

The open notes are the structural pitches of the melody, which coincide with the word/syllables of the songs's first verses as indicated; the filled-in notes are the surface elements of the melody.

elsewhere, on the 2nd or 5th scale degree, it is an open cadence). What gives these songs their individual identity is the particular way each one traverses this melodic contour, primarily through different patterns of passing tones to fill in falling 3rds that circle around the main melody notes. Five of the six examples are in a triple meter, so these songs also share a lilting rhythmic swing as the melodies make their descent ("I Can" is in a duple meter).

These closely related songs reveal a more general trait about one of Dolly's melodic approaches. Although she does not always follow the same pattern found in these six songs, she often begins lines or verses with an active melody and harmonic progression and then prolongs the penultimate or final melody note and chord in the second part of the lines or verses. For example, she used a similar procedure in "More than I Can Say" and "Unlikely Angel," two songs that share a melody that is a step-wise descent from the 5th scale degree to the 1st, as in the melodies in Example 2.1.

In "More than I Can Say" the melody is sparse, almost chantlike. The first measure is intoned on one pitch, the 5th scale degree. The melody descends to the 2nd scale degree in the second measure, and the remainder of the line, measures three and four, is sung on this pitch and culminates in an open-ended cadence. This melody repeats for the second line of text and ends on a fully closed cadence on the 1st scale degree. For her recasting of this melody in "Unlikely Angel," Dolly maintains this melodic outline, although she emphasizes the 3rd scale degree instead of the 2nd at the ends of the lines, both of which terminate in a fully closed cadence on the 1st scale degree. Additionally, in the second half of the verses of "Unlikely Angel" (at "thought I could never love again" and "how long have you been there for me"), Dolly embellishes the prolonged 5th scale degree of her original melody by circling down a 3rd and back up as in Example 2.1.

Both songs also share a contrasting section. Here, the melody moves up from the 5th scale degree, striving for, but not reaching, the upper tonic note only to fall back to pitch 5 (at the line "and when I need you" in "More than I Can Say" and at "unlikely angel" in "Unlikely Angel"). But the energy renews and the line finally rises to the upper tonic for the emotional payoff. After this expansion of the musical space to the upper part of the range, the line quickly drops back to the lower register. In contrast to the somewhat pensive quality of the relatively static opening lines, this section soars with feeling.

When asked about this pair of songs, Dolly remarked, "that was a beautiful melody. I often go back and use melodies that I think are still really good, that tend to want to lend itself to whatever I'm writing then."[37] Despite their shared melody, the close relationship between these songs is barely recognizable because of their very different arrangements. Dolly recorded "More than I Can Say" in 1987 on *Rainbow*, her last album to focus on pop music. The song is cast as a slow ballad with lush orchestration and reverb. Dolly returned to this melody for her 1996 film *Unlikely Angel*. The new lyrics frame the plot of the film (a deceased country music star trying to earn her wings), and the musical setting is folklike. Dolly's version for the film was not released, but she later recorded the song on *Blue Smoke* in 2014 using an old-time style band with prominent fiddle, mandolin, and dobro. This song pair, with their disparate arrangements and affects, showcase Dolly's workshop in action. The beautiful melody she had written for "More than I Can Say" languished on an album that was one of her least successful. It was a felicitous choice for a folklike song for her "Unlikely Angel" country singer character, and the upbeat, old-time version on *Blue Smoke* continued Dolly's emphasis on traditional folk, and mountain styles on her more recent recordings.

Dolly often speaks about her desire "to be somebody important in time; I want to be somebody that left somethin' good behind for somebody else to enjoy."[38] Perhaps because she had no children, one of the ways Dolly views her songs as her legacy is by thinking of them as her children. "I get the mothering experience from writing songs. It's like giving birth every time."[39] "I think God meant for me not to have children. My songs are my children, and I've given life to three thousand of them."[40] She spoke in similar language when discussing a contract she signed with Porter Wagoner in 1970. The contract gave him 49 percent of Owe-Par, Dolly's publishing company, and 15 percent of her record royalties. But her songs were specifically named as not being part of the agreement. Dolly explained, "I just had to protect my songs if something happened to Porter. They were always up for grabs. Everybody always wanted my songs; everybody knew there would be something there someday. So I tried to protect them for myself, from the world as you would your children."[41] In this context of Dolly's views on her musical legacy as offspring, Pamela Wilson's comment here—about Appalachian women, song, and children—takes on an added resonance. "Songs, like stories, have been a vital part of the cultural economy of Appalachian women; producing songs, like producing children, has been important to their social identities."[42]

Possibly as a result of her Appalachian heritage, with its rich ballad tradition, Dolly is a storyteller through song, and much of her music is narrative: "I just had a gift of writing. . . . I just knew how to put it into story form."[43] Dolly's skill at storytelling is a hallmark of her songwriting. Whether calling on her Appalachian heritage with a mountain-style ballad of betrayal and death, often with a gothic flavor, or weaving a country song of heartbreak and abandoned love, Dolly keeps listeners hooked through the last line of her songs, often delivering a gut-punch at the end. And writing story songs, as she would call them, is her favorite way to compose.

> That's more natural for me than trying to just do a few words in a simple song. To tell a story, I can rhyme words really good, and to me, it's the same as writing a book. So I really enjoy it. Usually, I just start out writing and I think, "I'm going to write and I'm not going to think about how long it is or how many verses I got before I get to the chorus, or how many times I go back to the chorus. I'm just going to write what I think and what I feel, then if I have to tear it down and fix it up to make it commercial, then I'll do that." But it's much easier for me to write the story songs. Boy, I can tell you a story in a minute. Honestly, I can sit down and write a big long story song much easier than I can the other kind—the more commercial, typical songs.[44]

Thus, Dolly creates instinctively—"not going to think about how long it is"—and then shapes her songs as an artisan—"tear it down and fix it up."

The term *songcatcher* is sometimes used to describe Appalachian ballad singers—those musicians who can pick up a tune and a story with little effort. Dolly is a songweaver, catching a tune and rhyme here, an image there, and entwining them into musical vignettes with ease.

The Back Stories of "Coat of Many Colors"

Dolly has told the story of the painful incident that inspired "Coat of Many Colors" in several ways, exploring her memories as through a prism. With each variation of the story, our understanding of the song, and Dolly herself, is enriched.

Her first recording of the song on *Coat of Many Colors* included an extensive liner note, written by Dolly, which detailed the story of her mother sewing the coat and the teasing from her classmates. Dolly was especially excited to wear the coat because she was to have her school picture taken that day. She wrote, "I cried but I was so proud of my coat and the thought of having my picture

FIGURE 2.1. Dolly Parton wearing her "coat of many colors," school photo (Sevier County, Tennessee, c. 1955). Courtesy: Dolly Parton Enterprises.

made for Mama that I smiled through my tears and the tears are plain in the picture and so is the smile."[45] Dolly included this sepia-toned photograph on the album's back cover and a colorized, painted version of the photograph on the album's front.[46] This painterly re-creation reveals the colors of the coat, not made from little squares like a beautiful, brightly colored crazy quilt (like the outfits Dolly wears to emulate the coat), but rather a couple of large dull-hued corduroy panels of single, but different, solid colors. The album's painted image also clearly includes and enhances Dolly's tears on her right cheek and under her left eye.

"Coat of Many Colors" was included on the LP release of the 1975 compilation *Best of Dolly Parton*, but the photograph and the liner notes from the original album were not reproduced. However, there was a new element. The lyrics to the song, which were printed in the inner gatefold of this album, included an additional final verse that Dolly has never sung on any recordings, although in 2017 she included this verse in her reading of the story in the bonus track on the children's album *I Believe In You*. The new lines, from an adult perspective, tell of Dolly's eventual success, luck, and happiness. She recalls the precious memory of her mother as paramount in life, echoing what she wrote at the end of her 1971 liner note.

FIGURE 2.2. *Coat of Many Colors* album front cover, 1971.

FIGURE 2.3. Dolly Parton in contemporary "coat of many colors." DFree/Shutterstock.com

In a 1977 interview in *Rolling Stone*, Dolly told a different version of the story: a painful encounter with the other children who terrorized her with actions much harsher than what she wrote about in the song.

> That was a very sad and cutting memory that I long kept deep within myself. I remembered all the pain of it and the mockery. How the kids had tried to take my little coat off and I was just sprouting . . . boobs, you know, and I didn't have a blouse on under it because I had done *well* just to have a little jacket to wear. So when the kids kept sayin' I didn't have a shirt on under it, I said I *did* because I was embarrassed. So they broke the buttons off my coat. They locked me in the coat closet that day and held the door closed and it was black dark in there and I just went into a screaming fit. I remembered all that and I was ashamed to even mention it and for *years* I held it in my mind.[47]

What is striking about this story is Dolly's visceral vulnerability and fear. She felt a physical threat that surpassed her sadness about her coat being mocked. In fact, the scrappiness of the coat is not the focus; rather, it is her fear of being physically exposed. Her potential nakedness and embarrassment about that is what filled her with such shame that she could not speak about the incident until she wrote the song many years later.

When Dolly again told the story in her autobiography, she focused more on her excitement and how much she preened around the house in the coat the day before she wore it to school. In this version, there is no mention of the school picture or the ordeal of kids tearing at her coat and locking her in a closet. Rather, she took the high road through this abuse and maintained her sense of strength and faith in God:

> The teacher came in and noticed I was being picked on, so she tried to help. "Don't you want to put your coat in the cloakroom?" she suggested, but I would not. They would not shake my pride in my coat, my love for my mother, my faith in myself. I would not have it. I would sit there and be hot and wait them out. I would wait until school was over and walk proudly from the building wearing my coat like a banner of pride. I would walk with my head high into the autumn afternoon and show my coat to God. He would know how special it was, how special I was. He did. He liked the way it looked with his autumn leaves. He admired the way it complemented his evergreens and the rich brown earth of the path. He watched carefully to catch glimpses of it from his side of the clouds as I marched proudly home. He loved the way it looked on his Dolly Parton.[48]

Of course, we do not know which of these stories comes closest to the actual event. But what is significant are the ways that Dolly has represented the incident throughout the years. For her 1971 album, early in her career as a solo country artist, Dolly paints a picture of heartbreaking, childish taunts, and her smiling-through-tears response explains and sweetens the photograph. This story would resonate with many and would be particularly well-received by country music fans who desire singers both to write about their own experiences and to demonstrate evidence of their hardscrabble life. The later story about being physically attacked and locked in a closet is Dolly at her most vulnerable. By then a genuine star, more secure in her place in country music, Dolly was willing to reveal more and, perhaps, not protect her fans from a harsher image of her childhood. Finally, her most upbeat version of the story is consistent with her autobiography, which is breezy and lighthearted, projecting an image of Dolly as vulnerable but ultimately strong and confident. This is the Dolly most people know.

Along with these versions of the back story of the song, there is also the question: what became of the coat? Although it is widely reported that the original coat is on display in the Chasing Rainbows Museum at Dollywood, Dolly says otherwise: "mama tore that [coat] down and sewed it into a quilt or blanket or something else. We do have a little replica of it my mom made from

FIGURE 2.4. Replica of the "coat of many colors," Chasing Rainbows Museum, Dollywood (Pigeon Forge, Tennessee, July 14, 2018). Photo: Lydia Hamessley.

memory as best she could remember at the time. But that was just a memory in my head."[49] This replica, in its glass case in the museum, matches the image on the 1971 album. The original papers with the song's lyrics are placed next to the coat.[50] Dolly wrote the song while on tour with Porter Wagoner, and the only paper she could find was attached to his flashy suits—dry cleaning slips.

On the wall behind the case is an almost lifesize, sepia-toned photograph of children looking directly at the camera, laughing at and taunting the viewer who is placed in the position of being teased and bullied. Adjacent to this mural is a panel with the text of the song. Thus, the coat is not just another artifact in Dolly's museum, which is stuffed with her wardrobe items, photographs, awards, and memorabilia. In this intimate alcove, the coat is thoughtfully displayed to highlight the song's message about bullying.

Dolly has continued to mine this childhood memory into other creative expressions. In 1996, she transformed the song into an illustrated children's book. The lyrics conclude with the added, unrecorded verse about Dolly's successful life and her precious memory of her mother. She dedicated the book: "To my mother, Avie Lee Parton; to all the good mothers everywhere; and to anyone who has suffered the emotional pain of being made fun of, may this book be healing."[51] For a new 2016 version of the book, Dolly wrote an anti-bullying

FIGURE 2.5. Alcove display of the "coat of many colors" replica and mural, Chasing Rainbows Museum, Dollywood (Pigeon Forge, Tennessee, July 28, 2019). Photo: Lydia Hamessley.

song, "Makin' Fun Ain't Funny," which she sang with a group of children. The song was available as a free download with a purchase of the book or by visiting Dolly's website.[52]

The story of the song was also the subject of a made-for-television movie, *Dolly Parton's Coat of Many Colors*, which first aired on NBC in 2015. Dolly wanted to create a family film that celebrated the strength and love of her own family. In this version, the coat (a much more colorful one than the replica of the original) is a plot device in a story about the grief and ultimate healing of Dolly's family after the death of her newborn brother Larry. Dolly was devastated by his death because Larry was to be her baby, following a common practice in large families of "giving" a new baby to an older child to care for along with her mother. In the film, the scraps start out as a quilt for the eagerly awaited baby, and after his death, a heartbroken Dolly places the quilt on Larry's grave. Later, Dolly's mother sews the quilt pieces into a coat in an effort to overcome her depression and to cheer up Dolly, who had not sung since Larry's death. At this point, the plot follows the song's lyrics with the story of Joseph and Dolly's excitement about wearing the coat to school.

Of the three versions of the event Dolly had previously told, the most disturbing one gets dramatized in the film. Dolly is teased at school, and the teacher does try to get her to hang up the coat to diffuse the situation. But Dolly confesses that she is not wearing anything under the coat, so she keeps it on. Later, when the teacher is away from the classroom, the other kids who

FIGURE 2.6. Dolly Parton (Alyvia Alyn Lind) lying on Larry's grave. *Dolly Parton's Coat of Many Colors*, 2015.

FIGURE 2.7. Dolly Parton (Alyvia Alyn Lind) in her "coat of many colors" arriving at school. *Dolly Parton's Coat of Many Colors*, 2015.

had initially teased Dolly come into the room and tear at the coat, stripping it off her. An older boy carries a screaming, half-naked Dolly, wearing only her bloomers, to a small closet and locks her in as she cries, "I'm afraid of the dark." It is a chilling scene in this family-friendly movie. Another child, Judy Ogle, fights off the bullies, opens the closet door, and, bathed in a halo of light, returns Dolly's coat to her. Their newfound friendship is further cemented as Judy turns to leave. "Don't go," Dolly pleads; "I don't want to be alone." Judy replies, "You ain't alone." In the next scene, Dolly gently cleans Judy's bloody split lip she got in the fight, and later in the film, Dolly says of Judy watching over her, "that's angel work." Judy is clearly cast as Dolly's savior.

In this version of the story, no school photograph is taken; rather, Dolly was wearing the coat on the day she was to read aloud an essay she wrote about how she was going to grow up to a be star. Further, Dolly does not wear her coat proudly after the humiliation. Instead, she runs home from school with Judy, strips off the coat, accuses her mother of lying to her about its beauty, and vows never to wear it again. The film ends, of course, with redemption: Dolly understands her mother's special love sewed into the coat, and she wears it proudly; the family's grief heals after Larry's death; Dolly makes a friend for life in her champion in the film, her real-life best friend, Judy Ogle; the bullying kids are understood, forgiven, and befriended; and Dolly forgives God for what she believed was his own bullying of her and accepts God's forgiveness for her

FIGURE 2.8. Judy Ogle (Hannah Nordberg) and Dolly Parton (Alyvia Alyn Lind) in the closet scene. *Dolly Parton's Coat of Many Colors*, 2015.

lack of faith. In the final scene, Dolly, wearing the coat, chases a butterfly as it takes wing after alighting on the newly made cross on Larry's grave.

This film does much more than retell the story of the coat. In it, Dolly also constructs a narrative about who is centrally important in her life and what events continue to have a deep resonance for her. Dolly intentionally gives Judy Ogle a pivotal role even though she is not present in any of Dolly's other accounts. Best friends since the third grade, Dolly and Judy have been inseparable most of their lives. Judy is Dolly's constant companion and personal assistant, and Dolly places Judy—"one of my most special angels"[53]—in a position of strength and honor in her film. Moreover, Dolly makes Judy a witness to the pain she felt when she was bullied, mirroring the way Dolly is often a witness to others' pain as a songwriter. Dolly also chose to incorporate and foreground her baby brother's death. She was devastated when Larry died soon after birth, and this tragedy clearly has had an effect on her songwriting. In this version of the story, Dolly places Larry's birth and death at the center, and she even has Judy secretly place wildflowers on Larry's grave as Dolly sleeps in vigil there. By linking Judy's friendship with Larry's death and weaving them both into her iconic coat-of-many-colors story, Dolly makes a powerful statement about their importance in her life. Yet again, she sculpts the story of the coat into the message she wishes to deliver in looking back on her childhood as a seventy-year-old woman.

Singing the Song

Dolly's 1971 recording of "Coat of Many Colors" illustrates the way Dolly combines her keen sense of storytelling with a memorable melody and harmonic structure that belie its seeming simplicity. The song is in verse-chorus form, but Dolly starts with an intro that creates a sense of community with her listeners. Rather than opening her tale with lines about her mother sewing the coat, Dolly begins in the present and journeys back through time to her childhood, almost lost in thought: "Back through the years I go wandering once again." While not exactly a "come all ye" introduction common in many traditional ballads, this approach similarly gathers her listeners into the story circle. In her second line, we arrive at the point in her life in which the story is set—"back to the seasons of my youth"—and she begins to remember the box of rags that kicks off the central story of her mother using the small scraps for a coat.

This four-line intro is an invitation to the listener to join Dolly in her memories. In order to create a hushed sense of expectation as one does at the beginning of a good tale, Dolly nearly recites rather than sings these lyrics, with the almost chantlike opening two lines centering on one note, the 3rd of the tonic chord (I). This melodic stasis is matched by the harmony that rocks between the tonic chord and the subdominant chord (IV) that we get on the word "youth." Since the IV chord includes the tonic note and quickly returns to the I chord, it does not engender a sense of harmonic movement. This same melodic and harmonic pattern repeats for the third and fourth line, closing out the intro with the open-ended IV chord. The narrow range of the intro, only the interval of a 5th, also contributes to the introspective mood. All these musical choices carve out a space for reflection and invite the listener to focus on the words of the story. The effect is one of quietness and remembrance brought about by the melodic and harmonic stillness as Dolly and we enter her recollections of the past.

The four lines of the intro, with its static melody and harmony, flow seamlessly into verse 1, which continues the melody of the intro and sustains the I chord over the first three lines. Here, she describes the rags that her mother will fashion into a much-needed winter coat. With the fourth line of the verse, "it was way down in the fall," Dolly is fully within the story. She punctuates this moment with a dominant chord (V), the first real harmonic movement of the song that propels the verse forward. The remaining second half of the verse—in which Dolly's mother sews the coat—features a more rapid harmonic rhythm through the three chords of the song and a slightly wider range than the intro. After telling the Bible story in verse 2, Dolly moves to the chorus, which describes

Listening Outline 1: "Coat of Many Colors," *Coat of Many Colors,* **1971**

0:00	Intro	Back through the years...	Acoustic guitar solo to start, fingerpicked; then a shaker and bass.
0:27	Verse 1	There were rags...	Intro seamlessly moves into verse. The listener becomes aware there was an intro only after the verse is repeated. "Way down in the fall" is on the V chord—the first time the harmony effectively moves away from tonic.
0:51	Verse 2	As she sewed...	An organ enters in subtly sustained chords creating a sonic "church," "Bible story," gospel-inflected feeling.
1:15	Chorus	My coat...	Backup singers on the first line, wordless harmony follows and then they sing the words again just on the repeat of "my coat of many colors," highlighting the title. Organ throughout.
1:41	Verse 3	So with patches...	Modulation up a whole step; no organ.
2:07	Verse 4	And oh I couldn't understand it...	Dolly often speaks this verse in most other recordings and performances.
2:31	Chorus	But they didn't understand it...	Lyrics change slightly to further the story. Backup singers again emphasize the title lyrics. Organ returns, bringing back the idea of the Bible story.
2:55	Tag	Made just for me...	Backup singers continue; plagal (Amen) cadence; organ continues.

her feelings of pride and includes the key lines, "Although we had no money I was rich as I could be/In my coat of many colors my mama made for me." Dolly writes a much more songlike melody for the chorus with a range spanning an octave, in contrast with the almost recited character of the narrow-ranged verses. To create a smooth transition back to verse 3, Dolly closes the last line of the chorus with the same melody that concludes each verse, effectively refocusing our attention on the continuation of the story.

There are two more verses and a final chorus in the second half of the song. In verse 3, Dolly sings of hurrying off to school, filled with pride as she nonchalantly reminds us of the "patches on my britches" and "holes in both my shoes." The end of the verse relates the jeering and laughter of her classmates. With verse 4, we get Dolly's confusion at this teasing and then her response about the real meaning of riches and poverty, which she concludes with an imperfect rhyme of the words "sewed" and "clothes."

The final line of verse 4 is an allusion to the adage "worth more than gold," so listeners might get ahead and fill in the word *gold* that would more closely rhyme with *sewed* and signify real riches. But then Dolly goes a different way (though she is likely playing with our expectations) and concludes the line with *clothes*. The kids teasing her did not have riches like gold any more than Dolly did. They most likely just had clothes that were not patched together as much as Dolly's coat. So the unexpected rhyme draws attention to the fact that Dolly's tormentors were not rich in two ways: they did not have real riches in the form of gold, and they did not have the genuine riches of the coat that was the symbol of Dolly's mother's deep love for her. In an adroit shift of rhyme, Dolly humbles those kids. Finally, by conflating the likely rhyme expectation, *gold* and *clothes*, Dolly links the wealth of gold with her own sense of being rich in wearing her coat. (In the song's lyrics printed in the liner notes for the 1975 compilation *Best of Dolly Parton* and in her reading of the story for her children's album, *I Believe in You*, Dolly uses the word *gold*.) The song ends with the chorus, but with the first four lines changed to include the moral of the story: "one is only poor, only if they choose to be." The chorus concludes as Dolly again links the coat with the emotional riches that surpass the family's economic poverty.

It seems a good decision not to have recorded that additional final verse discussed earlier.[54] The song is a visceral depiction of childhood feelings brought about by adult reminiscences. In the intro, the adult goes back in time to relive the event from the perspective of a child, and she invites listeners to join her. Had Dolly ended with that extra verse from the adult perspective, it would have worked with the adult intro to form a symmetrical frame for the story. But it would have broken the spell of the immediate and heartfelt story of the child's experience. The song is more powerful when concluded with the child's words. When Dolly performs "Coat of Many Colors" in concert, she does frame it from the adult standpoint in her comments to the audience. But within the song, this verse would be overkill and risk being too sentimental. Much of the power of the song is that it does not give in to the maudlin. Dolly does not describe in great detail the torment she suffered from the other kids in order to ratchet up the pathos; indeed, they get only one line for their teasing. Rather, she focuses on her childlike confusion tempered with her conviction that her mama was right: she was rich in her little coat.

The power of this song for Dolly's fans cannot be overstated. Dolly said: "I cannot tell you how many times someone has walked up to me to tell me how much the song meant to them."[55] By opening the song with a walk back through her memories and inviting us to join her, Dolly brings individual listeners into the circle of community, in effect calling everyone together out of their isolation. Thus, for Dolly, as well as her listeners, the coat is not a coat of rags, but a communal symbol of love and acceptance in the face of ridicule and shame, no matter the reason.

Dolly once said, "I want to be known as a great writer—now that's a dream of mine. I like to describe my writing as being simply complicated. It's got enough depth to be appreciated and enough simplicity to be understood."[56] By either measure, she succeeds with "Coat of Many Colors."

Chapter 3
"My Tennessee Mountain Home"
Dolly's Appalachian Musical Heritage

"This whole world of Appalachian music
means the world to me because it is what
shaped me. It was my mountain songs and
that mountain heritage."

Dolly's Appalachian heritage is the foundation of much of her music.[1] She often says mountain music "is the music that I sing the best and enjoy the most."[2] Her songs that reflect her mountain heritage distinguish her body of work from that of many country music artists of her generation. In this chapter, I explore the music of Dolly's childhood and examine the elements of her musical expression that flow from this mountain music.

Dolly's girlhood home in the Smoky Mountains of Eastern Tennessee was filled with the sounds of traditional tunes and songs as well as gospel hymns her family sang in church. Country music, courtesy of the Grand Ole Opry, was less prevalent in the Parton household since the family did not have electricity in Dolly's early years.[3] As she said, "I don't remember being influenced by anybody in Nashville."[4] So it is not surprising that many of Dolly's songs bear the imprint of traditional Appalachian music. Her musical world was centered around her family: "Daddy always loved music, but he never really thought it could put any food on the table." Her mother's side of the family was different: "They live to play music and will let nothing, earning a living, for example, stand in the way of that."[5]

The women in her mother's family were especially musical. Dolly's maternal great grandmother Lindy ("Mammie") Owens played "all the old instruments like the dulcimer, the banjo, the guitar."[6] Dolly believes her musical talent came through Mammie, explaining: "She'd just make music out of anything. And they say that I'm more like her than all the others, 'cause she used to make up all kinds of songs and all that."[7]

Dolly's mother sang many of the old ballads and songs such as "Barbara Allen" and "Bury Me Beneath the Willow." She usually sang unaccompanied although she could play dulcimer, autoharp, and guitar. Dolly recalled, "she didn't have time to sit around much and do that, 'cause there was so many kids. . . . Mama would sing while she was doing her chores. She'd sing when she was sad. She'd sing when she was happy. She would sing when she was sick. But she was just always singing."[8] Dolly also said her mother was "the one that taught us all."[9]

Dolly was also influenced by her maternal Aunt Dorothy Jo (Owens) Hope, who was a gospel singer and songwriter. She cowrote several songs with Dolly early in her career, including one that became a hit for Dolly and Porter Wagoner: "Daddy Was an Old Time Preacher Man." The song honored Dolly's maternal grandfather, Jake Owens, who was an important musical influence in the family. He played several instruments, including the piano, fiddle and guitar, "almost any instrument he picked up."[10] His fiddle had been passed down to him through several generations from his great-grandfather Solomon Grooms.[11] Grandpa Owens was a Pentecostal minister and singing teacher, and, according to Dolly, "he was a master at that old shape note music." Dolly never learned to read shape note music, but she was "always intrigued" by that "wonderful art" she heard when her grandpa sang with his brothers, sons, and others in the church.[12] Rev. Owens also wrote gospel hymns: "Singing His Praise" was recorded by Kitty Wells, and Dolly included his "Book of Life" on her album *The Golden Streets of Glory* (1971).[13]

The community Dolly grew up in was also teeming with music: "We all loved to sing, and everybody played all that music, whether we were at a barn dance, a hoedown, at the election, everybody played. Not just my family, but all the musical people in the community. There was always a band. There was always somebody picking and a-playing somewhere." Dolly heard "all those old fiddle and banjo tunes that everybody played—every kind of fiddle tune and banjo tune that you could think of. You couldn't think of one that we didn't know or that we didn't play." When asked to name a few, she quickly reeled off these tunes:

"Leather Britches"
"Log Cabin Blues"
"John Hardy"
"Rabbit in a Log"
"Rock the Cradle Lucy"
"Cotton-eyed Joe"
"Shortenin' Bread"
"Soldier's Joy"
"Sourwood Mountain"
"Lost Indian"
"Mississippi Sawyer"
"Old Joe Clark"
"Sally Ann"
"Sally Goodin" ("that was a big one")
"Shoot that Turkey Buzzard"
"Turkey in the Straw"
"Whiskey Before Breakfast"
"Whoa Mule, Whoa"

Dolly loved to dance to these tunes: "like the old buck dance they called it. And the clogging and just old country dancing." She also recalled that "a lot of people did all the old songs and ballads. But they'd also sing a lot of the country songs, and a lot of those old, old songs that we just grew up with. That was all just common to us."[14] Thus, Dolly was immersed in mountain music as a child—in her family as well as in her community.

Dolly's song, "My Tennessee Mountain Home," provides a glimpse into Dolly's idyllic view of her childhood in the mountains. From her front porch setting, she sings about playing with June bugs, the aroma of honeysuckle, songbirds, and flirting in porch swings. Here, "life is as peaceful as a baby's sigh" and "crickets sing in the fields near by."

Dolly's picturesque view of mountain life contrasts with the many negative stereotypes of Appalachia in the public imagination. "Appalachia may likely have replaced the benighted South as the nation's most maligned region," Ronald D. Eller writes. "Always part of the mythical South, Appalachia continues to languish backstage in the American drama, still dressed, in the popular mind at least, in the garments of backwardness, violence, poverty, and hopelessness once associated with the South as a whole. No other region of the United States today plays the role of the 'other America' quite so persistently as Appalachia."[15] This region has frequently been the object of harsh stereotyping in popular culture through television and films (*The Beverly Hillbillies*, *Hee Haw*, *The Dukes of Hazzard*, *Deliverance*, and *Wrong Turn*). As Pamela Wilson points out, "Parton parodies these popular images in her persona, even as she promotes the more 'authentic' cultural elements that reflect her heritage, particularly the culture of Appalachian women."[16] In fact, in 1978 Dolly posed for a poster scantily clad as a mash-up of Jane Russell and Daisy Mae of the *Li'l Abner* comic strip. But Dolly's parody of Appalachia resides almost completely in the way she presents herself and her body, appealing to a "Backwoods Barbie" image not too removed from hypersexualized Daisy Mae.

It is different with Dolly's songs. While she may invoke negative stereotypical images of Appalachia, such as the moonshiner, the mountain hermit, or incest—"Daddy's Moonshine Still," "Joshua," and "Robert"—Dolly does not move into parody or ridicule in them. "Daddy's Moonshine Still" is not a revelry in mountain dew, but rather a biting indictment of the damaging effects of bootlegging: wives old before their time and sons killed in car crashes while running moonshine. The stereotype of the moonshiner becomes painfully real in Dolly's hellish description of that life. Likewise, Dolly humanizes the figure of the untamed, threatening mountain man in "Joshua," her first #1 hit. Unafraid, the singer gets to know Joshua and learns they are both alone in the world. Eventually, they fall in love and make a home in his mountain shack. Both songs, from the same album, are talking blues with similar melodies accompanied by a driving bass and active electric guitar lines. To this usually strophic form, Dolly includes sung choruses that allow her narratives to linger on each song's central character or image.

In "Robert," the singer is a young poor woman whose rich suitor, unbeknownst to him, is her half-brother. Dolly sets up the listener to react with sympathy for this young couple by not revealing their kinship until the end of the song. With its folklike guitar intro and straightforward three-chord country sound, the song offers no hint of the averted incestuous relationship between the woman and her half-brother, so the listener is jolted by the song's reveal. Rather than poking fun at the incest stereotype, Dolly does not allow her characters to cross the line into incest, thereby challenging this offensive view of Appalachian familial relationships.

Dolly does not convey her Appalachian heritage by invoking negative stereotypes of mountain life. Instead, she resists these images by writing lyrics that often idealize her mountain past and making musical choices that are frequently rooted in traditional tunes, sonorities, and genres. Through these songs that draw on her deep internalization of Appalachian musical traditions, she offers alternative, complex portrayals of Appalachian culture that validate and uplift people who are too often portrayed in demeaning ways.

In this chapter, I begin with her album *My Tennessee Mountain Home* as an autobiographical act, examining the way she reconstructs her past through the songs and images of the album and extends the reach of the album through its tangible equivalent, Dollywood. Next, I identify the elements of mountain music that Dolly incorporates in a number of her songs, and I explore the way she links her mountain music to Britain and Ireland. I then focus on her bluegrass trilogy of albums, *The Grass Is Blue*, *Little Sparrow*, and *Halos & Horns*.

My Tennessee Mountain Home

Dolly writes about mountain life in many ways: idealistic, nostalgic songs of close family, unspoiled nature, religious faith, and simpler times—as well as songs of stark realism that portray violence, ruptured families, alcohol, and poverty. Fans and critics often view these songs as true depictions of life in Appalachia. Pamela Wilson reminds us, "A great deal of the 'Dolly' discourse . . . has been devoted to authenticating her 'country' life history and cultural roots, particularly the conditions of poverty, rural isolation, and familial heritage in which she developed."[17] One example comes from Connie Berman:

> Dolly's lyrics are autobiographical tone poems; intelligent yet poignant reminiscences of her life in the mountains, growing up poor, growing up different. Her songs can clutch at the heart; they are sad, grieving, sometimes speaking of deprivation, loss, deceit, and things gone wrong, twisted awry. The songs reveal a different side of Dolly Parton from the girlish, giggly, positive, and exuberantly optimistic person she is at an interview. Underneath that glittery veneer, there is the Dolly who has suffered greatly, and this suffering often fills her songs.[18]

While Berman may be right that some of Dolly's songs are autobiographical, Dolly consistently remarks that they are not all based on her personal experiences but often reflect the situations and conditions she observed growing up in the mountains.

Dolly often includes an "Appalachian set" in her concerts. With the stage lights lowered, she sits down with her banjo, dulcimer, or autoharp, as though inviting the audience onto her front porch. Within this rustic setting, she tells picturesque stories of her family and their mountain life, and her songs flow as musical extensions of her reminiscences. Dolly's performance of these songs—part memoir, part nostalgic yearning—creates an image of her mountain life that she can present to her listeners as authentic. As Richard Peterson explains, "authenticity is not inherent in the object or event that is designated authentic but is a socially agreed-upon construct in which the past is to a degree misremembered."[19] I find this concept of misremembering a useful way to illuminate Dolly's expressions of her mountain heritage since she does not fabricate her past; instead, she reconstructs it by appealing to and adapting her childhood memories. The accuracy of Dolly's mountain stories and the authenticity of her music are not the issue, but rather it is her skill at designing and tapping into mountain scenarios and sounds that her audiences want to, and can, accept as authentic. One of her most concentrated and successful efforts at constructing her Appalachian identity is her autobiographical concept album *My Tennessee Mountain Home* (1973).

The Songs

This album's songs are tributes to her family, her community, and her everyday life growing up in the mountains. Seemingly fueled by Dolly's homesickness after her move from the mountains to Nashville, the songs are filled with nostalgic, happy memories combined with her longing to return to simpler times while following a dream that keeps her from returning home. Dolly begins by reading the first letter she wrote to her folks back home a few days after her arrival in Nashville. In "The Letter," a solo harmonica wistfully plays "Home, Sweet Home." Dolly's voice is subdued as she tells her family how lonesome and homesick she is. We can hear her putting on a brave face, especially when she swallows hard after several lines. But she remains committed to her dream of becoming a songwriter. Next are three nostalgic songs about her mama and daddy—"I Remember," "Old Black Kettle," and "Daddy's Working Boots"—followed by the gospel-inflected "Dr. Robert F. Thomas," a tribute to the doctor who delivered Dolly.

On the heels of these sweet memories of a simpler life, Dolly places her new version of "In the Good Old Days (When Times Were Bad)," which has a slower tempo than her first recording of the song from 1969. In it, Dolly reminds us that her memories are not all pleasant. As Connie Berman notes, "The song is more blistering of her youth than any memories Dolly could ever recapture in conversation."[20] Dolly next presents a different image of her childhood with "My Tennessee Mountain Home," the hit of the album that reached #15 on the country chart. Almost as if thinking aloud while revisiting the past, Dolly sings the opening lines in a free, speechlike rhythm to just a couple of strums from an acoustic guitar. Little by little, the guitar becomes more active, more instruments gradually appear, and backup singers join Dolly on the title line in the chorus, as if to invite listeners to sing along. The banjo figures prominently for over half the song, played in a more rustic old-time rather than bluegrass style. The steel guitar punctuates Dolly's lyrics about songbirds, and a harmonica joins Dolly with a countermelody for the final verse. The song ends much as it began, with a dreamy quality as the full texture thins to just harmonica, banjo, and guitar playing while Dolly hums along. A lone whistler takes us to the fade-out.

The next three songs are more nostalgic reminiscences of home: "Wrong Direction Home," "Back Home," and "The Better Part of Life." This last song is similar both to the title song and her previously recorded "The Greatest Days of All," all of which are celebrations of Dolly's idyllic memories of the past. In "The Better Part of Life," Dolly also makes a clever reference to her song "In the Good Old Days (When Times Were Bad)" with these lines:

> Remember all the fun we had
> Back when they say times were bad
> And life was good to us and things were fine

The album's final song, "Down on Music Row," chronicles her move from the mountains to her success in Nashville. The first verse, accompanied by harmonica, features some clever rhymes and poetic enjambment (rhyming "Nashville" with "wait 'til") that showcase Dolly's skill at writing lyrics precisely at the moment in the song when she refers to her songwriting. In her second verse, Dolly recalls the lean times she faced in Nashville: eating a stale pastry outside her future record company RCA before visiting the Country Music Hall of Fame. Here, the harmonica is replaced with a steel guitar, musically signaling her move from the mountains to Nashville.[21] A modulation after the chorus, a classic country music convention, also marks this shift in locale. Yet, even at this point, Dolly does not completely abandon the mountain sound. The verses that follow bring back the banjo and harmonica as Dolly pounds the pavement searching for producers for her songs. To show her determination, Dolly speaks some of her lines to the accompaniment of a single picked guitar, a technique she often uses to signal her seriousness. She finally gets Chet [Atkins] and Bob [Ferguson] of RCA, her eventual real-life producers, to listen to her songs (to the accompaniment of Nashville sound-styled backup singers), and they confirm she will be successful. Dolly continues to speak, rather than sing, these lines that mark her acceptance in Nashville as a songwriter. She sings the final chorus to the accompaniment of the full band.

Porter Wagoner had discouraged Dolly from writing such folksy songs about everyday life in the Appalachians, believing that fans would rather hear love songs than ones about Dolly's mountain nostalgia and childhood poverty. He flatly told her "Dolly, nobody gives a shit about 'Mama's Old Black Kettle,' or 'Daddy's Working Boots.' *Who cares?*"[22] But Alanna Nash called the album "moving" and "a classic,"[23] and Bob Powel wrote he could "almost smell the hay and taste the grits cooking for breakfast."[24] *Rolling Stone* called it "a rare tour de force, but also one of the few really successful concept LPs . . . in any genre,"[25] and Chet Flippo said it was "her most nearly perfect album. . . . It's a bittersweet look backward at a life and a tradition she was bound on leaving, . . . a matter-of-fact tribute to a people and a way of life that are vanishing."[26] *My Tennessee Mountain Home* was and still is considered to be among Dolly's best.

Despite its loving view of the past, *My Tennessee Mountain Home* went beyond simple nostalgia. Released the year before Dolly left Porter Wagoner's show and launched her solo career, the album distanced Dolly from her role as Porter's "girl singer" and sidekick, authenticated her mountain identity, and strongly affirmed her as a songwriter who would record "all them songs that I wrote" as she sang in "Down on Music Row."

Iconography

Beyond the songs themselves, the album authenticates Dolly's mountain identity through its images in the liner notes and on the cover. On the inner gatefold of the album are photographs of Dolly posing with her maternal grandfather Rev. Jake Owens, with Dr. Robert F. Thomas, and with her Parton grandparents; two childhood photographs of Dolly (one is the coat of many colors school picture reproduced in Chapter Two); and two paintings, the cabin where she was born and her father's worn boots "after a hard day's work." Also included are two formal portraits of her mother and father, each accompanied by a note they wrote about Dolly as a child. This detailed illustration of Dolly's early life and family certifies her as a bona fide mountain woman.

The album cover's photograph of Dolly's childhood Locust Ridge home also authenticates her mountain roots. The family moved to this home when she was quite young.[27] Here, Dolly boldly presents an unvarnished look at her childhood home, a boxed house typical of those found in the Smoky Mountains in the late nineteenth through the mid–twentieth century. It is a style that many view as "an architecture of poverty" according to Michael Ann Williams.[28] Unlike in the songs on the album, around this house there are no butterflies, whippoorwills, or kids laughing and running around chasing fireflies. We see a drab dirt and

FIGURE 3.1. *My Tennessee Mountain Home* album front cover, 1973.

rock-filled yard with a small cluster of pink flowers growing in and around a pile of discarded tires and tire rims. The old wringer washing machine on the dark porch—and the chair with the bucket nearby—reminds us of the daily domestic labor of the people here. Yet, Dolly reports the house looked better in this photograph than it did when she lived in it—another "mis-remembering." "We never had a tin roof so nice, they've added that. . . . They got some grass now, too," she remarked. "I remember always wantin' a nice yard, 'cause, with 12 kids like us wasn't no way grass could grow within a given area. I remember . . . Momma sayin' 'Run fetch the broom and sweep the yard.'"[29] Pamela Fox notes that "Parton's life story . . . verifies her own authenticity by recuperating class abjection,"[30] and this album, with its songs and images of harsh but romanticized mountain life, certainly does that.

Dollywood

A little over a decade after the album's release, Dolly expanded the reach of *My Tennessee Mountain Home* when she created Dollywood in 1986 with co-owner Herschend Enterprises. As with the album, Dollywood plays a central role in validating Dolly's claims to her mountain heritage, authenticating her stories, songs, and childhood memories through their reenactment and replication within the park. Most significant is a replica of Dolly's Locust Ridge home. Prominently located in Dollywood, the replica—like her song "My Tennessee Mountain Home"—is an idealized version of life growing up poor in the mountains, a further "mis-remembering." In the original photograph, the house is open to the elements. The replica is nestled among lush trees with a small front garden, and the house's construction is altered slightly to give it a more finished, appealing look. As Dolly remarked, "Our house never looked so damn good, I'll tell you that."[31] The description of the house on the Dollywood website makes the privations seem minor inconveniences: "You'll get a true feeling of what Dolly means when she speaks of her Tennessee Mountain Home upbringing as you visit this two-room replica of her Locust Ridge childhood home. Though it lacked electricity and running water, love was abundant in this tiny little mountain house that Dolly and her family called home."[32]

Just as in the album, Dollywood creates a picture of Dolly's life in the mountains and her path to Nashville. Songs like "Back Home," "Wrong Direction

FIGURE 3.2. Replica of Dolly's "Tennessee Mountain Home" at Dollywood (Pigeon Forge, Tennessee, July 14, 2018). Photo: Lydia Hamessley.

Home," and, of course, "My Tennessee Mountain Home" find their counterpart in the re-creation of Dolly's childhood home. But its sparse furnishings, newspapers lining the walls, and cramped living conditions remind visitors that life in this place was difficult. The reality of physical labor is also present. A pair of worn work boots lie under the bed, and cast iron skillets hang from the kitchen wall, recalling "Daddy's Working Boots" and "Old Black Kettle." Working people are celebrated through the artisan workshops in Dollywood's Craftsman's Valley, and the natural world that Dolly valorizes in her musical reminiscences of home is an important focus of the park's rides and eagle sanctuary. The park's chapel is named after Dr. Robert F. Thomas, and Dolly's tremendous musical success, which began "Down on Music Row," is a backdrop to the entire enterprise of Dollywood.

Dolly once made this poignant statement: "the worst thing about poverty is not the actual living of it, but the shame of it."[33] She strives to lessen its shame by recasting the economic hardships of her childhood in her songs. Dolly does not deny the reality of poverty; rather, she focuses on representing poverty in ways that transcend the embarrassment and humiliation she says it brought. Dolly's idealized presentation of her mountain life in Dollywood mirrors the way she reconstructs the poverty of her childhood in much of her music, lessening its sting of shame by focusing on the love of family, their strong faith, and the beauty of nature.

Thus, the reconstruction of her childhood home as well as the replica of her coat of many colors and the stories Dolly tells in songs, concerts, and interviews are not inauthentic, but are intentional mis-rememberings of Dolly's experiences that fans accept as authentic. Dolly confirmed this notion of constructed authenticity when she described Dollywood as "a Smoky Mountain fantasy to preserve the mountain heritage."[34] The same could be said of *My Tennessee Mountain Home*.

The Sounds of Dolly's Appalachian Heritage

Dolly identifies her musical core as Appalachian: "That was just part of the fabric of our lives, those old songs. And so I grew up just loving that; feeling it, knowing it, and it's just embedded in my psyche and my heart and in my soul."[35] However, the music of Appalachia is such a conglomeration of styles and genres that country music historian Bill Malone asserts "there is no such thing as 'Appalachian music.'" Pointing to the diversity of ethnic and racial cultures that have always existed in the mountains, he reminds us that "ancient ballads, gospel songs, ragtime pieces, and Tin Pan Alley ditties coexisted in the repertoires of mountain musicians, with no apparent sense of contradiction."[36] Yet despite this wide array of musical expression, for many people, indeed, in the wider popular imagination, the music of Appalachia conjures up images of banjos and ballad singers, bluegrass bands and hoedown fiddles. These stereotypical ideas have arisen and remain strong for several reasons: a desire to identify a type of roots music that can embody an idyllic, rural American past; the effects of Hollywood and television depictions of rural America that are often represented as Appalachian; the marketing boon that such romantic associations bring to any music classified as Appalachian.

Even though Appalachian music is so diverse as to be, in Malone's view, nonexistent, for Dolly and her listeners, there is a set of musical styles, genres, and sonorities that is understood as traditionally Appalachian. This is music Dolly describes as old-world. These stereotypical sounds have been linked with mountain music though they do not represent the full range of Appalachian musical expression. To describe this sound of Appalachia, critics and listeners use a variety of terms for musical styles that often overlap: *mountain, old-time, early country, hillbilly,* and *bluegrass.* These styles are closely related through their shared roots in old fiddle tunes and string band music that blend English, Scottish, and Irish tunes and harmonies, particularly modal harmonies, with the rhythmic drive of the African-derived banjo and blues-inflected styles. Also part of this Appalachian tradition are ancient English and Scottish ballads such as "Barbara Allen."[37] Dolly acknowledges mountain music's "connection with all that music brought over from the old world. All that is a link."[38]

Dolly made the relationship between Appalachia and Britain and Ireland clear on her album, *Heartsongs: Live from Home* by speaking about this musical inheritance and blending her lineage with this history:

> Well hello and welcome to my Smoky Mountain Home. Boy it's always good to be home. . . . You know, this album is influenced by music from all over the world: Ireland, England, Scotland, Wales. And music made up right here in our own Smoky Mountains. You'll be hearing a lot of old songs, and a lot of songs that I've written that sound old.

Here, Dolly not only makes a connection between Smoky Mountain music and that of Britain and Ireland, but she asserts, as she often does, that some of her own compositions sound like these "old songs." "That's the easiest stuff for me to do. It goes back to my childhood. . . . And those old songs were the ones we heard the most. So it's just embedded in me and it's the easiest thing in the world. That's the stuff that comes out of me the easiest. To take some new stuff and make it sound old."[39]

What are the echoes of this mountain musical heritage that "come out of" Dolly so easily? When asked to describe this sound, she spoke in terms of feelings:

> It's old world, it's old feelings, and it's old stories. It's kinda like a great actor that can really sell you on what it is they're portraying. Well that's sorta like it is with this music. You act it out, you feel it out, you get all the feelings of it to the surface, and you can hear that, and it touches people. It touches me to sing it. And it touches me when I've touched somebody by singing it and see that I have. It matters. And when I talk about the harmony and the melody sounds old, that's what I mean.[40]

I want to explore the specific musical choices Dolly makes to evoke this depth of old-world feeling. How does Dolly make her "new stuff" "sound old"? It is too simplistic to identify only the sounds of fiddles and banjos that sometimes infuse her arrangements. The answer also lies in Dolly's use of musical genres, sonorities, and styles that are heard as traditionally Appalachian: ballads, modal melodies, and old-time and bluegrass styles.

Ballads

Ballads, to put it simply, are songs that tell a story.[41] Child ballads (after the nineteenth-century literary scholar who collected them, Francis James Child) have characters and titles like Barbara Allen, Lady Margaret, Lord Thomas and Fair Ellender, The House Carpenter, and The Elfin Knight. They are stories of a far-off time in England and Scotland and are filled with the supernatural, fantastical settings, bravery and deceit, and love gone wrong, often in tragic, violent, and even gory ways. Ballads are typically strophic: each verse is sung to the same melody and there is no chorus, though some include refrain lines at the ends of verses. Often ballads are quite long, some running to dozens of verses. They are usually sung from a third-person perspective in a dispassionate way with little to no moralizing. The fine grain of ballads is in the dialogue and descriptions of actions, not in explaining motives or exploring emotions.

Appalachian ballads had a significant musical influence on Dolly: "Come All You Fair and Tender Ladies," "My Dear Companion," "Barbara Allen," "East Virginia Blues," "Down in the Willow Garden," and "Knoxville Girl." Dolly's mother sang "all those old stories. Mama told us that's how people used to carry the news, they used to write it in songs, carry it from village to village to say what had happened. A lot of the stuff in those old-world songs were true stories that happened. And I believe that she was right about that." The profound emotions of old-world music Dolly spoke about was also a part of her experience of hearing her mother sing ballads. She recalled, "it was so lonesome when Mama would sing."[42]

The reach of the ballad tradition in Dolly's songs is evident in her skill as a storyteller. But beyond that, there are echoes of the ballads in Dolly's songs in their form and their use of language. Dolly says composing story songs is her favorite style of writing. Some are ballads, but others are not if judged by a purely technical definition. Many are not strophic but have verses, choruses, and bridges; often the story is told in first-person; and usually there is an emotional quality and sometimes a moral. Nonetheless, Dolly's story songs reveal strong traces of her ballad inheritance. As she said,

> A lot of people write a formula. . . . That's what I was taught when I was young and started in Nashville. It was pretty much two verses and a chorus, but I never could get everything I wanted to say in two verses and a chorus [laughs]. So to me, some of the best songs I write just ramble on and on and on. They're more like stories. People say, "Oh, you shouldn't write a song more than three minutes long because they won't play it on the radio." But some of the songs I've written are like four and five minutes long.[43]

"Mountain Angel," at almost seven minutes long, evokes Appalachian ballads. It is a tale of betrayal, heartbreak, madness, death from grief, and ghosts. Told in the third person, this lengthy, strophic song (though with choruslike contrasting sections) is the story of a young woman's seduction, pregnancy, and abandonment by the man she loved. Her heartbreak transforms her into a mountain witch, and she roams the hills mourning her dead baby at its grave until she dies there. This song, which one critic termed "downright gothic,"[44] calls to mind the trope of the bereaved sitting on a loved one's grave, haunted by the ghost of the dead, as found in the ballad "The Unquiet Grave."

"Mountain Angel" also includes another characteristic of ballads: textual motifs and epithets that sound archaic to modern ears—formulaic phrases such as "come all ye," "milk white steed," "cold clay lips," and "false-hearted lover." Dolly describes the young woman in the song as having "skin as fair as lilies, hair as golden as the corn," and the man who seduces and abandons her as a "wicked handsome stranger." Many other lines use similar language. Madness and the supernatural also play a role here as they often do in ballads. Local folks believed the baby was a child of the devil since the "mountain angel" had been seduced by "Satan's insane lure." The song ends with the spooky sound of Dolly's voice keening as she embodies the dead woman's ghost that haunts the mountains where she and her baby died. Buckingham, who produced the song, commented: "'Mountain Angel,' that's one that she wrote that sounds like an old traditional song."[45]

Dolly sometimes uses this type of figurative language in new songs that do not seem, on the surface, to have an Appalachian setting or prototype. For example, in the context of ballads, the lyrics of "Jolene" have a new resonance.

> Your beauty is beyond compare
> With flaming locks of auburn hair
> With ivory skin and eyes of emerald green
> Your smile is like a breath of spring
> Your voice is soft like summer rain

In "Daddy," Dolly challenges a father's adultery in a similar old-world idiom.

> I'm your oldest daughter, my age twenty-three
> Your new love is even younger than me
> She's young, she's pretty, her hands soft as dew
> While Mama's are withered from working for you

Dolly's song "My Blue Tears" also features archaic language. Here, the singer has been abandoned by her lover and cannot face cheerful birdsongs. Her verse imploring the sun to disappear is particularly rich with evocative, old-world language:

> Bring not your light into my dark gloom yellow sunshine
> Waste not your warmth on the coldness in here
> O trouble me not, go ye elsewhere
> Go light your blue sky and I'll shed my blue tears

Dolly uses the ancient trope of birds linked with heartbreak in several of her songs. A prime example is "Little Sparrow," Dolly's adaptation of the traditional song "Come All You Fair and Tender Ladies," to which she added a chorus; traditional versions are strophic. Buckingham commented about Dolly's skill at reworking these older songs: "even when she would do things like 'Silver Dagger,' it was taken partly from an old traditional mountain song that of course nobody owned, and Dolly wrote new lyrics to go along with some of the old lyrics like that."[46] "Little Sparrow" is so indebted to the language and atmosphere of old mountain songs that it could pass for an ancient air. As she said about "Little

Sparrow," "when I wrote that song, it was like those old songs of yore."[47] A comparison of Dolly's lyrics with traditional versions makes this connection clear.[48]

"LITTLE SPARROW," DOLLY PARTON	"FAIR AND TENDER LADIES," COLLECTED BY CECIL SHARP
All ye maidens heed my warning	Come all you young and tender ladies
Never trust the hearts of men	Take warning how you court young men
They will crush you like a sparrow	They're like a bright star in a cloudy morning
Leaving you to never mend	They'll first appear and then they're gone
If I were a little sparrow	Oh that I were a pretty little swallow
O'er these mountains I would fly	Or had I wings that I could fly
I would find him, I would find him	Then away after my true love I'd follow
Look into his lying eyes	I'd light upon his breast and flutter
	And tell him of deceiving me
I would flutter all around him	
On my little sparrow wings	
I would ask him, I would ask him	
Why he let me love in vain	

Modal Tunes

Many songs that made their way to the Appalachian Mountains from England, Scotland, and Ireland were modal. Modes are scales that comprise arrangements of pitches different from major scales. The most commonly used modes have a flatted 7th scale degree and are often harmonized with the flat-seven chord (♭VII). Thus, modal songs have distinctive melodic qualities, and their harmonic progressions (as heard in "Jolene," for example) are different from the three-chord, classic country harmony of "Coat of Many Colors." This modal sound strikes many as "folksy" or, in the case of my discussion of Dolly's music, "Appalachian" or "mountain." Even though modes are found in all genres and styles of music, the use of modal scales is frequently associated with music of the past, "the old world," or the folk. (For further information about modes, see Appendix C.)

In conjunction with their so-called ancient sound, modal tunes are also often heard as poignant, perhaps more somber, than non-modal music. Dolly had this to say about her frequent use of modal scales and the ♭VII chord in particular: "Well that's just that old mountain sound. It's the sorrow chord I guess, in a way. It's the feeling chord and emotional chord. . . . It just kinda takes you to that sorrowful place that you can get out of, but you go back to it. And I just know I'm prone to feel that. My body just goes there, my psyche is just trained for that. My heart goes there. And, I think it's a pretty chord. . . . I like how that feels, and how it sounds."[49]

In trying to account for this modal character of some of Dolly's music, Steve Eng wrote that some of her songs have "an antique 'Greensleeves' feel."[50] Eng heard the modal sound in Dolly's music as similar to this well-known melody that uses the modal ♭VII chord throughout.[51] In fact, Dolly reshaped the tune of "Greensleeves" for "Sandy's Song,"[52] which she set to newly written lyrics in the formulaic language of a riddle ballad:

> I'll love you 'til green grass turns lavender blue
> And all the stars fall from heaven and vanish like dew
> When horses and chariots chase down the wind
> Well that's when I'll leave you, I'll love you 'til then

Here, Dolly plays with the image of blue grass—the shifting of the color of grass from green to blue—a trope she later revisited in her bluegrass albums. Dating from her early pop crossover period, "Sandy's Song" is heavily orchestrated with strings and English horn, but the "Greensleeves" melody and chord progression are unmistakable. By choosing this well-known tune, Dolly drew attention to her connection to English folk song—and her ongoing connection to traditional music—within an album that contained mostly pop songs by other writers.

One of Dolly's songs that revels in modal harmonies is "Shattered Image," first recorded in 1976. The verses and chorus of the song both begin in a major key, but when the last line of each verse and chorus is repeated, usually some variant of "shatter my image with the stones you throw," Dolly dips the harmony and melody down to the flatted 7th scale degree and chord (♭VII) of the Mixolydian mode, and she also closes the song with a fade-out on these shifting harmonies. In this version, Dolly adds a banjo to her hard-driving country band at the second verse.

She rerecorded this song, with an additional verse, for inclusion on her third bluegrass album, *Halos & Horns*, and the fiddle provides a mountain touch. Dolly also emphasizes the modal harmony even more by extending the final line fade-out with its modal sound to over one minute and fifteen seconds. Here, in the album's bluegrass context, Dolly gets down to the business of enjoying the *sound* of that modal harmony. The last third of the track features Dolly and the fiddle riffing on the line "shatter my image with the stones you throw" to the undulation of the Mixolydian flatted 7th chord (♭VII) moving to the tonic (I) and back.

In yet another recording of the song from 2012, Dolly sang the first verse as she played the dulcimer, "an instrument with a long history in the Appalachian Mountains whose very presence signifies a return to traditional roots."[53] Modal harmonies are easy to play on the dulcimer, and its sound is especially evocative because the melody is played on one string while the other one or two strings remain open as drones, a sound Dolly particularly enjoys. When Dolly built her first makeshift instrument from an old mandolin and piano strings discussed earlier, she described it as "more like a dulcimer, really. And when I strummed it, it sent up a droning sound that I could sing to. I wrote a lot of songs with that old mandolin."[54]

A number of Dolly's early songs feature modal sonorities, even though they are not particularly Appalachian in their lyrics or arrangement. One example is "I'm in No Condition," which depends on its shifting harmonies—into and out of modal areas—for its emotional effect. This song is a model of Dolly's musical economy: there are only two melodic lines, A and B. (Listening Outline 2 shows the formal structure of the song.) The A melody line is harmonized exclusively with Mixolydian modal chords—the major tonic (I) and the flatted 7th chord (♭VII)—which alternate throughout. In this example from the first verse, in the A lines the ♭VII chord harmonizes the italicized text, and the tonic chord areas are not italicized. The B line uses non-modal chords. The very clear bass line makes these harmonic shifts, the same ones used in the intro, easy to follow.

A¹ Don't look at *me* with love *in your* eyes
A² Go look at some*body that can* make *it worth*while
B I'm hurt from a love affair I didn't want to end
A³ I'm in no con*dition to* try to *love* again

In each A line, the I and the ♭VII chord alternate throughout, giving a relentless quality to the lines that evoke the hopeless mental condition the singer is in, unready to love again after a breakup. The melody of the third line, B, is a contrast to the A melody. It goes higher in Dolly's range and becomes more harmonically active, abandoning the modal ♭VII chord in a seeming effort to escape the insistent pull of the modal sound of the A melody.

These two verses contrast with the next section, the song's chorus. Here, as Dolly repeats the title line, she sings a variant of the B melody twice in a move that reprises the desire and attempt to break out of the unrelenting modal pull downward. But the second B line does not break free, yielding back to the modal sound on *time*. This section then concludes in the lower register with the A melody for two lines. The aggressive country sound of the steel

Listening Outline 2: "I'm in No Condition," *Hello, I'm Dolly*, 1967

0:00	Intro		Instrumental lick, harmonized with only I and ♭VII.
0:06	Verse 1	Don't look at me...	A^1 open-ended cadence on the 3rd scale degree.
0:11		Go look at...	A^2 moderately closed cadence ending on the 1st scale degree approached from above.
0:18		I'm hurt...	B.
0:24		And I'm in no condition...	A^3 firmly closed cadence ending on the 1st scale degree approached from below.
0:32	Verse 2	Don't smile at me...	$A^1A^2BA^3$; same as verse 1.
0:58	Chorus	I'm in no condition...	$B^1B^2A^1A^3$.
1:21	Instrumental		Reuse of music from intro; steel guitar marks the return to the chorus.
1:30	Chorus	I'm in no condition...	$B \cdot B^2A^1A^3A^3$; repeat of chorus; last line repeated for closure.
2:01	Outro & Fadeout		Reuse of music from intro.

guitar takes the lead briefly and drives the melody to try again by repeating this contrasting section. Once more, the B lines try to break free only to fall back into the modal area as before. The song closes with one extra A line that leaves Dolly where she started: "in no condition to try to love again." The song ends with a fade-out of the music from the intro as the ♭VII and I chords rock back and forth. By rearranging just two melodic ideas with their contrasting harmonic implications, Dolly shifts the emotional pull throughout the song from a sense of despondency to an attempt at escape and then a fall back into heartbreak.

Dolly wrote many songs that included the modal ♭VII chord in the 1960s and 1970s. Some of the most outstanding are "Everything's Beautiful (In Its own Way)," "You're Gonna Be Sorry," "The Bridge," "Don't Let It Trouble Your Mind," "Down from Dover," "When Possession Gets Too Strong," "Hillbilly Willy," "Walls of My Mind," "Early Morning Breeze," "The Greatest Days of All," "Barbara on Your Mind," and "The Bargain Store." Dolly used this modal sound less frequently in her pop crossover albums in the late 1970s, 1980s, and 1990s; however, a few notable examples are: "The Man," "Sandy's Song," "What Will Baby Be," "Crippled Bird," "Camel's Heart," and "Only Dreamin'."

All but one of these songs use the Mixolydian mode with its major tonic (I) chord, as in "I'm in No Condition." But "The Bargain Store" is in the rarely used Dorian mode with a minor tonic chord. This mode has a bittersweet, unusual quality that many hear as particularly Appalachian and "old world." Alanna Nash said the song's "eerie melodic structure hark[s] back to the old Elizabethan ballads,"[55] and one commenter said it sounded "exquisite—almost medieval."[56] There are only two chords in this song: the minor tonic (i) and the major subdominant chord (IV), and this IV chord is what gives the Dorian mode its distinctive sound. The major IV chord is the result of the 6th scale degree being raised in this scale (which also features a flatted 7th scale degree like the Mixolydian mode). Dolly sings the raised 6th scale degree in the chorus. In the following line from the song, the raised 6th is underlined and the flatted 7th is italicized: "The bargain store is *o*pen come inside, you can easi*ly* afford the price."

In addition to the "old-world" sound of the Dorian mode, Dolly's use of the word *unto* in the first line is striking: "My life is like unto a bargain store." Dolly credits both elements, the mode and the archaic word choice, with making the song sound old. When asked if she used the word *unto* in order to give "an archaic, Biblical, eternal weight to a dime-store confession . . . or did she just need two syllables to make the line scan," Dolly replied: "Aha! No, I purposely did it. I could have said any number of things—it's easier to sing 'My life is like a bargain store.' I like doing old-timey songs. It's in that minor key, which sounds old world to me, that lonesome drone."[57]

Dolly often weaves modal touches into her music: "It was natural when I wrote to reflect back to the old songs we used to sing, and part of my melodies kind of carried that old-timey flavor without me realizing it until after they were done. And I still do that—those folky-type melodies are the best of all."[58] Buckingham reminds us that this modal language is an integral, but largely unspoken, part of Dolly's musical language: "I can say without a doubt we never sat down with guitars and started talking about modalities, Mixolydian or whatever. Never. Now it's just understood among the musicians. The musicians understand that. I understand it. But it's not like 'ok, let's make this Mixolydian.' You either play it or you don't, and Dolly plays it and sings it and writes it. It all comes out of her head and heart, and fingers."[59]

Mountain Music: Old-time and Bluegrass

Often, all it takes for music to be heard as Appalachian is the presence of stereotypical mountain instruments. When country music includes the fiddle

and banjo, these instruments frequently connote an old-time, hillbilly, or mountain sound, and, in conjunction with other Appalachian musical elements, this
resonance becomes stronger. Almost without fail, critics and fans use *bluegrass*
to describe music that features these instruments. This term is often used as a
generic stand-in for mountain music, roots music, or any music with an old-time
sound.[60] But bluegrass is a particular genre distinguishable in varying degrees
from other mountain music, notably old-time music, and it is critical to this
discussion of Dolly's work to clarify the elements of these styles.[61]

Old-time music, as it is called today, traditionally focuses on the fiddle and
banjo with the fiddle playing the melody and the banjo providing a driving
rhythmic pulse and a chordal backdrop played in either a clawhammer or a
two-finger style. Other instruments include the guitar, upright bass, and mandolin; the autoharp, both hammered and mountain dulcimer, banjo uke, and
harmonica sometimes make an appearance. Tunes are played at a danceable
tempo, often accompanying square dances and flat-footing or clogging. When
the players sing, they use a naturalized vocal style, often in unison rather than
harmony.

Bluegrass, which originated with Bill Monroe in the 1940s,[62] takes this old-
time string band music, along with gospel hymns and the songs of early country
music, and makes some significant changes. The typical instruments are the
banjo, mandolin, fiddle, guitar, and bass, along with the resonator guitar (Dobro).
The players take turns leading the melody in a show of virtuosity, and the music
is often very fast-paced, no longer conducive to dancing. The vocals are quite
high in pitch (thus the term *high lonesome sound*) and are often in three-part
close harmony, which is indebted to gospel singing. Finally, the banjo style is
altered from the old-time clawhammer and two-finger picking styles to the
three-finger, rapid-note style associated with the playing of Earl Scruggs.

Early on, these divisions between musical genres were not rigid, and Dolly
heard both styles as a child. But the distinctions between bluegrass and old-
time mountain music were fluid then, as she said: "some of what was later called
bluegrass, it was just country music then, or mountain music."[63] Today, for many
people bluegrass, old-time, and early country music still blur. Of course, not all
old-time and early country music is Appalachian, and bluegrass is a commercial
genre that, while associated with Appalachian culture, is played and heard in all
regions of the United States and throughout the world. Bluegrass, nonetheless,
is "self-construct[ed] as a music securely located in the distant past."[64] Thus, in
the popular imagination, old-time and bluegrass, as well as early country music,
are consistently conflated and associated with the Appalachian region and an

idyllic mountain past. As Ron Pen explained, it "is the music that America continues to come home to in order to renew its ties to the earth, the country, and a sense of community."[65]

Dolly's Bluegrass Trilogy

Between 1999 and 2002, Dolly released three albums that placed her within the mainstream of the bluegrass world and set in motion a new phase of her career. Critics described *The Grass Is Blue*, *Little Sparrow*, and *Halos & Horns* as Dolly's return to her Appalachian musical roots. But Dolly had drawn upon old-time and bluegrass styles for her songs throughout her career, from her earliest days.

Precursors to the Bluegrass Trilogy

Three albums are particularly important as precursors to her bluegrass trilogy: *Trio*, *Heartsongs: Live from Home*, and *Hungry Again*. Dolly recorded the Grammy-winning 1987 album, *Trio*, with Linda Ronstadt and Emmylou Harris. Ronstadt described the album as "old timey music" and "more agrarian music." Commenting on the mountain music authenticity that Dolly brought to the project, Harris remarked, "We wanted to bring that part of her voice, that part of Dolly, back into Appalachia. And using it to our purposes too. Having Dolly's voice there, and just Dolly's presence there made us authentic."[66] The blend of the three women's voices in harmony recalled earlier country and old-time acts such as The Coon Creek Girls and The Carter Sisters. The album included traditional hymns and old-time songs such as "Farther Along," "Rosewood Casket," and "My Dear Companion" along with "Hobo's Meditation" by Jimmie Rodgers and "Wildflowers," which was written by Dolly and alluded to the Carter Family's recording of "Wildwood Flower" with its title and prominent autoharp accompaniment. The country music industry recognized *Trio* with the Album of the Year Award from the Academy of Country Music and the Vocal Event of the Year Award from the Country Music Association.

In 1994, Dolly released *Heartsongs: Live from Home*, which highlighted ballads and folk hymns such as "Barbara Allen," "Mary of the Wild Moor," and "Wayfaring Stranger" along with Dolly's songs about her mountain past, such as "Applejack" and "My Tennessee Mountain Home." She also included "Smoky Mountain Memories," a new version of "Appalachian Memories," which was inspired by stories of Appalachian families who moved north in search of better jobs but who ended up feeling displaced and disheartened. Some, like Dolly's father who went to Detroit, returned to the mountains, preferring hardship over loneliness. Several arrangements include the dulcimer and autoharp, and the album featured renowned bluegrass musicians, such as Alison Krauss, and traditional Irish players and singers.

Four years later, Dolly recorded *Hungry Again*, which included bluegrass artists Rhonda and Darrin Vincent. The recording has a back-to-roots feeling with its bluegrass and old-time-tinged tracks such as "The Camel's Heart," "Time and Tears," and "When Jesus Comes Calling for Me." For the album's resonant finale, Dolly wrote "Shine On" set to the tune of "Amazing Grace," which was recorded "up home at our old church, the House of Prayer, where my grandfather, the Reverend Jake Owens, was pastor many years."[67] Several of her family members sang harmony on the recording. Even Dolly's photo for the album's cover shows her looking surprisingly down-home, wearing overalls, very little makeup or nail polish, and her hair in a long braid. This rustic look emphasizes her mountain past, a striking change from her usual glamorous image. Alanna Nash called the album not just "Dolly's return to her rural roots. It's the sound of an artist who's found herself again."[68] And Linda Ray wrote that "Parton has rediscovered the fountain of youth. . . . [She] gleams brighter than morning sun in the rustic, righteous realness of her original idiom—the sounds of her Tennessee mountain home."[69] It is noteworthy that these critics linked the album's focus on Dolly's mountain heritage with a renewal of her core identity and musical vitality.

Earlier in her career, Dolly had recorded Jimmie Rodgers's "Muleskinner Blues," a classic country, yodel blues favorite from 1930 that had become a bluegrass staple. It was released on *The Best of Dolly Parton* (1970) and was Dolly's first solo to break into the top ten on the country chart, going to #3. Jocelyn R. Neal suggests that in the late 1990s, when Dolly "was firmly ensconced in the pop-country sounds," she "relied heavily on the legacy of 'Muleskinner Blues' as a Bill Monroe classic, and that one connection (and one song in her past) helped reinvent her." "The bluegrass audience accepted her as one of their own," making possible a new phase of Dolly's career in the late 1990s and 2000s with her bluegrass trilogy.[70]

The Grass Is Blue, Little Sparrow, and Halos & Horns

THE GRASS IS BLUE   The genesis of *The Grass Is Blue* was an informal marketing survey. Dolly explained, "I knew all these songs from when I was 10 years old, but I just never thought there was an outlet for an entire album. Then the album's producer [Steve Buckingham] told me that they [Sugar Hill Records] had done a survey asking 'Who would you most like to make a bluegrass album

FIGURE 3.3. First day of recording *The Grass Is Blue*. L-R: Jerry Douglas (resophonic guitar), Sam Bush (mandolin), Stuart Duncan (fiddle), Bryan Sutton (guitar), Dolly Parton, Steve Buckingham (producer, guitar), Jim Mills (banjo), Barry Bales (upright bass). (Sound Kitchen, Nashville, Tennessee, August 1999). Photo: Rob Draper. Courtesy of Steve Buckingham.

that has never done one?' Something like 10 to 1, the results said Dolly Parton."[71] By coincidence Dolly and Buckingham had been on the same flight to Los Angeles in June 1999, and he asked Dolly if she would "ever consider the possibility of doing a straight ahead bluegrass album." She agreed saying, "I know this music. I can do it because I know this music." Dolly had a full schedule that summer, so in late August the album "was recorded entirely within a week and mixed over the next ten days. It was released in October 1999, which was unheard of in the quickness of the turnaround." The album was highly praised by critics and fans; Buckingham noted, "It was the most critically acclaimed album of her career."[72]

Several songs on the album are Dolly's bluegrass versions of country and pop songs: "Travelin' Prayer," "Cash on the Barrelhead," "I Still Miss Someone," "Train, Train," and "I Wonder Where You Are Tonight," and the bluegrass standard, "I'm Gonna Sleep with One Eye Open," by Lester Flatt. Dolly incorporated a more old-time sound with her rendition of mountain singer Hazel Dickens's "A Few Old Memories," her sister Rachel's gospel song "I Am Ready," and her own re-working of the traditional ballad "East Virginia Blues" as "Silver Dagger."

Dolly also wrote four songs on the album. "Will He Be Waiting for Me" is a new recording of the song from her album *Touch Your Woman*. Its bluegrass arrangement highlights the clever wordplay on *will* and *won't* ("will he be waiting for me, he will be won't he") along with its persistent internal rhymes. "Steady as the Rain," written in the 1970s for Dolly's sister Stella, works beautifully as a bluegrass number since, as Dolly said, "I wrote it on the banjo, that's why it has that steady rolling sound."[73] The similar watery metaphor in "Endless Stream of Tears" is also well suited to bluegrass treatment.

The real prize on the album is the heartbreaking waltz "The Grass Is Blue," which reveals Dolly in top form as a songwriter. Buckingham recalled she went right to work on song ideas for the album:

Dolly started sending me song ideas, new ideas. She'd literally be on her bus with her cassette deck and her guitar, and she'd be writing songs and she'd send them. But she was also sending other old mountain bluegrass tunes that she wanted to record. One day she called me and said, "I have written a great song for the album," and she literally played the song "The Grass Is Blue" to me over the phone with her playing guitar, the phone sitting in front of her and singing, and that's how the title came about.[74]

In the song, Dolly portrays the emotional instability of heartbreak by using interacting rhetorical and musical strategies of repetition, opposites, inversions, and deception.

In order "to survive" being abandoned by her lover, the singer must "pretend that the opposite is true." This coping strategy is laid out in the first verse. The choruses then outline several lists of opposites mostly derived from nature: "rivers flow backwards, valleys are high, mountains are level," and then "truth is a lie." The chorus continues with this emotional deception—she is fine and does not miss her lover—and it ends with the refrain, "the sky is green, and the grass is blue." The second verse imagines the possible effect of this self-deception: one will eventually break down and move "into that realm of insanity's bliss," a lyric marked by its sophisticated vocabulary. The chorus returns with different words, but the rhetorical strategy is the same: a list of opposites from the natural world followed by the singer's emotional opposites and the refrain. Propelled by an instrumental riff, the chorus repeats immediately. It again has new words, although Dolly brings back the initial image she used in the first chorus ("rivers flow backwards"). The song concludes with a tag reiterating the title line, "the grass is blue." The title's wordplay, with its triple meaning, is inspired. It is a clever way to say bluegrass; it is a vivid statement of a contradiction; and *blue* is the overarching sentiment of the song. No matter how many opposites the singer tries, the sorrow does not cease, and the song ends on *blue*. These exquisite lyrics alone would be enough to place this song among Dolly's best. But her musical setting is equally outstanding in the way it sets the lyrics and embodies their meaning, and her performance intensifies the song's emotional effect.

The melody of the song's two verses is pentatonic and in the lower range of the scale, which establishes an introspective atmosphere suited to the lyrics and matches the singer's restrained emotions. The choruses, though, are where

Listening Outline 3: "The Grass Is Blue," *The Grass Is Blue*, 1999

0:00	Intro		Solo strummed acoustic guitar.
0:07	Verse 1	I've had to think up...	Lyrics about survival strategies by thinking in terms of opposites; solo acoustic guitar only.
0:41	Chorus 1	Rivers flow backwards...	Mandolin enters and harmony singers enter. Images from nature that are opposites followed by an emotional response. "I'm perfectly fine" repeats the melody of line 1. Ends with the refrain "the sky is green and the grass is blue."
1:11	Instrumental Interlude		Full band; fiddle and Dobro play variants of chorus melody.
1:41	Verse 2	How much can a heart...	Lyrics about sorrow causing both heartbreak and a mental break.
2:17	Chorus 2	There's snow in...	More images from nature that are opposites again followed by an emotional response. The melody is a variant of chorus 1, now staying higher in the range on "ice" and "I'm glad."
2:50	Chorus 3	And the rivers flow backwards...	Begins with a repeat of line 1 of chorus 1, but the line moves up on "backwards" rather than down. New lyrics continue with opposites, including bird imagery. Unusual repeat of "now," where the lines again move up rather than down. The refrain line ends on a deceptive cadence on "blue" at 3:19.
3:22	Tag	And I don't love you...	The first line is almost whispered. The last line of the refrain is sung in a free rhythm ending on "blue" at 3:32 with another deceptive cadence. The final melody note wavers and then slides down at 3:35.

FIGURE 3.4. Studio chart of "The Grass Is Blue." Courtesy: Steve Buckingham.

the emotional work and eventual mental collapse occur. Reaching all the way up the octave as the first chorus begins, Dolly writes falling melodic lines for each opposite, and each statement in turn begins at a lower pitch level. This pattern occurs twice in each chorus, and it is easy to predict and sing along with. Dolly then manipulates this melody in subsequent iterations. The second chorus, with changed words, appears immediately after the second verse has raised the possibility of crossing over into "insanity's bliss." This time the melody of the chorus remains in the higher range a bit longer. There is still a descent from the high octave, but Dolly prolongs the upper register for *ice* in the second line and *I'm glad* on the sixth line. The rising emotional tension is palpable, though not overplayed.

But things escalate at the end of this second chorus. Instead of moving to a third verse or bridge as one might expect, Dolly writes another chorus, urged by the instrumental fill between choruses. Here, the musical lines do not fall; they climb up in the opposite direction. Recall that for this third chorus, Dolly retrieves the image "rivers flow backwards." The shift in the musical direction, where the melody ascends rather than descends, is on *backwards*. Dolly goes beyond presenting opposites through lyrics, she also depicts them musically. The second line remains in the higher register until it finally falls to conclude the first half of the chorus. Dolly gathers her energy and self-denial for one final attempt at self-deception in the second half of this chorus. She again pushes the melody line up rather than down, accentuating this change in direction with an unusual repeat of *now* used in two different syntactical ways. This repetition of *now* occurs in the comparable melodic spot that *backwards* did in the first phrase. A change in rhythm at these two places also highlights these moments and intensifies the emotional desperation. With these changes to the final chorus, the emotional instability described in the second verse is now embodied in the more desperate way Dolly presents these opposites, as if willing the self-deception to work.

Ultimately, her efforts to fool herself fail. Her heartbreaking and false assertion, "I'm over you," is immediately followed by the repeated lie that "the sky is green and the grass is blue." To underscore the point, the chorus ends on a minor chord with a deceptive cadence on "the grass is blue." This musical deception mirrors her attempt at emotional self-deception, while it also, paradoxically, reveals her true feelings of sadness. This cadence is a common musical move: approaching the conclusion of a song with a deceptive cadence on a minor submediant chord (vi) and then repeating the line with a final cadence on the major tonic chord (I). But in a final act of deception, Dolly again breaks an expected pattern. When she sings "the grass is blue" for the last time, she pauses before singing the final word and note, giving the listener ample time to "hear" (or predict) the last chord and melodic pitch on the expected major tonic, the same chord that had ended the previous chorus. And then Dolly, again, does the opposite: she concludes with yet another deceptive cadence. This final minor chord is the same chord that begins each chorus, which suggests that she is no closer to finding resolution than she was when the song began. Barely able to find the right note, Dolly vocally "searches" for the final pitch before singing it and then, as if in exhaustion, lets that pitch drop, sliding into silence.[75]

"The Grass Is Blue" is a gentle waltz in a major key. Bluegrass is full of these sweet, lilting melodies. In this style, Dolly starts with a simple idea—let's pretend everything is OK—and then musically depicts the emotional and physical exhaustion required to imagine that everything is normal when everything is wrong. With each chorus, Dolly tries to put on a brave face, and by the third chorus she sounds desperate when singing the inversion of the melody in a high range. These moments are clearly the "blissful" climax of the song. At the close of the song, after the two final pushes in this high register, she no longer has the energy to lie to herself. The first deceptive cadence on a minor chord is, paradoxically, the sad "truth" of her situation, and the final deceptive cadence marks a complete inability to lie anymore (though still giving the listener the opposite of what is expected). And as she searches for that final note, she seems to have lost her moorings completely, barely able to hold the note after she finds it. It is a remarkable performance.

The Grass Is Blue won a Grammy for the Best Bluegrass Album in 2000, and Dolly performed at the awards show. But it was Dolly's recognition by the International Bluegrass Music Association [IBMA] that really floored her. She performed at that awards ceremony, and *The Grass Is Blue* won the IBMA Album of the Year. Buckingham recalled, "That's the most surprised I've ever seen her, and the closest to being speechless I've ever seen her. She never expected that, and it meant so much to her that the bluegrass community accepted her for doing this. And believe me, she can do it because that's the roots of her music, mountain music and bluegrass music. And old-time country music. So we started planning the next album, *Little Sparrow*."[76]

LITTLE SPARROW   When *Little Sparrow* came out two years later, it was also highly acclaimed. While Dolly called *The Grass Is Blue* "a mountain, bluegrass, folk album," she characterized *Little Sparrow* as "a lot of this old-time mountain music."[77] Indeed, the music on *Little Sparrow* is not rooted in bluegrass as solidly as the songs on *The Grass Is Blue*, although she names Bill Monroe in "Bluer Pastures" in yet another green-turns-to-blue metaphor.

> Now I'm headed for bluer pastures
> Where the bluegrass waves sweetly in the wind
> Where the bluegrass music's always playin'
> To the haunting sound of Monroe's mandolin

Rather, as critics wrote, *Little Sparrow* "frequently goes right back to the source of bluegrass"[78] and "explores the darker, more fable-like side of the genre."[79]

Some of Dolly's originals on the album like "Little Sparrow," "Mountain Angel," and "Down from Dover" are directly drawn from and inspired by the ballad tradition. Her euphoric "Marry Me" is more old-time than bluegrass with its accompaniment of a barn dance complete with hoedown fiddle and old-time clawhammer banjo. It fades out with a square dance caller and the sound of flatfoot dancers. However, a driving bluegrass style is featured in the brilliant recasting of the rock songs "Seven Bridges Road" and "Shine," which received a Grammy for Best Country Female Vocal Performance.

The album has a reflective quality through her rerecording of "My Blue Tears" from *Coat of Many Colors*, as well as her version of "A Tender Lie" by Randy Sharp, a recording of "The Beautiful Lie" by David "Butch" McDade, and a rendition of the hymn "In the Sweet By and By." Noting that traditional and old-time musical styles permeate this "bluegrass" album, Dolly described *Little Sparrow* as "blue-mountain music. . . . It's the purest thing I've ever done."[80]

Buckingham linked the sepia-toned/black-and-white covers of *Little Sparrow* and *The Grass Is Blue* with an old-world atmosphere: "I wanted to make it look stark and sound stark." He also wanted these albums, with their old-world look

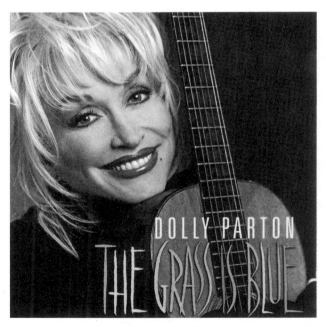

FIGURE 3.5. *The Grass Is Blue* album front cover, 1999.

FIGURE 3.6. *Little Sparrow* album front cover, 2001.

and sound, to "take the focus off, as Dolly calls it, the cartoon [of her persona] and put the focus back on her artistry: that voice, that singer, that musical talent, that songwriting talent, and the way she could interpret other people's songs from that [mountain music] genre."[81]

HALOS & HORNS The third album, *Halos & Horns* (which was not produced by Buckingham, but by Gary "Biscuit" Davis), was also "steeped in bluegrass and reflects her mountain roots." Bill Friskics-Warren recognized the traditional models for two of Dolly's songs, "Not for Me" and "Dagger Through the Heart," which he dubbed "neo-Appalachian ballads."[82] In "These Old Bones" Dolly performs in the voice of an old mountain woman who is a seer, and in "John Daniel" she sings about a charismatic old-time preacher. "Sugar Hill," named for the album's record label, celebrates a lifelong love story sung to the buoyant playing of the fiddle and banjo. Dolly also rerecorded her 1976 song, "Shattered Image." As in *Little Sparrow*, Dolly sang bluegrass covers of pop and rock songs, "If" and "Stairway to Heaven." The album also includes Dolly's responses to 9/11 with the powerful, gospel-inflected "Hello God" and the uncanny harmony and figurative images of "Raven Dove." The title track encapsulates the theme for the album: we are all sinners and saints, and each song references those identities.

Reflecting on these three albums, Dolly said, "I've found a comfort zone. If the music's real, people will always respond to it. Sometimes we get forced to go back to doing what we should do. . . . I had such a good time doing it, I know what the true me is."[83]

After the Trilogy

Soon after *Little Sparrow*, Dolly contributed a song to the album *Songcatcher: Music from and Inspired by the Motion Picture* (2001). The film—a fictionalized account of ballad collecting in the southern Appalachian Mountains in the early twentieth century—explores the Appalachian link to the music of Britain and Ireland. Dolly had seen and enjoyed *Songcatcher* and agreed to write a song, "When Love Is New," for the follow-up album.[84] Once again she turned to her mountain heritage for inspiration, saying: "I tried to write something that really sounded old. . . . As a songwriter it was easy for me, especially for those kind of songs. It's a new song that sounds like it's two or three hundred years old."[85] The song is modeled on traditional dialogue ballads. In this case, a mother (sung by Dolly) and a young daughter (sung by Emmy Rossum, who had starred in *Songcatcher* as a ballad singer) trade parallel verses about the daughter's new love. The young, starry-eyed woman asks for her mother's blessing to marry, but her mother answers with warnings of the man's certain infidelity. Dolly adds a contemporary touch by writing a chorus in which they both sing:

> Love is pretty when love is new
> Like a blushing rose in a dazzling dew
> Intoxicating like cherry sweet wine
> When love is new it's magic

The song's tune evokes traditional folk melodies, reinforced by the accompaniment of dulcimer, acoustic guitar, Dobro, mandolin, fiddle, and bass.

Dolly revisited mountain music in 2014 with *Blue Smoke*, "another rootsy, . . . stripped-down, catchy collection."[86] The title song plays with multiple associations: train smoke, the color and name of the mountains (Blue Ridge, Smoky Mountains), bluegrass music, and sadness. For this song, Dolly reworked her folklike melody from "These Old Bones" into a driving blend of country and bluegrass with gospel-inflected harmony vocals. She also included a traditional murder ballad, "The Banks of the Ohio" (to which she added additional lyrics) further invoking an old-time feel. In 2016, her recording of the sentimental ballad she knew from her childhood, "Little Rosewood Casket," appeared alongside traditional music on the Appalachian tribute album *On Top of Old Smoky: New Old-Time Smoky Mountain Music.*[87] Dolly had earlier included the song on her *Trio* album from 1987.

Dolly said, "you cannot make any money singing bluegrass or this old mountain music." But when she recorded *The Grass Is Blue*, *Little Sparrow*, and *Halos & Horns*, she had the financial freedom to record the kind of music that "means the world" to her.[88] As she said, "I know [*Little Sparrow*] won't sell as much as pop or country. But those 100,000 people that buy it are good enough for me. I'm gonna try to do an album like this every two years or so because it's who I am, what I love. I could never make enough money to buy that feeling out of my soul."[89] When *The Grass Is Blue* and *Little Sparrow* were released, Dolly made a direct link between their mountain music repertoire and her Appalachian roots in extreme poverty: "It's the music that brought me to Nashville. But you couldn't make a living doing it. I had to get rich so I could sing like I was poor, which is what I've done."[90]

Dolly initially made this remark as a way to be clever about how her bluegrass and mountain music albums would not be lucrative. But this "true statement," as she called it, is also a window into Dolly's artistic identity and journey. She knew mountain music, which she "worships," would not get radio or television play and that her dreams of stardom would not come true unless she performed music that appealed to a wider audience. But when freed from the commercial aims of the music industry, Dolly looked back to "that old mountain music," her "first and true love."[91]

———— ～ ⌒ ————

Appalachian music shaped Dolly, but she said "it goes deeper than just the music. . . . It was a lifestyle, it was a way of life."[92] Dolly was nurtured in a musical family and community for whom singing and playing music was an everyday occurrence. Her family helped her make instruments, gave her a guitar and taught her chords, encouraged her songwriting, and immersed her in a rich legacy of music—ballads, fiddle and banjo tunes, hymns, old country songs—that laid the groundwork for her own songwriting. Certainly not all of Dolly's songs spring from her mountain roots, but it is this heritage she holds most dear.

Chapter 4

"These Old Bones"

Dolly's Mountain Identity and Voice

"When I sing I feel like that I'm part of the
mountains, I'm part of that whole sound."

Many of Dolly's songs draw upon elements of mountain music,
as demonstrated in Chapter Three.[1] However many critics who
write about Dolly's music often rely on generic and stereotypical
mountain tropes to characterize her songs and her vocal style rather than
discussing specific musical characteristics. In this chapter, I explore how critics
have woven Dolly's musical style into a larger narrative about the history of
Appalachian music, and I allow Dolly to stake her own claim to her mountain
voice and identity.

As discussed, Dolly often links her mountain music and vocal quality to the
music of Britain and Ireland. Just prior to singing "Little Sparrow" in concert,
she said:

> This music is best suited for my voice. It's music of the heart, of the soul. I think
> most writers, especially mountain people like me, it comes from that old world
> of tragic songs that were brought over from England, from Ireland, and those
> Scottish ballads. That's just programmed into us. It's just in our psyche.... And
> I just love to sing sad songs; I love to write sad songs. I write a lot of new songs
> and people'll say, "that's an old song, ain't it?" I say "no, that's my song. Just all
> that English blood in me carried over."[2]

This notion about the origins of Appalachian music is not Dolly's alone. In the late-nineteenth and twentieth century, it was part of a larger cultural project that sought to define the Appalachian Mountains as the site of "our contemporary ancestors," defined as those early pioneers who were descendants of British emigrants and to whom Americans could look to find an idyllic and usable past.[3] These beliefs about the origin of Appalachian culture and music also play a role in the way critics identify Dolly's music as Appalachian.

The Elizabethan Myth

For more than a century, writers, cultural critics, and composers have conflated Appalachia with Elizabethan England. These ideas gained wide circulation through Charles Morrow Wilson's 1929 article in *The Atlantic Monthly*:

> We know a land of Elizabethan ways—a country of Spenserian speech, Shakespearean people, and of cavaliers and curtsies. It is a land of high hopes and mystic allegiances, where one may stroll through the forests of Arden and find heaths and habits like those of olden England. . . . Elizabethan English, as well as Elizabethan England, appears to have survived magnificently in these isolated Southern uplands.[4]

Appalachian music played a significant role in reinforcing these ideas. In his 1915 article, "Shakespeare's America," William Bradley wrote, "Old English and Scottish popular ballads are not the only legacy of the Old World to the New that time has kept more or less intact in the dark hollows of the Kentucky hills."[5] In identifying Appalachian people and their music as Elizabethan relics, both cultural and music critics were looking to uplift the region by associating it with an imagined, honorable past that recuperated the supposedly uncultured and degraded mountain folk. Thus, the presence of the ballads in Appalachia—"the literature of the illiterate" as Frost wrote[6]—demonstrated the hidden nobility of the region. This well-established belief lived on in the folk music revival of the 1950s and 1960s as the ballad tradition and folk tunes of Appalachia became well-known and popular through artists like ballad singer Jean Ritchie and folk singer Joan Baez. Eventually, music critics applied this Elizabethan myth to Dolly.

Writers had often described Dolly's songs with phrases like "Appalachian ballads" and "old world." For example, in 1978 Bruce Cook wrote:

> Dolly has captured the high lonesome sound of Appalachia. It is the kind of chill, pure vibrato you can hear to this day if you go deep enough into the hills

and listen to the old women in sunbonnets who sit on their porches, twang on dulcimers, and sing the ballads they learned at their grandmothers' knees.[7]

Others went even further, pushing beyond the Appalachians to Europe. *New York Times* critic John Rockwell wrote, "Her music is often colored by the modalities and rhythmic abnormalities of old English folk songs,"[8] and Toby Thompson remarked, "Here [in Appalachia] medieval hymns are taught by the shape note method, folk tunes persist."[9] Eventually, these ideas coalesced, and critics began to characterize Dolly's mountain music as specifically Elizabethan. For them, *Elizabethan* was shorthand for Dolly's Appalachian heritage as well as her use of British-derived ballad forms, the modal inflections in some of her songs, and occasionally her idiosyncratic vocal quality.

The earliest use of the term *Elizabethan* in conjunction with Dolly's music that I have found dates from August 1977 in an article in *Rolling Stone* by Chet Flippo. He described her vocal style as "a shimmering, childlike trill, influenced mainly by church music and by the Elizabethan ballads her mother sang."[10] A few months later, Jack Hurst referenced Elizabethan ballads in his discussion of Dolly's musical influences: "Dolly's style grew out of her exposure to . . . Elizabethan ballads preserved for centuries by isolated Appalachian mountaineers."[11] Within a year, two other writers had picked up this language.[12] One of the quirkiest instances of this term is in Alanna Nash's 1978 biography of Dolly: "Just as [the song] 'Coat of Many Colors' has its foundation in the old English folk tunes, it retains the rhythmic aberrations of the Elizabethan ballads handed down through the centuries, although they are hardly noticeable in her delivery." Nash also claimed "Jolene" "harks immediately back to the purest of Elizabethan form."[13] She seems to credit the modal harmony of the tune for this observation.

One wonders if Flippo's remarks—and their widespread perpetuation—were inspired by the wave of colonial revivalist spirit in the United States during the Bicentennial celebrations of the mid-1970s. Moreover, it appears that after Flippo's use of the term, anyone who tried to account for Dolly's Appalachian musical sound and heritage simply latched on to the concept of Elizabethan and left it at that. As mentioned earlier, Steve Eng resorted to Elizabethan-tinged language about "Jolene," saying: "the minor-chord melody has an antique 'Greensleeves' feel to it." He also characterized "Coat of Many Colors" as "one more 1960s-style old English ballad," and wrote "Down from Dover" could be "mistaken for an Old English or Scottish ballad" because of its "folk chord progression."[14] Meanwhile, Flippo continued to use *Elizabethan* in his subsequent writing about Dolly,[15] and his language was reproduced in prominent online biographies of Dolly,[16] providing an established terminology borrowed by writers in 2007, 2014, and 2018.[17]

Dolly has never used *Elizabethan* to describe her music in her interviews. Instead she speaks about lyrics and sonorities: "A phrase like 'Come all ye fair and tender maidens' rolls as easily off the tongue of an ironworker in a Liverpool pub as it does off that of a sharecropper in the Smokies. A bow being pulled across the strings of an Appalachian fiddle makes the same kind of baleful moan as bagpipes wafting through the highlands. Our roots and the deepest parts of our very souls are tied to the music."[18] Buckingham recalled, "I never heard the word *Elizabethan* come out of her mouth. It was 'music from the old country' or 'old-timey music'—those are the words I remember."[19]

Writers who use *Elizabethan* about Dolly's music hear something distinctive that prompts them to identify some of her songs and her sound as Appalachian. But they make both category and history errors when they misunderstand Dolly's Appalachian heritage as Elizabethan, using this misnomer that has been attached to Appalachia for over a century.

Dolly's Mountain Voice

When Flippo first introduced *Elizabethan* to describe Dolly's music, he said her voice had "a shimmering, childlike trill."[20] Once again, critics followed his lead and described Dolly's voice by using romanticized allusions to her mountain upbringing, as these examples illustrate:

> Dolly has captured the high lonesome sound of Appalachia, . . . [a] kind of chill, pure vibrato.[21]
> The vibrato and light twang of her voice evoke the Anglo-Saxon ballads of the Southern Mountains.[22]
> The clear sound of her lovely mountain tremolo voice and her hillbilly glam image have become a permanent part of the tapestry of twentieth-century American popular culture.[23]

These are certainly accurate descriptions of some of Dolly's distinctive vocal characteristics—she uses a range of vocal qualities, including a tight vibrato that writers describe as trembling, a tremolo, and a trill. Further, Dolly sometimes uses a very light tone in her upper register that might be construed as childlike, and she occasionally sings in a child's voice.

However, these writers often define Dolly's vocal quality as a mountain sound not a country music sound. We are lucky to have recordings made by traditional women ballad singers from Appalachia, and very few sing in a voice that matches these critic's descriptions of Dolly's voice.[24] Most use little vibrato; instead, they sing with a straight tone in a naturalized chest voice that may strain for the top pitches. Stephanie Vander Wel suggests this type of sound "signals an authentic sonority located within the vernacular expressions of rural, white, southern culture."[25] We are also fortunate to have a recording of Dolly's mother who presumably "crooned" those Elizabethan ballads.[26] Dolly had her parents and seven of her siblings as guests on an episode of her television show *Dolly!* (1976). In one segment, they sang the traditional song "In the Pines" to Dolly's guitar accompaniment.[27] Dolly's mother sang part of a verse alone without vibrato in a strong, nasal chest voice that no one could label crooning. Dolly described it as "straight-ahead mountain sounds."[28]

Dolly used this style of mountain voice in her song "These Old Bones" on *Halos & Horns*. There are two characters in the song: an old mountain woman who is clairvoyant, and a young woman, her daughter, who was taken by the county soon after she was born. Dolly uses two different voices for these roles. She sings in her usual voice for the young woman, but she models the voice of the mountain woman after her mother's. "Mama had a great mountain voice," Dolly said.[29] "I grew up hearing my mom and those old mountain women that sound like that. And when I did that [song] I wanted to pay tribute to my mom, 'cause that's how Mama sounded."[30] Dolly's version of this voice does sound very much like her mother's vocal style. This raw, edgy sound stands in sharp contrast to Dolly's normal singing voice. The difference is pronounced as the two voices are juxtaposed in the opening moments of the song.

Dolly begins the song with the chorus sung in a mountain voice like her mother's. Then, in the first verse, she switches to her usual vocal style, which seems urbane, smooth, and refined in comparison. The two voices continue trading parts: Dolly uses her normal voice in the verses and her mountain voice for the chorus as well as spoken lines in some of the verses. After the old woman dies, the two voices sing the final chorus in a duet with the mountain woman on the melody and the young woman singing harmony. It is an uncanny and moving moment—a musical fusion of Dolly's voice and her mother's voice, and a passing on of the gift of clairvoyance from mother to daughter in the song.

"These Old Bones" refers to the old mountain woman but also to the animal bones that the old woman throws to see into the future. The mountain voice of the old woman dominates the final minute of the song. In the background and in her normal voice, Dolly freely riffs on the title line of the song to the melody of the chorus while the mountain woman talks at length about her gift of sight.

She cackles as she skirts any responsibility for unhappy events that she predicts, and she closes the song saying the bones are "just for show," "the magic is inside you; there ain't no crystal ball." The song fades out with the sound of the bones rattling as they are thrown one last time to the accompaniment of the old-time, clawhammer banjo that has been present throughout.

Although Dolly had entertained her family for years with imitations of her mother's voice, she said it was not easy to inhabit that identity in the recording studio. She was adamant that her old woman persona and voice not be ridiculed. "I'm dead serious about this," she said to the recording engineer. "Turn the lights down. I don't want you looking at me, because I've got to become the old woman." It is touching to imagine Dolly feeling vulnerable and exposed in a recording studio as she sang both "with" and as her mother: "it'll be like me and Mama!"[31] Here was a moment where Dolly's artificial and real worlds met: Dolly the glamorous singer embodying her mountain singer alter ego.

Since Dolly's usual voice does not sound like a stereotypical mountain voice—like her mother's—why, then, do writers say her voice has a mountain sound? Starting with Dolly's Appalachian identity they ascribe mountain descriptors to her vocal style. In essence, their thinking is: Dolly is from the mountains, she has an unusual vocal quality and style, so her voice must be an authentic Appalachian mountain voice. Thus, Dolly's unique voice becomes the starting point for identifying a mountain vocal sound, and critics then define Appalachian vocal style based on Dolly's singing rather than exploring what qualities and elements of Appalachian singing Dolly does bring to her distinctive vocal style.

For instance, the vibrato that critics hear in Dolly's voice is not a characteristic of most traditional Appalachian ballad singers. While Dolly's voice does have a natural vibrato (which she sometimes suppresses), there is nothing specifically Appalachian about that vocal element. Rather, I believe what these writers hear in Dolly's voice—what they also call a trill or a tremolo—are nuanced vocal embellishments, essentially mordents and turns, that she uses to punctuate certain words. Dolly calls them "my little curls."[32] She describes her voice and these embellishments as akin to "that mountain sound that those people sing. And that's just built in my whole body: those old mountain twirls and twists and things."[33]

These moments, rather than her vibrato, are related to traditional Appalachian singing. Such "elaborate vocal gestures," according to Sammie Anne Wicks, are an element of the "old way of singing." Wicks describes this style, which dates back to "the late seventeenth ... century in England, New England, and the American South," as a "long-breathed, melodically elaborated and bracingly loud vocal art, pitched in the upper registers of the voice, and applied to the singing of Christian hymns by Southerners."[34] Writing in 1911, Joseph James said the style was filled with "twisted rills and frills of the unnatural snaking of the voice."[35] Jean Ritchie described mountain singing as "'decorating' a song with shakes and quivers in the old way, shaking up a note and quivering down."[36]

Dolly uses these embellishing techniques in many of her songs, from her country and pop tunes to her mountain-inspired ballads and songs. For example, a close listen to the opening verse of "The Bargain Store" reveals several places where Dolly uses ornaments: the first syllable of *bargain*, the last syllable of *merchandise*, and most obviously on *for*. Another example is on her 1971 recording of "Down from Dover." In the third verse she ornaments *told* and the final word *Dover*. Her stirring recording of "Crippled Bird" is a catalogue of vocal embellishments of all varieties, including her use of a sobbing timbre. Her quivering ornaments are especially pronounced in the first verse on the words "*time to* mend," in the second verse at "*words* could say," and in the third verse at "*deep* and sharp," "*pain*ful," and "*true* blue *bro*ken *heart*."

Dolly's use of these embellishments is a complex technical facet of her vocal style, similar but not identical to her quick vibrato. Further, she does not sing in only this one style. There are many examples, such as "Dumb Blonde," where she sings without these light curls—sometimes in a straight tone, sometimes with vibrato. This is where we can hear the influence of her mother's mountain style of singing, which did not include vocal ornaments. When Dolly sings in this way we also occasionally hear another element of traditional mountain singing, the presence of a "lift or wail at the end of a line of verse," often called "feathering."[37] This sound is the physical result of singing a fully supported note and then abruptly stopping the note while the breath support is still at its maximum, resulting in a slight rise in pitch. Dolly uses feathering on occasion, especially when she sings in a straight-tone vocal style—the "hillbilly nasal twang"[38]—which she often places within a hard-shell country aesthetic.

"Only Dreamin'" is filled with Dolly's vocal embellishments I have identified as Appalachian—the curling ornaments and a full-throated, naturalized voice with a strained feathering throughout. For example, in the opening lines, Dolly sings the note on *know* and *tears* with her straight-toned voice, but as this first chorus ends, she uses an ornament on *know* (the second time the word is sung). She repeats this ornament in the following verse on *kiss* and almost immediately thereafter on *dream* and again on *know* at the end of the section. Her most striking use of a straight tone is in the final chorus when she pushes up the octave on *know*. The vocal feathering at the end of this word is obvious. Related to her embellishments, and also a hallmark of Dolly's songwriting prowess, is the way she sings *teardrops* and *tears*. Both words have long, descending melismas, or strings of notes, to depict tears. In "Only Dreamin'," Dolly performs her own version of an Appalachian voice: filled with twists and twirls, powerful and raw but more refined than her mother's voice, and not at all childlike and trembling. (See Appendix D for a full analysis and Listening Outline of "Only Dreamin'.")

Dolly feels most at home vocally when singing in a mountain style, incorporating her curls and twists: "I can sing all kinds of stuff, and I've been lucky that I've got enough power in my voice that I can sing all styles of music. But when I get back home to these [mountain] songs, I just feel it through and through and through and through and through."[39] Buckingham suggested that Dolly had assimilated the singing styles she heard and created her own sound:

> She'll talk about Dollyizing something. It's not thought out. It just flows that way, the curls at the end of notes, the trills, that type of thing. Vocally, in just strictly octaves, it's not a huge range. But her range of riffs, whatever you want to call it, vocally, it's endless, it's bottomless, it just goes on. And it's not like she says, "ok, I'm going to trill this little note," or "I'm going to bend this note up." That's not part of the process that I've ever experienced with her. It's always just, that's the way it was. That's the way it flowed out.[40]

Dolly confirmed that although these vocal embellishments are a hallmark of mountain singing, her use of these ornaments is also something specific to her: "That's just my personality of voice, I guess is as good a way of saying it. That's kinda like acting. That's how I express my feelings, 'cause I'm able to do things with my voice, little trills, little curls, it feels natural like I want to go to those places." Dolly defined herself as a "stylist," saying: "They're stylists in this world and then there are singers. And usually you either like a stylist or you don't. 'Cause a lot of people don't like to hear me sing, but a lot of people do, thank God."[41] However one describes it, Dolly's vocal style has been a significant element in the construction of her mountain identity.

Why has Dolly's music and vocal quality so often been described as Elizabethan and mountain? I believe the answer starts with the deep-rooted practice of overlaying Appalachian culture with an Elizabethan identity. Next, critics hear Dolly's style as different from other country artists of her generation. For instance, Loretta Lynn shares a similar Appalachian upbringing with Dolly, but no writer has suggested that her songs sound like Appalachian ballads, much less Elizabethan ones. Lynn's music does not have as many characteristics that echo traditional styles as Dolly's. Her songs and naturalized voice are strongly indebted to a hard country, honky-tonk sound (a sound that Dolly also uses at times). Critics who hear British and Irish influences in Dolly's mountain music are not off the mark. But rather than specifically identifying qualities related to the "old way" of singing—as well as her compositional style that incorporates modal harmonies and traces of balladry—they use the Elizabethan misnomer attached to Appalachia for over a century. In doing this, they also construct Dolly as a bearer of an old-world, Anglo-Saxon heritage that some view as the root of country music. Further, Dolly's mountain voice, reified with these old-world resonances, also marks her as morally uplifted in the same way the Appalachian region was figuratively uplifted through an association with Elizabethan England. As Toby Thompson wrote in 1976:

> [Dolly's] fibrilating [*sic*] soprano pump[ed] out Nashville tearjerkers and down-home spirituals with a sincerity that was heartrending. . . . Back on the kitchen radio, Loretta Lynn or Tammy Wynette were sure to be bitching about something—their voices grating, acerbic, cranky as alley cats squalling under a drainpipe, but Dolly flushed all that away with a vibrato clean as mountain rain. . . . We courted Loretta's music in barrooms and poolhalls, but Dolly's was a voice you could take home to mother.[42]

Through this sexist language, Thompson valorized female purity, hearing a mountain innocence in Dolly's voice that was a moral contrast to the honky-tonk singing of Lynn and Wynette.

Elizabethan or Irish? Dolly's View

Dolly makes many self-reflexive comments about the relationship between her music and vocal style and what she calls old-world music:

> I could not be prouder than to be a Smoky Mountain girl. And I really do think that my style of music, my vocal style, especially when I sing the old-timey songs, the old country songs, there's just something about these hills that have a sound, and I think so much of that is because of so many people that came here from the old world; the old flavors from Scotland and Ireland. The Welsh flavors and England and all those great old songs.[43]

She feels a special affinity for the music of Ireland, identifying "Only Dreamin'" as sounding Irish and being an "old-world kinda song."[44] To create an even more recognizable Irish sound, her recording of "Only Dreamin'" incorporated a harmonium for a drone along with tin whistle and bodhrán. For her 1994 album, *Heartsongs: Live from Home*, Dolly and Buckingham highlighted her music's connection to "Celtic music from Scotland, Ireland, England, and Wales," and the Irish band, Altan, joined the bluegrass musicians on the album:

> It was a match made in Heaven as the fiddles, guitars, and dobros interacted with the Irish "squeezebox," uilleann pipes, whistles, and bouzouki. We often found that a song known by the Irish musicians under one title would be familiar to the bluegrass musicians under another title. One of the songs we recorded was the ancient ballad "Barbara Allen." While I sang the lyrics in English, Mairéad Ní Mhaonaigh of Altan sang the Gaelic translation. The combination was unbelievable. . . . [T]he impact and connection of this timeless and classic music will live forever.[45]

This link with Ireland was made explicit again on *Little Sparrow*. Buckingham explained, "I mixed in Altan because it was such a connection between the music that came out of England, Ireland, and Scotland and came to the United States, especially in the southeast Appalachian mountains and down into the Smoky Mountains. It's the music Dolly heard as a kid." Buckingham incorporated uilleann pipes on the album because their "sound, the modal sound, no thirds, that type of thing, was very familiar to her. So when you hear that sound of the uilleann pipes, it's like the dulcimer, the banjo [with their] drone sound."[46]

Four songs on *Little Sparrow* also included players from Altan: "In the Sweet By and By," "Down from Dover," "My Blue Tears," and "Mountain Angel." "In the Sweet By and By" features Mairéad Ní Mhaonaigh again singing verses in Gaelic and Altan musicians on whistle, accordion, and Irish bouzouki. These same instruments accompany "Down from Dover," and Irish singer Maura O'Connell sings harmony vocals. (O'Connell had previously sung on Dolly's 1993 recording of "What Will Baby Be," which also included the subtle presence of uilleann pipes, introduced by Buckingham.) Dolly said she "wrote a few pieces [for *Little Sparrow*] that lend themselves to an Irish treatment,"[47] and she wanted to include "more mountain music, more things with Irish flavor" on this album rather than getting "pigeonholed just into bluegrass."[48] Dolly succeeded in having listeners make the association with Irish music. One critic wrote *Little Sparrow* "frequently goes right back to the source of bluegrass—Celtic music."[49]

The Irish press is an enthusiastic partner in Dolly's efforts to link her music with Ireland. In one newspaper, Dolly commented, "I have a huge following in Ireland, they completely believe the songs I sing and I can feel that when I'm there, too. I really feel like I'm home when I come to Ireland." Indeed, the author of the article asserted the Irish "feel a profound kinship with country" music—since country music supposedly has Celtic roots—and so they are especially fond of Dolly.[50] Dolly explained: "[Fans in the U.K.] swear that I sound just like them. So I think that's one of the keys to my success is that they just kind of claim me as a homegirl. . . . [There's] just kind of a sadness and a longing in the voice that they have and in the voice that I have and grew up with."[51] The heart of Dolly's connection to Ireland is in what she described as Irish music's lonesome qualities—"they tell such sad stories you can just feel it"—that grows out of a hard life Dolly views as similar to own early years: "They had such hard times and very much like us, just poor people with big families, hard living, and you just hear it in their voice like how I think it is with African American music, you feel all the sorrow of all the centuries, and you just feel the heart, the gut, and the soul of it all."[52] Dolly perceives hardship and sorrow as a profound connection between Appalachia and Ireland, and she believes the similarity of experiences led to the similarity in musical expression.

Jean Ritchie said the Celtic label in reference to mountain music is "an umbrella term that people use, not always knowing what it means. It's a very descriptive word. It unites people in that feeling."[53] Thus, *Celtic* functions similarly to *Elizabethan*—as a shorthand for a style of music and a cultural feeling that is hard to capture—and *Celtic* is now a more prominent term than *Elizabethan* in characterizing Appalachian music.[54]

In aligning her music with this connection to Britain and Ireland in particular, Dolly has tapped into a style, a sound, and a story that resonates with her fans and continues to fuel her career. In a comment about her album *Heartsongs: Live from Home*, Dolly viewed this musical "old world to Appalachia" story as embodied in her life story. "I've been waiting all my life to do an acoustic album of the songs I grew up lovin' and singin'. The album has songs from the Old World—England, Ireland, Scotland, Wales—as well as songs from the Smokies and some that I have written that were influenced by all these places. It's the album I hope and believe I will be most remembered for, and *it goes nicely with this story of my life*."[55]

"Appalachian Memories": Return to Roots

"Even when I'm writing a modern song," Dolly said, "I'll find myself pulling stuff from those days before I ever left home. The days of Mama and Daddy and my grandmas and grandpas, and church days. All I ever have to do is close my eyes and just kind of go inside."[56] When *The Grass Is Blue* was released it was called "a return to the Appalachian Mountains," and *Little Sparrow* "was lauded as her return to pure mountain music."[57] Some critics and fans suggested Dolly "is at her best when she returns to her Appalachian roots."[58] But Dolly made it clear that mountain music was not a new phase in her career: "It's not like I came in the back door with this music. I've been doing it on my front porch for years."[59]

For many, these recordings re-contextualized some of Dolly's other songs such as "Coat of Many Colors" and "My Tennessee Mountain Home," clarifying "that the sounds we've always associated with Dolly at her best grew out of bluegrass and related styles. So, her venture into this music takes on the nature of a journey home."[60] Dolly's so-called return that these critics described was undoubtedly her homecoming after her crossover pop albums and more urbane country recordings. But Dolly had never completely abandoned her roots, as she explained:

> Well *return* to roots, I guess I never really left my roots. I think that's the thing that's kept me sane all these years no matter what else I've done. . . . I've always stayed true to my roots and true to myself and that music is the most natural form. Now there's no pressure, since I'm not doing it to make a living anymore 'cause I've managed to do a few things like Dollywood and my production company where I can make a living doing other things. So I had decided I was going to do some more traditional things. . . . I just wanted to get back to real stuff.[61]

In these remarks, Dolly sounds a lot like those folks in her song "Appalachian Memories" who left the mountains seeking better paying jobs, but who always kept sight of who they were, staying strong by holding their memories of home close and eventually returning home to the mountains. As she said, "I'm an all-around girl. I'm happy that I can go uptown now and then, but I still will always love the mountain music best."[62]

Dolly asserts that mountain music is not merely an influence from her past, but that it is literally inside her. She speaks of physically embodying this musical heritage that gives her a specific genetic and artistic identity. "I'm on the right track as far as the people who like to hear me do really heart-felt, gut music. . . . This is really who I truly am," Dolly says. "It's my roots, my Smoky Mountain DNA. It's in every fiber of my body. When I open my mouth to sing these songs, it amazes me the feeling I get here in my heart and down inside my soul."[63] Dolly believes this profound emotional quality makes her mountain music powerful for many listeners: "I love being able to express my feelings and my heart in that way. And I think that's one of the reasons people respond to me singing that kind of music. They really feel it."[64] Dolly's "Smoky Mountain DNA" is not an empty metaphor; it is Dolly's claim about her core identity and the source of her musical power.

Chapter 5
"I Will Always Love You"

Songs about Love

"My heart is very tender. I just have strong
muscles around it."

Dolly enjoyed a banner year in 1974.[1] Four of her most well-known songs about love were #1 hits: "Jolene" in February, "I Will Always Love You" in June, "Please Don't Stop Loving Me," a duet with cowriter Porter Wagoner, in October, and "Love Is Like a Butterfly" in November. It was also the year she set out on her solo career, leaving *The Porter Wagoner Show*, and her departure was the genesis of her most celebrated love song.

"I Will Always Love You"

Widely lauded by fans and critics—"as perfect a love song as Parton or anyone will ever write"[2]—"I Will Always Love You" was not written about romantic lovers. Dolly composed it to convince Porter she needed to separate from her business relationship and singing partnership with him. When she joined his show in 1967, Dolly planned to stay for only five years since she wanted to pursue a solo career. When she finally announced she was leaving after seven years, Porter balked. Dolly wrote "I Will Always Love You" as a way to get through to him:

> He wouldn't listen to nothing at that time because he was so angry and spiteful and so mean about the whole thing that he wouldn't allow me a conversation

to try to explain why I was doing what I was doing. I thought, "Well, the only way I'm going to be able to express it is to write it." Everybody can understand a song. There were so many things I wanted to say, there was so much emotion, feeling and heartache on his part and on my part. Once I started it, the song seemed to pour out.[3]

Dolly's message was clear: "If I should stay I would only be in your way" and "we both know that I'm not what you need." When Porter heard Dolly sing the song, he cried and said he would let her go on the condition he produce the song.[4] In 2007, Dolly again sang it to him during his 50th Anniversary Celebration at the Grand Ole Opry. Porter was dying of lung cancer, and Dolly, struggling a bit with emotion, cupped his chin in her hand and wiped tears from his cheek when she sang "goodbye, please now, don't you cry."[5]

However, now for most performances, Dolly shifts the direct address of the song from Porter to her listeners, which forges an intimate bond between her and the audience. She explained: "Now because of my fans and the way they react, it's my love song to them at the end of my show."[6] She closes her concerts with "I Will Always Love You," and its final hushed verse, tenderly spoken, hovers over everyone as a benediction:

> I hope life treats you kind
> And I hope that you have all that you ever dreamed of
> And I wish you joy and happiness
> But above all of this, I wish you love

This blessing is also the last thing visitors see when they exit Dolly's Chasing Rainbows Museum at Dollywood.

When Elvis Presley and his management heard Dolly's recording of the song in 1974, they approached her about Elvis recording it. But the deal was to include Elvis buying half of the song's publishing rights. Although she would have loved Elvis to record it, Dolly went against others' advice and did not sell it since the song was already her most lucrative copyright. Always protective of her songs, Dolly explained her difficult decision. Her songs were both personal creations as well as investments in her future: "I cried my heart out, it was going to kill me. I always joke that my songs are like my children—I expect them to support me when I'm old. I'm from a very poor family, six boys and six girls, and none of my people ever had any money. So when I started making money I thought that my songs are what I'm going to leave to my mom and my dad and my brothers and sisters. I have no children of my own. My catalogue is what I'm going to leave behind to my relatives."[7] "I would not give up the publishing, and thank God I didn't, because that song made me more money than all of the others put together. . . . Plus I would've lost half the pride in it."[8] Her decision proved to be a savvy business move.

The song went to #1 a second time in 1982 when she rerecorded it for *The Best Little Whorehouse in Texas* (the first time a song went to #1 on the country chart twice in two different recordings by the same performer). Dolly recorded a third version in 1995 as a duet with Vince Gill on *Something Special*; their version charted at #15 and was awarded Vocal Event of the Year by the CMA.[9] In 2007, Dolly's recording from 1974 was inducted into the Grammy Hall of Fame. Most people likely know the song through Whitney Houston's recording for the 1992 film *The Bodyguard*. This version, a powerful, soulful interpretation compared with Dolly's more tender country rendition, was #1 on the *Billboard* Hot 100 chart for 14 weeks, and it reappeared on that chart at #7, peaking at #3, after Houston's death in 2012. "I Will Always Love You" was one of three songs featured in the "Forever Country: Artists of Then, Now and Forever" music video celebrating the 50th Annual Country Music Association Awards in 2016. Dolly's song had the last word as the sea of country singers parted, revealing Dolly singing the song's final lines before closing with her twinkling smile.

The lyrics of "I Will Always Love You" reflect a sense of loss or change in a relationship while taking the high road with strength, generosity, and kindness. Dolly's musical setting intensifies these sentiments. The song has a powerful hook in the chorus with its double repetition of the title line and the chords of the classic '50s progression (I, vi, IV, V) found in hundreds of popular songs, most notably "Heart and Soul."[10] This harmonic progression taps into a musical-cultural memory for listeners, even those who may not consciously recognize it. Dolly's chorus is different from numerous songs with this progression in how she aligns the two lines of lyrics across the two repetitions of the harmonic pattern. In "Heart and Soul" for example, one line of text aligns with one iteration of the progression; line two of the song starts at the beginning of the repetition of the chord progression, on the tonic (I):

> I   vi IV   V
> Heart and soul, I fell in love with you
>
> I   vi IV   V
> Lost control the way a fool would do

But Dolly avoids such a symmetrical relationship between text and harmony. Instead, she prolongs the first line of text so the harmonic progression returns to the tonic chord before the second line of the chorus.[11] By using the tonic as a pivot point, she propels the motion forward into the second line with her artful misalignment of text and harmony:

```
I    vi    IV  V      I
And I ... will always love you

vi    IV  V      I
I will always love you
```

Dolly explained why she thought "I Will Always Love You" is so timeless. "Well, I think it has [endured] for two reasons. One is, it's a very simple melody, really easy to sing, like holding the notes. Even if you can't sing, you can sing, Iiiiiiiiii-Iiiii will alwaaaaays love yooou.... Plus there's the message." She continued, "I think everybody can connect with it, whether it's their lost love affair, or a partnership, or when children go off to college, or when people die. I've had so many people say, 'Oh, we played "I Will Always Love You" at my dad's funeral or at my mom's funeral,' so I think it's something everybody can relate to for one reason or another."[12] The song is "full of every kind of emotion you could imagine.... When you are able to write all those feelings, that's what I think truly makes the classic songs."[13] As Dolly said, "there are many kinds of broken hearts, and I'm a very sensitive person, so I write about it."[14] Thus, "I Will Always Love You" has an emotional flexibility, applicable to many kinds of loving relationships.

Unlike "I Will Always Love You," most of Dolly's love songs are explicitly about romantic love. She writes love songs that seem like fairy tales of unbridled joy or quiet contentment in discovering and nurturing a relationship, but, just as often, she delves into the many ways relationships are broken and the happily-ever-after fades and vanishes. While temptation, betrayal, cheating, and jealousy all appear in her songs, the aftermath of a breakup is often the subject—usually from the heartbroken perspective of the abandoned lover but sometimes from the sassy viewpoint of the person who leaves in an I'm-taking-my-life-back cloud of dust.

I begin my study of Dolly's love songs with those that enact fairy tales, and I juxtapose these fantasies with Dolly's real-life relationships with the two people closest to her: her husband Carl Dean and her lifelong friend Judy Ogle. Dolly's creative world and personal world overlap in complex ways in her love songs, and her unconventional views of love, marriage, and friendship inflect many of her love songs. So is it important to consider Dolly's primary relationships in order to have a richer understanding of the wide range of her songs about love that I explore later in this chapter.

Fairy Tales and Real-life Love Stories

Fairy tales loom large in Dolly's construction of her image, as well as in many of her love songs and other creative projects. She often relies on the familiar figures and formulas of fairy tales, as in the opening of her autobiography: "Once upon a time and far, far away, back in the hollers at the foothills of the Great Smoky Mountains of East Tennessee there lived a little girl with yellow hair, blue-green eyes, fair skin, and freckles."[15] By beginning her personal story as a fairy tale, she invoked a set of expectations: this charmed little girl will overcome obstacles, be transformed in some way, and arrive at a happy ending. And, indeed, this is the way Dolly usually tells the story of her life.

In some of her songs, Dolly also reimagines fairy tales, and her album *The Fairest of Them All* is a prime example. The cover photo complements the album's title. Dolly, dressed in an extravagant, even outlandish pink princess dress, reinterprets the "mirror, mirror on the wall" scene from *Snow White*. She ostensibly gazes at herself in the mirror, searching for confirmation of her beauty as in the story. But in fact, she looks directly at the viewer, confirming instead our shared knowledge of the conventional fairy-tale script. Rather than asking the customary question of the mirror, "who's the fairest of them all," Dolly gives us the answer directly: she is the fairest. This tableau is a meta-moment in which Dolly watches us watching her reenact this story, a self-reflexive move that exposes the artifice of the fairy tale. Moreover, Dolly rewrites *Snow White* to suit her flamboyant fairy princess persona—in the original it was the evil queen, not the young woman, who used a mirror to confirm her beauty. Dolly may have intended the cover art and title of the album simply to be a comment on her image. As she once said, "I like looking like I came out of a fairy tale."[16] But the title and photograph invites, even encourages, listeners to hear the album's songs as fairy tales as well.

The songs on the album question fairy-tale expectations. Dolly wrote ten of the eleven tracks on the recording, and not one is a happily-ever-after story. Time and time again the handsome prince goes off script, as does the fairy princess in a few instances. In two songs of lost love, the prince abandons the woman: in "But You Loved Me Then" the woman remembers earlier happy times

FIGURE 5.1. *The Fairest of Them All* album front cover, 1970.

in a fairyland before her lover left, and in "Daddy Come and Get Me" a young woman begs to be rescued from a mental asylum after suffering a breakdown because of her cheating man. Both "Chas" and "Robert" are stories of inappropriate love affairs: the prince is a family member. In "When Possession Gets Too Strong," "Just the Way I Am," and "More than Their Share," the woman resists the conventional script and refuses to be controlled by her prince in an unequal relationship. Three songs explore the consequences of unwed pregnancy, scenarios in which the prince seduces but does not marry the young woman: "Mammie," "I'm Doing This for Your Sake," and "Down from Dover." Dolly often writes songs about difficult relationships and lost love, but it is unusual for her to fill an entire album with them as she did here. Moreover, Dolly broke from her usual practice with the album's title. Her recordings typically are named after one of their songs. Instead, with *The Fairest of Them All*, Dolly framed all the songs on the album as fairy tales, even though none of them used fairy-tale language or characters.

Several years after this album, Dolly wrote "Where Beauty Lives in Memory," which specifically referenced fairy tales. Here, a woman, whom Dolly compares to Cinderella, is driven into a fantasy world waiting for a handsome prince who had once loved her. Over the span of forty years, the woman repeats the line from *Snow White*, "mirror, mirror on the wall, who's the fairest of them all," watching her beauty fade as she waits for his return. She eventually loses touch with reality and hallucinates: "inside her mind she sees him at the door" and she "falls dead upon the floor." Dolly was inspired to write this fairy tale by her real-world memories: "I knew a woman who was beautiful and she was married to this man and she was crazy about him but he would do bad things to her and he got to tellin' people she was crazy. She almost grieved herself to death and now she is like a child, and she still talks about him, she has kind of gone back in time. She still thinks she is as young and pretty as she ever was. It just touched me so deep and I could just imagine that happening to *me*."[17]

Dolly's recollection provides insight into how she shapes real-world experiences to create her music. She placed this story that got under her skin into a fantasy world, and her choice to use fairy tales to transform her memories of this situation—as well as those on *The Fairest of Them All*—speaks to the power of those archetypes in Dolly's songwriting process. These fantasies give Dolly access to well-known characters, scenarios, and expectations that she can use to frame her original stories. Consequently, some of Dolly's songs take on a mythic quality that also reinterprets fairy-tale models and exposes the folly of believing in fairy-tale happy endings. However, Dolly does not dismiss the possibility of romance and happiness, and she writes many songs that revel in the joy of love, as I discuss later in the chapter.

As noted, Dolly often speaks of herself as a modern-day Cinderella. The first part of the Cinderella story is easy to overlay on Dolly's early years in poverty. But what was Dolly's happy ending? Her prize was not the handsome prince, but rather her own musical autonomy and success: "I grew up to be a fairy princess of a sort, more of a Cinderella story, the rags-to-riches kind."[18] Dolly may often write songs about a prince, but he was not her goal. In her personal fairy tale, she seeks freedom, independence, fortune, and self-expression. Thus, Dolly was not looking for, and has not lived, a fairy-tale marriage.

Dolly met her husband Carl immediately after she moved to Nashville in 1964. When they married two years later, it was on her own terms. She told him: "I love to cook, but I'm gonna make enough money for somebody else to cook. It's not gonna be my duty and it's not gonna be my job and I damn sure ain't gonna clean house and I'm not washing no dishes because I'm not ruining my fingernails. I'm gonna write songs and I'm gonna sing. I may be a good woman, but I'll be gone most of the time, and I am certainly not gonna be your average housewife."[19] By Dolly's accounts, they have remained happily married for over 50 years. She celebrated that anniversary in 2016 with the release of an album of love songs, *Pure and Simple*. The couple spends much of their time living apart, and Carl never accompanies Dolly in public. Interviewers often ask her about their relationship, and Dolly's descriptions of her life with Carl and her thoughts about why their marriage has lasted so long do not always satisfy fans and critics who want to hear about grand passion. A comment like "my husband and I have always liked each other" is not the stuff of fairy-tale marriages.[20] Dolly consistently refers to Carl as a close friend, a good buddy, and a real nice man, and she says the secret of their marriage is mutual friendship, respect, and independence. "My husband's very private," Dolly says. "He's a great guy, and he's not demanding, and he enjoys his time alone and neither one of us wants to be stuck in each other's face all the time."[21] Several of Dolly's love songs reflect this progressive view of marriage with lyrics that focus on camaraderie, mutual regard, independence, and honest communication rather than romantic fairy-tale scenarios.

Dolly's expansive approach to marriage accommodates her close relationship with Judy Ogle, who has been an almost constant presence of love throughout Dolly's life. Dolly and Judy met in the third grade at Caton's Chapel school in the mountains. Judy, like Dolly, grew up poor. Despite their similar backgrounds, the girls were opposites in personality. Judy was a quiet and shy counterpart to Dolly's exuberant persona. They became instant friends, both being "fish out of water" among their classmates,[22] and they arranged to take all their high school classes together. Dolly explained, "I wanted to think, dream, create, sing, write. Judy [who was more athletic and physical] was fascinated by that part of me. I did the thinking and planning, and she played it out. We made a great pair."[23] One of their plans was that when Dolly became a star in Nashville, as they were convinced she would, Judy would join her there and work with her. Eventually, after a stint in the Air Force, Judy did move to Nashville to join Dolly.

"She is my best friend," Dolly says, "and the two of us have been as close as any two sisters could ever hope to be."[24] She is also one of the few people who works closely with Dolly when she is writing songs: "More often than not, the first person to put pen to paper to write down one of my songs has been Judy Ogle."[25] Their connection, combined with Carl's invisibility, has led people to speculate for decades that Dolly and Judy are in a sexual relationship. But Dolly counters with the argument that two women can be very emotionally close, perhaps even more than with their husbands, and not be gay: "Most people can't understand two women being so close and devoted to each other."[26] As early as the mid-1970s, Dolly had this to say about her close bond with Judy and her response to the rumors that had already begun: "She's like an extension of me, like my shadow. And I'm like an extension of her. We can look at one another and know what the other is thinking. She's devoted to my music and I'm devoted to her because of that. . . . She believes in my dreams as much as I do, and the Bible says that if two people agree upon the same thing with utter faith, it shall be done."[27] Not content with Dolly's consistent answers over the years, interviewers continue to ask about her relationship with Judy. One recent answer sums up Dolly's responses: "I love her as much as I love anybody in the whole world, but we're not romantically involved."[28]

Both Judy and Carl are Dolly's emotional support. When one interviewer suggested that her husband was "a stabilising force in her life, a rock," Dolly corrected him. "God has been good to me. He gave me Carl Dean. And that was the perfect man that I needed. And he gave me my best friend Judy Ogle. And those two people actually have been the rock."[29] Dolly's song "Sweet Lovin' Friends," with its light-hearted lyrics of a loving friendship, mirrors the way Dolly often explains her marriage to Carl as well as her friendship with Judy.

> We're just sweet lovin' friends
> That's what we've always been
> Just breezin' along like the wind
> Just sweet lovin' friends

For Dolly not all affairs of the heart are sexual: "People think you can't love but one person."[30] "I have many wonderful relationships with men and women that are love affairs of a sort. I mean, sex and love are two different things."[31] She said, "Maybe some men think I'm a flirt, but if I'm a flirt, then I do flirt with everybody—men, women and children. I love people. If it's not right to love, then what do we have?"[32] Accordingly, Dolly takes an expansive view of love—in her personal life and in her songs.

Despite Dolly's personal disinterest in a fairy-tale marriage, many of her love songs are mythic in the way that they portray a woman's desire for the love of a faithful man. Sometimes the story ends happily, even if there is ultimately no prince. But often wishes do not come true (they "come false as well" as she wrote in "What a Heartache"), and the story ends in betrayal, heartbreak, and broken relationships. Dolly taps into a range of ideas and beliefs about relationships in her love songs: duos with Porter Wagoner that enact heterosexual marriage; idyllic love songs filled with the beauty of nature and sexual desire; songs of heartbreak that foreground bird imagery; cheating songs; and songs of strength and personal agency within romantic relationships. In the next sections I take up each of these scenarios.

Marriage Duos with Porter

Dolly's early career was dominated by her partnership with Porter Wagoner. When he hired Dolly, Porter was not looking for a duet partner. He and Norma Jean Beasler, Porter's previous "girl singer," had not been a duo, and Porter was disinclined to sing duets because of the tensions he felt arose in such partnerships. But his audiences did not accept Dolly immediately, often yelling "We want Norma Jean!" as Dolly sang. After one especially boisterous night, Porter tried to console Dolly who was crying "just like her heart had been broken." It was then Porter decided they would sing duets: "I felt like singing together would help Dolly get accepted much quicker."[33] Dolly agreed, and the arrangement worked so well they became one of the most popular duos in country music in the 1960s and 1970s. Audiences soon came to love and accept Dolly as a soloist, but the Porter/Dolly duo was such a successful audience favorite—they had a "real good blend . . . almost like blood kin"[34]— that they released eleven duet albums during their partnership from 1968 to 1974, and two more after their split.

When Porter hired Dolly, she had been married to Carl over a year, and the three of them met to discuss the inevitable rumors that would swirl. Porter told Dolly and Carl "people were bound to suppose she and I were sleeping together. We all agreed we didn't want [such rumors] to happen. And we all felt sure it wouldn't."[35] However, those rumors did circulate. At one point, this gossip in Nashville upset Dolly so much that she wrote "Shattered Image" about her pain in being tossed around in the rumor mill. Dolly recalled, "people weren't taking me seriously and just thought I was Porter's whore or something. And that really hurt me, because these people don't know me."[36] The song's scenario has a clever double meaning in the ways one's image, both real and figurative, can be shattered and ruined.

Because many of their duets were about heterosexual romantic relationships, there were also rumors the two were married. In these songs, Porter and Dolly sing as husband and wife, sometimes as contented lovers, but more often as a bickering couple or as disillusioned partners who have drifted apart. These different views of marriage, many of which Dolly wrote, coexist on albums as if to give listeners a menu of possibilities reflecting their own relationships back to them. Porter and Dolly further projected the image of a married couple since they sang several songs in the role of parents, as I discuss in Chapter Seven.

Dolly's most light-hearted and humorous approach to marriage in these duo recordings appears in the bickering songs. For example, in "Fight and Scratch," Porter and Dolly verbally tussle, arguing and sassing one another over the mundane things that drive partners crazy. Each one throws in spoken comments of good-natured derision as the other sings, and often the songs end with a fade-out of traded spoken insults. Dolly gives as good as she gets—these are not songs of women as victims. Rather, they depict the mutual irritation that comes with time and familiarity, while often suggesting that the squabblers are enjoying themselves, as in "The Fighting Kind": "We delight in pickin' fights 'cause our love's the fightin' kind." Other songs in this category are "Run That by Me One More Time," "I've Been This Way Too Long," "I've Been Married (Just as Long as You Have)" (cowritten with Porter Wagoner), and "We'd Have to Be Crazy." They released one of these good-natured "a-quarrellin' and a-fussin'" songs just about each year as humorous novelty pieces.

Alongside this high-spirited view of marriage, their duo albums also included songs of emptiness, of lovers who have drifted apart. Numbness, rather than bickering, dominates as the partners acknowledge there are no feelings left between them as in "No Reason to Hurry Home." Similar sentiments loom in "I'm Wasting Your Time and You're Wasting Mine," "It Might as Well Be Me," "Oh, the Pain of Loving You," "In Each Love Some Pain Must Fall," "Somewhere along the Way," and "Too Far Gone." These songs are filled with hollow feelings of detachment as passion fades not to hatred or anger, but to boredom and disinterest.

Dolly answers such songs with ones about the excitement of finding new love as in "Is It Real," "Lost Forever in Your Kiss," and "Love Have Mercy on Us." Other songs offer a Biblical slant with an Adam-and-Eve inevitability to love that lasts into eternity such as "There'll Be Love," "Together Always," and "You." More compelling and complex are Dolly's songs that look past the first flush of excitement in new love. In several, Dolly goes beyond fairy-tale, starry-eyed language and writes about relationships in a surprisingly pragmatic way. In "Two of a Kind," the lovers trade spoken lines about the realities of sadness, disappointment, and jealousy, as well as respect, honor, and admiration in their relationship—all qualities that go into a love that might last forever.

Two songs in particular resonate strongly in the context of what Dolly has said about her marriage to Carl being based on friendship and mutual respect. The country waltz "A Good Understanding" opens with these lyrics: "When we married we agreed that we'd both do as we please/Just as long as we done each other right." Avoiding temptations, the singers agree they have "a good understanding." Even more intriguing is "Between Us." Here, the lovers are new, just getting to know one another. But rather than writing of insistent sexual passion that sweeps them away, Dolly suggests a different way of embarking on a relationship—by talking. She sings there should be no "deep dark secrets," "false disguises," or "hidden feelings," since "an honest love is a love that will survive." Wishing for an "open-minded understanding," Dolly asks more for companionship than passion:

> In our love let's share a friendship between us
> Always close enough to talk things out
> Let's be honest with ourselves and with each other
> And our love will never know mistrust or doubt

One of Dolly's biggest hits with Porter was a song they cowrote, "Please Don't Stop Loving Me," which topped the country chart for one week and spent several weeks in the top ten. It was also Porter and Dolly's only #1 hit as a duo. The lyrics have a nice twist since, in contrast to its lively walking bass and breezy melody set to a Bakersfield shuffle, the title suggests a breakup. But the verses, sung alternately by Dolly and Porter, are actually about a happy relationship. The chorus confirms the couple's commitment by naming the unthinkable: that life without the other would not be worth living. The song ends on the title line, but there is no hint the relationship will dissolve. Nonetheless, the song raises the possibility of romantic failure.

The most intriguing types of love song Dolly wrote and recorded with Porter are ones with a romantic surface, but that are not explicitly about lovers. Several of these songs could describe any type of close relationship: the love and caring between friends, parent and child, siblings, coworkers, teammates, and caregivers and patients. The lyrics of some of these songs—"I Am Always Waiting," "Come to Me," and "The Fire That Keeps You Warm"—are in the same vein as "Bridge over Troubled Water" by Paul Simon. They are about being a constant presence, safe harbor, and comfort for another person. In 1974, the last year of their partnership as a duo, Dolly and Porter released "Together You and I," a song filled with images from nature—oceans, stars, the sun, flowers—that embody the depth and breadth of Dolly's expansive views of love. It appeared just a few months after "I Will Always Love You," and both songs celebrate enduring love that need not be romantic, though with different valences. "Together You and I" is a joyful celebration while "I Will Always Love You" recognizes the pain of loss.

Given Dolly's ambivalent personal connection to fairy-tale, heterosexual marriage, it is not surprising the love songs Porter and Dolly sang which express the most happiness are ones Dolly wrote in this expansive, all-embracing language that transcends a conventional romance script. Despite her reliance on fairy-tale tropes in some of her songs about romantic relationships, Dolly is clear about the difference between these fantasies and the reality of relationships with all their complexity.

Songs of Tender Love and Sexual Desire

In her songs as a soloist, Dolly explores a wider range of scenarios about love, with many more nuances. Although she has written hundreds of songs about love, those expressing unambiguous happiness are not as plentiful as one might imagine. But one of her signature songs, "Love Is Like a Butterfly," is emblematic of the exhilaration of love. Perhaps on first hearing, the song's intricacies may be lost in its sweet lyrics and light pop style. One writer even said the lyrics were "throwaway" and there was "nothing earth-shattering in melody."[37] Yet the song reveals the complexity of her ideas of love.

In comparing the physical and emotional consequences of love to the fluttering wings of a butterfly, Dolly captures a mixture of joy and restlessness: the many moods of love and a fluttering heart are like a butterfly's "soft wings in flight." But what stands out even more than these physical and emotional responses is that love is *rare*: "Love is like a butterfly, a rare and gentle thing" and "how very precious, sweet, and rare." While the song is apparently about romantic love, its frequent appeal to love's rarity calls to mind statements Dolly made about her childhood. Although there was much love from her parents, Dolly said it was unusual to be singled out for affection because there were so many children, coupled with so much poverty. "I never got enough personal attention when I was a child," Dolly said. "Not enough caressing. How can you pick up 12 children?"[38] But she soon discovered her musical talent gave her "the attention [she] had longed for."[39] Music filled the void when time for love and affection was limited.

"Love Is Like a Butterfly" is brimming with images from nature, particularly in the final verse. Dolly writes about sunshine and springtime before ending the song with "together we belong like daffodils and butterflies." But this hearts-and-flowers scenario is not just another cliché. Dolly has always found butterflies particularly meaningful. "I guess it was 'cause we didn't have nothing pretty, so I looked to nature for beauty. To me butterflies were fancy dressed-up girls going to a party. . . . The butterfly doesn't hurt anything or anybody. It goes about its business and brings others pleasure while doing it."[40] The song's opening line "love is like a butterfly, soft and gentle as a sigh," also brings to mind a line from another song that captures her sense of contentment in an idyllic natural setting: "In my Tennessee mountain home, life is as peaceful as a baby's sigh." So while the song celebrates romantic love, it also taps into feelings of tenderness and affection, reflecting these desires from Dolly's childhood when love was rare and beauty emanated from nature.

The music of "Love Is Like a Butterfly" reflects this gentleness. In a smooth, light country pop style, the song features a rocking bass, finger-picked acoustic guitar, subdued piano and steel guitar, and an almost ethereal vocal backup that is a gauzy wash of sound more pop than country. Dolly's voice is light as she navigates the melody that flits around in leaps rather than steps in the chorus, especially the opening line, which is triadic and spans just over an octave. The melody of the verses is clearly derived from the chorus' melody, but without as much triadic outlining. Dolly additionally sets the chorus apart with two modal turns to the flatted 7th chord (♭VII) at "like its satin wings" and "rare and gentle thing." This harmonic move also tempers the unremitting sweetness of the tune with a more poignant, bittersweet quality.

The chorus also includes a moment of polyphony, an element of musical dexterity, when Dolly trades parts with the backup singers. In the first chorus, the backup vocalists lightly sing just the words of the title as Dolly sings the full first line of the chorus. These vocal lines are traded in the second chorus, and the polyphony is more evident since Dolly's "backup vocal line" is still at the forefront. Also setting the chorus apart is the piano riff that fills in between the two halves of the chorus, just after each modal shift to the ♭VII. It is a quickly descending chromatic line in parallel major 3rds. So just after the harmony takes an unexpected modal turn at the two cadences, the piano lightly ruffles the harmony a bit further before returning to the tonic chord (I). This riff has a shimmery, glinty edge to it, clearly meant to evoke shiny butterfly wings.[41]

"Love Is Like a Butterfly" was a #1 hit on the country chart and #38 on the adult contemporary chart. It was the theme song for Dolly's first variety show, *Dolly!* (1976–1977), and it was her signature song for some time. Dolly's nickname is "The Iron Butterfly," and this imagery is apparent in much of her branding. She also has at least one butterfly tattoo.[42] Dolly revisited this image in her song "Butterflies," which she sings with a light touch over a loping, perpetual motion accompaniment that reflects the excitement and idealism of new love. In a bubbly pop style, Dolly sings fairy-tale lyrics of magic wands, castles, diamond-studded chalices, and golden harps.

Two other examples of happy love songs date from much later in her career. "Marry Me" and "Berry Pie" are an intriguing pair with their similar musical settings and exuberant celebrations of new love. In "Marry Me," the singer has met a boy at a barn dance. They have kissed, and they are going to be married. It is a whirlwind romance, and one might doubt whether it will last (as I discuss in Chapter Six). But within the song itself, her happiness knows no bounds, and she sings a spirited melody to the accompaniment of fiddles, clawhammer banjo, and the sound of flatfooting dancers. "Berry Pie" sounds like a prequel to "Marry Me." Here, the singer has her eye on a boy, and she decides to get his attention by baking a pie for him. This song has the same energy and musical style of "Marry Me" (with a little extra touch of Irish whistle). "Berry Pie" also includes Dolly's signature style of yodeling in which she sings agile lines, on *yo-del-lay-ee*, high in her range without actually flipping her voice over the break to create a true yodel. Her yodeling is a wordless celebration of happiness and, like the sound of the dancers in "Marry Me," places the song within a rustic mountain or country setting.

Dolly's catalogue is filled with such starry-eyed love songs: "Joshua," "River of Happiness," "Bobby's Arms," "You Are," "More than I Can Say," "Something Special," "Sugar Hill," and "Pure and Simple." Although many of these songs, along with "Love Is Like a Butterfly," have a gentle tenderness, even bordering on the naive, other songs celebrating love are openly sexual. Dolly was candid about her feelings about sex in her autobiography: "I was always very open-minded about sex, and I'm glad that I still am. I have always loved sex. I've never had a bad experience with it. I am a very emotional person, and to me it's another way, a very intimate and wonderful way, of showing emotion. It was never dirty to me. After all, God gave us the equipment and the opportunity. There's that old saying 'If God had meant for us to fly he'd have given us wings.' Well, look at what he *did* give us."[43] As a woman who was always curious about sex and felt alive in her own sexuality, Dolly openly embraced sexual desire in a number of songs.

"Touch Your Woman," the title song of her 1972 album, is an uninhibited country song about a woman who celebrates the sexual connection she has with her partner even after an argument or at the end of a long day: "touch your woman, everything's gonna be alright." The last verse makes clear any ambiguity about what is desired: "You know exactly what it takes to keep me satisfied/You know exactly what I need and I always go to sleep in peace." Dolly's skillful manipulation of musical and sexual tension is evident in the way the song engenders desire and prolongs a sense of resolution. Each of the first two lines of the verses cadences solidly on the tonic chord, and the melody remains low in the range. But Dolly builds tension in the final two lines of the verses by moving through new harmonic territory with a strong descending bass line that culminates in a dominant-seventh chord (V^7) at the end of line three. Rather than resolving this chord as listeners expect, she detours back to the subdominant (IV) and then returns to the dominant chord at the end of the verse, setting up an even stronger desire for the tonic chord. This harmonic tension, prolonged over two lines, is finally released in the chorus on *touch*. The rising melody, coupled with the descending bass, of these last two lines of the verse adds to the drive for both musical and sexual resolution.

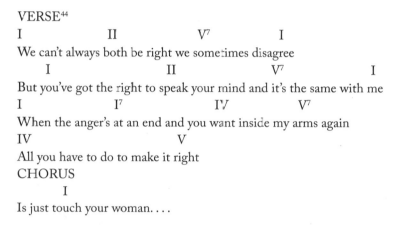

VERSE[44]

| I | | II | | V^7 | | I |

We can't always both be right we sometimes disagree

| | I | | II | | V^7 | | I |

But you've got the right to speak your mind and it's the same with me

| I | | I^7 | | IV | | V^7 |

When the anger's at an end and you want inside my arms again

| IV | | V |

All you have to do to make it right

CHORUS

| | I |

Is just touch your woman. . . .

Five years after "Touch Your Woman," Dolly recorded "It's All Wrong, but It's All Right." It was a bolder statement about sexual desire since it was a candid invitation for a one-night stand, not about sex within an established relationship:

> Hello, are you free tonight?
> I like your looks, I love your smile
> Could I use you for a while?
> It's all wrong, but it's all right

Dolly thought the song would seem amusing because it was so clearly "dirty," as she said. "Just how plain can I be? . . . But there was some question about it. Even in this day and time [the late 1970s], when you can say everything, country music is a little bit more delicate and I respect that."[45] The song was the second #1 hit from *Here You Come Again*, one of Dolly's earliest albums that focused on a pop sound. The first #1 hit was the title song, written by Barry Mann and Cynthia Weil, in which the singer finds her ex-lover's looks and sex appeal irresistible. The following year, Dolly heated up even more with the disco-style

"Baby I'm Burnin'," a frenetic windup to sex: "hot as a pistol of flaming desire." The song was also the theme song for her second variety show, *Dolly* (1987–1988).

The upbeat country song "Wait 'Til I Get You Home," cowritten with Mac Davis, pays homage to Charlie Rich's song "Behind Closed Doors" from 1973 with Dolly's line, "we'll make some shadows on the ceilin' tonight by candlelight behind closed doors." On the same album, *White Limozeen*, she recorded "Why'd You Come in Here Lookin' Like That," written by Bob Carlisle and Randy Thomas. In this song, powerful sexual attraction undermines the singer's ability to get over her past love. In 1998, she combined sexual desire and hunger with her effort to reinvigorate her career in *Hungry Again*, an album comprised solely of her original songs in traditional, acoustic, and bluegrass styles. The title song laments the loss of sexual desire in a relationship and wishes to recapture its magic: "Let's love like we're hungry again, bring back the passion we had back then."

Songs of Heartbreak

True love and sexual passion make for good songs. But more compelling for Dolly are scenarios in which lovers are heartbroken. Just as she uses the butterfly as a positive expression of love, Dolly accompanies broken hearts and memories of lost love with birds, particularly the sparrow. For example, in "Little Bird," Dolly's lyrics are cheerless but wrapped in a veneer of images from nature and the light country pop style of "Love Is Like a Butterfly." Here, "memory is a little bird" that can "fly me away back to yesterday." In "My Blue Tears," the singer implores a little bluebird to fly away because her sadness makes hearing the bird's song too painful. In her 1971 version of this song, Dolly evokes an early country, Carter Family sound in the loping guitar and close harmony singing; the heartbreak is barely palpable in this recording. But in 2001, she reimagines the song for *Little Sparrow* with a slower tempo and thinner instrumental and vocal textures that convey the singer's despair. "Pleasant as May" uses similar images: summer sunshine is dim and the birds' love songs are no longer sweet. Dolly's simple triadic melody has a childlike, innocent quality that adds a poignant twist to the sorrow of the lyrics.[46]

Two songs, "Little Sparrow" and "Crippled Bird," are particularly sophisticated in their use of the image of the bird for heartbreak. As discussed in Chapter Three, "Little Sparrow" is Dolly's re-creation of "Come All You Fair and Tender Ladies," which advises young ladies to "take warning how you court young men." This ballad continues with the wish to become a little sparrow and fly away to confront a man about his deception. But Dolly pushes the sparrow imagery further in her version of "Little Sparrow," not only seeking to become the little bird that confronts a false-hearted lover, but directly linking the broken-hearted maiden to the fragile bird that is crushed. Further, in "Crippled Bird," the bird is not merely a symbol of the young woman; rather, the bird is heartbreak itself:

> A broken heart like a broken wing
> It must have its time to mend
> I am like a crippled bird
> In hopes one day to fly again

For both songs, Dolly reworks the melody of "Wayfaring Stranger." (See Appendix D for a full analysis.) She recalled this folk hymn from her childhood "left an impression in me. I remember hearing that song all my life." In particular, she remembered once hearing an old man sing it alone in church, saying "it was the saddest, most beautiful, most lonesome thing I'd ever heard."[47] For the opening phrases of both songs—"Little Sparrow" and "Crippled Bird"—Dolly draws on the first phrase of the hymn's melody, which is marked by a rise of a perfect fifth and a descent back to tonic. She also relies heavily on the distinctive melodic gesture of the third phrase of the hymn, with its leap of a fourth from the 5th scale degree to the upper octave as heard in her improvisatory intro to "Little Sparrow" and its chorus. In "Crippled Bird," the pathos reaches an almost unbearable point in the chorus with its similar plaintive reach to the upper octave in the first line:

> Oh, to die, 'twould be a pleasure
> Slow to heal, but quick to cry
> Fragile as a sparrow's feather
> Crippled bird too blue to fly

This folk melody, combined with the archaic language of the first line of this chorus, creates a strong old-world feeling. The last verse of "Crippled Bird" describes the loss of her love as "cold and shameful" and her grief as "deep and sharp." Weaving in the color blue, which she often links to birds, she concludes the verse with the image of a "true blue broken heart" before repeating the chorus with its keening first line.

"Crippled Bird" is a tearjerker of a song, dangerous in its expression of devastating grief. Buckingham recalled when they recorded the song "it was emotional for everybody involved. The lyric, the sound, everything."[48] Part of the power of the song is that it seems so familiar with its use of archaic language and melodic gestures derived from "Wayfaring Stranger." The song's appeal to an older musical style is, surprisingly, not undercut by its full orchestral accompaniment. Indeed, the violin lines seem vaguely Celtic. But despite, or perhaps because of, its old-world sound, the emotion of the song is immediate and powerful.

Dolly's melody for "Crippled Bird" so aptly captured grief, desperation, and despair that she reused it sixteen years later in "Only Dreamin'" with its similar situation of heartbreak. In this song, the only recourse is to "dream about the pleasures that we shared in days gone by." Unable to face the truth, the singer dreams of her lover's return, but faces reality in the heartrending final verse: she will wake alone from her dream. Nevertheless, she resolves to continue pretending otherwise, as she does in "The Grass Is Blue." In both, the singer is filled with such pain and longing that willful denial and creative self-deception is the only solution, the only way to ease the pain. Like "The Grass Is Blue," "Only Dreamin'" ends the way it began, trapping the singer in her new reality. Although it uses no bird imagery, "Only Dreamin'" is an inspired re-creation of "Crippled Bird." These songs are two versions of the same love story, both set to Dolly's imaginative reworking of "Wayfaring Stranger": "Only Dreamin'" is an attempt at denial about the loss of a love that increases in emotional intensity as the song progresses; "Crippled Bird" is the raw despair throughout. (See Appendix D for a fuller comparison and analysis of these two songs.)

In commenting about "Only Dreamin'" (and, by proxy, the melodies of "Crippled Bird," "Little Sparrow," and "Wayfaring Stranger"), Dolly said, "I love that lonesome, mountain, Irish sound."[49] "Wayfaring Stranger" depicts the image of a lost soul, and Dolly links this figure with heartbreak in these three songs through their shared melody. When asked about this melodic similarity, Dolly said, "I do write a lot of songs around that melody. It just went so deep inside my soul that it just must be embedded. I think it's a beautiful melody."[50]

Cheating Songs

Dolly writes many songs about betrayal in a relationship. Together these songs "constitute an almanac of human misbehavior and misery."[51] She typically tells the story from the point of view of the one who has been cheated on, often plunging the singer into a morass of degradation, such as "Teach Me to Trust," "Dagger through the Heart," and "Daddy Come and Get Me." Only a few songs are about women who cheat in a relationship, but these are noteworthy examples: "My Hands Are Tied," "He Would Know," "Can't Be That Wrong," and "I Can't Be True." In "Star of the Show," from 1979, Dolly writes a sassy, disco-style number that explores love as "an act we perform." It includes an intriguing verse that not only furthers the song's cheating scenario, but that could be read as a comment on performance and independence more generally.

> I don't play second fiddle in nobody's band
> And I'm no backup singer and I won't be a fan
> And I'm nobody's co-star I just play leading roles
> And I don't want the part, don't want a part
> Won't play a part unless it's star of the show

These lines echo Dolly's statements about her fairly recent departure from Porter Wagoner's show, and her use of this metaphor for her cheating song was likely inspired by her desire to be a star in her own right.

Of all her cheating songs, "Jolene" is the pinnacle of her expression about the "other woman" in both its lyrics and its music. Remarkably, Dolly wrote the song in the same writing session as "I Will Always Love You,"[52] and she tells several stories about the genesis of "Jolene." The name came from a young fan of Dolly's, a little girl about eight years old—with "this beautiful red hair, this beautiful skin, these beautiful green eyes"—who wanted an autograph. Dolly told her "you're the prettiest little thing I ever saw" and asked for her name. When the girl replied, "Jolene," Dolly said, "Jolene. Jolene. Jolene. Jolene. That is pretty. That sounds like a song. I'm going to write a song about that."[53]

In the song, a woman begs another not to "take my man . . . even though you can." Dolly claims this scenario is based on a tall, red-headed bank teller who had a crush on Dolly's husband. "He just loved going to the bank because she paid him so much attention," Dolly says. "It was kinda like a running joke between us—when I was saying, 'Hell, you're spending a lot of time at the bank. I don't believe we've got that kind of money.' So it's really an innocent song all around, but sounds like a dreadful one."[54] In concert (and in some interviews) Dolly tells the story of the bank teller in a way that suggests the two women physically fought and that Dolly stood up to the teller and defended herself. "She pulled my wig off and almost beat me to death with it," Dolly said. "I fought that woman like a wildcat. I had another wig, but I didn't want another man."[55] But other times on stage Dolly says, "Here's a story about this little redhead girl that was trying to steal my husband. Years went by, and now I wish to hell she had [laughs]."[56] But little of the aggressiveness of these stories is in the song itself.

As is often the case, Dolly was likely inspired to write "Jolene" by using casual events from her life: she was intrigued by an unusual name and a pretty woman flirted with her husband. She admitted the song "was based on a thread of truth, but it was so frayed by the time I got finished with it, it didn't even matter."[57] Nonetheless, from these kernels, Dolly wrote a song exploring the feelings of an insecure woman who, faced with a threat, pleads with the other woman rather than fighting with her. However, the insecure, pleading persona Dolly portrays in "Jolene" does not match audiences' expectations of Dolly the "Iron Butterfly." So Dolly tells us a different story to make us laugh: she did not put up with any guff from this interloper, and she inverts the classic "take my wife, please" joke, wishing Jolene *had* stolen her husband. Dolly's more aggressive stance in her remarks in interviews and concerts allows her to authenticate her claim that the song is based on a real event from her life while disavowing for herself the song's image of an insecure woman.

"Jolene" was Dolly's second #1 hit, and she left *The Porter Wagoner Show* soon after that. Two decades later, she recorded a second version on *Something Special* in 1995. This recording retains the same opening lick, though orchestrated with strings, heavy reverb, and acoustic distance. In 2018, Dolly released yet another version of "Jolene" accompanied only by orchestral strings for the soundtrack of *Dumplin'*. According to Dolly, "Jolene" has been covered more than any of her other songs in just about every style imaginable. In 2004, *Rolling Stone* ranked it #217 on its list of the 500 Greatest Songs of All Time,[58] and in 2014, Dolly's 1973 recording of "Jolene" was inducted into the Grammy Hall of Fame. In 2017, the a cappella group Pentatonix, joined by Dolly as featured artist, won a Grammy for Best Country Duo/Group Performance for their recording of "Jolene." The song was also the inspiration for the first episode in Dolly's 2019 Netflix series *Heartstrings*, which dramatized a version of the song's story.

Always an audience and karaoke favorite, what accounts for the song's massive popularity among fans, performers, and critics? Its singable chorus is the hook of the song: as Dolly said, "it's just the same word over and over, even a first-grader or a baby can sing, 'Jolene, Jolene, Jolene, Jolene.' It's like, how hard can that be?"[59] Thus, "Jolene" calls to mind Dolly's comment about her songs being simple enough to be understood and complex enough to be appreciated. "Jolene" uses a limited musical palette, and its powerful opening instrumental lick and unrelenting, repeated chord progression and chorus has, according to one *Rolling Stone* reviewer, a "sense of accelerating dread."[60] Listeners are immediately captivated by the unusual modal harmony that seems to propel us into another time (the song has "an antique 'Greensleeves' feel"[61]) and the emotional stage is immediately set with the opening minor modal guitar riff that is an integral part of "Jolene." Dolly "made up the little lick on the guitar," and it was difficult for the studio musician to master.[62] She described this opening as "a great chord progression—people love that 'Jolene' lick. It's as much a part of the song almost as the song."[63] This finger-picked, acoustic guitar lick appears in the intro, between phrases in the chorus, more subtly between some of the verses, and at the outro. Its syncopated nervous energy, combined with its unvaried repetitions, captures the sense of rising anxiety and the fervent pleading in the lyrics.

The song has two sections. The chorus repeats *Jolene* followed by a plea for her not to take the singer's man. Several verses quickly outline the situation: the other woman is beautiful, irresistible, and powerful; she alone controls the outcome. Common to both chorus and verse is an unchanging chord progression. With each iteration of this progression, the melody rises steadily from the 1st scale degree (tonic) to the midpoint of the phrase—to the penultimate flatted 7th chord (♭VII)—and then falls back to the tonic pitch.

i   III   ♭VII   i   ♭VII.   i
Jolene, Jolene, Jolene, Jolene, I'm begging of you, please don't take my man

In the chorus, the name Jolene is sung four times, rising up through the full octave with a chord change for each *Jolene*, and this harmonic motion enlivens the plea. The last repetition of *Jolene* occurs at the apex of the phrase on the tonic chord (i). From there, the melody quickly falls back over a prolonged ♭VII chord to the lower tonic note and chord only to try once more. This assertive rise and doomed, acquiescent fall embodies the singer's pleas and her likely defeated position at the hands of Jolene. Furthermore, Dolly's vocal harmonies during the fall back from the ♭VII to the tonic in the chorus (at "I'm begging of you" and "please don't take him") consist primarily of parallel 4ths and 5ths, intervals that create a hollow sound. Also, each time the tonic chord is reached at the end of a line, the vocal harmony closes on the interval of an open 5th—the absence of the 3rd of the chord in the voices creates an unsettled, unresolved feeling. These harmonic choices create an archaic air that complements the modal setting of the song.[64]

The verses follow this same harmonic progression; however, the melody does not reach up to the full octave. Each verse is three lines, and the melody rises only to the 5th scale degree over the course of the first two lines, which are declaimed rather quickly. The drop to the tonic note accompanies the final line of each verse, most of which describe Jolene's power over the singer. This unrelenting rise and fall of the melody (in both chorus and verse) over the repeated chord progression gives "Jolene" its memorable and haunting mood and adds an obsessive quality to the pleading lyrics. By the end of the song, with one last

Jolene and the minor guitar lick played on the fade-out, the song comes full circle. Dolly does not give Jolene a voice to respond in any way.

Dolly remarked about the freshness of the musical style of "Jolene," noting that when it was released, "that was the first time I noticed people sayin', 'That's different than what you been doin'.' But I had been fightin' for that sort of thing for years. I had all these songs I was writing', and I was developin' musically, as far as a different style of pickin' and hearin' different sounds in my mind was concerned. 'Jolene' was the first good example of the fact that you can be yourself and still improve on whatever you do."[65] The minor modal melody and harmony that Dolly uses in "Jolene" are partly what sets this song apart from her previous songs in terms of the "different sounds" Dolly mentions.

What also accounts for the new quality in "Jolene" is Dolly's somewhat unconventional approach to the cheating song. It is a more complex response to cheating than depicted in many of her others. In "Jolene," the singer is not just a passive victim of her man's betrayal, crying alone about her loss. Instead, she speaks directly to the other woman. There are several ways to interpret this encounter.

In one reading, the singer seems to give Jolene all the power in their meeting rather than fighting her competitor. The singer is simultaneously powerless and gutsy, but her assertiveness devolves into pitiable pleading with Jolene not to take her man. Dolly's approach is a stark contrast to Loretta Lynn's classic honky-tonk style and barroom setting of "Fist City." Lynn is no victim. She aims to fight the other woman for her man: "I'm here to tell you gal to lay off of my man if you don't wanna go to Fist City." But in "Jolene," Dolly portrays a woman's inadequacy and inability to compete with other women. The bank teller "had everything I didn't, like legs—you know, she was about 6 feet tall. And had all that stuff that some little short, sawed-off honky like me don't have," Dolly said. "So no matter how beautiful a woman might be, you're always threatened . . . by other women, period."[66] In contrast, the singer in another Loretta Lynn song, "You Ain't Woman Enough (To Take My Man)," shuns inferiority. She declares "he took a second look at you but he's in love with me." The feeling of inferiority is strong in "Jolene," and Dolly has commented that the song will stand the test of time because many people can relate to feeling inadequate in relationships. Yet, it seems hard to reconcile this reading with the song's popularity among fans who exuberantly sing along with Dolly in concerts, laughing and dancing.

On the other hand, there is a way to read "Jolene" that does not rely on the singer's inferiority but rather on Dolly's unwavering direct address to Jolene. By saying to Jolene, "I had to have this talk with you," Dolly makes it clear she is not simply obsessing about the situation psychologically and "talking" to Jolene in her mind. She speaks directly to Jolene, imploring her not to take her man and revealing that her happiness depends on Jolene who seemingly has all the power in the love triangle. It is a complex maneuver. Dolly, as the wronged woman who says she is inferior, paradoxically wields all the power in this scenario, and Jolene is left without a voice. Dolly's rhetorical power is also exerted by naming the other woman. Jolene is not just any "other woman." In her direct address, Dolly calls Jolene out by name, which is something Dolly does not often do in her songs. In a kind of psychological sidestep, Dolly speaks from the position of the wronged, powerless woman while taking charge of the situation by confronting her rival directly and by name. This emotionally complex direct address to the other woman is what fans sing along with the loudest: the quadruple naming of Jolene.

A third way to read "Jolene" is to focus on the admiring description of the beauty of the other woman. In this approach, Dolly also veers from the standard cheating song. For example, in "Fist City," Lynn insults her rival, singing "the man I love when he picks up trash he puts it in a garbage can." But in "Jolene," Dolly outlines the other woman's beauty in a rhapsody of archaic language reminiscent of an ancient love ballad, as discussed in Chapter Three, and the modal musical setting reinforces this old-world feeling.

> Your beauty is beyond compare
> With flaming locks of auburn hair
> With ivory skin and eyes of emerald green
> Your smile is like a breath of spring
> Your voice is soft like summer rain
> And I cannot compete with you, Jolene

This language seems to be more than just a description of a beautiful woman who is a threat. Rather, these lines can be heard as love lyrics to a woman as an object of desire. The twist is, of course, that it is the female singer, and not her man, who sings these lines, thus complicating the gender and sexual dynamics of the song. In this context, the direct address to Jolene creates a sense of intimacy. The song is laden with yearning and desire, but who and what is desired? Does the singer project her desire for her man onto Jolene? Is the singer as captivated by Jolene's beauty as her man is?

Nadine Hubbs has explored this issue, calling "Jolene" a "moving transformation of female heterosexual rivalry into homoerotic reverie."[67] When sung by

Dolly, the song's chorus is the heterosexual story ("please don't take my man"). But the lingering on Jolene's name, combined with that rhapsodic first verse, fills the song with homoerotic desire. Accordingly, LGBTQ+ audiences have long embraced this song. Dolly often welcomes these fans in concert by singing a snippet of "Jolene" with these words: "Drag queen, drag queen, drag queen, drag queen. . . ., I'm begging of you please don't take my man." She usually does this when she acknowledges all the people in the crowd dressed in drag as Dolly, often saying "It's a good thing I was born a girl, otherwise I'd have been a drag queen." Humor aside, "Jolene" not only resonates with Dolly's LGBTQ+ audiences, Dolly herself uses "Jolene" as an opportunity to welcome her LGBTQ+ fans, and she forges a bond with them through the intimacy of her direct address, as she does with "I Will Always Love You." In both songs—with their easy-to-sing-along-with choruses—Dolly conveys the complexity of intimate relationships by inviting her listeners into the exchange.

Songs of Strength and Personal Agency in Love

Dolly has written a number of songs in which a wronged woman asserts herself and leaves a relationship. As Helen Morales observed, Dolly provides "progressive models for a girl to identify with. In Dolly's fairy tale, it's no use waiting for a Prince Charming; a girl has to make her own luck."[68] Several of Dolly's early songs are from the viewpoint of a woman who fearlessly leaves a relationship in which she feels ignored or mistreated. "When Possession Gets Too Strong," cowritten with Louis Owens, is a sort of "you don't own me" anthem. Here, the singer balks at emotional abuse, declaring "if you try to control me then you won't ever know me" and "I'll take you just like you are and I'll expect the same." Unwilling to live in "chains," she states plainly that she'll "be movin' on." The song is musically reminiscent of "I'm in No Condition," with its modal, folklike sound throughout. The austere modal sonority that dominates most of the song gives way to a more typical country sound each time Dolly sings the title line in harmony with her backup singers in a show of strength. The result is a convincing statement of female independence and self-determination as she resists the abuse.

In "You're Gonna Be Sorry," Dolly muses about how her man will feel when he realizes that he will "miss the kiss that you're forever turnin' down." After all of his "dirty deals" and staying out all night, she is "busy makin' plans for checkin' out." In a style and setting strongly reminiscent of "I'm in No Condition," and "When Possession Gets Too Strong," "You're Gonna Be Sorry" features an active bass line, a recurring acoustic guitar riff, and Dolly's characteristic modal turn to the flatted 7th chord (♭VII) for a bittersweet bite. The song fades out with the title line punctuated by the guitar lick that suggests the singer's impending departure. Dolly explored these same sentiments in 1975 in "When I'm Gone": her lover has decided he is bored and no longer finds her exciting, so she chooses to end their relationship. This up-tempo bluesy number also uses modal harmonies at the ends of lines. There is not much of a fade-out here for Dolly's self-assured lyrics; she sings her last *gone* and is gone. The abrupt ending confirms that she, indeed, has left.

In "The Camel's Heart," Dolly confronts her cheating partner by reimagining the conceit of "the straw that broke the camel's back." She also uses other straw clichés, singing that she has "been grasping at straws" with her lover, but he has drawn "the short end of the straw . . . and lost it all." The catalyst is his new affair, but she does not blame the other woman. Rather, Dolly sings, "She's just the straw that broke the camel's heart/It's not her fault, it's yours we fell apart." The song was included on her 1998 album *Hungry Again*, which emphasized her roots and country music sound over her earlier pop recordings. "The Camel's Heart" has a gentle bluegrass setting, though with prominent percussion. Dolly's expansive melody floats over the spirited rhythm of the band, giving credibility to her steady and firm resolution that she is done with the relationship and plans to leave. The song's modal touches, again, sound the sadness in the song even as the singer establishes her independence.

Two of Dolly's songs from later in her career are even stronger proclamations of strength at the demise of a relationship. In "I'm Gone," from 2002, Dolly writes her cheekiest exit from an emotionally abusive relationship. He was "hateful, rude, and rough," and she felt "unwanted, unwelcome and unloved." So she packs some amenities for the road: "some chewing gum and candy, some magazines and snacks," some extra money, and "a change of clothes." On her way out of town she tosses her wedding band from the train as she yearns for freedom. Despite the circumstances, though, this song is also one of her funniest. She writes a tour de force list of excuses for her man to use when explaining where she's gone:

> You can tell the truth or you can lie
> You can say I left you or I died
> Say I'm in the Himalayas on some spiritual quest
> And could spend years lookin' for the light
> Say I'm in the witness program with the F.B.I.
> Say a U.F.O. abducted me from home

You can say what you choose, but I tell you the truth
You can say for sure I'm gone

After another litany of all the possessions that she says he can keep, basically everything they owned including their pillows, she finishes with this zinger: "When you lay your head on that big feather bed, you can rest assured I'll be gone." The bluesy, bluegrass setting of this song energetically sends her on her way, while the band provides the mechanistic, driving sound of the train.

In 2008, Dolly wrote an even bolder song of female empowerment, "Get Out and Stay Out," for the Broadway show *9 to 5: The Musical*. Before this time, Dolly had never written for the theater, and she expressed some concern she was not up to the task of writing for a Broadway show. "Get Out and Stay Out" proved that she had the musical flexibility and skill to succeed in this style as well. One critic commented on the quality of the songs Dolly wrote for the show: "It shouldn't surprise anybody she's taken so well to the stage: She's always been a storyteller first and foremost. Her countrified pop, enhanced by fiddle and pedal-steel guitar, fits perfectly on Broadway. Of all the mainstream artists who've tried their hand at show music in the past few years, she may be the most convincing."[69] Indeed, Dolly's score was nominated for both a Tony and a Drama Desk Award.

"Get Out and Stay Out" was the 11 o'clock number, performed by Stephanie Block, that regularly brought down the house. Block had the Judy Bernly role (played by Jane Fonda in the film) of the housewife who returned to the workplace after her husband left her for his secretary. Buoyed by her friendships with women and her newfound confidence at the office, she throws her husband out when he attempts to return home after being discarded by his "new love." Singing that although she used to need him, want him, and love him, now the "table's turned" and "it's your time to squirm." But unlike in "I'm Gone," the singer does not leave; instead, she remains and tells *him* to "get out and stay out." After describing all the ways she attended to his needs at her own expense, she sings her final declaration: "I'm taking back my life." It is a song of raw strength, self-confidence, and fearlessness. These two songs, "I'm Gone" and "Get Out and Stay Out," extend the more passive sentiments of her songs from the 1960s and 1970s—"you'll be sorry when I'm gone"—to forthright statements of independence and assertiveness—"I'm leaving" and "get out." These later songs give the woman an active voice in the decision to end a dysfunctional relationship.

Twenty years earlier, Dolly had recorded "The Salt in My Tears," seemingly a precursor to "Get Out and Stay Out." In both, Dolly sings about regaining her self-respect after realizing her mistake in making sacrifices for a man who turned out not to value her. In the song's music video, Dolly turns the tables on her attractive hunk of a man who is offered up as eye candy for her viewers. He wears tight jeans, a white sleeveless T-shirt, and has chains around his ankles as he mines lakeside salt with a pickax. The same year as *9 to 5: The Musical*, Dolly released "Shinola," a song that continued the sentiments of both "I'm Gone" and "Get Out and Stay Out." Singing that her man's "attitude stinks" and that is he "arrogant, cocky and rude," Dolly calls him out saying she doesn't "need this crap," explaining before she leaves that "a woman needs someone to hold her, not someone to just lay her down."

These songs of self-reliance form a strong counterweight to those that Dolly writes in which the singer is dejected or humiliated by the loss of a relationship. We can turn to two of her earliest songs to see the remarkable sense of self-awareness and autonomy Dolly expressed about romantic disappointment even at the beginning of her career. In "Don't Let It Trouble Your Mind" (1969), Dolly writes from the perspective of someone who recognizes her relationship is not working and is strong enough to say it, even though it means losing her partner. Dolly's opening verse—with its internal rhymes, the archaic air of the second line, and its incisive diagnosis of the psychology of the situation—is particularly remarkable:

> Our love affair is bittersweet, insecure and incomplete
> And I've often wondered why your leaving's been so long delayed
> It's all become so complicated, maybe you feel obligated
> And out of sympathy for me you've stayed

After singing that she would "rather live alone than live with someone who doesn't love me," the singer takes the initiative to end the relationship in the refrain, "and if you don't love me, leave me and don't let it trouble your mind." As she does in many of her songs, Dolly uses a modal sound at the end of the chorus that captures a bittersweet feeling. The sentiment is strong, forthright, and, above all, not angry.[70]

Another early statement of autonomy in a romantic relationship is "My Kind of Man." Dolly plays with the listeners' expectations with her title, leading us to believe the song will be about the qualities she wants in a lover. But instead, she asserts herself, singing "If I'm not your kind of woman being just the way I am, then I know you're really not my kind of man." The song is a feminist statement in a classic country two-step setting, with the singer telling her partner that if he loved her, he would not want to change her. By the end of the song, she is heading for the door: "I can only be myself but if you want something else, then I can see no reason I should stay." Dolly released this song in 1973, the year before she made a remarkably similar statement in "I Will Always Love You."

Although Dolly writes many songs in which women are dejected by the loss of a love, her catalogue includes a significant number in which the woman remains strong and whole at the end of a romance, sometimes being the one to make the break when the relationship sours. In the context of these songs of empowerment, "I Will Always Love You" takes on an even richer, more complex meaning. This ultimate love song is, paradoxically, about facing the fact that a relationship is not working. What makes the song so popular is that it beautifully expresses the endurance of love despite the need to separate. One can face the end of a relationship while remembering and valuing the love that was and still can be shared.

Dolly recalled her feelings from when she wrote the song for Porter Wagoner: "So I just, out of a broken heart of not being heard or anything, knowing I had to make major decisions that would ultimately change my life forever, and his for that matter, I wrote that song one night out of great grief and depth and just trying to say the right things to say goodbye."[71] Dolly knew her business partnership with Porter was no longer working, and the song was her way to tell him she was leaving. Soon after she wrote the song, Dolly reflected on the influence Porter had on her career:

> I don't like to think that he made me a star, I like to think that he *helped* me become one. Porter's a brilliant man who I admire and respect a lot for what he knows. Through him I was able to become all the things that I've become. You take it by steps and when it got to the point where I felt a need to go on my own because I wanted—my dream was to have my own show. . . . Now that I'm on my own, I'm becoming more of what I really am instead of having to be just a part of somebody else.[72]

So from its inception, "I Will Always Love You" was linked to Dolly's desire for personal and musical autonomy, the goal of her fairy tale. Not only a love song, "I Will Always Love You" was her personal song of independence and freedom.

Chapter 6
"Just Because I'm a Woman"

Songs about Women's Lives

"I love seeing women do well. I'm so happy that I did well as a woman."

In 1978, Dolly was asked if she supported the Equal Rights Amendment.[1] Her response to the interviewer from *Playboy*: "Equal rights? I love everybody."[2] Of course, Dolly knew what the question really was: is she a feminist? It was a provocative question that gave Dolly little room to maneuver. The interviewer must have believed Dolly took a feminist viewpoint with her recordings of songs like "Dumb Blonde," "Just Because I'm a Woman," "You're Gonna Be Sorry," and "When Possession Gets Too Strong." But rather than allowing her songs about resilient women to speak for her, the interviewer hoped to get Dolly to identify as a feminist, which would have been professionally risky for her at the time. She had little to gain and much to lose by doing that.

In the mid-1960s, country music fans had enjoyed feisty women songs by Loretta Lynn such as "Fist City," "You Ain't Woman Enough to Take My Man," and "Don't Come Home A-Drinkin' (With Lovin' on Your Mind)," though there is a hint of prurient enjoyment in the promise of a "cat fight" in the first two songs. But when Lynn recorded "The Pill" (written by Lorene Allen, Don McHan, and T. D. Bayless) in 1975, she crossed the line into a territory explicitly linked with feminism. The song was banned by dozens of radio stations and denounced by ministers.[3] One country music critic wrote the song was "in poor taste" and

"Loretta should let the welfare workers tell folks about the pill while she concentrates on recording some good, clean country music songs."[4] While "The Pill" was a hit (it reached #5 on the country chart), Lynn never identified as a feminist although she acknowledged her desire for equal treatment: "I'm not a big fan of Women's Liberation, but maybe it will help women stand up for the respect they're due."[5] And Lynn was married with a prominent husband and six children.

So when Dolly, childless and married to a man who was rarely seen, was pressed on her gender politics, she deftly opted out of the question by redefining the issue in ways that worked for her: "Everybody should be free: If you don't want to stay home, get out and do somethin'; if you want to stay home, stay home and be happy."[6] And: "I don't even understand that women's liberation stuff, don't know what it's about. I'm a lucky person. I'm liberated, free spirited, free minded, but it's not something I promote or push—just a natural way I've always lived."[7] She then lived life on her own terms, which included writing songs that answered the question, "are you a feminist?"

In 1977, Pete Axthelm wrote this droll but apt assessment of Dolly's gender politics: "Aside from her talent, she represents a vanishing natural resource—the mountain woman who understood independence and manipulation of men long before the first city girl got her consciousness raised."[8] Ten years later, Gloria Steinem acknowledged Dolly's feminism with a definition even Dolly could embrace: "People who haven't listened to Dolly Parton or to feminism may be surprised to learn that they go together. . . . If feminism means each of us finding our unique power, and helping other women to do the same, Dolly Parton certainly has done both." In 1987, Dolly was named one of *Ms.* magazine's Women of the Year in part "for bringing jobs and understanding to the mountain people of Tennessee." Steinem stated Dolly's feminism was linked to her class and region: "She has crossed musical class lines to bring work, real life, and strong women into a world of pop music usually dominated by unreal romance. She has used her business sense to bring other women and poor people along with her."[9] The popular feminism that Axthelm and Steinem describe is rooted in Dolly's Appalachian and working-class identity, not "intellectual rhetoric," in Pamela Wilson's words. The "sentimental, emotional, and nonthreatening" nature of Dolly's songs, which can be written off as "comical and ineffectual," actually has a subversive power.[10]

Several decades later, Dolly responded to the perennial question of her feminism by broadening her scope: "I think people should be allowed to be themselves and to show the gifts they have, and be able to be acknowledged for that and to be paid accordingly. You know, I love men, but I love women too and I'm proud to be a woman. I just really try to encourage women to be all that they can be and I try to encourage men to let us be that."[11] When a call-in viewer on *Larry King Now*, in 2016, asked her if she was a feminist, Dolly answered: "I'm very feminine and I'm all for women. I just never followed that as a political statement. You know, I never thought I had to beat the men down to raise the women up. I just try to raise the women up and do what I can. I am very proud to be a woman. I'm very proud of all the accomplishments that women do."[12] And in 2018, Dolly contributed a song to *27: The Most Perfect Album*, a collection of songs about each of the twenty-seven amendments to the Constitution. Dolly wrote "19th Amendment (A Woman's Right)" about the suffrage movement: "We had to fight for women's rights/We won the right to vote."

Message Music

Dolly's songs about women's experiences reflect the complexity of women's lives without seeming to take an overt political stand. "I have always felt that I have an [even] greater mission," Dolly said. "I'm not a political person, but I write a lot of message music, a lot of message songs, and I do believe in the time to come that I can be very helpful. In fact, that's what I want to do."[13] More recently when responding to questions about feminism, she points to her songs for her answer, in particular "9 to 5" and "Just Because I'm a Woman."

"9 to 5"

In 2016, Dolly spoke about her pride in the satirical comedy *9 to 5* when Larry King asked if she was a feminist. The 1980 film was the brainchild of Jane Fonda. Rather than making a drama, which Fonda felt would be too political, she produced a comedy that included Dolly and Lily Tomlin. Dolly remarked that Fonda believed Dolly's inclusion in the film would attract southern audiences. But Fonda gave Dolly more credit than that:

> Anyone who can write "Coat of Many Colors" and sing it the way she does has got the stuff to do anything. This was not a woman who was a stereotype of a dumb blond. I felt that she could probably do just about anything she wanted, that this was a very smart woman. We developed a character based on who she is and what she seems like. Did we coach her? No. Her persona is so strong, you get somebody mucking about with that and making her self-conscious, and it could be negative. Even though we're from different backgrounds and different classes, we're very alike in many ways. Dolly's not political, but her heart, her instincts—she's just on the side of the angels.[14]

As Dolly sat for hours on the movie set waiting for shots and lighting to be worked out, she played with ideas for the theme song for the film. Using her long acrylic nails for percussion that mimicked the clicking of typewriter keys, she came up with an opening rhythmic riff, and she packed the verses with sophisticated lines using clever rhymes and rich images that are punctuated with the sounds of typewriter keys and bells: "Tumble out of bed and stumble to the kitchen/Pour myself a cup of ambition."

"9 to 5" spent two weeks on the Billboard Hot 100 chart and went to #1 on the country chart, eventually going platinum. Other accolades included two Grammy Awards for Country Song of the Year and Female Country Vocal of the Year as well as a nomination for the Academy Award for Best Song. The song was also featured in the 2009 Broadway show, *9 to 5: The Musical*, for which Dolly received a Tony nomination for Best Original Score with its seventeen songs. "9 to 5" remains a crowd-pleaser, and no Dolly concert would be complete without it.

With its relatable, incisive, and witty lyrics, "9 to 5" gives working people, particularly women, a voice, although it is not a call to action. Dolly keeps the lyrics focused on the continuing situation of many working people. Nevertheless, there is defiance in the sassy, upbeat music that engenders spirited participation by her audiences who sing and dance along to the bluesy, syncopated chorus. To boost this effect and to honor the many women who worked on the movie—extras, office workers, technical staff—Dolly "had all the girls come down to sing along on the real record," she said.[15] The power of communal singing to raise consciousness and inspire action should not be underestimated, particularly when the song's lyrics dramatize injustice.

When the film came out, Dolly downplayed its political elements, saying it was not a "message movie." "A lot of people thought it was just going to be women's lib; I wouldn't have been involved if I'd thought it was gonna be a sermon of some sort. Not that I'm not for rights for everybody, I'm just sayin' I didn't want to get involved in a political thing. It's just a funny, funny show. I think it's very obvious what it's sayin'. It's mostly about this boss and these three women—not bosses in general or the plight of secretaries."[16] But years later, in 2016, she said, "I'm proud to be part of that *9 to 5* where we were actually preaching that equal pay for equal work. And we've come a long way, but a long way to go."[17] Despite her reluctance to define her beliefs as feminist, Dolly is committed to women's rights even though she always contextualizes this within the rights of all people.

"Just Because I'm a Woman"

When Dolly left the mountains in 1964, she knew she was making an unusual move for an 18-year-old girl at that time "I didn't want to get married. All I had ever known was housework and kids and workin' in the fields. But I didn't want to be domestic, I wanted to be *free*. I had my songs to sing, I had an ambition and it *burned* inside me. It was something I knew would take me out of the mountains. I could see worlds beyond the Smoky Mountains."[18] Dolly did not have a larger political framework for her ideas. She had a dream compelling enough for her to cast aside cultural assumptions and norms about how a young mountain woman should live. So Dolly speaks about her career in terms of personal fulfillment. "I feel I'm a lucky person to be able to do what I want to do. I'm not doin' it to spite anybody or to say that I'm doin' it because I'm a woman. I'm just glad that I can do what makes me happy. I don't voice my political beliefs."[19] As Pamela Wilson put it, "Feminism, class, and regional/ethnic consciousness become personal rather than political, rhetorical, or structural issues for women like Dolly Parton."[20]

Dolly's marriage is a compelling example of her personal feminist consciousness, which she expressed in her song "Just Because I'm a Woman." Dolly understood marriage could be an obstacle for her success, and, as we saw in Chapter Five, she believed a stereotypical 1964 marriage would not give her the freedom she needed to become a star. Her producer, Fred Foster, also believed this, but for different reasons. When Dolly told him she planned to marry Carl, Foster asked her to wait a year because the company was devoting considerable resources to promoting her, and he did not feel they would get the payoff from their investment if she were married. But Dolly did exactly what she wanted, not allowing the gendered expectations of conventional marriages of the time to affect her decisions.

Before she married, Dolly was clear with her husband Carl that she was not going to be the kind of wife who remained home, cooking and cleaning. "We won't have the kind of marriage other people have because my music is going to take me away from home a lot, and the bigger I get the more demands will be made on my time." Dolly told Carl "he had to be willing to accept this" and she "had to know in [her] heart he could live with it."[21] After Carl assured her he did not object to her conception of how their marriage would be, they crossed the Tennessee state line to Georgia and married despite Foster's wishes. The wedding notice was not carried in the Nashville newspapers, and she kept her marriage a secret for a year.

Dolly's progressive marital arrangement with Carl turned out to retain one traditional element that surprised her: Carl had expected that Dolly had not had sex with anyone but him when they married. Dolly explained, "See, I had had sex before we met, but I hadn't mentioned it, and he hadn't asked. We were married for eight months, happy as we could be, and all of a sudden he decides to ask. I told him the truth, and it broke his heart. He could not get over that for the longest time. I thought, 'Well, my goodness, what's the big damn deal?'"[22] This situation inspired Dolly to write "Just Because I'm a Woman" in which she challenges some men's expectation that women should not have any sexual experiences before marriage. In a classic country style Dolly gently, but firmly, confronts her man about his hypocrisy. She not only declares "my mistakes are no worse than yours just because I'm a woman," but also asks him to "think of all the shame you might have brought somebody else." Dolly takes Kitty Wells's hit from 1952, "It Wasn't God Who Made Honky-Tonk Angels," a step further by not only pointing out the part men play in the sexualizing of women, but also asserting there is no shame in a woman's sexual experience as compared to a man's.

Dolly's argument is not a plea for forgiveness or absolution. Rather, it is a statement of fact and a condition of the continuation of the relationship: "listen and understand" and "just let me tell you this, then we'll both know where we stand." Dolly responds not only to her own husband, but she speaks more generally about the hypocrisy of the sexual double standard: "what's the big damn deal?" Dolly often says she uses songs to express her thoughts and work through emotional issues. But she also espoused a political viewpoint in "Just Because I'm a Woman" through her personal story. Dolly "took a stand for personal and female equality that was almost unthinkable in conservative Nashville," Alanna Nash suggests. "The mere *hint* of liberation was the kiss of death to a girl singer's career, but Dolly faced it head-on, as she would many controversial subjects in her writing; her progressivism was at one time thought to be the reason the Country Music Association waited until 1975 to name her Female Vocalist of the Year."[23] In 2019, Dolly used "Just Because I'm a Woman" as a touchstone when asked yet again about her views on feminism. She said the song "addressed the issues that we're addressing now. And that I've, all through the years, I've written all these songs that were to strengthen and to empower women."[24]

Dolly has sung, if not spoken, her mind about a number of women's issues. By writing songs that spring from, but move beyond, her personal experiences and observations, she has empowered women to follow their ambitions, encouraged them to stand up for themselves in their lives and relationships, laid bare the devastating and sometimes fatal consequences of the sexual double standard, and denounced a system that ostracized women for certain sexual behaviors. Regardless of whether she identifies as a feminist, Dolly's convictions are clear. She reaches her fans through her music, not the soapbox, and changes minds through her eloquent songs, which expose sociocultural practices that lead to gender inequities and the mistreatment of women.

Dolly's Image

In tandem with her message songs, Dolly uses one of her strongest subversive strategies: her hyperfeminine image. As Steinem wrote about Dolly's feminism, "her flamboyant style has turned all the devalued symbols of womanliness to her own ends."[25] Dolly uses the supposed disconnect between her exaggerated appearance and her savvy business sense and musical talent to her advantage. She explained, "When I started out in my career, I was plainer looking. I soon realized I had to play by men's rules to win. My way of fighting back was to wear the frilly clothes and put on the big, blonde wigs."[26] Dolly speaks openly about the constructed nature of her image: "I'm careful never to get caught up in the Dolly image, other than to develop and protect it, because if you start believing the public persona *is* you, you get frustrated and mixed up. Like, I suppose I am a sex symbol, but that idea is funny to me because I see Dolly as a cartoon. . . . Oh, sure, I *feel* sexy, and to some people I come across as *extremely* sexy, but Dolly's as big a joke to me as she is to others."[27] And the jokes are numerous.

Many critics seem unable to discuss Dolly's songs and career without also making reference to her physical appearance, her bosom, hair, makeup, and long fingernails. The number of crude and even vulgar comments, usually by men, in what would otherwise be serious reviews is staggering. In contrast, feminist critic Margo Jefferson, writing for *Ms.*, referenced Dolly's image with more nuance: "I think of Dolly as a genial, playful female impersonator, offering audiences—women in particular, if we choose to share the joke—a survey and catalog of feminine fantasy and gimcrackery: Walt Disney princesses, Flo Ziegfeld showgirls, Lillian Russell, Daisy Mae; the golden icons of Hollywood as a child might see them—Mae West, cheerful and hearty in her bawdiness; Jayne Mansfield, a vision of shining platinum unmarred by the struggle to be a sexual icon; Marilyn Monroe without the broken blossom air that encourages cruelty."[28] Dolly herself encourages these responses with her own never-ending jokes and one-liners. Ultimately though, Dolly gets the last laugh: "Well, I certainly got hit on a lot. And a lot of men thought I was as silly as I looked, I guess. You know, I look like a woman, but I think like a man. And in this world of business that has helped me a lot because by the time they think that I don't know what's going on, I done got the money and gone."[29] Exchanges like this are what earned her the nickname "Iron Butterfly": the sparkling exterior with a sharp business acumen that gets the job done.

Dolly also speaks eloquently about what lies beneath this image: "I've created this and played it up—the makeup, the whole persona. I've overexaggerated and made things worse. But I've had a good time doing it, and it all came from a serious place: a country girl's idea of what glamour is. But this isn't all I am. It's not even most of what I am. Hopefully, people can see beneath the hair to know there's a brain, beneath the boobs to know there's a heart, and behind all the other stuff to know there's some talent."[30] She drew on these very words for her song "Backwoods Barbie." As Carrie Havranek argues, "Parton was no fool. Her desire to create and control her own image showed a shrewd, subversive feminist, even if she never outwardly identified herself with the rhetoric of the women's movement. She instead appealed to both her male and female fans through her keen intuition of people and through the emotional components of her songs and the stories they tell."[31]

Dolly's songs that focus on the lives and experiences of women reveal not only the brain, heart, and talent beneath Dolly's star image but also the ways that, according to Wilson, Dolly draws "upon a model of feminine action in which women subvert, and gain strength from within, the dominant patriarchal system . . . to create opportunities for women to control their lives within it."[32] Dolly creates these opportunities in several ways that I now explore. In some songs, she inverts gender roles, allowing women to inhabit stereotypically male terrain or adopt male attributes and actions. In a significant number of songs, Dolly replays the tension between domesticity and independence, often by reimagining her mountains-to-Nashville story to include a longing for the boy back home. These songs affirm Dolly's gender-appropriate ties to her mountain home while allowing her to follow her dreams. Other songs grapple with issues confronting some women who remained in the mountains: being labeled trash for their sexual behavior and facing the devastating consequences of unwed pregnancy. These songs also give us further insights into why Dolly constructed her hyperfeminine look and persona. Finally, in "Eagle When She Flies," Dolly composed a powerful portrait of women that encompasses the multiplicity of women's identities and roles.

"I'm a Lady Muleskinner": Gender Role Inversions

Despite her glamorous image, Dolly has occasionally played the male role in her performances and songs, juxtaposing her hyperfemininity with traditionally masculine lyrics. In the following examples of these gender role inversions, Dolly sings about female power and independence by rewriting the male role for a woman or inventing a scenario for a woman performer. Rather than singing as if she were, for example, a male muleskinner or outlaw, she recasts and performs these roles as a female character. Through her subversion of these songs' original contexts, Dolly creates images of female agency and independence.

One of Dolly's earliest hit singles at #3 was her version of "Mule Skinner Blues," a song made famous by Jimmie Rodgers and later Bill Monroe. Although Dolly was not the first woman to record this hard-driving classic, her version included her own newly written lines that identified this muleskinner as female. In her performance on *The Porter Wagoner Show*, Dolly opens the song with the traditional long-held note on "good moooooooooorn-in' captain," which was a classic hypermasculine move by male singers that lets "the singer exert physical dominance over the song."[33] She also yodels like the boys, though she admits "I was never able to do that really pure, true yodel."[34] Dolly does not quickly or repeatedly flip her voice back and forth over the break between her chest voice and her head voice in a true yodel (like Jimmie Rodgers does in his recording of the song or, say, Patsy Montana in "I Wanna Be a Cowboy's Sweetheart"). Rather, Dolly's yodel is similar to Bill Monroe's in his performances of "Mule Skinner Blues" where he sings long notes entirely in his falsetto voice with an occasional *yip* as punctuation. Dolly's yodels are almost completely in her soprano range on the syllables *yo-del-lay-ee*, and, like Monroe, she holds the high note while the band vamps. Yodeling is an integral facet of "Mule Skinner Blues" demonstrating power and mastery, and Dolly's yodel puts her in charge.

Despite these masculine markers, as she begins the second verse, we learn she is not the typical muleskinner: "Well I'm a lady muleskinner." Her spoken line "I come from Tennessee" also identifies Dolly herself as the muleskinner. Another original verse further establishes the gender of this muleskinner: "Well I've been working down in Georgia at a greasy spoon café/Yeah just to let a no good man get every cent of my pay." She then speaks these lines as the band vamps—"and I'm sick of it and I'm gonna quit and I'm gonna be a muleskinner"—and ends the verse with another yodel. Dolly said, "I thought the little verse that I threw in would make it a little more Dolly-ized and a little more girl-ized."[35]

There are a number of accounts about how Dolly came to record this song, but most emphasize it was done on a whim and would be "funny for a girl" to sing it.[36] Humor is precisely what masks the power in this performance. The guys in the recording studio and the band may have been laughing, but Dolly, holding a guitar and singing the song in her sunshine yellow dress and sparkling high heels on *The Porter Wagoner Show,* was dead serious through her twinkling smile.[37] Even though she was not the first woman to record the song, Dolly's version was notable for its gender reversal; previous recordings by woman had not recast the muleskinner as female. Jocelyn R. Neal argues, "the *idea,* if not the historical fact, that Parton was the first woman to personify the whip-cracking, yodeling muleskinner was critical to her success and the song's reception, and it highlights the radical shift in gender roles that her performance facilitated."[38]

Dolly again reversed gender roles in her murder ballad "J. J. Sneed," cowritten with her Aunt Dorothy Jo. In traditional murder ballads, women are almost always the victims of boyfriends, suitors, or fiancées, usually because they are unwilling to marry or pregnant.[39] But in "J. J. Sneed," Dolly turns the table and the woman kills her lover. Both are outlaws. J. J. has cheated on her with another woman, so, after describing their time together robbing banks, with the singer doctoring J. J.'s bullet wounds, she declares "but now you have betrayed me and for that you're gonna die." Dolly's murder ballad conforms to the traditional strophic ballad form, and the last line of each verse repeats with a dip into modal harmony. The song has a sparse accompaniment: finger-picked acoustic guitar for a folklike quality, with bass and light percussion providing a subtle loping rhythm that keeps the action continually unfolding.

Dolly also performs most of the ballad in an indifferent and detached manner. But, in an unusual move for a traditional murder ballad, she lingers in the last verse just before and after she kills J. J. In a free rhythm to a few strums of the guitar, she sings "the good old days are over as we stand here in the rain." Then she almost speaks rather than sings "gonna shoot you" in the next line: "J. J. I'm gonna shoot you now, I hope you feel no pain." On this last word, the bass and percussion reenter, playing eight pulses of heartbeat rhythm before she flees from the posse "on her trail," though there is no sense of urgency to her escape. As in many murder ballads, the singer knows she will pay for her crime, so she bids farewell to J. J., saying she will soon join him in death. Dolly's matter-of-fact lyrics and unemotional delivery recall the impersonal characteristics of the classic murder ballad. But her unusual momentary dwelling on the shooting—slowing down the pace enough for the listener to visualize the woman dispassionately killing the man—subverts the typical approach to murder ballad performances. In "J. J. Sneed," it is the woman who calls the shots.

Dolly took a different approach in her version of the traditional and often-recorded murder ballad, "The Banks of the Ohio." Rather than reversing the roles, making the woman the murderer, Dolly wrote an introduction to the ballad that frames the story as a flashback from a woman's perspective. As Dolly explained, "I wanted to record it years ago, and I thought, 'I don't like to sing a song that's just like a *man*, you know, just from a man's standpoint. . . . I'm clever. I'm a writer. So why don't I just kinda box this in a little bit and just kinda present myself as a reporter or a writer that goes into prison to talk to this guy?"[40] Dolly was not interested in this rewrite only for her own use. She hoped her changes to the lyrics would "make it a little more personal where more women could sing it. So I'm hoping that as years go by, more women might want to sing it."[41] Indeed, in these songs, "Muleskinner Blues," "J. J. Sneed," and "The Banks of the Ohio," Dolly modeled ways for women to flip established gender scripts and reimagine their own participation from a place of power and authority.

Domesticity or Independence

Dolly often writes about women taking control of their lives in her semiauto-biographical songs about the yearning for a life of ambition and independence beyond the mountains. As a young woman forging a career in the early 1960s, Dolly knew she had to walk a fine line between her Nashville dreams of being a star and the mountain girl identity that would mark her as authentic. Inspired by her own real-life journey from the Appalachian Mountains to Nashville and on to Hollywood, Dolly has written a number of songs tracing her path that eventually culminates in success, despite homesickness and loneliness. These songs focus on the pull between remaining in her country home—adhering to gender norms for a mountain woman—and leaving for the city to follow more worldly goals. In her songs, Dolly usually tempers this break with gendered expectations by asserting she is still a country girl at heart as she remembers fondly the old home place and those she left behind.

In the following examples, Dolly returns again and again to this tension between home and her dreams, between domesticity and independence. She often navigates these opposing forces in her country-to-city songs by recalling the boy back home. In maintaining this gender-appropriate tie to home—assuring listeners she is still a country girl at heart with a mountain boy waiting for her—Dolly inhabits both worlds. In some songs, she focuses on the dangers of city life and her regret at leaving a boy behind. In others, she finds happiness in her new life, though still thinking fondly of home. By simply appearing to adhere to the expectation of domesticity through the figure of the boy back home, the women in Dolly's songs are able to exert a great deal of freedom as they follow their dreams beyond the mountains. Thus, Dolly presents a compelling negotiation between traditional cultural norms and feminist independence.

Dolly recorded her most well-known boy-back-home song twice: "My Blue Ridge Mountain Boy." This country song tells the story of a girl who yearned to go to the big city. She leaves, breaking the boy's heart back home, and ends up in New Orleans as a prostitute who recalls the kindness of the one she left behind. Ultimately, she cannot return home, ostensibly because the boy, tired of waiting for her, has married. But her return home would be tricky in any case given what she has been doing in the city. Certainly, without having a boy waiting, a homecoming seems impossible. Danger and nostalgia intermingle in the lyrics and the musical setting. In both recordings, Dolly evokes a mountain past with banjo and fiddle (1969) or harmonica (1982), both of which give way to a country sound with the steel guitar. The later recording is a country pop rendition with a heavy backbeat. The song sounds a cautionary tale, striking in its frank suggestion of prostitution and loss of home and family that result from leaving the mountains.

In "Will He Be Waiting for Me," the singer regrets leaving home and the boy who loved her. Once she decides to return, she rushes through the wooded mountains back to her remote home place, uncertain about what she will find. Her bucolic imagery in verse two suggests a premodern sense of place:

> Shadows from the trees shade the path that I am walkin'
> As I make my way back up that windy road again
> The smell of mountain laurel fills the air with sweet perfume
> My heart beats faster as I near my journey's end

The verses, packed with words, create a sense of breathlessness, and Dolly sets the opening lines of each to minimal melodic and harmonic movement: lines 3 and 4 repeat the music of lines 1 and 2; each line centers primarily around one pitch; the tonic (I) chord dominates with only momentary shifts to the subdominant (IV) that simply prolong the tonic. These musical choices make the singer's racing thoughts seem even more single-minded.

Dolly first recorded the song in 1972 on *Touch Your Woman*, but her rerecorded version on *The Grass Is Blue* (1999) more vividly captures the singer's anxious return to the mountains. The song's full bluegrass treatment pushes the momentum toward home with a faster tempo that enlivens the run-on word play "will he be waiting for me, he will be, won't he," making the question sound desperate. This phrase is woven into the verses as well as the chorus, which adds to the relentless uncertainty about what awaits at home. Further, the asymmetric phrase lengths in the bluegrass version embody the nervous, butterflies-in-the-stomach feeling as Dolly rhythmically and formally over-runs a more square phrase structure, which is especially noticeable following the second line in verse two, quoted earlier. In contrast, the earlier version's symmetric phrase structure lends a more complacent air to the song's question which, in neither version, is answered.

"When the Sun Goes down Tomorrow" is a rollicking song in which Dolly thumbs a ride, trying to get back home from the city. She again sets her verses, with their pileup of words, very simply. Each line is almost chanted on a single note, and the three-chord harmony moves along to a relatively mild rhythmic accompaniment. But things get moving in the chorus, inviting listeners to sing along, especially to the final line—"when the sun goes down tomorrow I should be home"—the refrain in both the chorus and the verses. In the chorus, as Dolly sings about going "back to the place I dream of," the melody becomes much more active and the rhythm section gears up, propelling her home. In the midst of this melodic and rhythmic energy, Dolly references two commonplace phrases in "there's no place like home sweet home" with a syncopated rhythm that stretches the words "home sweet home" in a momentary reverie. While this song does not focus on the broken-hearted boy back home, he is mentioned in the chorus as she anticipates reuniting with him.

When Dolly wrote the song "Tennessee Homesick Blues" for the film *Rhine-stone* in 1984, she reused three lines from "When the Sun Goes down Tomorrow":

> New York City ain't no kind of place
> For a country girl with a friendly face
> When you smile, people look at you funny, they take it wrong

"Tennessee Homesick Blues" covers the same ground as the former song. But it expands the nostalgic remembrances of home, painting many more images of idyllic mountain life—complete with Dolly's yodel—than "When the Sun Goes down Tomorrow," which focuses more on the city and the desire to return home. Also, rather than pining over a boy back home, in "Tennessee Homesick Blues," Dolly longs for her mother and father, home cooking, the comfort of her featherbed, and the country church. In this way, the song is reminiscent of her nostalgic songs on her album *My Tennessee Mountain Home*.

All of Dolly's boy-back-home songs mitigate a woman's desire to live a life of her own by suggesting she still has ties to a mountain patriarchy and is unchanged, still a backwoods girl at heart. Dolly presents this idea of enduring, internalized mountain values in "White Limozeen," a country-to-city story, but now without the boy back home or even a desire to return home. Here, the woman is a Daisy Mae who has gone to Hollywood and lives in a glamorous world. But despite her fame and riches, she remains a down-home girl, maintaining her mountain identity and values. Country music lyrics rarely depicted the kind of female success Dolly's story presents here, and as Pamela Fox argues, "these autobiographies' success stories rank as distinctly gendered 'failures' of country authenticity." Thus Dolly, in order not to "lose [her] claim to 'home' altogether,"[42] asserts her unchanged mountain girl identity, both for her own persona as well as for the mountain girl in "White Limozeen." Rather than pining for home or the boy left behind, she celebrates simultaneously her success *as well as* her mountain roots, no longer needing to choose between the two worlds she claims to inhabit. Nonetheless, Dolly positions herself in an oversized luxury car—an uptown, shiny extension of her wigged, rhinestoned image. If she were to visit her mountain home, it would be in that

FIGURE 6.1. *White Limozeen* album front cover, 1989.

urbane limozeen, with its ingenious down-home spelling that blends her two worlds.

"White Limozeen" was released on the album marking Dolly's return to a country sound after her extended pop crossover period in the late 1970s and 1980s in which she had musically left Nashville for Los Angeles. Perhaps the song was Dolly's way of saying she had never left country music despite her pop albums. *White Limozeen*, which went to #3 on the country chart, also included the song "Take Me Back to the Country" by Karen Staley. It repeats the sentiments of "Tennessee Homesick Blues" in its bluesy pop country setting of lyrics about dirty cities and the desire to return home. As Dolly often said in interviews at the beginning of her crossover period: "I'm not leaving country, I'm taking it with me." What better way to "come home" to country but to write a song, "White Limozeen," in a pop-inflected country style, saying she had never left?

In 2011, Dolly released her song "The Sacrifice," about the high cost of working for a dream. As with many of her songs, her lyrics reflect her own path. But this song does not trace her mountains-to-Nashville story; rather, it is from the perspective of someone who has already made her dream come true and is content with her life. In this song from later in her career, Dolly no longer had to demonstrate her connection to home by singing of the boy left behind and mountain nostalgia. Here, Dolly sings as someone who has realized her goals and now looks back to see what she gave up, willingly, to get there. The song does not dwell on regrets. Instead, it asserts that one must make choices and sacrifices to attain dreams: constant work with few vacations, time spent traveling rather than being with family and friends. Dolly had to leave some doors closed. And she chose to forgo some experiences others might take for granted, in particular having children.

Pamela Fox states that country music "ideology equated femininity squarely with the domestic sphere, especially motherhood."[43] Although Dolly often refers to her songs as her children, she rarely uses songs about motherhood to establish her authenticity, despite its centrality in traditional mountain culture. She and Porter Wagoner did record several of Dolly's songs about children, singing the roles of parents, but the majority of these songs were about the death of a child, as I discuss in Chapter Seven. Dolly's solo songs about motherhood were similarly dark; most often, the mother was unmarried and abandoned by the baby's father. The result was usually the death of the child, although sometimes the child was given up for adoption.

Dolly expressed ambivalence about having children herself. In early interviews, she said she and Carl, of course, wanted to have children. That would have been the right answer for country music fans at the time; she could hardly have said otherwise. But years later, after it became clear she was unable to have children, she spoke about this issue in a different way. "I went through a depression of not being able to have children, *because I don't know for sure that I even wanted them.* You know I used to talk about it and I used to want them. But it was when I couldn't have them, then I got that guilt thing that that's the woman's duty, you know every woman should have children or at least have a child."[44] Early in her career, she could still imagine having children and present herself publicly as a potential mother. But even then she admitted she would have children only "when I feel that I am ready to give up part of my career."[45] Dolly's songwriting and performing always came first. As she said to Alanna Nash, "I don't miss havin' children, let's put it that way."[46]

Dolly continues to write songs about mountain girls who dream of something beyond their "tattered dresses" and "brogans," as in "Something More" written for Dolly Parton's Lumberjack Adventure Dinner & Show in Pigeon Forge, Tennessee. This unreleased song retells Dolly's story.

> She knows there's something out there and she'd like to play a part
> And yet she knows inside she's just a mountain girl at heart

She concludes by singing she will always miss her home no matter how far away her dreams take her. In her country-to-city songs, Dolly portrays herself as an unchanged mountain girl, unspoiled by her contact with the world beyond the Smokies. The sheer number of these songs speaks to the centrality of this image in the way Dolly represents her gendered connection to her mountain roots.

Dolly's White-Trash Femininity

Although Dolly wrote many songs in which women escape the mountains to follow their dreams, she also wrote about women who remained behind. Many of these songs are about poor women who are subjected to a sexual double standard and are abused and abandoned by men. Several of these songs deal with the shame about female sexuality that results in tarnished or ruined reputations, while others explore the stigma of unwed pregnancy. These are songs about women who Dolly has said would have been considered trash by their communities. In this section, I explore the way Dolly talks about the term *trash* and how she navigates her complex relationship with white trash identity in her personal image and through her songs.[47]

Dolly had this to say about the term *white trash*:

To me that's not an insult. We were just mountain people. We were really redneck, roughneck, hillbilly people. And I'm proud of it. "White trash!" I am. People always say "Aren't you insulted when people call you white trash?" I say, "Well it depends on who's calling me white trash and how they mean it." But we really were to some degree. Because when you're that poor and you're not educated, you fall in those categories. But I'm proud of my hillbilly, white trash background. To me that keeps you humble; that keeps you good. And it doesn't matter how hard you try to outrun it—if that's who you are, that's who you are.[48]

Dolly embraces her white trash roots, saying it is part of what contributed to her character. Accordingly, she often portrays the dignity of poor and working-class people, and many of her songs, like "Coat of Many Colors" and those on *My Tennessee Mountain Home*, idealize her impoverished childhood. So Dolly does not always write lyrics that construct trash as an outcome of poverty. Nonetheless, trash identity has poor and working-class resonances. To be trash, one is usually poor. But not everyone who is poor is trash, and Dolly writes about this contradiction in "Backwoods Barbie."

"Backwoods Barbie": Dolly's Images of Trash

Dolly wrote "Backwoods Barbie" for the Broadway musical version of *9 to 5: The Musical*. Sung by the character of Doralee (whom Dolly played in the movie version), the country-style song reads as a manifesto for Dolly's star persona of "too much makeup, too much hair," and it reveals the complex nature of her image. She sings about her poor childhood and her desire to be pretty, but she also cautions the listener: "Don't let these false eyelashes lead you to believe/ That I'm as shallow as I look 'cause I run true and deep." Although Dolly often says her outward image is separate from the "real" Dolly, she also blurs that line with comments like, "Sure I look like a cartoon. But you know, it started out very honest and sincere, and it still is, basically. . . . I just can't stand to look plain 'cause that don't fit my personality. . . . I guess you could say I created this person, this character. And I like her, I mean, the image is something I made up, but it's not like the image is separate from me. I still know who the little girl from Sevier is. I never lose sight of her."[49] Thus, Dolly asserts she is certain of her core identity—the little girl from Sevier—even as it has merged with the cartoon.

From early in her career, Dolly expressed this paradox about her image: she both is and is *not* the image she projects. "Some folks see my artificial look and think I have no depth. But my inner sadness and joy are as real as my hair and nails are fake. That's what I like—looking like one thing and being another."[50] However, one of the lines in "Backwoods Barbie" recognizes how this image can backfire: "Yes, I can see where I could be misjudged upon first glance/But even backwoods Barbies deserve a second chance." As Dolly explained in a 1978 press conference, "people . . . have to get over the shock of my image before they can get real serious about my music, which is sad, because the whole purpose of the image was a gimmick to catch their attention, and then to let them know there was a person underneath it that did sing, and write songs, and was very serious about her music."[51] The second chance Dolly sings about in "Backwoods Barbie" challenges her listeners and viewers to take her music seriously, despite her exaggerated appearance.

But why this particular image in the first place? As she sings in "Backwoods Barbie," "the way I look is just a country girl's idea of glam." For Dolly, this image is linked to a white trash identity: "I patterned myself after this woman that was the town tramp back home. She had blond hair and high heels and red fingernails and lips, and to me she was like what movie stars were to other kids. We'd see her, and I'd say, 'Oh, look, she's got plastic goldfish in her heels!' and my mama would say, 'She ain't nothin' but trash, nothin' but trash,' and I thought, 'Ooh, that's what I'm gonna be when I grow up—trash!'"[52] To Dolly, this look was cosmopolitan and urbane. She also saw versions of this sophistication in some of her aunts who came to visit on occasion: "They had purses filled with lipstick and powder and eyeliner and all kinds of things we had no access to. This was the real ammunition in the battle of the sexes."[53] Dolly viewed this trash persona—with her heavy makeup, high hair and heels, painted fingernails, and generous bosom—as an alternative to her own decidedly unglamorous and poor existence in the mountains of eastern Tennessee. Women there did not get a second chance but were marked as trash after encounters with men left them abused, discarded, alone, often pregnant, and sometimes dead. It did not matter that these women were not prostitutes or "town tramps"; once used up by men, they were trash.

A couple of Dolly's early songs are about young women who brought this kind of shame to their families by sneaking off with boys. In "I'm Not Worth the Tears," a slow two-step, country number with Nashville-sound style backup singers and prominent slip-note piano, Dolly sings about the shame a young woman brought to her family. Regretting that she went along with a boy who led her on, she sings about her family: "Now they cry, but I'm not worth the tears they cry for me." The song drips with feelings of shame and worthlessness: "I'm not worth the salt in one tiny tear." Many years later, Dolly borrowed this image for her song "The Salt in My Tears." Singing that the man who had mistreated her was not worth the salt in *her* tears, she took charge in another gender role inversion similar to "J. J. Sneed."

Also in 1970, Dolly released her recording of "Mammie," which fleshes out this scenario even more. Mammie is apparently the girl's grandmother who delivered her. Tragically, the girl's mother died in childbirth, and Mammie is now raising her. After a verse in which the girl sneaks out of the house to meet a man, we learn her back story, as well as her mother's:

> They tell me my mama could not name my dad
> So I guess it was natural for me to be bad

Unlike in "I'm Not Worth the Tears," the girl finds redemption after Mammie's death, pledging to be good. The way Dolly portrays the Mammie character is noteworthy. Because Mammie witnessed her own daughter's shame, she is especially devoted to her granddaughter and prays she can raise her right. Mammie had taught her granddaughter to sing and play the guitar, and the song's opening, a solo strummed banjo, combined with the title "Mammie," might lead some listeners to imagine that Mammie is an African American woman who is raising the singer. However, Dolly is more likely writing a story of shame as it passes through generations. Dolly's own maternal great-grandmother, who played banjo and wrote "incredible songs,"[54] was called Mammie. "Mammie" is an example of Dolly's songwriting process in which she weaves together stories she witnessed growing up with the details and musical sounds of her own family and life.

One of Dolly's #1 hits, "The Bargain Store," paints a vivid portrait of a woman who feels used up and discarded by men, but who expresses no shame. Here, Dolly uses the metaphor of a bargain store to represent the hurt and broken parts of a woman who still wants to give and receive love. When the song was released, it was banned by some country radio stations because they believed it was a veiled reference to prostitution; clearly the woman depicted here was trash to country radio. Dolly discussed her intent in the song with an interviewer from *Rolling Stone*:

> I just thought ... well, why don't a person compare your body and your mind and your heart to objects, like an old broken heart sittin' on a shelf and some plans and dreams as if they were things you could see. [She starts singing:] "My life is like unto a bargain store/And I might have just what you're lookin' for/If you don't mind the fact that all the merchandise is used/But with a little mendin' it can be as good as new." That means that I have been in love before

and kicked around and banged around and had my head and my heart broke, my cherry stole, but I can grow *another* one if that's what you want. [She laughs a loud, exuberant laugh.] When I said the bargain store is open, come inside, I just meant my *life* is open, come into my life, so I wasn't even thinkin' of it as a dirty thing. I just felt at that time I had been probably kicked around some. . . . I felt black and blue and I just wanted to heal back up and mend myself back together and get on with my life.[55]

The most distinctive characteristics of this song are its Dorian mode and the archaic use of *unto*, as discussed in Chapter Three. Dolly said these elements make the song sound old, which situates this woman in an old-world mountain culture.

Abandoned Pregnant Girls and Dead Babies

Several of Dolly's earliest songs deal with the devastating consequences of unwed pregnancy. She was attracted to this story line as a very young songwriter. One of her earliest songs, "Girl Left Alone," was written when she was not yet a teenager and released when she was thirteen. The song paints a gloomy, if somewhat ambiguous, portrait of a girl in trouble. The song, cowritten with her Aunt Dorothy Jo and Uncle Bill Owens, is a short, strophic, first-person description about a girl who is alone, estranged from everyone who loves her. Although she never names the trouble, it seems likely the girl is pregnant and must pay for her mistake. The final stanza raises the possibility of happiness only in heaven after her earthly suffering. Young Dolly's voice is full-throated, with a nasal quality, as she belts out the lyrics to this honky-tonk waltz. Her impersonal vocal performance demonstrates her familiarity with traditional ballad performance practice.

"The Bridge," from 1968, is a first-person ballad about unwed pregnancy, and it is as gripping as a murder ballad. I advise readers who have not heard this song to listen to it now *before* reading my analysis.

"The Bridge" is reminiscent of "I'm in No Condition" in several ways. Both stories of desertion and heartbreak use Mixolydian sonorities, and, for both, Dolly writes only two melodic lines for the verses: line A in a low register and line B in a higher register. In "I'm In No Condition," the B melody abandons the modal chords, suggesting the singer's attempt to escape her troubles. However, in "The Bridge" Dolly harmonizes both the A and B lines with Mixolydian modal chords—the major tonic (I) and the flatted 7th chord ($\flat$VII)—which alternate throughout. By maintaining the modal chords for all the lines of the verses, Dolly gives "The Bridge" a relentlessly hopeless quality, more desperate than the feeling of "I'm in No Condition." And the chorus of "The Bridge," which includes only a single dominant chord (V) among the I and ♭VII chords, does little to alleviate the singer's despair as it surrenders to the modal chords at the cadence. In this example from the first verse, the ♭VII chord harmonizes the italicized text; all other text is set to the I chord. As in "I'm in No Condition," the prominent bass line makes these harmonic shifts—the same ones used in the intro—easy to follow:

A The moon is big and *yellow and the* stars are *all a*-glow
A From the bridge, I see *reflections in the* waters *far* below
B You kissed me for the *first time here and* held me *awfully* tight
A And the bridge became our *favorite place, we* came here *often in the* night

The song begins with the chorus: a young woman stands on a bridge reminiscing about how she and her lover used to meet there. In the following two verses, she recalls how passion and desire overtook them and they ran to a meadow where they made love. The chorus that follows, with slightly changed words, tells us more: she is once again on the bridge, but now she is alone. Then in one final verse, the story comes to its shocking conclusion. Standing on the bridge, left "with our unborn child," the woman slowly approaches the edge. In what seems to be a reprise of the closing words of the first chorus, the next line, "Here is where it started" does not conclude with "on the bridge," as in the first chorus. Rather, the final line of the song parallels the previous line with "and here is where I'll end it."

The effect is stunning, even shocking. By bringing back the original words and melody of the opening chorus, Dolly sets up the listener to expect the same lyrics in the final chorus: "Here is where it started *on the bridge*" would create an ambiguous ending. Does she jump or not? But instead, Dolly takes the listener right to the edge of the bridge with her, and then she jumps! "Here is where it started *and here is where I'll end it.*" This final line is unexpected: it is a longer line that repeats the melody of the previous line, and then it is abruptly cut off with no sense of melodic, rhythmic, formal, or harmonic closure. In effect, the listener witnesses a suicide.[56] Moreover, this is not a third-person recounting of the story. Dolly writes from the perspective of the woman on the bridge, and everything occurs in real time: her memories, her despair, and her leap into "the waters far below." The silence at the end is sudden and unanswered; there is no moral; she is simply gone. The song's modal sonority, with its atmosphere of an earlier time and place, heightens the pathos. And it is this sonority, combined with the dark story, that prompted Steve Eng to hear the melody as "spooky" and "minor-chord folky." Eng also hears Dolly's feminism in "her calmly insistent,

Listening Outline 4: "The Bridge," *Just Because I'm a Woman*, 1968

0:00	Intro	Instrumental	Harmonized with only I and ♭VII.
0:08	Chorus	The bridge...	Note the last line: "here is where it started/on the bridge."
0:23	Verse 1	The moon...	First two lines are low in the range; line 3, "you kissed me," moves into the upper register.
0:58	Verse 2	One night...	Line 3, "from the bridge we saw," again moves into the upper register. More prominent percussion enters.
1:35	Chorus	The bridge so wide...	Note the changed words that reveal plot development.
1:53	Verse 3, Lines 1-2	Tonight...	Modulation up a half step. More prominent drumbeats echo her beating heart and escalate the tension.
2:14	Verse 3, Lines 3-4	My feet...	Line 3 again moves higher. The first half of line 4 sets up the final cadence with what seems to be a reprise of the chorus text ("here is where it started/on the bridge"), but it ends differently, abruptly, and without harmonic resolution.

if not very militant, view of female sexuality, namely, that women should enjoy the same freedom as men in life, in love."[57]

Several critics, including Eng, suggest a connection between "The Bridge" (1968) and Bobbie Gentry's "Ode to Billie Joe" (1967)[58] because in both songs someone jumps off a bridge. However, they differ in several ways. "Ode," a talking blues song, is a detailed picture of ordinary life filled with people and conversation (though ultimately there is little communication or understanding). The characters speak in the present about past events with a sense of detachment. Yet with all the details in the lyrics, the song is ambiguous: what were they throwing off the bridge? Why did Billie Joe jump? Dolly's song, on the other hand, is a solitary account in the present moment. There is no information about who the speaker is; there are no details about her life beyond her pregnancy. But there is no ambiguity about what happened. It is clear she jumps, and the listener knows why. They are also different musically. As fits the disconnection between family members in "Ode," Gentry's talking blues feels laid-back and weary, its strophic nature matching the daily monotony of life on the farm. Gentry's dispassionate delivery masks secrets the violin countermelody only suggests. But Dolly's song has a chorus and verses for different musical effects, narrative details, and commentary. The energy of the song, with its pounding percussion heartbeat, builds relentlessly to its chilling, suicidal end.

"Down from Dover" is another first-person ballad about a young unmarried girl, pregnant and abandoned by her lover.[59] This time the girl does not commit suicide; instead, she believes her lover will return even after she is ostracized by her parents.

> My folks weren't understanding, when they found out they sent me from
>   the home place
> My daddy said if folks found out he'd be ashamed to ever show his face
> My mama said I was a fool, she did not believe it when I told her
> Mama, everything's gonna be all right 'cause soon he will be coming down
>   from Dover

Deserted by everyone she loves, she finds work at a farm and pathetically writes to her mother with her address to give to her lover when he returns. With no companionship or help, she delivers the baby alone. Dolly's lyrics eloquently illustrate the heart-rending scene of the birth, the baby's death, and the young woman's realization, made clear through her dead little girl, that the baby's father has forsaken her:

> My body aches, the time is here, it's lonely in this place where I'm lying
> Our baby has been born, but something's wrong, it's too still, I hear no
>   crying
> I guess in some strange way she knew she'd never have a father's arms to
>   hold her
> So dying was her way of telling me he wasn't coming down from Dover

The song ends here, with no consolation or closure. Unlike "The Bridge," "Down from Dover" does not reveal the eventual outcome. Instead, listeners are left with the image of a bereft young woman holding her dead baby.

"Down from Dover" is strophic with no chorus to interrupt the hopelessness of the young woman's situation. The narrative spins out in strings of images through two limited melodic lines that are more like chant than song since long stretches of lyrics are sung to a single note. Each verse has four lines, and the first, second and fourth lines are musically identical. The melody of these lines—in the lower range of the mode—is a descending pattern of four notes over a repeating modal chord progression.[60] This repeated musical line is unrelenting in its embodiment of the girl's plight and ultimate fate: each line starts anew only to fall again. The only respite is the contrasting third line, which is

I know this dress I'm wearing doesn't hide the secret I have tried concealing

Melody note:	D	C	B	A
Scale degree:	1	♭7	6	5
Bass/Chord:	D	C	G	D
Chord symbol:	I	♭VII	IV	I

When he left he promised me he'd back by the time it was revealing

Melody note:	D	C	B	A
Scale degree:	1	♭7	6	5
Bass/Chord:	D	C	G	D
Chord symbol:	I	♭VII	IV	I

The sun behind a cloud just cast a crawling shadow o'er the fields of clover

Melody note:	G	F#
Scale degree:	4	3
Bass/Chord:	G	D
Chord symbol:	IV	I

And time is running out for me I wish that he would hurry down from Dover

Melody note:	D	C	B	A
Scale degree:	1	♭7	6	5
Bass/Chord:	D	C	G	D
Chord symbol:	I	♭VII	IV	I

EXAMPLE 6.1. "Down from Dover," melodic/harmonic patterns. This chart represents the structural pitches, chords, and the scale degrees of the melody and bass line. It does not account for the ornamental bass line and chord changes at the ends of each line.

more static and consists of only two melody notes that are a bit higher. Dolly sings this line on a single note over the subdominant (IV) chord before falling to a note over the tonic (I) chord on the final word of the line. Her attempt to break out of the persistent descending pattern does not work, however, and she returns to the melody of lines one and two. It is worth recalling that the lyrics of the third line in the first verse were the ones Dolly wrote first. Dolly highlights the image that inspired the song's composition by stopping all melodic and harmonic motion, creating a sonic space for her pictorial lyrics to shine.

As with "The Bargain Store," country music radio in the 1970s was squeamish about the implications of "Down from Dover." Dolly observed: "'Down from Dover'—that was so ahead of its time, but nowadays that would be very tame on the radio. You certainly could talk about a girl having a baby. We released that as a single and they wouldn't play it on the radio. They wouldn't play it because it was so suggestive and it was about a pregnant girl and it was so against what country radio was at that time."[61] At that time, country music would not endorse such an explicit, critical, and sympathetic portrayal of the tragic effects of a young girl's exile for a sexual transgression. By humanizing the situation in her ballad, Dolly exposed and denounced the cultural views that led to such unfair treatment of women.

The album *Little Sparrow* contained an intriguing trilogy exploring these disastrous effects of unwed pregnancy for some women. This trilogy—"Down from Dover," "Mountain Angel," and "Marry Me"—depicted comparable scenarios in which women have trusted, or are about to trust, men who have the power to destroy their lives. These songs represent poor or working-class women who are too easily considered trash by their communities as well as mainstream American culture, and Dolly gives them each a voice.

"Mountain Angel" is a lengthy ballad about an abandoned pregnant girl. It includes not only the dead baby of "Down from Dover," but adds the mother's eventual madness and death from grief. As discussed in Chapter Three, the song conjures up images of revenants from ancient ballads, and it has a spooky feel with Dolly's wordless, keening voice at the end. The song features fiddle, banjo, mandolin, and Dobro for its Appalachian sound, and, like most ballads, is in the third person. This gothic, cautionary tale about the dire consequences of having a child out of wedlock resonates with a feminist reading.

"Marry Me," placed between "Down from Dover" and "Mountain Angel," celebrates the excitement of falling in love. The story is from the first-person perspective of the young woman who has met a boy at a barn dance and is convinced he will marry her. The song is an up-tempo, major key hoedown with no hint of modal inflection. But for listeners, this one may seem the most Appalachian with its prominent banjo, fiddle, mandolin, and percussive dance accompaniment. Stylistically, this is a very different kind of mountain music than "The Bargain Store," "The Bridge," and "Down from Dover" with their poignant stories and modal sonorities. Far from being an introspective song, "Marry Me" is optimistic and inspires movement and joy.

However, its placement between two songs of shame and death that result from the abandonment of an unmarried pregnant girl casts a pall over its optimism. In a different context, one could take "Marry Me" at face value: the boy and girl meet, fall in love, kiss, and will marry. But on *Little Sparrow*, "Marry Me" reads like a prequel to "Down from Dover" and "Mountain Angel." Here, we encounter the girl when she believes *this* boy is the one. He's "gonna marry" her she sings over and over. But the subtle change at the end—"he's done kissed me on the mouth, so he's *gotta* marry me"—is significant. She has given herself to him ("he knows a lot about love and stuff"), and that seals the deal—he *must* marry her. Is that not what both young women in "Down from Dover" and "Mountain Angel" also believed? We know how those stories ended:

I loved him more than anything and I could not refuse him when he
>   needed me
He was the only one I'd loved, and I just can't believe that he was using me
He wouldn't leave me here like this, I know it can't be so, it can't be over
He wouldn't make me go through this alone, he'll be coming down from
>   Dover

In "Down from Dover" and "Mountain Angel," Dolly exposes and critiques a system that punishes women for their sexual behavior. One critic wrote about Dolly's "epic tales of love and loss in which [she] creates a landscape littered with the broken hearts of women who have lost everything after loving the wrong men."[62] "Marry Me" is an augury of more heartache in this landscape.

Dolly was inspired to write these tragic songs of young pregnant girls from her own experiences of watching these situations unfold. "I knew a lot of young girls getting pregnant, and usually in the mountains people would pretty much turn you out; you were trash and a whore and your daddy and mama wouldn't let you come home, so you'd have to go to some home for unwed mothers or a relative who'd take you in. I'm touched by everything, and that used to bother me: how cruel and awful must that be, how lonely they must feel. That was great fodder for a song."[63] In her songs about these scenarios, Dolly brings to life the high price these women pay for their sexual transgressions: their public shaming as "trash and whores."

The Look and Sound of Trash

Dolly frequently situates these stories in the sonic landscape of Appalachian poverty, with the instruments and modal sonorities often associated with the mountains. Through her songs about forsaken women thrown out of their homes, pregnant and alone, we hear musical echoes of the poverty Dolly experienced as a child and the way she saw some women treated. The image of these young women—misused, abandoned, and often destitute—is not the kind of trash Dolly says she re-created with her hyperfeminine look modeled on the town prostitute. Often calling herself a "white trash princess" rather than "poor white trash," Dolly links her personal style of trash to glamour and wealth instead of plainness and poverty. Thus, Dolly uses the word *trash* in different ways. The term *white trash* comprises a tangle of racial, gender, and class identities sometimes combined with particular sexual behaviors. The meaning shifts. But when used as an epithet toward a woman, the term often refers to one who is both poor and sexually immoral.

In Dolly's experiences and in her songs, the idea of trash likewise covers a lot of territory about gender and class. It could describe poor, plain mountain girls who found themselves unwed and pregnant, as in "Down from Dover." But it could just as easily be used for those fancy-looking women who were, or were assumed to be, prostitutes, or at least "bad girls," as in "Backwoods Barbie." At times, Dolly uses *trash* to describe her appearance that she modeled on the women her mother called trash: "I always liked the look of our hookers back home."[54] But at other times, she claims she was not trash since to her *trash* signified the mountain girls who were sexually free with the boys. As she once said to David Letterman when looking through her high school yearbook, "[I] looked like the real trash that a lot of the girls were."[65] Here, she juxtaposed her own image of trash—the hyperfeminine look of hookers—with that of the plain-looking girls who, unlike her, did "sleep around," to use the language of that time. Dolly claimed she *looked* like trash because she bleached and teased her hair, used too much makeup, and wore too-tight clothing. But she insisted she was *not* trash since she was a good girl who did not "sleep around."

So Dolly distinguished the hypersexual appearance of trash from the sexual behavior of trash. "I don't mean to look trashy and whore-y, it's just that I don't think I do," she explained. "And even if I do look like a whore, I sure don't feel like one."[66] This paradox is why she and her audiences laugh when she says in interviews, "that's what I wanted to be when I grew up: trash." We laugh at the thought of a poor little girl saying she wants to be trash when she does not fully understand its sexual implications. We laugh at the ultra-wealthy woman who has not grown up to be trash by either class or sexual measures. And we laugh because Dolly's highly sexualized appearance as trash is so exaggerated, so cartoonish, it is more of a joke than a come-on.

In her 2016 made-for-television movie, *Dolly Parton's Christmas of Many Colors: Circle of Love*,[67] Dolly gave viewers a glimpse of the model for her image of trash. Dolly played the small but pivotal role of the "painted lady." This woman is gaudily made up (even more than Dolly usually is) with bleached hair, heavy makeup, long nails, high heels, and tight clothing. But she also has money. In the course of the movie, she tries to give $20 to a young Dolly who is busking on the street corner to earn a few nickels and dimes, only to be shooed away by a "moral" shopkeeper. Her car is a shiny red Thunderbird convertible, which she drives to the Parton home to deliver Dolly's only wish for Christmas: bright red, patent leather shoes. In this look of the town tramp, young Dolly saw an alternative to the colorless and poor existence of her day-to-day life as a child. The painted lady recognized a kindred spirit.

From this extended quote of Dolly's, we discover another reason why this hyperfeminine image was so appealing to her:

FIGURE 6.2. Dolly Parton as the "painted lady," *Dolly Parton's Christmas of Many Colors: Circle of Love*, 2016.

FIGURE 6.3. Dolly Parton as the "painted lady" with Alyvia Alyn Lind as young Dolly, *Dolly Parton's Christmas of Many Colors: Circle of Love*, 2016.

Womanhood was a difficult thing to get a grip on in those hills, unless you were a man. My sisters and I used to cling desperately to anything halfway feminine. . . . We could see the pictures of the models in the newspapers that lined the walls of our house and the occasional glimpse we would get at a magazine. We wanted to look like them. They didn't look at all like they had to work in the fields. They didn't look like they had to take a spit bath in a dishpan. They didn't look as if

FIGURE 6.4. Dolly Parton, front center, with siblings and cousins (Sevier County, Tennessee, 1955). Courtesy: Dolly Parton Enterprises.

men and boys could just put their hands on them any time they felt like it, and with any degree of roughness they chose. The way they looked, if a man wanted to touch them, he'd better be damned nice to them.[68]

In Dolly's mountain world, and in a number of her songs, traditional womanhood looked like poverty, hard work, and rough handling by men, while femininity looked like wealth, privilege, and respectful treatment by men. The outward appearance of a woman's class identity played a role in this equation. Women who looked poor were fair game for men, while hypersexualized women who looked rich, even if poor, were insulated from this abuse. If that feminine look was called *trash*, well so be it; that was what Dolly was going to be. Dolly constructed an image that for her would rise above her poverty and the sexual mishandling by men she witnessed as a young woman.

This rationale provides deeper insight into Dolly's glamorous persona. It is protection and power, the real ammunition in the battle of the sexes. Dolly's exaggerated cartoon look, as she would call it, allows her to disarm men with whom she works. She explained, "the certain type of woman I am, I guess they all thought I was a whore, 'cause I looked like it [laughs] and I was a good ole girl. I'd go in and I'd tell a joke as bad as they would. I kind of fit in and I was just one of the boys, so to speak, even though I was very feminine and all that too. It's a little different than if I would have been a very strict and straight-laced business woman. Anyhow, I didn't have those problems."[69] Here again, Dolly links her glamorous look with that of a whore, and by extension, trash. And she credits this image, along with her sense of humor about it, with her ability to work easily with men without a lot of hassle. Thus, while Dolly's sexualized look opens her up to jokes and leering, it also, paradoxically, insulates her from male abuse and the kinds of tragic stories she composes.

Dolly says she learned a lot about how to deal with men when she was a child. She usually laughs off the "macho redneck attitudes" of her father, brothers, and other men in her life growing up. But her oldest sister, Willadeene, "hints that the effects of their male-dominated world might have been more serious. 'We girls have complexes to this day over the way the boys treated us then.'" As Dolly said, "I grew up in a house with five sisters, giving my love and baring my soul to them and knowing that there was a kindness, a sweetness and a depth to them that I didn't get from my brothers."[70] She feels this camaraderie with women in her professional life as well: "For some reason, I have better luck when I work with women. I guess I have a good sense of sisterhood."[71] Having learned from family experiences about how to deal with male aggressiveness, Dolly often speaks about how she has handled unwelcome attitudes from men during her life. "I think being brought up in a big family and all those brothers, and my father and being very close to my uncles, I think I had a good understanding of men, so I knew how to maneuver and not allow myself to get caught in that trap."[72] And when things did escalate and she "got jumped on on occasion," she said she "always knew how to diffuse a situation without injuring their pride."[73]

Dolly mastered this skill early in life. Cas Walker, who was the host of a radio show Dolly sang on from the age of ten, recalled, "Course, Dolly's got a lot of good traits, but she's got one real good one. She just never did let nobody start mullin' over her. No one could feel around on Dolly. She stood her own—kept her hands to herself and made everybody do likewise. There just wasn't no such thing as walkin' up and layin' your arm around Dolly. She was just unusual that-a-way and was from the time she was just small."[74] Dolly says "when I was a young girl working in those honky-tonks, I was pretty much left on my own to fight off all them good ole boys. I just used my good, common horse sense, all of that stuff that I'd learned as a mountain girl. I could always talk my way out of pretty much anything. And didn't do anything or get nothing done to me that I didn't ask for or didn't want."[75]

As Pamela Wilson reminds us, Dolly "does not distinguish the abstract condition of being female from her personal experience as a Southern Appalachian, working-class woman."[76] Dolly's creation of her hyperfeminine image of trash is not just about gender and sex, but also about class. Dolly was singled out for abuse in school because of her coat, a handmade garment stitched together from rags that was a sign of her poverty. Having it ripped from her body linked both sexual and class shame. Accordingly, Dolly's trashy image is also a response to poverty. As a child, she was aware of her deprivation:

> The reason I like my hair and pretty clothes is it's something I never had [as a] a kid. . . . As children, we had to wear britches with the hind end out of them and patches all over. The faded denim and stringy hair and scrubbed faces. It was fine, but we had no choice. So then, I automatically thought when I get grown up, I'm going to have pretty clothes and pretty jewelry and pretty make-up and pretty hair-dos. I wanted to know what it feels like. . . . I know what it feels like to live down to earth—to be earth people. I still am inside.[77]

Her often-quoted quip "It takes a lot of money to look this cheap" speaks directly to the way Dolly links her glamorous trashy look with wealth and an escape from mountain poverty. Thus, Dolly's appearance is a way to publicly demonstrate an upward mobility in income if not social class.

The day after Dolly graduated from high school, she left the Appalachian Mountains for Nashville, not only physically but, in some senses, musically. Her trashy glamour of high hair, makeup, and nails was more at home on *The Porter Wagoner Show* with the rhinestones and steel guitars of Nashville country music than in the mountains. Similarly, her songs of female agency, power, and defiance are often in a classic country, honky-tonk, or hard-shell style of music. However, when Dolly writes of women who would be considered trash by their mountain communities—women in poverty who are abused and abandoned, who bear children alone, and who sometimes die of grief or suicide—she often goes home to her musical roots, which she links with poverty: "When I came out of the Smoky Mountains, I tried to make a living doing [mountain music], but I couldn't. I had to prostitute myself in certain ways musically in order to make a living. It's almost like I had to get rich in order to sing like I was poor again."[78] This wealth is gained through "prostitution," through singing music she felt would sell, whether or not she personally enjoyed it. The protection provided by her constructed, "trashy," "whore-y," glamorous image, as well as the financial power gained through some of her strategic musical choices, allowed her to sing mountain music and to tell stories of poor women who did not choose to be labeled trash.

Women's Strength

At some point, women who are composers face the question, how has being a woman affected your career? Dolly responds the way many of these composers do: it has not made much of a difference. Thus, Dolly's white trash persona is in opposition to the way she views herself as a songwriter and musician. In her public presentation as an entertainer and celebrity, she projects her hyperfeminine image. But when she focuses on her identity as a songwriter, gender is irrelevant: "First of all, I never thought about whether I was a girl or a boy," Dolly said. "I was a songwriter, I was a singer, and I think you get treated pretty much with the respect that you have for yourself."[79] Dolly's self-respect is rooted in her belief in the quality of her music coupled with her inexhaustible work ethic. She always felt the caliber of her songwriting formed the basis of how people ultimately judged her, despite her distracting image. Linda Ronstadt recalled Dolly taught her that lesson: "you don't have to sacrifice your femininity in order to have equal status. The only thing that gives you equal status with other musicians is your musicianship. Period."[80]

In navigating the male-dominated music industry, Dolly chose to take men's flirtations and jokes as a compliment. She also capitalized on her hyperfeminine appearance while moving on to more important matters. When the leering began, Dolly's strategy was, "hey now, you can look all you want to. I'm just gonna stand here and let you look for a minute. But I came here on more important business. You know, it's like, I might look like trash, but I got a little more going for me than that."[81] As Samantha Christensen put it, Dolly "controls male desire just as she controls her own success."[82] She often shifted these ogling moments to the task at hand by explaining that she had a song, a creative idea, or a product that would make her and her male business partners a lot of money. Rather than being intimidated by men, "I just would walk right in with my songs or with my business ideas, and I never felt the effects of being a woman, or felt that I was kept down." But Dolly acknowledged not everyone was unaffected by sexism. "I'm so lucky now, I see that, but I never had the problems that a lot of other people did."[83]

Although Dolly does not readily identify as a feminist, she has a great love and respect for women, and her songs demonstrate her commitment to gender equality. Throughout her career she has written songs expressing a woman's desire to break free from the constraints of home, family, and enforced domesticity. And some of her most powerful songs expose the hypocrisy and often tragic consequences of the sexual double standard, particularly in the context of the mountain poverty of her youth. Whether they are old women or young girls, independent superstars or mountain women, wives, lovers, mothers, or grand-mothers, Dolly conveys the complexities of women's lives. When Dolly writes of women who are in pain, she often uses the metaphor of the sparrow. But the eagle is her avatar of a woman's strength and her hard-won freedom.

In the late 1970s, when she was making her controversial crossover move into pop music, Dolly used eagle imagery to describe her feelings: "I was just dreamin' big dreams. The decisions were hurtful to make. The changes I made weren't against the people I was with, but I just had to make these changes. It was hard for me to do it, and I suffered, but the suffering has been worthwhile. I don't like to hurt nobody's feeling, and I have a great love for all the people involved. But now I feel like an eagle who's trying to fly as high as it can."[84] Not long after her break with Porter Wagoner, Dolly wrote "Light of a Clear Blue Morning" about her newfound freedom after being under someone else's musical control. Again, her strength came in the form of an eagle, symbolizing, in her words, her "total self-expression and daring to be brave." The song "told how I was feeling at the time," Dolly said, "feeling like a captured eagle, and an eagle is born to fly, and now that I have won my freedom, like an eagle I am eager for the sky."[85]

About ten years later, Dolly explicitly used the eagle as an emblem of women's strength in "Eagle When She Flies." Dolly said she based her song on her rela-tionship with her mother, sisters, and grandmothers. "It's about the strength of women and the stuff that they had gone through, and what we went through together."[86] Referencing both the sparrow and the eagle, Dolly portrays her ideas about the fragility as well as the toughness of women who are "gentle as the sweet magnolia, strong as steel," as sung at the song's climax. Dolly also said the song conveys how she navigated her multiple roles as a private individual and as her public persona of "Dolly Parton": "It was about me, like 'being a sparrow when she's broken, but an eagle when she flies,' meaning you're so sensitive, but yet when it's time to fly, when Dolly Parton has to be Dolly Parton, she has to go out there and shine and smile and do positive interviews and things that people ask. But when I hurt, and when I have my personal problems to deal with, they're hard to bear. My burdens are very hard to bear. So it was re-ally about that. It was a very personal song."[87] Here, she reveals that her public persona—the image she can never drop and must resolutely maintain even during difficult times—is aligned in her mind with the image of the eagle, the avatar of protection and power, qualities inherent in her image.

"Eagle When She Flies" is an understated anthem of female power set in a slow waltz meter. With a subdued steel guitar, piano, and intermittent choral backup singers, the song hints at a gospel sound, particularly at the refrain line at the end of each verse:

> And she's a sparrow when she's broken
> But she's an eagle when she flies

This refrain is also set apart rhythmically from the surrounding lines. Each verse is eight lines long, with the first six lines each comprising two measures. But the last two lines, which are the refrain, are four measures each. Dolly creates this rhythmic extension by elongating the words *broken* and *flies*, the counterparts to sparrow and eagle. The harmony of these two lines subtly marks the sparrow and eagle: *sparrow* is set to the gentler sonority of the subdominant chord (IV) while *eagle* is marked by a very strong move to the stability of the tonic chord (I). This refrain is also set to rising melodic lines in contrast to the descending contour at the ends of lines in the verses.

Eagle When She Flies reached #1 on the country chart, and it was quickly certified gold and then platinum a year later. These numbers were likely driven by the #1 single from the album, "Rockin' Years," written by Dolly's brother Floyd Parton. Dolly sang it in a duet with Ricky Van Shelton who also released the song on his album *Backroads*, 1991. Dolly's song, "Eagle When She Flies," reached only #33 on the country chart. She explained, "Male DJs on the radio would not play that song. They hated it. It didn't do well with me singing it, because they thought it was against men and not about women. . . . It was really just about the life of women. It had nothing to do with men."[88] The absence of men in the song was the problem since some male DJs believed that this signaled a general dismissal of men if not outright male bashing. Dolly once said, "I need my husband for love, and other men for my work. But I don't depend on any man for my strength."[89] This was her sentiment in "Eagle When She Flies," and while it left some men cold, it touched the hearts of many women.

———⌒⌒———

The questions about feminism asked of Dolly in the 1970s continue to be asked fifty years later. While her answers have broadened, she still does not use the term *feminist* when talking about herself and her beliefs. When asked in 2019 during Women's History Month about her 60-year career as a barrier-breaking female artist, Dolly replied: "I had these songs. I had this dream. I had this talent, so I just went for that. So I think that would be my advice to all the women out there. Just believe in yourself and know who you are. Stand your own ground and don't take no for an answer. Just respect yourself. Respect each other as women. And respect the good men and appreciate them. And do what you need to do about the rest, about the others."[90] Although Dolly speaks in personal terms about her own journey rather than addressing the obvious feminist implication of the question, there is a hint of feminist resistance in her last sentence.

Despite her reticence to speak about matters she views as political, through her music Dolly reflects the complexity of women's lives. Often interviewers, sensing a feminist sensibility in her songs, press her for answers: What does she think? What does she believe? Dolly is charming and open, but she reveals only what she chooses, quite carefully and deliberately. Critics often look only to "her parodic authenticity [and] her performance of white (trash) womanhood"[91] when trying to understand her views about women's lives. But by limiting their observations and questions only to the facet of Dolly that she herself would call cartoonish, they miss out on the central way Dolly communicates her convictions—her songs. By considering Dolly's songs about women, one gains a fuller picture of her complexity and her principles

Most of Dolly's songs are not autobiographical or overt "message songs." But when listened to as a group—attending to their common threads of imagery, situations, emotions, and ideas—their messages coalesce, revealing what Dolly believes is important. Her songs encompass a rich, nuanced expression of women's lives and struggles. So, it is not necessary to ask Dolly if she is a feminist. The answer lies in her songs.

Chapter 7
"Me and Little Andy"

Songs of Tragedy

"I like ballads. Real strong, pitiful, sad, cryin' ballads."

Dolly always sleeps with a light on.[1] She says her experience of being locked in a closet at school led to her lifelong fear of the dark.[2] But many of her songs revel in dark scenarios. Some are set within a loving family, but more often the family is dysfunctional. She writes tales of abuse, broken homes, and abandoned, orphaned, and dying children. These songs often end in madness, suicide, or death. Some critics describe these songs as gothic, "rooted in the British ballad and broadside traditions,"[3] and Margo Jefferson also linked Dolly's darker songs to the ballad tradition: "Like the traditional Southern balladeers, [Dolly] is drawn to tales of death, violence, and deceit: women are betrayed by men; children are abandoned by parents. And like them, she can tell a plain story with dramatic fervor."[4] Dolly explained, "We used to hear all those stories back home. And if they weren't singing those sad-ass songs, they were telling stories about it," and "that makes an impression on a little child."[5] She recalled "Mama always sang those old songs, those cryin', hurtin' songs. . . . I have such a feeling for those songs."[6] She also remembered her mother and great grandmother Lindy telling "Raw Head, Bloody Bones" bedtime stories that spooked and delighted the kids.[7]

Dolly's imagination was sparked by these stories, and she began writing her own dark songs as a child—she recalls one "about a boy getting killed in the war."[8] As a budding songwriter she believed she would need to write tragic songs "in order to be a mountain singer."[9] Dolly still credits her Appalachian upbringing with her propensity for writing dark songs: "It's just that old mountain way. Basically, I have a happy heart, but I haven't been dead nor blind, neither. I grew up with all these stories, from all these sisters, cousins, aunts, and uncles. I've seen more sorrow than one person ought to see in a lifetime, whether it's been my sorrow or someone else's. So I can write funny stuff like 'He's Gonna Marry Me,' and then turn right around and kill the baby."[10]

Dolly was writing tragic songs from the earliest days of her career on *The Porter Wagoner Show*; she said, "back then, most of the stuff I wrote was dark and sad."[11] Her later albums continued to highlight her "sad-ass" songs, particularly those that emphasized bluegrass and mountain music. But even when she moved into pop styles on her albums, she often included a song that would mine the depths of human suffering, such as "Me and Little Andy." It is one of Dolly's most well-known tragic ballads: six-year-old Sandy and her puppy Andy have been abandoned and seek help in a storm. Although taken in and fed by a kind stranger, she and the puppy both die. Few people have an unambiguous response to this song. While some find the song touching, others belittle its sentimentality.

It is precisely this song's capacity to engender such strong reactions that reveals what is at stake in Dolly's dark songs—the willingness to take a stark, unflinching look at situations that are discomforting, even harrowing, despite whatever emotions might arise. Dolly writes songs inspired by tragic stories even though she finds them distressing: "I watch the news and I'm just tore apart by some of the stuff I see, some of it I can't bear to watch. I have to flip the channels around because I can't stand to see little starving kids or the idea that somebody beat up a kid or starved a kid or all the horrible things in the world. And I have to write those things too."[12] Rather than turning away completely from disturbing scenarios, Dolly often filters these contemporary stories through the Appalachian ballad tradition. She recalls that many of the old sad songs and tragic ballads she heard as a child were versions of true stories, sung as a way to disseminate news, and they were often cautionary tales. Dolly said singing such songs is "just the way of the mountains. You grow up singing those old sad songs. You don't even think they're sad."[13] The routine singing of these tragic ballads ingrained their messages while lessening their horror, and Dolly's original songs about sorrow, abuse, and neglect function similarly.

Many of Dolly's songs tell bleak, enigmatic stories that keep listeners hooked until the final lines when she reveals the twist: the child and the puppy died, the orphan home burned down, or the bedtime prayer became a suicide note. Nearly all of Dolly's tragic songs are domestic stories, and most are about children. A significant number portray the damaging, sometimes fatal outcomes, including suicide, that neglectful parents, abuse, and divorce have on children and families. She also writes songs about the dehumanizing effects of orphanages, linking orphaned children to her songs about unwed pregnancy. Abandoned children haunt her catalogue. However, some of her songs feature happy youngsters, cherished by loving parents in good homes, but who nonetheless die; the majority of these songs were duos with Porter Wagoner. Following my exploration of these different types of songs, I suggest some models Dolly draws from, and I return to "Me and Little Andy" to offer some thoughts on how it is both an anomaly as well as a quintessential dark song of Dolly's.

Broken Families

"Blue Valley Songbird" is related to those like "My Blue Ridge Mountain Boy" and others about a young woman who leaves her country home to follow her dreams in the city. In it, Dolly sets this story to an acoustic waltz with prominent mandolin and steel guitar. But the nostalgic musical setting of "Blue Valley Songbird" is ironic since the singer recalls an abusive and broken home. The woman runs away from her abject family life as much as she runs toward her dreams of fame in the city. Her father was cruel to her, and her mother does the only thing she can: tells the girl to leave home at the age of fifteen and try to make it on her own as a musician. The song was featured in the made-for-television movie *Blue Valley Songbird*, which dramatized this story.[14] Dolly creates a similar scenario in "A Gamble Either Way," which is about a young woman who is dispossessed, on the road, and alone from the age of thirteen. In effect, an orphan during her childhood, she falls into prostitution as her only option as a teenager.[15]

In several songs, Dolly writes about the pain of a home broken by divorce and neglectful parents. In "Miss You–Miss Me," a girl sings to her divorced parents in a leisurely paced song, sparsely accompanied with finger-picked acoustic guitar, mandolin, and plaintive fiddle. Dolly evokes a little girl voice as she often does when singing from a child's point of view. She also takes the opportunity to include a little wordplay on the word *miss* along the way: "Your little miss is missing out on you/And you're both missing out on so much too." The song was performed by Desiree Ross in *A Country Christmas Story* (2013). In this made-for-television movie, Ross plays a teenaged, biracial singer from the Appalachian Mountains whose performance at Dollywood reunites her broken family. As she follows her dream to become a country singer, the film also highlights the role of African American musicians in country music.[16]

Dolly also tackles parental neglect in "What Will Baby Be." Here, she sings a litany of ways that a home with fighting parents will affect a young child. She effectively sets the song to a gentle lullaby of a melody with a modal harmony that rocks between the tonic (I) and the flatted 7th chord ($\flat$VII). The 1993 recording of the song, released on *Slow Dancing with the Moon*, evokes a lush, Celtic sound with uilleann pipes and the harmony vocals of Irish singer Maura O'Connell. Dolly had earlier recorded an unreleased version of the song in 1972 during a session in which she recorded "My Tennessee Mountain Home" (later released in 2009). This version, much more hard-edged in its lyrics and accompaniment than her softened 1993 recording, is in a country style with active percussion that suggests more turmoil in a family with no love. Rather than a generalized sense of family neglect, Dolly's earlier version outlines the trouble more graphically and with a hint of balladlike language in the first line: "The babysitter is a fair young maiden/Lovin' baby's daddy where baby can see." Dolly juxtaposes these disturbing scenarios with the baby's innocence by using a tinkling keyboard that sounds like a child's music box. In both versions the final message is the same: "What baby is when baby grows up/Depends entirely on you and me."

Suicide

For some characters in Dolly's songs about broken homes and unhappy families, the pain of dispossession, abandonment, and loss leads to suicide. "Blackie, Kentucky," a bouncing, folklike song featuring finger-picked acoustic guitar, begins the way several of Dolly's songs do: a young woman leaves her rural, poverty-filled existence in the mountains for a better life. But unlike other examples, here she leaves with a man who promises her riches but soon isolates her completely from her family and friends in his fancy house. Scornful of her family's poverty, the husband does not allow them to visit, and refuses to let her travel home. Bereft of everyone she holds dear, she vows to commit suicide, speaking rather than singing the lines in which she writes her husband a note asking that he bury her in Blackie, Kentucky so her family and friends can visit her grave. Dolly folds into the last lines a hint of a bedtime prayer—now I lay me down to sleep—as she imagines being buried back home.

Dolly had previously used some of these tropes and performance techniques in another song of suicide. "'Til Death Do Us Part" opens with Dolly speaking, with a lump in her throat, to the faint accompaniment of a church organ. She reveals that her husband is in love with another woman, and she relives the moment of her wedding when she placed a ring on her husband's finger and heard his vow that included the traditional oath, 'til death do us part. When the song proper starts with Dolly's singing to the strains of a crying honky-tonk accompaniment, we learn that she has decided to take that vow seriously and to kill herself. The wedding vow becomes her suicide note, once again combined with a bedtime prayer:

> Tonight I lay me down to sleep forever
> With this small empty bottle and broken heart
> I keep the vow I made I won't forsake it
> I promised 'til death do us part

While lyrically clever and musically poignant, "'Til Death Do Us Part" does not pack the punch of "The Bridge." At the end of "'Til Death Do Us Part," the woman is still alive and singing. In contrast, the singer in "The Bridge" commits suicide at the end of the song.

The singer of "Gypsy, Joe and Me" also commits suicide on a bridge. After cobbling together a family of sorts with her boyfriend Joe and her dog Gypsy, the homeless singer leaps from a bridge after Gypsy is killed by a passing car and Joe dies from exposure to the cold. Dolly's setting of these lyrics remains upbeat, even as the situation becomes grimmer and grimmer. The buoyant bass line continues unchanged until a brief stop-time as the singer plans her suicide at the edge of the bridge. But the jaunty swing of instruments returns as the song fades out, perhaps in a musical move to reflect the singer's final dreams of happiness after death. Once again, Dolly brings a young woman to a bridge's edge to end her life.

Abandoned Children and Orphans

"Me and Little Andy" is perhaps Dolly's most well-known tragic song, and the story is the epitome of pitifulness. Sandy, who is neglected by her parents, seeks shelter, food, and solace from a stranger in the midst of a howling storm made vivid through wind sound effects at the beginning and end of the song. Dolly sings the song in two voices: her usual voice as the adult who takes in Sandy and her little girl voice as Sandy who interweaves descriptions of her broken home with nursery rhymes.

> Patty cake and bakersman
> My mommy ran away again

> London bridge is fallin' down
> My daddy's drunk again in town
> And we was all alone and didn't know what we could do

Sandy also speaks some of these lines to the accompaniment of light, arpeggiated music-box chimes that match her childlike chanting, blending fantasy and harsh reality into a single stream. The stranger gives the girl and puppy a bed for the night, but in a move right out of a gothic tale, Sandy and her little dog die before morning:

> But that night as they slept the angels took them both to heaven
> God knew little Andy would be lonesome with her gone
> Now Sandy and her puppy dog won't ever be alone

In his astute analysis of the sentimentality of this song, Mitchell Morris wrote: "Sandy's matter-of-fact statement about her missing parents and especially her declaration, 'If you don't love us, no one will,/I promise we won't cry,' offer an appallingly accurate depiction of the honesty we often find in children, but in the song we know that these words are also Parton's transparent bid for our emotional investment. We might laugh to make sure that the song does not work on us."[17]

When the song was released, many critics decried its maudlin nature. One notable response comes from Bruce Cook who called the song "as heinous as any of her past offenses against good taste."[18] During her live concerts at the time, Dolly had to fight her management to keep the song on the set list. Don Roth, one of the tour musicians, remarked, "You and I may be very jaded and sophisticated and think that song transcends the boundaries of good taste, but that's Dolly song. And the average person out there will cry when she sings it."[19] Laura Cunningham acknowledged the song's extreme rhetoric, though she explained that it is Dolly's performance in concert, Dolly's transformation *into* Sandy, that rescues the song from ridicule and launches it into our hearts:

> [The song is] more than a tear-jerker, it's a tear-yanker. Most singers couldn't get away with it, but Dolly does—denying her physical appearance to become, on stage, a six-year-old girl. . . . Dolly, as the song's narrator, does have a bed—and the little girl and her puppy lie down and die in it. The song would be to throw up over if Dolly performed it in a cutesy way. But her little girl is not a Shirley Temple moppet. Her voice projects another kind of child—a starved, terrified

Listening Outline 5: "Me and Little Andy," *Here You Come Again*, 1977

Time	Section	Lyric	Description
0:00	Intro		Acoustic fingerpicked guitar solo to start; the sound of wind enters and continues through verse 1.
0:05	Verse 1, 1st half	Late one cold and stormy night...	The first two lines are identical in a descending stepwise melody with static harmony over the tonic (I) chord.
0:17	Verse 1, 2nd half	I wondered who could be outside...	The tonic finally moves to the subdominant (IV), and the change in melody and the speeding up of harmonic rhythm matches the action of the narrator. A single high chime marks the verse.
0:30	Verse 2	Before I could say a word...	Accompaniment adds strings and bass. Sandy's voice is spoken by Dolly in a little girl voice. A single high chime marks the verse.
0:54	Verse 3, 1st half	Ain't ya got no gingerbread...	The first half of the verse is spoken in Sandy's voice with a music box accompaniment of arpeggios.
1:06	Verse 3, 2nd half	Patty cake and bakersman...	The second half of the verse is now sung in Sandy's voice to a nursery rhyme and Sandy's explanation of her situation. Strings replace the music box. Note the subtle stop time at 1:18 when Sandy asks to stay. A single high chime marks the verse.
1:24	Verse 4	Gitty up, trotty horse...	Sandy continues to sing and speak nursery rhymes along with more lyrics about her drunken father. The string accompaniment becomes rhythmically agitated with a strong bass in imitation of the trotting horses; the accompaniment smooths somewhat in the second half of the verse. Note the subtle stop time at 1:47 when Sandy asks to stay again. A single high chime marks the verse.
1:53	Interlude	Brief instrumental section	Bell-like electric piano and strings allow for a moment of thought before the story continues.
1:56	Verse 5	She was just a little girl...	Narrator continues full-voiced with a few words spoken. Full strings and a dotted rhythm in the prominent bass increase the tension. Note Dolly's voice break at 2:17 on "ever" for a heightened emotional effect.
2:21	½ Verse Tag	Ain't ya got no gingerbread...	The return of the first half of verse more whispered than spoken in Sandy's voice. Her voice fades to nothing by the last syllable. The music box accompaniment is replaced by atonal, ethereal wind chimes and the sound of the wind as in the intro. Wind sound continues for a brief moment after Sandy's voice fades out.

orphan . . . unwanted and slightly resentful. Dolly, with her diamonds, her rose, her salmon chiffon, disappears, by some magic in her voice, and is replaced by a ragged, knock-kneed little girl. All around me, there are sniffles.[20]

John Rockwell agreed: "Miss Parton conceives the song and then performs it in a way that quiets cynicism."[21] If we take Dolly's melodramatic performance seriously, the song touches us beyond our nervous laughter, even as the "conventions of sentimentality mount with every verse."[22] Perhaps Dolly's transformation in performance is based on her memory of chanting the line "ain't you got no gingerbread" as a toddler when she would visit Martha Williams, a woman who baked gingerbread and hoecakes for the Parton children as a special treat.[23]

Dolly also has memories of being spooked by ghost stories as a child: "I can remember hearing some of the old folks talk about 'haints' and tell some of the old tales that had been passed down through generations."[24] A number of elements in "Me and Little Andy" invites listeners to hear the song as a ghost story. The inexplicable death of the child and dog after they have been fed and warmed suggests that perhaps they were already dead. Their appearance in the midst of a storm we can hear, the knock on the door in the night, the eerie singing of nursery rhymes to the tinkling accompaniment of a music box, and the enigmatic deaths all suggest a classic ghost story scenario where the narrator encounters an already dead soul looking for comfort. Further, after the child and puppy die, the song ends with Sandy still speaking, in her singsong manner, in an almost disembodied whisper. Her voice dies out to the sound of wind and chimes that are not part of the tonal framework of the song like the tinkling music box. The chimes are eerie—random and dissonant. With pitches that are alien to the tonality of the song, they reverberate through the movement of wind, not human touch, thus conjuring up this other-worldly effect.

Dolly recalls that it was a terrifying ghost story of a woman killed on the mountain and still screaming up there that inspired her song "Mountain Angel."[25] If we place "Me and Little Andy" in this tradition of Appalachian Mountain ghost stories, which are filled with rhetorical excess and a sense of the uncanny, then the criticism that the song is maudlin is beside the point. Aware that the song risks scorn from the cynical listener, Dolly often admits the song is "plumb pitiful." Fully embracing its dark nature, Dolly also says the song "goes over with almost everybody. It's not just country, it's real. Of course, you can't dance to 'Little Andy.' But who'd want to? Life ain't all a dance."[26]

Although the little girl in "Me and Little Andy" is not technically an orphan, she has, in effect, been orphaned by neglectful, absent parents. Further, the image of a little girl named Sandy who owns a dog named Andy conjures up Little

Orphan Annie and her dog Sandy. Orphans and unwanted (or unplanned) children appear in many of Dolly's songs. Some merely mention the singer's orphaned status and suggest that orphans can grow up to have happy lives. For example, the singer in "Joshua" is drawn to the mountain man because they are both loners: she had spent her childhood in an orphanage. In "These Old Bones," the singer was taken from her mother by the county. As an adult, the daughter meets her mother on her deathbed and happily carries on her gift of clairvoyance. But few of Dolly's songs end well for orphans.

As discussed in Chapter Six, Dolly saw how, in her mountain culture, young pregnant girls would be turned out of their houses or sent to a home for unwed mothers or to sympathetic relatives. Such ostracization from family and community was Dolly's inspiration for one of her favorites, "Down from Dover," a song that surprised one writer "because it was so dark."[27] In this song, the baby dies and the mother tries to cope alone. In another, "Mountain Angel," she is driven to madness after the baby's death. However, Dolly also wrote songs about the heartbreak of giving up a baby for adoption and the plight of orphans, which was another outcome of unwed pregnancy. On the same album that contained the original version of "Down from Dover," she included "I'm Doing This for Your Sake." In this honky-tonk style song, heavy with a crying steel guitar, another young woman has been seduced and impregnated by a man who promised marriage. After he leaves her, the singer gives away her baby girl. Unwilling to make the child pay for her mother's mistake, Dolly poignantly links heart and home as she leaves the child behind: "In this home so far away from home I leave my heart today/'Cause home is where the heart is and with you my heart will stay." In "Love Isn't Free," Dolly also explored adoption, but from the perspective of the unwanted six-year-old girl who knows she was given up by her mother. In these songs about unwed pregnancy, the baby survives only to live in misery in orphanages.

Dolly exposes the suffering and despair of life in orphanages in one of her most disturbing scenarios. "Evening Shade" paints a grim picture of abuse at the Evening Shade orphanage. The evil matron, Mrs. Bailey, terrorizes the children, which also recalls the Little Orphan Annie story. Dolly writes these excruciating lines to set up the justification for the children's shocking actions at the end of the song: "Little Susan Bradley, one night had wet her bed/Mrs. Bailey took the razor strap and beat her half to death." This cruelty was the last straw for the song's young narrator, herself an orphan, who hatches a plan with the other children to burn down the orphanage with Mrs. Bailey in it. This classic country song, with a heavy backbeat, fiddle countermelody, and backup vocals, makes no musical comment to match the desperate and ghastly actions of the children. With no change in accompaniment or melodic material, the song runs its course matter-of-factly to its conclusion with Evening Shade ablaze. It is only at this point that the song slows, the relentless energy dissipating as Dolly sings the last line, with accusation in her voice, in a kind of stop-time ritardando: "Evening Shade was burning just like the hell it was."

Doomed Children—Dolly and Porter Duets

When Dolly was nine years old, her mother was pregnant with her ninth child. As was often the case in large families, older children were given the responsibility of helping with new babies, and this child was to be Dolly's. Dolly's mother had been ill during the pregnancy with spinal meningitis, and the baby boy, Larry, died soon after he was born. As we saw in Chapter Two, Dolly was devastated. "I guess I was angry at God," Dolly recalled. "Why was my baby dead? Why did everything that was mine have to die? I couldn't eat. I couldn't sleep. For the first time in my life, I couldn't sing. I wouldn't leave Larry's grave. I would take a lantern up on the hill and sit there most of the night talking to him and crying." Eventually, Dolly accepted that "his spirit [was] something apart from his body, something not bound to that grave that I kept mourning over but set free to live a perfect existence in heaven. . . . In my childlike way, I came to understand that death is only frightening to those of us left behind. . . . I sang again, now with a voice made richer for having known loss."[28] Despite her acceptance, Dolly has never stopped thinking of Larry as a vital part of the family, and when asked about her siblings, she always replies that there were twelve children in the family, which includes Larry. She also reproduced in her autobiography the family photograph taken of Larry in his little coffin, a vestige of nineteenth-century sentimental mourning practices. Further, she made Larry's death the centerpiece of her made-for-television movie, *Dolly Parton's Coat of Many Colors* (2015), as discussed in Chapter Two.

Certainly any child who grew up in the mountains when Dolly did would have been exposed to death, but the loss of "her baby" was an especially significant event that Dolly conjures up in her many songs about dying infants and children. Some, like "Down from Dover" and "Mountain Angel," have at their heart the death of a baby or child who is the result of an unwed pregnancy. In other songs, like "Me and Little Andy," a child is abandoned, neglected, and even abused. But Dolly has also written a number of songs about dying children who are deeply loved and wanted by both parents, as Larry was.

Most of these songs, which include lengthy spoken sections, are duets with Dolly and Porter in the role of loving, heartbroken parents. Dolly explained: "Me and Porter like to sing those old sad songs, he liked to do recitations, and I liked to sing those pitiful songs, so the more pitiful I could make them, the better we liked them."[29] These types of recitation songs were popular in country music from the 1930s to the 1960s, with a few appearing in the 1970s. Like those Dolly wrote, they often featured sentimental subjects, most notably dead children. For example, Hank Williams first recorded "The Funeral" in 1950 under the name Luke the Drifter. He adapted the lyrics from a poem of the same name by Will Carleton.[30] In 1970, Little Jimmy Dickens made a mark with his recitation "(You've Been Quite a Doll) Raggedy Ann," written by Red Lane. Dickens, in the role of a weeping father at his little girl's grave, usually held his daughter's favorite doll and spoke directly to it in performance.

Many of Porter and Dolly's duets about dying children join the company of these sentimental recitation songs. In them, the child (almost always a girl) dies, usually of natural causes, and often the child has a death wish or expresses a desire to be in heaven. Musically emphasizing the child's innocence, Dolly sets most of these lyrics to a lilting waltz rhythm. One of the most notable examples of these songs is "Jeannie's Afraid of the Dark," which Porter claimed was the most requested song he and Dolly performed. It is a poignant story of a little girl so afraid of the dark that, after visiting the graves of relatives, she begs her parents not to bury her when she dies because it is dark underground. When Jeannie then dies on a dark, stormy night—the only explanation is her fear of death—her heartbroken parents do bury her, but they place an eternal flame on her grave so she will not be in the dark.

Although Dolly sings most of the song as a solo, it is Porter, not Dolly, who bears the responsibility of breaking the bad news to the listener by freely speaking the final verse of the song as Dolly hums along with background singers. Dolly ends the song by singing "our Jeannie's afraid of the dark" one last time. The spoken section is an effective storytelling device that highlights the tragedy by breaking musical expectations. Moreover, it conveys a gendered response to the child's death. Often, heightened emotion is displayed through singing, while speaking can seem more impersonal and dispassionate; although the speaking voice can still convey a range of feeling, in these duets it also implies self-control and perhaps stoic emotional distance. The father, Porter, is still rational enough to communicate by speaking, while Dolly embodies the mother's emotional response through her continued musical utterances. However, she has no words, no ability to speak, when Jeannie dies. Dolly and Porter repeated this pattern in a number of their songs as parents, with Porter speaking about the child's death while Dolly hums, sings, or remains mute.

A year after "Jeannie's Afraid of the Dark," Dolly and Porter recorded "Malena," which is melodically and rhythmically related to "Jeannie," as discussed in Chapter Two. "Malena" recalls Dolly's fascination with butterflies as the little girl in this song chases them, wishing that she had wings to fly. When her loving parents tell her that is only possible in heaven, the look in Malena's eyes changes, suggesting her desire to die. Dolly again sings most of the song as a solo, but Porter speaks the final verse to the accompaniment of lush background vocals, telling us that on her birthday Malena made a wish for wings. That same night the angels granted her wish, and she is now able to fly.

In "Mendy Never Sleeps," once again a beloved daughter dies, but the story takes a darker turn. Here the girl is a rebellious teenager who has begun sneaking out of the house to smoke and drink. The song was written and is clearly placed in the hippie, flower-child era of the late 1950s and early 1970s: Mendy has long straight hair and wears miniskirts, and the song is accompanied by prominent electric guitar, bass, and the keening of a musical saw that sounds psychedelic. The lyrics suggest that Mendy has moved on to drug use: her eyes are glassy, she is pale, and she cannot sleep even though she stays out late partying.

The song shares its opening melodic gesture with "Jeannie's Afraid of the Dark" and "Malena," but its modal harmonies differ. With its lilting rhythm and modal chords rocking back and forth, the song constructs a feeling of inevitability, at once static and yet inexorably moving toward tragedy. In the final verse, Mendy grows weak and then dies in her parents' arms. The drums and electric guitar become more insistent throughout this verse, mirroring the parents' growing fears until the final line, a twist on the title, which they sing freely and with no accompaniment: "Oh Mendy, please don't go to sleep." The electric guitar, bass, and saw return to play out the song with the same eerie quality as the final, atonal wind chimes at the end of "Me and Little Andy." In both songs, an uncanny sound portends death.

A decade later, Dolly and Porter recorded "Little David's Harp," one of her few songs that feature a dying boy. David, with his heavenly smile, was blind from birth but able to play the harp so that it sounded like angels singing. When only seven, he dies during a storm, as Sandy did in "Me and Little Andy." David then finds peace in heaven playing in God's angel band. His parents hear his harp playing every year on his birthday, Christmas Day. The recording of the song, dating from Dolly's crossover pop period, is awash in harp arpeggios and glissandos and angelic background vocals. Like the previous examples, the song is a lilting waltz, and Porter again speaks the final verse that tells of David's death.

It is David's disability that could explain why Dolly rarely writes songs about little boys who die, focusing instead on girls. It is too easy to claim that Dolly writes about girls autobiographically. She also taps into a larger set of cultural/literary tropes. In Victorian literature and fairy tales—with characters like long-suffering Little Dorrit and the abused and neglected Little Match Girl—the plight of innocent girls traditionally engenders more unambiguous pity in the reader than the suffering of boys who are expected to withstand and overcome hardship on their road to manhood. When boys are the object of this pity, they are often feminized through disability, like Colin Craven, the wheelchair-bound boy in *The Secret Garden*. And Tiny Tim Cratchit with his crutch can only watch the rough-and-tumble boys play in the snow. Both Tiny Tim and David are vulnerable and are therefore acceptable male objects of sympathy. Dolly's penchant for writing about the suffering of girls places her lyrics in this literary tradition as she adheres to these sentimental gender stereotypes.

Porter and Dolly did not always sing as loving, attentive parents. Porter sometimes plays the role of a father who abandoned his family and who is later discovered by his child. In "Mommie, Ain't That Daddy?" a young child sees a beggar and asks her mother, in Dolly's little girl voice, if the man is her father. The mother replies yes and wonders if she failed him. Porter then takes over, speaking all of his lines for the rest of the song. He explains that he was an alcoholic who left his family.

Things end on a happier note in "I Get Lonesome by Myself," a recitation with musical accompaniment. Porter sings only two lines at the beginning, and then he and Dolly trade off speaking the parts of a father and young daughter. Again, the father has abandoned the family, and the six-year-old girl is left alone, locked in a dingy apartment while her mother is out drinking, a familiar scenario of Dolly's. The man sees the lonesome little girl waving at him, and he goes up to her room to talk with her. She explains that her father left and now her mother drinks from heartbreak. When the man recognizes himself in that story and shows the child a picture of himself and his wife and baby, she completes the tale as she sees herself and her mother in the photo and realizes the man is her father. She and her dad now wait for her mother to come home, reiterating the title line: "I Get Lonesome by Myself."

As in "Me and Little Andy," Dolly uses her little girl voice throughout this song. She speaks her lines in a speech rhythm to very little accompaniment, and the sound of a tinkling music box envelops the child's words. Porter, on the other hand, speaks his lines to a fully accompanied country waltz. Although the worlds of the father and daughter are marked by musical differences, as they discover their connection, more and more of the little girl's words are accompanied by the band as their lives come back together.

For one of their earliest recordings, Dolly and Porter portrayed neglectful parents, an usual role for the duo. In "The Party," Dolly sings the first half of this classic country song as she and Porter leave their little boy and girl home with a babysitter so they can go to a party on a Saturday night. Porter then takes over and recites, rather than sings, the rest of the lines. As the party gets wilder with drinking and dirty jokes, the father has a strange feeling that they should get home to their kids. When they arrive, the house is in flames. The children had wanted to go to church the next morning, but now it is only their bodies that are taken to church. Porter ends the recitation abruptly with a final punch, "Though we'd left the party early, we still got home too late." As in most of their duets, Porter again delivers the bad news. But here, Dolly does not even hum the melody at the end. Her voice is absent once they leave their home that night, as though she is incapable of expressing her grief and guilt, too ashamed to speak or sing.

Dolly and Porter do not play the role of parents in "Ragged Angel" unlike in their other songs about dying children. Instead they sing as observers of a scene similar to "Me and Little Andy." Here, Cindy wanders the streets looking for food. With no father and a mother who leaves her alone in their shabby home, Cindy has only a paper doll for company. Unlike Sandy, this poor girl does not seek help, but dies "cold and hungry on the floor." When Dolly reworked the story of "Ragged Angel" for "Me and Little Andy" seven years later, the paper doll became a puppy named Andy, a name easily paired in this context with the earlier "ragged" image—Raggedy Andy. And Cindy became Sandy, a name that forms a pleasing rhyme with the puppy's name. In both songs, God calls the little girls to heaven:

> That night God came for the ragged angel
> And now Cindy won't ever be cold and hungry, no not anymore, ragged
>   angel
> **"Ragged Angel"**
>
> God knew little Andy would be lonesome with her gone
> Now Sandy and her puppy dog won't ever be alone
> **"Me and Little Andy"**

Because they are not the grieved parents, Porter does not tell the listener about Cindy's death as he does in so many of their other songs. Instead, Dolly speaks the lines. This reversal of roles also indicates that they are not singing as Cindy's mom and dad. When Porter and Dolly perform as parents, Porter always reveals the outcome, as if the father, not the mother, is the one strong enough to speak of the tragedy. In "Ragged Angel," Dolly's sliding, descending line in the verses is syrupy, sung in harmony with Porter and backed by ethereal voices. "Me and Little Andy" may be considered cloying by some, but it is a more successful song that Dolly crafted from this earlier version. Its setting is vivid, the nursery rhyme adds an allegorical element, and the melody is folklike and singable. Further, Dolly's use of a little girl voice for Sandy adds an uncanny quality more effectively than the angelic background vocals of "Ragged Angel."

Models for Dolly's Dying Children Songs

Often, Dolly's songs of dying children are viewed as maudlin. But their emotional excess is better appraised in the context of the rhetorical tradition of nineteenth-century sentimental parlor songs that Dolly would have heard as a child. Intended for home performance by amateurs at the piano—usually women—parlor songs had simple melodies and accompaniments. The lyrics often focused on children and the home, as in "Home, Sweet Home," which Dolly borrowed for some of her own songs. Many of these parlor songs were intended to have an ennobling influence through their vivid images of stories told through pathos and moralizing. One sub-genre of these songs is the sentimental mourning ballad that recalls a deceased person. This preoccupation with death—manifested in practices such as "mourning pictures and brooches, sentimental songs and poems lamenting dead children, elaborate mourning practices and fashions, and the custom of spending time with dead family members by picnicking in cemeteries"[31]—as well as spirits who return from the dead, was common in the mountains.

Sentimental parlor ballads, like "Little Bessie" and "Put My Little Shoes Away," also entered the bluegrass tradition, and they inspired bluegrass songs such as "I Hear a Sweet Voice Calling" and "There Was Nothing We Could Do" that similarly featured the death of an ill child who is mourned by loving parents.[32] Although the child does not express a desire to die, she accepts death and her certain heavenly home. In other examples, like "The Little Girl and the Dreadful Snake" and "The Water Lily,"[33] the child wanders from home into danger and is killed.

Several of these sentimental songs entered the oral tradition, and Dolly heard some in the mountains. She recalled her mother singing "Little Rosewood Casket," and Dolly recorded it twice.[34] When she was about seventeen, Dolly recorded "Little Blossom," an anti-temperance ballad.[35] Her version softens the political message of the original parlor song with its preachy final lyrics about the dangers of drink. Dolly instead focuses on the little girl who dies. But Blossom is not a ghost or a child who dies in her sleep from neglect. Blossom is brutally killed by her father, who beats her with a chair, after she enters the saloon and tells him she is hungry. The story bears a similarity to "Me and Little Andy." In both songs, a little girl leaves her home looking for help after her mother has left her alone and her father is out drinking.

Included on the same 1963 recording was a song, "Letter to Heaven," which Dolly wrote as a teenager. In this solo song reminiscent of a parlor ballad, Dolly constructs the scene from a distance rather than as a participant as she did in many of her duets with Porter. And, unlike many previous examples, in this song the little girl's mother is dead; she is looked after by her grandfather. One day, the child asks her grandfather to write a letter to her mother in heaven telling her she misses her and will be seeing her soon. She gets her wish when, on the way to mail the letter, she is struck and killed by a car. The postman, who finds her body and the letter, has the final word: "Straight up into heaven this letter did go/She's happy up there with her mommy I know." As in many of her songs of this type, Dolly sets the lyrics to a waltz meter that suggests lightness and innocence. Accompanied in a soft, slip-note piano, steel guitar, strummed acoustic guitar and bass, the song is balladlike with its strophic form and third-person narration. Young Dolly's voice does not change as she sings in a full-throated style that reveals little emotional response to the ghastly hit-and-run tragedy, like a mountain ballad singer using an impersonal performance style.

Dolly rerecorded the song seven years later and made a few changes that augment the emotional effect of the story. First, the accompaniment is more folklike and sparse, as Dolly lightly sings with only an acoustic guitar and bass. She also performs the piece at a slightly faster tempo, perhaps to accommodate the additional verse she includes. Her new lyrics wrench the story even further into a death wish as the little girl not only states she hopes to see mother soon, but also that she prays every evening: "That God up in heaven will answer my prayer/And take me to live with my mommy up there." This version intensifies the little girl's sweetness with an over-dubbed harmony line above the melody to the lyrics spoken/sung by the child. Dolly's harmony voice here suggests a more childlike timbre in the reenactment of the scene rather than a dispassionate description as in her earlier version. (When Dolly sings the third-person narration, she does so without any vocal harmonies added.) The harmony line returns with the postman's final words, recalling the voice of the child as we learn she is going to join her mother in heaven. The song fades out as Dolly hums the melody, with the same over-dubbed harmony line of the child's voice.

As these examples demonstrate, many of Dolly's songs of dying children tap into this genre of nineteenth-century sentimental parlor songs and their blue-grass descendants. What sets many of Dolly's songs apart from these examples is how often the girls in her songs are either neglected or express a desire to die in order to find happiness.

Rethinking "Me and Little Andy"

Commenting on her approach to tragic songs, Dolly explained, "Usually, if you notice, all my sad songs have happy endings. They go to a better place where they're real happy."[36] And this is true for many of Dolly's songs that end with the child going to heaven, now able to fly, to walk, or to be with her mother. Dolly's Pentecostal religious background informs these songs that look to a heavenly reward for earthly suffering and that take comfort in the certainty of faith and redemption. "Many of her songs float lightly on dark currents"[37] nicely captures this juxtaposition of hope and pain. However, not all of Dolly's sad songs have happy endings, despite her assertion to the contrary. Some like "Down from Dover," "Mountain Angel," "Evening Shade," and "I'm Doing This for Your Sake" offer no consolation at their close. These songs are forged out of the ballad tradition of gothic tales that takes an unsentimental perspective. Dolly does not write with the same emotional distance in her stories found in many traditional ballads. Nonetheless, she often writes tragic, perverse, and disturbing tales without alleviating the characters' sorrows and troubles at the song's conclusion. These are dark songs through and through.

"Me and Little Andy" bridges the dichotomy of Dolly's songs that console versus songs that remain dark to the end. Consolatory songs, like "Malena" and "Letter to Heaven," are impossibly sweet and sentimental. The children are angelic even before death, and they are mourned by loving parents who cared deeply for their children and who lost them through no negligence or abuse. Songs that end with continued despair, like "Evening Shade" and "Down from Dover," do not give in to sentimental excess, and there is no solace for the orphans or the unwed, abandoned mothers. "Me and Little Andy" stretches the conventions of both types of song: it is sentimental but not consolatory.

In the song, Sandy is more earthly than angelic. She is acutely aware she has been abandoned, and she holds her puppy, clinging to her one source of comfort and love. Although cold and hungry, Sandy has the wherewithal to seek help. She does not sweetly and innocently accept her fate, much less seek out her death. She asks for food and shelter and receives them. Unlike most of the abandoned children in Dolly's songs, Sandy is rescued, taken in by a caring stranger. But she still dies, and that is the real twist of the song. Going against the grain of most of Dolly's songs, this abandoned child is saved, but then dies with no loving parents to grieve her. Instead, we, the listeners, are the mourners here, left with no consolation. And the last voice we hear is Sandy's as she continues to ask for help at the end. She is not singing about finding solace in heaven, nor are there grieved parents who cry at her grave. She is still an abandoned, lonely little girl who is cold and hungry. She makes her appeal directly to us, and it is no wonder that many are moved to tears in their inability to help. Sandy herself supplies us with words to express our own feelings: "we was all alone and didn't know what we could do." And in a brilliant move to "make it as sad and pitiful as [she] could,"[38] Dolly further twists the knife by having Andy, the puppy, inexplicably die as well. He, like Sandy, was rescued, fed, and warmed. But he is linked to Sandy's grief and loneliness, and it is only through the dog's death that we have any assurance that Sandy is in a better place: "God knew little Andy would be lonesome with her gone/Now Sandy and her puppy dog won't ever be alone."

Had Dolly ended the song here, we might have wept "Old Yeller" tears, comforted by the image of Sandy and her puppy in heaven—yet another of Dolly's songs of children who die and "go to a happier place." It is evidence of Dolly's storytelling skill and emotional savvy that she brings back Sandy's words and voice to haunt us and to undercut any sense of consolation as she whispers her final plea to the sound of eerie, dissonant wind chimes.

> Ain't ya got no gingerbread
> Ain't ya got no candy
> Ain't ya got an extra bed for me and little Andy

Our sense of powerlessness in the face of such child neglect, as well as the lack of solace at the end of the song as we have come to expect in these sentimental songs, makes us uncomfortable. And this squirming helplessness prompts some to call the song sappy and mawkish.[39] But Dolly does not flinch. She forces us to confront the situation and make a choice: either enter into the song and cry, or scoff and look away. This emotional dilemma sets "Me and Little Andy" apart from her other dark songs.

———⌒⌒———

"Don't you love them old sad songs? I do."[40] Reflecting on why so many stories she heard as a child were grim, Dolly wondered, "maybe it was just human nature to create horrifying stories so the real horrors of survival in such a place didn't seem quite as frightening."[41] What Dolly calls human nature is one response to suffering, and this is a plausible explanation. A different response might be to invent fantasy worlds that not only distract from the "horrors" but recast them in a positive light, which Dolly does in her songs about idyllic mountain life. In them, she chooses to see beauty and kindness rather than pain and injustice.

In other songs, however, Dolly meets the "horrors" head on. Why write these stories that do not assuage or distract? As discussed in Chapter Two, Dolly sometimes composes for her personal benefit, as a kind of therapy. "Coat of Many Colors" is one example. But in her dark songs, Dolly also acts as a witness—a figure who sees, hears, and confirms other people's stories, not only her own. Zora Neale Hurston wrote, "There is no agony like bearing an untold story inside you."[42] As a witness, Dolly can write and perform songs that express otherwise silent pain, the untold stories of ordinary people, particularly women and children, who are silenced, devalued, and thrown away. Having one's story mirrored back by another person in this way can be cathartic and a foundation of healing, and Dolly's celebrity and upbeat, loving persona amplifies this mirroring effect. This is why some fans view Dolly herself as a healer, as I discuss in the next chapter.

Dolly's songs about abuse, neglect, and tragedy expose social problems, validate the experiences of those who suffer, and evoke an emotional response in her listeners, but she always focuses the larger issue through the lens of an individual. Dolly also knows how much her listeners like to dwell in these dark places of scary stories that might mitigate personal "horrors." She understands the desire to be spooked by a grim tale or to weep at a pitiful one to confront and heal one's own pain, and she recognizes that these tragic songs can arouse empathy in her listeners who may also become compassionate witnesses to the pain of others.

When asked if these dark songs go against her image as an optimistic, upbeat person, Dolly replied that they do. However, she also said that they do not "go against who I am. There are many sides to me. . . . I've often said that you have to work at being happy, just like you have to work at being miserable."[43] Dolly has always been moved to write about disturbing situations in ways that would wrench as much pathos from the song as she could. This is Dolly in her songwriting workshop, crafting a sad song for maximum impact. Perhaps this explains why Dolly claims all her sad songs have happy endings. As she said: "God, if it wasn't for my ability to write and sing and express [sad things] . . ., just the feeling of having it come out, to be able to vocalize that, it kind of permeates every little cell in your body and somehow it kind of works it all out, and I don't feel near as bad after I've written it."[44] For Dolly, the work itself, the act of songwriting, is what brings about the happy ending.

Chapter 8
"Light of a Clear Blue Morning"
Songs of Inspiration

"I try every day to leave the world a little
better, a little brighter."

Dolly loves sparkle.[1] As a child she was always on the lookout for the
iridescence of butterflies and the glint of broken glass she would find
in the dirt yard of her mountain home. "When my daddy used to
plow the fields," she recalled, "and the sun would shine down, that quartz stuff
would glisten, and I was sure we had struck diamonds."[2] She also believed "that
some real treasure would come to the surface that would pay the way out of
poverty for all of us."[3] As an adult, Dolly sparkles in her rhinestone wardrobe,
long fingernails, and extravagant hair. Her flash and glitter confirm her move
out of poverty into stardom: "I guess I did invent that part of me. I was always
fascinated with fairytale images. Half of a show is the lighting and the shine
and the sparkle. Stars are supposed to shine and maybe I just want to be a *star*."[4]

Dolly composes songs that sparkle—inspiring songs celebrating the beauty
of the world, particularly when viewed through the eyes of a little girl in a
homemade coat who had only the colors of nature to satisfy her desire for
beauty. While Dolly's darkest songs console by grappling with human struggle
and sorrow, assuring listeners they are not alone, many other songs are joyful,
uplifting responses to the harsh realities Dolly confronts in her saddest songs.
She explains:

We're meant to be happy, but we have to work at that. I was born with a happy heart. I wake up every day expecting things to be right, and if they're not, I get to making them right.... Sometimes people like to wallow in their sorrows and their sad tales, but I really believe that's detrimental to the lives we should be living. It's natural to have hurts and disappointments, but you have to deal with it—pray out of it, dream out of it, and get to living.[5]

One of Dolly's most popular inspirational songs is "Light of a Clear Blue Morning." Written in the aftermath of her break with Porter Wagoner when Dolly sought her musical independence, the song speaks to anyone who faces troubles and seeks hope. She explained how the song came to her:

As I left [Porter's] office and began to drive toward my home . . ., it began to rain. So did I. I cried, not so much out of a sense of loss, but from the pain that almost always comes with change. It was a sad kind of freedom. Then I began to sing a song to myself, "It's been a long dark night and I been waitin' for the morning. It's been a long hard fight, but I see a brand-new day a-dawnin'. I've been looking for the sunshine, ain't seen it in so long. Everything's gonna work out just fine. Everything's gonna be all right that's been all wrong. And I can see the light of a clear blue morning." And I swear to you on my life, the sky cleared up, it stopped raining, the sun came out, and before I got home, I had written the song "Light of a Clear Blue Morning." It was my song of deliverance. It was my song of freedom, and I knew that God was in it. I knew that I was free.[6]

The song traces this emotional shift with its slow, gospel-like opening that builds to a transcendent, joyful conclusion. Its "caring lyrics" are not religious,[7] but its message of hope and its musical journey from despair to ecstasy reflect the Pentecostal tradition of Dolly's upbringing.

Some of Dolly's inspirational songs that I consider in this chapter are clearly religious, and, in many, Dolly incorporates hymn tunes and lyrics from her childhood. Other songs reflect on faith, turning to God in times of trouble or grappling with doubt. Dolly's faith embraces all people, and in this context I explore her ideas and songs about gender and sexual identity. In other songs, Dolly becomes a motivational speaker. Many of these examples are secular, though tinged with religious fervor. I also consider songs that reflect Dolly's belief that God is immanent in nature. Finally, I investigate the way Dolly intertwines her faith with music and sex and how she expresses ecstasy in her songs. In her uplifting songs, Dolly's optimism is infectious, leading many of her fans, and even some critics, to view her as a saintly healer.

Hymn Tunes and Lyrics

Dolly has vivid memories of the fire and brimstone preaching by her maternal grandfather, Rev. Jake Owens, in the Pentecostal church. "I can remember sitting in church and listening to what a worthless sinner I was, and feeling so ashamed."[8] "I used to be *real* scared of that and I think that inspired me or *depressed* me into writin' all these sad, mournful songs."[9] But despite her fears, she was drawn to worship through the music.

Early in her career, Dolly honored Rev. Owens with her song, "Daddy Was an Old Time Preacher Man," cowritten with her Aunt Dorothy Jo. In this upbeat gospel song, Dolly and Porter sing together, trade lines, and are joined by a choir. The song's charismatic preacher always had a full altar call at his long revivals, took no pay for his work, and preached simply so all could understand. One line stands out: "he preached hell so hot that you could feel the heat." These words recall Dolly's childhood fear during fire and brimstone sermons, and she particularly emphasizes the words "hell so hot" in her performance by accentuating the hissing "h" sounds.

The chorus includes brief interpolations of two different gospel songs: "In the Sweet By and By"[10] and "I'm On My Way to Canaan's Land."[11] At the mention of these iconic tunes, the melody shifts briefly to each hymn, and Dolly's memories become even more vivid as the accompanying choir participates in the call and response of these hymns. The final chorus extends this "you are there" effect as the entire first line of one hymn, not just the title, is sung: "in the sweet by and by we shall meet on that beautiful shore." This extended chorus is repeated to the exuberant accompaniment of an added tambourine, and the praise song continues into a third chorus that fades out.

"Sacred Memories" is another of Dolly's songs that incorporate hymns.[12] Here, Dolly interweaves the music and lyrics of three well-known gospel hymns, and she mentions two more. Each solo verse describes a scene from Dolly's childhood memories, followed by a hymn she sings with choral accompaniment. Verse one takes Dolly back to "that little country church that I love so much." She remembers singing songs in church and then moves seamlessly into "This World Is Not My Home." In fact, the music of the verse itself is so similar to this hymn tune, the distinction between Dolly's memories and the hymn blur.

In the second verse, Dolly, accompanied by banjo and harmonica, recalls the hymns sung when she was saved ("Lord I'm Coming Home") and baptized ("Amazing Grace"). She then quotes a line from "Amazing Grace" before continuing with her next hymn: "and oh how sweet the sound when everybody would join in and sing my favorite song 'If We Never Meet Again.'" Unlike in the first verse, where the hymn flowed directly from the opening lines of the verse with no change in the full accompaniment or energetic rhythm, here the quoted hymn, "If We Never Meet Again," is sung with only a subdued piano and bass in a dramatically slower tempo. The effect is of an a cappella gospel hymn, even though the singers are lightly accompanied. The band and upbeat tempo return at the last word of this verse, and Dolly concludes the song with a verse about her memories of her mama singing "clear and loud" her favorite song, "Power in the Blood." The choir returns yet again to join Dolly in this hymn's exuberant call and response chorus.[13]

On some albums, Dolly included religious songs and hymns from her childhood for their cultural, not just spiritual, connotation. She used the tune of "Wayfaring Stranger" for several secular songs, as discussed in Chapter Five. She also used its melody for the instrumental frame of "Appalachian Memories" and recorded it again, along with "What a Friend We Have in Jesus," on her album *Heartsongs: Live from Home*. She included "In the Sweet By and By" on *Little Sparrow*. Both albums highlighted Dolly's mountain music, and the inclusion of these two hymns enriched and completed Dolly's portrait of her musical culture. Another notable recording of an old-time gospel hymn of Dolly's childhood is "Farther Along" on *Trio*. The hymn fit in with the old-time cultural resonances of the other songs on the album and closes the recording on a spiritual note.

One noteworthy religious song of Dolly's is "When Jesus Comes Calling for Me." Like "Sacred Memories," it contains textual references to hymns, but musically it is more like a traditional Appalachian tune than a gospel hymn. Dolly opens the song by speaking the first two lines in an easy manner, accompanied by strong percussion and laid-back bass and harmonica. This somewhat lazy, front-porch feeling, enhanced by the song's restrained tempo and deliberate rhythm, enhances Dolly's portrait of Zeke, an old man who has lost his family and is nearing death. Dolly starts to sing as Zeke's own words begin: "I'm just sittin' here thinkin' about Jesus, rockin' as my old chair creaks." Zeke's next lines are derived from hymn lyrics, yet are not exact quotes:

> Some glad day I'll fly away when Jesus comes calling for me
> It might be today, it might be tomorrow, maybe one day next week
> I'll soon be done with trouble and sorrow when He comes calling for me
> When Jesus comes calling for me

The first line above references the opening line of "I'll Fly Away": "Some glad morning when this life is o'er, I'll fly away." The third line suggests the hymn

"We'll Soon Be Done with Troubles and Trials." Another line in the second verse is from "Swing Low, Sweet Chariot": "A band of angels in a cloud of glory when Jesus comes calling for me."

But Dolly does not quote the music of these hymns, nor does she evoke a gospel sound. Her melody is reminiscent of the secular folk tune "Cumberland Gap" with its characteristic rise up the major triad to the 6th scale degree before reversing its triadic motion and descending to the tonic note. This common pentatonic melodic formula occurs throughout both the verses and chorus. The folklike melody is suited to this song, which is told not through the experience of worship in church but, instead, through images of rural daily life when Jesus may come calling at any moment:

> I might be in the graveyard walking, talking to my family
> Or I might be plowing in the field down yonder, just old Muley and me

Dolly used this same pentatonic melodic shape in other songs. "Marry Me" also incorporates the move up to the 6th scale degree and back while the melody of the sassy "If You Need Me" is an even closer reimagining of the "Cumberland Gap" tune. The connection between this folk melody and "When Jesus Comes Calling" is another instance of Dolly drawing on tunes from her past as raw material for new songs (as she did with "Wayfaring Stranger").

The hymns Dolly sang in church and the folk songs and tunes she heard at home also merge in other songs. For example, she referenced the tune of "Amazing Grace"[14] in two songs. "I Took Him for Granted" is a secular lament of a woman who has lost her love through her own neglect. Its melody is clearly derived from "Amazing Grace," and Dolly's vocal performance is in a gospel style. The lyrics are also a clever word play on the hymn text: "I once was blind, but now I see/I took him for granted, she took him from me." For "Shine On," Dolly set the melody of "Amazing Grace" to new spiritual words.

Despite Dolly's feelings of fear and alienation spurred by the fire and brimstone view of God, she found comfort in worship and especially in the music. In her songs, Dolly incorporates hymns not only as songs of faith, but for their memories of family and home. They allow Dolly to return to the place of comfort and safety of her childhood. The cultural resonances of these hymns are a source of strength apart from their theology. Like her other songs that mine memories of home—"Daddy's Working Boots," "Old Black Kettle," "My Tennessee Mountain Home"—these religious songs are part of Dolly's nostalgia for an idyllic past where troubles could be overcome by faith and family.

Reflections on Faith

Dolly's relationship to religion, faith, and spirituality is complex: "God and I have a great relationship, but we both see other people."[15] She fleshed out this humorous comment in her autobiography: "I am not a *very* religious person, although I grew up with a very religious background. I am highly spiritual, and there is a great difference. Often, I feel religion is so organized and categorized that it loses sight of the true love of the spirit."[16] As she said in her commencement speech to the graduates of the University of Tennessee: "I always call that spiritual center that we all have inside us, I call that my 'God core.' In a way, it's where heaven and earth kinda meet. So you should always listen to that 'God core' and care for others, and then you truly will be something special."[17]

Dolly's comments reflect what Deborah Vansau McCauley says about Christians in the Appalachian Mountains: "By 'religion,' mountain Christians usually mean organized religion or denominations, which they often call simply 'big churches.' In fact, they rarely speak of religion. Instead, they talk about faith as the conscious discipline of embodying through their personal speech and actions, their own words and deeds, God's gift of saving grace for themselves and each other."[18] Accordingly, Dolly once commented about growing up in the Church of God: "We never held to no doctrine really, except scripture. . . . We just believed to 'make a joyful noise unto the Lord,' and that's what we did."[19] One way Dolly enacts her spirituality is through the act of songwriting. She composes "alone because that's my time with God. That's my creative time. . . . My writing is just a very spiritual time for me."[20] She also expresses her ideas about faith in some of her songs seeking guidance during times of doubt.

"The Seeker"

Dolly's song "The Seeker" is a touchstone of her thinking about faith. In public remarks about her religious beliefs, she often draws on the lyrics of this song, italicized in the following quote: "I am certainly not a Christian" although "I do believe, I know there is a God and He is still the best friend I got in the world. . . . I just could not decide whether I wanted to be a Christian or not. So I was out in the kitchen a-cookin' and I started thinkin' about how serious that was, so—*I am a seeker, a poor sinful creature, there is none weaker than I am, I am a seeker and you are a teacher.*"[21] Thus, Dolly defines herself as a "seeker" who strives, but often fails, to live a Christian life.

"The Seeker" is a prayer for guidance and teaching. While asking for God's guidance, the singer acknowledges she is a sinner, a bad seed, a loser, and is weak. She juxtaposes herself as a seeker while God is a guiding spirit with multiple identities: teacher, reacher, keeper, leader, and her last hope. The song encompasses two different musical affects over an active bass line. Most of the verses are very restrained; the melody rises triadically, often with just one note prolonged per line. Additionally, the harmonic motion is static with the tonic chord (I) sounded for most of the verse, interrupted only by a subdominant chord (IV) that prolongs the tonic. The real harmonic motion comes with the dominant chord (V) at the cadence at the end of each verse. This sparse harmonic and melodic movement, combined with the bouncing bass line, creates an undercurrent of energy simmering below a tightly lidded surface. Significantly, these musically restrained verses outline the singer's weaknesses and deficiencies and align with the notion of a humble plea for guidance.

There are three instances, each of the three-line choruses, where this controlled energy begins to bubble up and the plea for guidance becomes urgent; the music intimates salvation is at hand. The melody suddenly rises, the dynamics increase, and Dolly sings with much more excitement in her voice for the first two lines:

> Reach out and lead me
> Guide me and keep me, Lord
> In the shelter of your care each day

Just as it seems she might unleash the music into a rapturous gospel moment, the intensity suddenly abates in the third line. And this siphoning off of energy occurs on lyrics that humble the sinner in God's sheltering care. Dolly repeats this pattern for these lyrics a second time after several more subdued verses. For the final chorus, she changes the lyrics, giving them a more pastoral depiction of salvation:

> You are a mountain
> From which there flows a fountain
> So let its water wash my sins away

But even here, the last line's energy ebbs, humbly falling back like the others. Each time this pattern occurs, the listener expects *this* will be the one when Dolly lets the music soar, like in so many of her songs, such as "Light of a Clear Blue Morning." This never comes about, and the song ends as it began rather than bursting open for a transcendent payoff. The song's effect then is not the emotional transport of salvation, but humility in accepting guidance. In this way, "The Seeker" is unusual since Dolly more frequently closes her uplifting songs with a sense of certainty.

"Raven Dove" and "Hello God"

Dolly returns to hymns and scripture in her songs when events shake her faith, as she did in "Raven Dove" and "Hello God." In these responses to the terrorist attacks of September 11, 2001, Dolly makes no direct references to the events of 9/11, unlike most popular and country songs about that day. With spiritual rather than patriotic lyrics, these songs are not on lists of 9/11 songs found online. Dolly's songs encompass feelings of fear, frustration, and hope greater than just a response to a specific event. This lack of specificity accounts for why fans across the political spectrum can embrace these songs.

"Raven Dove" is a hope for peace through God's intervention, not a song of vengeance, flag-waving, or musing about the lost towers and the voids left in New York City, Washington D.C., and Shanksville, Pennsylvania. Dolly writes of a raven of darkness being transformed into a white dove of peace, calling to mind the raven and dove from the story of Noah's Ark in which the two birds were harbingers of deliverance from the flood.[22] Musically, the song has two different affects like "The Seeker." Verses 1, 2, 4, and 6 are in a stop-time waltz rhythm with only two chords undulating between major and modal sonorities. The melody has a major 3rd, but it also contains the flatted 7th scale degree, and the harmony further includes a flatted 6th scale degree. This modal mixture creates a meditative and static atmosphere, particularly because the major key tonic note is played throughout as a pedal note, thus making the entire opening section a prolonged tonic harmony. This mixed-mode sonority also gives the song an old-world feeling that matches Dolly's use of archaic biblical language. To this music, Dolly imagines a world where "the hungry shall be fed, the aimless shall be led . . . the last shall be first."[23]

The melody of the contrasting verses 3 and 5, in a stronger triple meter, recalls the melody of the chorus of "The Grass Is Blue." In verse 3—"weapons to plowshares, hate turns to love"[24]—Dolly energetically sings a more expansive melody about a presence "descending from heaven, he'll sweep down to us in a radiant splendor." And for special effect, she singles out the word *radiant* with a quick flip of her voice up a 5th to a high G. This musical vitality quickly subsides, and the opening music returns as Dolly imagines a better day to lyrics borrowed from hymn titles (shown in italics):

> Oh, there will come a day when *I'll fly away*
> Forever to be in his keep
> Eternal life *in the sweet by and by*
> When raven dove, raven dove speaks

After this second meditation, the more spirited melody returns in verse 5 with lyrics drawn from scripture: "When lambs walk with lions, a child tames the beast, Nations shall gather and bow at his feet."[25] This verse is longer than its previous iteration, and the increased intensity is marked by the same shift of melodic direction Dolly uses in the final verse of "The Grass in Blue" when, at its climactic moment in the third verse at "rivers run backwards," the melody rises rather than descends. As the melody of "Raven Dove" rises unexpectedly, rather than descending as it had earlier, the energy grows until it bursts open into three *hallelujahs* marked by the same vocal flip up a 5th that Dolly had used on *radiant*. The song ends on a more subdued and pensive note with the return of the opening material as Dolly quotes from Revelation: "Raven dove, behold he cometh in the clouds, And every eye shall see him."[26]

"Hello God" is a plea for guidance in the face of the terrorist attack, which Dolly does not name explicitly. Rather, Dolly begins this gospel-style song with a crisis of faith: "Hello God, are you out there? Can you hear me, are you listenin' anymore? . . . I have questioned your existence, my resistance leaves me cold." The lyrics allude to the 9/11 attacks in the second verse, and yet Dolly does not place blame on the attackers alone with her use of the second person *we* throughout.

> This old world has gone to pieces
> Can we fix it, is there time?
> Hate and violence just increases
> We're so selfish, cruel and blind
> We fight and kill each other
> In your name, defending you
> Do you love some more than others?
> We're so lost and confused

Returning to the opening doubts of the song, Dolly moves into a chorus she sings three times to changed words, but all with the same sentiment: a plea for God's help in the face of humanity's mistakes—"the free will you have given we have made a mockery of." Although the striving and declamatory music remains the same through these three choruses, each one grows in intensity through the interpolations of the gospel choir that accompanies most of the second half of the song. As with other songs, Dolly references Biblical language, and the last verse ends with her final plea borrowed from scripture: "please forgive us, for we know not what we do." Dolly said the song is "about how we only run to God, just like you run to your parents, when you need something or when you're in trouble."[27] Although her faith is shaken, Dolly does not turn away from God, but prays in earnest for guidance and mercy in granting the human race "one more chance to prove ourselves to you."

Gender and Sexual Identities

As a child, Dolly "felt a need for God and always wanted to have a relationship with him." But she "was the ultimate nightmare for a fundamentalist Christian out to save souls" because she was "a kid with her own opinions," even though it was considered a sin to question what she was taught. She watched her grandfather as well as her devout mother and knew "the way they worshiped God worked—for them. . . . So I had no problem with wanting to be like them in that way. I guess what I resisted was the way God was presented," as a lightning bolt wielding angry old man.[28] "You kind of grew up in a horrid atmosphere about fear of religion," Dolly remembers. 'We thought God was a *monster* in the sky."[29] This terrifying picture, combined with the equally frightening fire and brimstone sermons, kept Dolly "constantly walking on the brink of the fiery pits of hell."[30]

In her fear and confusion, Dolly also experienced and ultimately resisted the culture of judgment in her church, where she was dogged by the constant questions: "Are you prepared to meet God? You could be killed on the way home today. Are you ready to be judged?" Dolly eventually concluded: "I guessed I had damned well better be ready to be judged, because it was obvious I was going to be every day of my life. To me, it seemed like a lot of people took the Bible too literally. But at the same time they were selective in which parts they clung to with such conviction. It seemed to me like the part about 'judge not, lest you be judged' got kind of swept under the rug."[31] Her childhood ideas about this hypocrisy have carried over to her beliefs, actions, and songs as an adult.

The most obvious way Dolly rejects a theology of judgment is in her attitude toward issues of gender and sexual identity. Dolly has a large LGBTQ+ fan base,[32] and she enjoys the connection she feels with that community. "They've made me the poster child, I think, only because I'm so outspoken as far as just being accepting of people in general."[33] Dolly also acknowledged that this position puts her outside the mainstream of many in the country music industry. In the 1990s, she had this to say about the way the industry treated k.d. lang when she came out as a lesbian: "A lot of the real dyed-in-the-wool redneck people are very conservative and very religious. . . . She's so out there that I think she frightened those people."[34] Around that same time, Sandollar Productions, a company Dolly started with her openly gay manager Sandy Gallin, won an Academy Award for Best Documentary Feature for the film *Common Threads: Stories from the Quilt* (1989).[35] It chronicled the history of the Names Project AIDS Memorial Quilt. Dolly's connection to the project was veiled. She admits "in show business you have to be diplomatic,"[36] and she manages to walk a fine line regarding LGBTQ+ issues. Dolly usually responds to questions about her support of the LGBTQ+ community with humor and statements about being nonjudgmental. For example, when asked why she did not cancel her *Pure and Simple* tour concerts in North Carolina in 2016 following the controversial HB2 legislation regarding the use of public restrooms by trans* people, she replied: "I think everybody should be treated with respect. I don't judge people. I try not to get too caught up in all the controversy of things. I hope that everybody gets a chance to be who and what they are. I just know if I have to pee, I'm gonna pee. I don't care where it's gonna be."[37]

Despite her diplomatic stance on these issues, she still faces criticism from some faith-based communities: "Having a big gay following, I get hate mail and threats. Some people are blind or ignorant, and you can't be that prejudiced and hateful and go through this world and still be happy."[38] For example, in 2005 her song, the sweetly flirty "Sugar Hill," was included on a compilation album, *Love Rocks*, to benefit the Human Rights Campaign. *The Baptist Press* called out Dolly, Mandy Moore, and The Dixie Chicks for their involvement in the project "that benefits the nation's largest homosexual activist organization." The title of the article mentioned only Dolly, singling her out for special censure, and a full list of participants was a thinly veiled threat of boycott.[39] Dolly's response to fundamentalist communities about their positions on LGBTQ+ issues is to question their ideas of what a good Christian is:

> I think we should be accepting and loving. We're all God's children. We are who we are, and we should be allowed to be who we are. . . . I keep saying, well if you're the fine Christian that you think you are, why are you judging people? . . . We're not God; we're not judges. . . . And we're not supposed to take vengeance on other people. That's God's job. So I got too much to do of my own to try to do God's work too.[40]

Dolly faces challenges in striking a balance among the range of religious beliefs and sexual identities of her fans. One of Dolly's nieces, Jada Star Andersen, who performs in the "My People" show at Dollywood, explained, "It's that thing where she is as loving as she can be about it, but there's also a lot of people in our family who don't like it. It's a line she walks."[41] Speaking about threats from the Ku Klux Klan regarding "Gay Days" at Dollywood—not founded or endorsed by Dolly, but not prohibited either—Dolly said "When it first started there were people giving us threats, I still get threats. But like I said, I'm in business. I just don't feel like I have to explain myself. I love everybody."[42] Responding to attention garnered by a 2011 incident at Dollywood's Splash Country water park near Dollywood when a woman wearing a T-shirt saying "marriage is so gay" was asked to turn the shirt inside out to conceal the message, Dolly issued a statement. She explained the policy was to limit the likelihood of fights about politics in the park and to protect patrons, including those wearing the clothing. Her comments included an apology: "I am truly sorry for the hurt or embarrassment regarding the gay and lesbian T-shirt incident at Dollywood's Splash Country recently. Everyone knows of my personal support of the gay and lesbian community. Dollywood is a family park and all families are welcome."[43]

When writer-director Duncan Tucker was making the film *Transamerica* (2005), about a transwoman, he asked Dolly to write a song for the film, saying "it should be a song that has to do with redemption. It should be a song you could sing in churches and you could sing in dancehalls."[44] The song, "Travelin' Thru," has a relentless forward locomotion brought about not only through its easy canter, jaunty bass line, catchy rhythmic hook, and short phrases, but also through the chorus with its kinetic repeat of the word "travelin'." In a clever variation of this frequent repetition, Dolly piles up rhymes in the line "As I'm stumblin', tumblin', wonderin', as I'm travelin' thru." Dolly casts the journey described in the song as a pilgrimage, and she references the hymn "Wayfaring Stranger," once more calling on the archetype of the lost soul striving for home.[45]

> Like a poor wayfaring stranger that they speak about in song
> I'm just a weary pilgrim trying to find what feels like home

She does not specifically name the nature of the journey of the main character in the film, but her lyrics take on an enriched meaning when heard in the film's context:

> I'm out here on my journey trying to make the most of it
> I'm a puzzle; I must figure out where all of my pieces fit

> Goodbye little children, goodnight you handsome men
> Farewell to all you ladies and to all who knew me when

God made me for a reason and nothing is in vain
Redemption comes in many shapes with many kinds of pain
Oh sweet Jesus if you're listening, keep me ever close to you

Dolly said she "wanted it to be a song that would stand on its own, even if there wasn't a movie, so it's really just about asking for help, asking for guidance."[46] "Travelin' Thru" was nominated as Best Original Song for an Academy Award and a Golden Globe Award, and it won Best Original Song from The Phoenix Film Critics Society.

Dolly explained her connection to this film, as well as to her LGBTQ+ audience, as rooted in her own sense of feeling judged as an outsider. She often says she felt different from others as a child, and she believes those experiences shaped her attitudes toward others. "I'm just a very open person. I'm not judgmental of anybody. Maybe that's just because I have always been different and always strived for acceptance and understanding."[47] In particular, Dolly knows the sting of judgment entrenched in the church of her youth: "It was a sin to even pluck your eyebrows, and they thought it was a sin for me to be there looking like Jezebel."[48] Thus, Dolly responds not with judgment of others, but with a live-and-let-live philosophy: she says she loves "the God core in all people. And I know that is in the center of us all, so I just try to accept people for who they are, whatever that is."[49]

Dolly put this creed in her song "Family," cowritten with Carl Perkins, some fifteen years before she wrote "Travelin' Thru." While the lyrics are outdated by current standards, her inclusion of gay family members was a progressive statement on her 1991 album, *Eagle When She Flies*.

When it's family, you forgive them for they know not what they do
When it's family, you accept them, 'cause you have no choice but to . . .
Some are preachers, some are gay
Some are addicts, drunks and strays
But not a one is turned away, when it's family

A more recent example of Dolly's inclusive stance is in her 2019 Netflix series, *Heartstrings*. Several episodes include gay, lesbian, and trans* people, and one, "Two Doors Down," centers on a gay man whose mother struggles to accept him. Dolly introduced the episode with these thoughts about her time on the road earlier in her career: "Being gone all that time from my home and family, well that was tough. But what I found out on the road was a whole new family with bands and crews that were made up of all kinds of people who were different colors, gay, lesbian, transgender, and all different faiths. But it didn't matter as long as we all loved each other and got along. And we did, and we still do."[50]

In their documentary *Hollywood to Dollywood* (2012), Dolly fans and gay twin brothers Gary and Larry Lane spotlight the way Dolly has touched, inspired, and sustained many people, particularly those in the LGBTQ+ community. Along their road trip from California to Tennessee, in their RV named Jolene, the Lanes met and interviewed people who attested to Dolly's comforting role in their lives. One interviewee was gay actor Leslie Jordan who had this to say about Dolly's appeal to gay men in particular:

> Gay men love flash. I don't know what that's about. But gay men like anything that sparkles and glitters. But there's a genuineness about her, and I think she's just like a big ole drag queen. You know, she gets up in the morning, and nails, and hair, and all that. . . . It's not easy growing up homosexual in the hills of Tennessee. I look back and it really is a wonder that I'm sane. . . . She would give a free concert once a year at the high school auditorium in Sevierville. This is *long* before Dollywood, . . . this'd be '72. This is before Dolly the movie star. She would come out on stage and she'd say [gesturing toward his hair], "What's a country girl without her haystack?" And we would scream and cry. . . . Oh, she'd sing "Jolene" and we'd cry. Then she'd sing "Coat of Many Colors" and we'd cry. . . . We just have our divas, be it Barbra Streisand or Bette Midler. They're always larger than life, you know, goin' all the way back to Judy Garland.[51]

Jordan's comments explain Dolly's appeal to the young, deeply closeted gay men who lived in isolation in the Tennessee hills in the early 1970s and, by extension, to the larger LGBTQ+ community. In his recollections Jordan became part of a "we" at Dolly's performances and part of a larger gay community that included Dolly in its pantheon of divas.

While some country music artists have more recently spoken out in support of LGBTQ+ persons, Dolly has been a prominent LGBTQ+ diva and ally for decades. She expresses her convictions about LGBTQ+ issues through songs, believing that "art can change minds."[52] She also speaks her mind in interviews: "Love is love. And everybody should be allowed to have their love however they have it," Dolly says. "We're just born to love, and we should always be open to it."[53] Through her commitment to this idea and by accepting everyone without judgment, she opens up a space for her listeners to do the same.

"Better Get to Livin'": Dolly as Motivational Speaker

Although Dolly was raised in a Pentecostal church, she says her faith is focused on uplifting people outside the context of organized religion: "I'm not a religious person, but I'm very spiritual. I just try to have a good attitude and bring everybody up with me."[54] Accordingly, some of Dolly's musical expressions of spirituality transcend her use of the lyrics and melodies of her Pentecostal background, and she writes inspirational songs that are secular. Many, like "Light of a Clear Blue Morning," have messages of hope and encouragement that are not overtly grounded in faith or theology. Dolly is explicit about her purpose for these songs: "I can't save the world, but I might be able to save someone today if I can put them in a better mood. The music's designed to be like a ray of sunshine for all those folks in the dark."[55] These songs are an antidote to her tragic songs that witness people's sorrow.

One such song from early in her career, "A Better Place to Live," is Dolly's country version of the hippie generation's sentiments found in songs like "I'd Like to Teach the World to Sing (In Perfect Harmony)" from 1971 and "Get Together" from the mid-1960s. Dolly sings breezily about all people joining hands and singing in harmony. A light-hearted riff on "la la la" in harmony with backup singers bridges the buoyant verses about making the world a better place. The more rhythmically accented choruses emphasize looking for peace through loving one another rather than judging. Another round of "la, la, la" closes out the song with a fade-out as everyone metaphorically sings together in this better world.

Decades later, a song with a similar message from *Better Day* (2011), "Together You and I," was released as a single and a music video. Dolly had used these lyrics in a 1974 country duo with Porter Wagoner, but for the 2011 recording she set the lyrics to a new upbeat melody. While the lyrics alone of this country pop song might be taken as a straightforward love song, as discussed in Chapter Five, in the video it becomes an anthem celebrating the connection among all people. Making the most of the metaphor of a bridge, much of the video was filmed on the John Seigenthaler Pedestrian Bridge in Nashville, Tennessee. Hundreds of extras of all ages, genders, races, sexualities, and ethnicities lined the bridge, one by one taking hands as Dolly walked the bridge, singing, and finally joining the line at the end, taking the hand of a little boy. Scenes of others joining hands in locations around the world were also included.

Dolly's inspirational book *Dream More: Celebrate the Dreamer in You*, based on her commencement address at the University of Tennessee, encourages readers to "dream more, learn more, care more, be more." Her song "Try" includes this philosophy:

> I've always been a dreamer and dreams are special things
> But dreams are of no value if they're not equipped with wings

When the book was published, one interviewer asked her whether she could imagine being a preacher herself one day. She replied, "I'd be a good motivational speaker. Incorporate my music and my stories and help uplift people.... But I'm not that religious."[56] One critic spoke directly to the notion of Dolly as motivational speaker: she is "like the life coach you never realized you needed."[57]

Dolly takes on this role in "Better Get to Livin'," cowritten with Kent Wells. In the video for the song, Dolly plays a performer in an old-style carnival sideshow who entertains her audience of depressed women by giving them a pep talk about getting their lives in order. At the outset, in her upbeat country pop style, she addresses the listener directly, saying she is often asked what her secret is to her good attitude. She explains and disperses advice—though claiming with a punning wink she is not the Dalai Lama—about not giving into negativity in life but, instead, focusing on the solution as found in the song's title. The chorus spins out clever rhymes on how to get down to the business of living, starting with forgiving. Elaborating on her trope of Dream More, she revels in rhyming wordplay:

> You better stop whinin', pinin'
> Get your dreams in line
> And then just shine, design, refine
> Until they come true

In the midst of this merriment, Dolly nonetheless reminds her listeners when things really get rough in life the answer is to pray each day. At this point, as the song is winding down in what seems to be its final chorus, Dolly veers sharply into a coda with this admonishment: "The day we're born we start to die/Don't waste one minute of this life." This line is striking: the message is sobering—we are already dying—but the music remains upbeat. Dolly guarantees this lyric stands out by singing a new descending melody composed especially for this line. Dolly simultaneously has listeners confront their own limited time on earth but keeps her warning lighthearted so the song still ends optimistically.

The lyrics of "Better Get to Livin'" target women in particular. In the video, Dolly's audience is all women; in the second verse, Dolly enacts a kitchen table encounter with a girlfriend who is crying about her life; and in the song's bridge Dolly outlines frustrations in life that are more stereotypically female than male: "your house is a mess and your wardrobe's way outdated ... overweight and underpaid, underappreciated."

Dolly's syncopated pop song from 1977, "Two Doors Down," somewhat obliquely shares its message with "Better Get to Livin'." It was one of her first crossover hits, an unusual example of one of her pop hits that she composed. Seemingly a lighthearted confection about partying, Dolly embeds another "better get to living" message in the song. Realizing that crying alone in her room after a breakup is useless, the singer decides to go down the hall to join the party. Once she pulls herself together, stops wallowing in post-breakup tears, and gets to livin', she finds a new love.

In "Shine Like the Sun," Dolly again pitches a motivational song to a female audience even though, as before, its underlying message need not be gender-specific. Written for *9 to 5: The Musical*, this song is the freedom rally of the main female characters. Doralee, Judy, and Violet each sing a verse about the way she has been mistreated by their sexist male boss. Doralee, Dolly's alter-ego in the show, sings an especially poignant and clever autobiographical verse:

> Under this hair is a brain not that you'd ever care
> And you only see tits but get this, there's a heart under there
> A heart that you've broken and ripped out more times than a few
> Well ole double-D Doralee's gonna stick it to you

Each character also sings a tailor-made chorus bookended with the more general message of the song's title: she will overcome the mistreatment and will "shine like the sun." For her own recording of the song on *Better Day*, Dolly reworked the lyrics, making them more general and retaining only one verse from the musical's version.

Dolly says she takes emotional risks to be able to write such affirming songs: "I've been through everything, you know, so I can write a positive song like 'Better Get to Livin'' because that's my attitude. But that doesn't mean I'm happy all the time. You can't be a deep and serious songwriter without feelings. You kinda have to live with your feelings out on your sleeve and get hurt more than most people. The fear I might get hurt means I might not be able to write another song."[58] Speaking about *Better Day*, Dolly said she "wanted to do an album that would be very uplifting and positive, as well as inspirational."[59] "I know I can sing a good sad song, but people hate to hear me sing them. I wanted to do something people would want to hear."[60] Of course, Dolly's listeners do not really hate her sad songs. As I suggest in Chapter Seven, tragic songs can be healing in different ways, and people welcome their restorative power. With her inspirational songs, Dolly takes the next step. After reflecting people's pain, she offers solutions for how to overcome difficulties with hopeful messages that can lessen suffering, and listeners find these songs equally affirming.

"Everything's Beautiful (In Its Own Way)": Finding Music and God in Nature

Dolly's earliest music-making was in response to sounds of nature. "I would hear the katydids, I'd kind of get into that rhythm. I would sing with that if we was popping snap beans, you know, anything that made a rhythm. Or the birds that were singing. I'd kind of do harmony along with them."[61] Dolly has always found inspiration and solace in the sounds, colors, and beauty of the natural world. Such bucolic settings are also where she experiences the divine: "I have never ceased to be amazed by nature. Anybody who spends any time at all observing nature has to believe there is a God."[62] She expresses this connection through a number of songs that do not draw on the Pentecostal language of worship but rather link the natural world and God. Making no mention of Jesus or heaven, and quoting no scripture or hymns, Dolly revels in the wonder that she sees in nature through a quasi-pantheistic lens. These songs are not just descriptions of flowers, landscapes, birds, and butterflies; rather, they are sketches of color, movement, and shape reflecting a spiritual presence.

Dolly's songs about God in nature can be understood as her way to move from religious doctrine to her "God core." In these songs, she escapes from the judging, frightening Christian God of her childhood—the monster in the sky—in a way that is reminiscent of Celie in Alice Walker's *The Color Purple*. Celie, who is afraid of a monotheistic God, experiences a conversion to a pantheist outlook when she accepts Shug's ideas that God resides in nature and everyone is connected to the divine. With her own nod to pantheism, Dolly once again draws on nineteenth-century tropes as she does in her dark songs. Dolly's romanticist celebration of nature is akin to writings of Wordsworth and the American Transcendentalists, that the divine pervades all of nature, and this belief is shaped by her Christian upbringing and her belief in God as the architect of creation.

"Everything's Beautiful (In Its Own Way)," one of her earliest songs written on a fishing trip with her husband,[63] is a classic example of Dolly's pantheistic lyrics about the divine beauty of nature. When Dolly first met Porter Wagoner, she sang it for him, thinking he was interested in buying some of her songs. He later said, "the song told me so much about her! I knew that if a person could sit down and write a song like that, they'd have to have a real soul inside 'em."[64] The first recording released of this song was her duet with Willie Nelson, which went to #7 on the country chart in 1982. Dolly had previously recorded a solo version of the song in 1969, but it was not widely released until 2009. It is unfortunate that this earlier version of the song has not received the attention it deserves, since it is a hidden gem in her catalogue.

Dolly once described "Everything's Beautiful (In Its Own Way)" as "kinda folky/sacred/country/pop."[65] The song, primarily in the Mixolydian mode, is indeed folksy with a lilting meter and melodic structure similar to "In the Good Old Days (When Times Were Bad)" as discussed in Chapter Two. The melody of the verses descends stepwise from scale degree 5 to 1 with one note per measure in the first and third lines. The primary sonority is the gentle rocking between the tonic (I) and the flatted 7th (♭VII) chords. These musical gestures suggest stillness rather than movement. For the chorus, Dolly breaks from this modal sonority and melodic pattern briefly, shifting to the major key for the chorus' first two lines. But she brings back the melody and modal harmony of the verse in the final two lines of the chorus, which ends with the title line as a refrain. It is not surprising that Dolly emphasizes this modal sonority—often linked in her music to her mountain heritage—since the rustic charm of the music is an apt setting for lyrics surveying the beauty of the natural world.

The relative stillness of the harmony and the narrow range and stepwise motion of the melody also match the sentiment of the lyrics, which are striking in several ways. First, Dolly composes a clever internal rhyme in every other line: *over/clover* and *moody/beauty*.

> When I look out over a green field of clover
> Or watch the sun set at the end of the day
> I get kind of moody when I see such beauty
> And everything's beautiful in its own way

This pace of the rhyme reinforces the lilt of the rhythm and enlivens the stepwise melody. Second, Dolly does not write only about conventionally beautiful images. She also describes the beauty of brown falling leaves and a "black summer windstorm that uproots the harvest and hurls it away." Even here, Dolly sees beauty in the destructive, angry, and dangerous side of nature. Finally, the lyrics mention God as the creator that makes "each thing beautiful in its own way." But this line occurs only once in the song, at the end of the final verse. As in many of her songs, Dolly saves the revelation for the conclusion. The introduction of a divine presence is heard at this point: synthesized strings suggesting an organ. Thus, Dolly emphasizes the natural world rather than God, though she eventually offers a divine explanation for all she sees.

"Early Morning Breeze" is a better-known example of Dolly's pantheistic approach to spirituality. In it, she sings of waking early and running to a sunny meadow where she visits with butterflies and delights in a variety of flowers that are still dew-kissed. As in "Everything's Beautiful," the lyrics focus entirely on the pastoral images until the last line of the second verse where she reveals the divinity in all this beauty. The meadow is Dolly's source of strength and her chapel where she feels close to God. "Early Morning Breeze," which she recorded twice in the 1970s, is a light country pop song with a prominent bass. The verses of both versions are more subdued than the lively chorus with its higher range and more active rhythm section. Dolly includes the modal flatted 7th chord (♭VII) once again for her melody of the closing refrain at the end of each verse and chorus: "early morning breeze."

Yet another song celebrating divinity in nature is "God's Coloring Book" from her 1977 album *Here You Come Again,* which was #1 on the Top Country Album chart for nine weeks. Although the album included her first major pop hits—"Here You Come Again" (written by Barry Mann and Cynthia Weil) and her own "Two Doors Down"—Dolly also recorded two songs rooted in her more traditional material: "Me and Little Andy" and "God's Coloring Book." In the latter song, Dolly muses about the various colors in nature—golden sunshine, silver dew, red and orange flowers, purple sunset—as well as the gray hair of an old man and a baby's pink cheeks. She also reprises an idea from "Everything's Beautiful" by including a black sky and brown leaves. However, unlike in "Everything's Beautiful" and "Early Morning Breeze," Dolly weaves God's presence throughout the song with the refrain in which she realizes the world around her is "God's coloring book." Further, she devotes one verse to prayer, as she did in only one line of "Early Morning Breeze." Dolly emphasizes her prayer by interrupting the flow and singing in a free rhythm accompanied only by a strummed guitar at every chord change. The rhythm resumes with her next lines, which sum up her expansive outlook on God's presence in nature: God completely surrounds her in this colorful world.

In contrast to the previous two songs, "God's Coloring Book" is a three-chord, folk-country song, and it does not include modal inflections. Instead, Dolly draws on a style reminiscent of "Coat of Many Colors." Like this earlier song about her childhood, "God's Coloring Book" is folklike and intimate, accompanied primarily by a finger-picked acoustic guitar and using a simple three-chord harmonic structure that emphasizes gentle moves to the subdominant chord (IV). The songs are also linked through their idea of God's love being manifest in colors—either in the natural world or through a coat lovingly made from scraps of cloth.

Critic Bruce Cook called "God's Coloring Book" pious and concluded that it was "as heinous as any of her past offenses against good taste."[66] Recall that when he wrote this critique, he also included "Me and Little Andy," as discussed in Chapter Seven. Just as Cook scoffed at Dolly's sentimental song of an abandoned child, he rejected Dolly's unabashed statement of her faith through nature as maudlin and unseemly. "God's Coloring Book" may not be to Cook's taste but, when heard in the context of Dolly's frequent comments on the comforting beauty of nature in her reminiscences of childhood poverty, its earnestness is understandable.

If we take seriously Dolly's conviction that God is immanent in nature, our understanding of her other songs that trade in these images is enriched. "Love Is Like a Butterfly" is the most obvious example, but Dolly's catalogue is filled with lyrics that use the natural world as metaphor, especially in songs about love, as discussed in Chapter Five. Whether celebrating the excitement of newfound passion, the comfort of a familiar touch, or the heartbreak of abandonment and loss, for Dolly, romantic feelings often intertwine with scenes of sunshine, birds, and butterflies. While some may believe these images from nature are clichés, they are not formulaic components of songwriting to Dolly. Rather, they reflect her pantheistic outlook that frequently colors her songs about both faith and love. Her language of butterflies, flowers, and rainbows is woven throughout her songs that combine spirituality and romantic love in a tangle of sensations and desires.

For example, in 1996, Dolly revisited "More than I Can Say" from 1987, giving it a new arrangement and lyrics for "Unlikely Angel," as discussed in Chapter Two. "More than I Can Say" is a hushed celebration of love, which Dolly compares to gentle breezes, rainbows, birdsongs, and sunrises in the opening verses. The chorus is a more expansive, soaring section about the steadfastness of her lover. When she returns to the more subdued melody of the verses, she replaces natural images with erotic ones, touching and kissing her lover's skin and making love that brings her "into ecstasy." The return of the chorus continues with lyrics that fuse friendship with sexual love that fulfills her fantasies. The song's beautiful melody and lyrics are set to a lushly-orchestrated arrangement of strings and winds.

"Unlikely Angel," with its subtle poetic enjambments, reprises the melody of "More than I Can Say," but without the complex orchestral harmonies. It has a folklike atmosphere, a slightly faster tempo, and is accompanied by a string band of guitar, mandolin, and fiddle, with light vocal harmony. "Unlikely Angel" also revels in love, but now the elements of nature are replaced with sacred imagery. God has sent an unlikely angel with heaven in its eyes, and Dolly wonders

"How long have you been there for me, I once was blind but now I see." These two love songs exemplify Dolly's practice of revisiting songs, mining them for melodic inspiration. They are also compelling illustrations of how Dolly blends love with the spiritual beauties of the natural world and the ways she merges love with the sacred. It is understandable that Dolly would return to her melody of "More than I Can Say" as a blueprint for "Unlikely Angel," since they both use pictorial language that gathers nature and spirituality into expressions of love.

"Pure and Simple": Faith, Music, and Sex

Dolly's complex relationship to religion, faith, and spirituality—whether as a struggling Pentecostal Christian, an ecumenical life coach, or a romanticist/pantheist who experiences the divine in nature—is further complicated by the way she intertwines her faith with music and sex. She writes in her autobiography: "All my life . . . I have been driven by three things; three mysteries I wanted to know more about; three passions. They are God, music, and sex. I would like to say that I have listed them in the order of their importance to me, but their pecking order is subject to change without warning. In my heart of hearts, I always know that God comes first. But in my body of bodies, some other urges can be absolutely irresistible."[67] For Dolly, these passions are inseparable in her experiences, her performances, and her songs. But the untroubled coexistence of these elements—God, music, and sex—was hard won.

As a child in her grandfather's church, Dolly often wondered what she had done that was so sinful she would be consigned to hell. She concluded the sin was sex, and not just the act of sex, something she had not yet experienced. She believed that "somehow just being aware that it exists feels like a grievous sin in itself. . . . The sex drive being as difficult to resist as it is, and having been so branded as evil, can give a thinking child a sense of helplessness."[68] But her attitude changed while she was still very young. As discussed earlier, Dolly often spent time in an old abandoned church playing a piano that had "a cracked sounding board and rusting strings" by banging the strings with a mallet to get a drone for her melodies. On the church walls someone had scrawled sexual graffiti. Her own analysis of these moments is revealing.

So, here in one place was God, music, and sex. My fascination was complete. . . . And so I would sing hymns to God for a while and look at dirty pictures for a while and pray for a while, and one day as I prayed in earnest, I broke through some sort of spirit wall and found God. . . . Here in this place of seemingly confusing images, I had found real truth. I had come to know that it was all right for me to be a sexual being. I knew that was one of the things God meant for me to be. I also knew that my dreams of making music, of traveling outside the Smokies and pursuing a greater purpose, were not silly childhood ideas but grand real schemes ordained and cocreated by my newfound heavenly father. I was validated. I was sanctified. I was truly reborn. I was happy. I thanked God long and loud for having shown himself to me. . . . I had found God. I had found Dolly Parton. And I loved them both.[69]

Relating this same story years later, Dolly added, "once I made that connection I never turned it loose. It's like a golden glowing thread for me that just runs through my life."[70] Dolly's sanctification, her rebirth, is rooted in her recognition and acceptance that her three passions—sex, music, and God—are not mutually exclusive but are, in fact, bound together in a powerful triad of desire, longing, and the transcendent.

How does Dolly express these entwined passions in her music? Of course, there are love songs that blend a divine presence with romance. As we have seen, her use of similar natural images for both romantic love and God reveal this connection indirectly, and her song "Pure and Simple" more overtly makes the link. Here, forgoing butterflies and sunshine, Dolly uses the words *sacred*, *sublime*, and *divine* to describe the way love feels, and she does not use these words metaphorically. In other songs, Dolly writes more explicitly about sexual desire: "Touch Your Woman," "It's All Wrong, but It's All Right," and "Baby I'm Burnin'." Moreover, Dolly's sexualized persona is usually the first thing most people notice. But the sexuality Dolly means when she links sex with music and God is not about her image or even her songs about sex.

Dolly is suggesting a more expansive experience, one similar to the concept of Audre Lorde who described the erotic as not only sexual arousal but also "the deepest life force, a force which moves us toward living in a fundamental way, . . . which moves us toward what will accomplish real positive change."[71] Dolly's sanctification and rebirth in that old abandoned church with its decrepit piano and dirty pictures is a real-world example of what Lorde means in this passage: "The erotic is a measure between the beginnings of our sense of self and the chaos of our strongest feelings. It is an internal sense of satisfaction to which, once we have experienced it, we know we can aspire. For having experienced the fullness of this depth of feeling and recognizing its power, in honor and self-respect we can require no less of ourselves."[72] Dolly had a sense that various parts of her life were coalescing, as well as a conviction that this new-found self-acceptance would chart the remainder of her life. Lorde would call Dolly's realization erotic knowledge: "once we begin to feel deeply all the aspects of our lives, we begin to demand from ourselves and from our life-pursuits that they feel in accordance with that joy which we know ourselves to be capable of. Our erotic knowledge empowers us, becomes a lens through which we scrutinize all aspects of our existence, forcing us to evaluate those aspects honestly in terms of their relative meaning within our lives."[73] As Dolly wrote, "The joy of the truth I found there [in that old church] is with me to this day."[74]

Dolly's descriptions of tapping into the erotic—for her the union of God, music, and sex—suggest she was in a state of ecstasy: the heightened emotional sense of being outside oneself, of being transported to another plane, of experiencing deeply but in ways that are usually indescribable. Judith Becker argues, "Religious ecstasy is often described in explicitly sexual terminology. . . . The strongest version of happiness in relation to musical listening and an example of extreme arousal is ecstasy. Usually associated with religious rituals, ecstasy, as extreme joy, almost by definition involves a sense of the sacred (although musical ecstasy can justly be claimed by some attendees at secular musical events such as rock concerts)."[75] All three realms—the religious, the musical, and the sexual—are pathways into ecstasy, and, according to Dolly, these three passions "overlap and intertwine within me."[76] Thus, the boundaries between these three experiences often blur in Dolly's music and lyrics: songs about romantic love evoke the divine; songs about the divine have a sexual energy. And images of the natural world flow easily in both, as demonstrated in her song pair "More than I Can Say"—with its inclusion of ecstasy—and "Unlikely Angel." The fusion of the sacred and the erotic is evident throughout her music and in the way she embraces the same erotic metaphors for ecstasy that have been used for centuries.[77]

The sensation of ecstasy in her music results from the way Dolly shapes the ebb and flow of energy in her songs, both in their composition and in her performances. Dolly describes her swirl into ecstasy in this way: "I just get *real* excited onstage, because I love to sing and perform. It takes me about three hours to come down. Your openin' tune is usually the one you get off on if you're goin' to get off. Sometimes I get so excited over a certain moment onstage, I could just swear that it's the same thing as sex. . . . Music is the closest thing to it to me."[78] Dolly's moments of heightened transcendence often occur in her performances of inspirational songs whether sacred or secular. This is not to say she does not bring emotional intensity to all her songs. But she imparts a greater measure of sublime energy to her songs like "Raven Dove," "Hello God," and "Light of a Clear Blue Morning" as each one traces a path from serenity through rising emotion, finally reaching a climax of sensations that feels boundless. These are heightened moments of ecstasy Howard Dorgan called "peak exuberance"—a "climactic plateau from which the speaker can climb no further." This state is brought about by an acceleration in "pace, volume, and intensity."[79]

Dolly follows this same course in her recordings of two songs she did not write: "He's Alive" and "Jesus and Gravity." Moreover, her restrained writing and performance of "The Seeker" reveals how much she understands this trajectory into ecstasy. She manipulates listeners' desire for this song to burst open in musical abundance, withholding this musical effulgence and thwarting their expectations. She moves to the precipice of this pleasure three times in the song, but never makes the leap into unbounded joy as she does in "Light of a Clear Blue Morning." When Dolly shapes her songs and performances in a way that leads to ecstasy, she replicates the gospel musical practices of Pentecostal worship: beginning with subdued pensive music, gradually increasing the energy, moving through a more exuberant section, and finally crossing over into extended musical ecstasy that eventually dissipates, bringing the worshipers back to earth.

This sort of musical ecstasy is brought about in part by the communal nature of Pentecostal worship. Likewise, Dolly's listeners play a role in this exchange. In terms of Lorde's conception of the erotic, Dolly's audience is integral to "the power which comes from sharing deeply any pursuit with another person. The sharing of joy, whether physical, emotional, psychic, or intellectual, forms a bridge between the sharers."[80] While many of Dolly's fans desire and celebrate this circulation of musical pleasure, all this emotional excess is deeply disturbing for some critics. Some, like Cook, feel that Dolly occasionally goes beyond the bounds of good taste with her music, which they believe is saccharine and overblown, trite and embarrassing, even intellectually weak. But this is often the response to the expression of ecstasy.

As Becker states, the manifestation of ecstasy "demands a surrender of impressive bearing and grand self-presentation. The price of ecstasy may be a loss of dignity" that invites the disdain of others.[81] Dolly embraces ecstasy in terms that again bring to mind Lorde's assertion that the erotic is "the open and fearless underlining of [our] capacity for joy."[82] Not shrinking from ridicule, Dolly is unafraid to express and share a range of undignified emotions with her audience. As McCauley writes in her study of ecstatic religious experiences in Appalachian Mountain religion, "not only did ritual ecstasy displace rationality but it was fundamentally a religious leveler, the great equalizer of all the participants, regardless of background or communal standing."[83] Similarly, moments of shared musical ecstasy create a sense of flow between Dolly and her listeners.

Dolly has always been willing to expose her "loss of dignity" and her emotional vulnerability in her songs and performances. Just as she was not ashamed to cry for "Me and Little Andy," she is unashamed to view the world as "God's Coloring Book" or to move into ecstasy in "Light of a Clear Blue Morning." While this kind of emotional display may cause some listeners to squirm in discomfort, many of Dolly's fans are drawn to her openness, experiencing emotional strength in Dolly's willingness to be vulnerable.

"Unlikely Angel": Dolly as Healer

Another way Dolly is sometimes viewed as undignified is in her outlandish physical presentation—extravagant wigs, heavy makeup, long nails, ostentatious clothing—which has been the object of much fascination and ridicule. Dolly has thought carefully about her choice of public persona, and she speaks eloquently about being made the butt of people's jokes:

> I don't like to be like everybody else. I've often made the statement that I would never stoop so low as to be fashionable. That's the easiest thing in the world to do. So I just decided that I would do something that would at least get the attention. Once they got past the shock of the ridiculous way I looked and all that, then they would see there was parts of me to be appreciated. I'm very real where it counts, and that's inside. . . . Oh I know they make fun of me. But actually, all these years people has thought the joke was on me, but it's actually been on the public. I know exactly what I'm doing, and I can change it at any time. I make more jokes about myself than anybody because . . . I am sure of myself as a person. I am sure of my talent, . . . and I am sure of my love for life. . . . I'm very content. I like the kind of person that I am, so I can afford to piddle around and doo-diddle around with makeups and clothes and stuff because I am secure with myself.[84]

Dolly's "ridiculous" facade allows her to access and share her "real" inner life. A large measure of her ability to connect genuinely with her audience is that she never drops that facade. She is never seen out of character, and paparazzi-type candid photographs exposing the "real" Dolly are rare if nonexistent.

Dolly guards information about her personal life as carefully as she protects her physical image. The result is that Dolly is a blank canvas for her listeners: she can be something to everyone. Her oversexualized persona grabs people's attention, but that is not what sustains their interest, nor is it actually real. As Dolly once remarked, "I'm too cartoonish to ever be a threat to wives and girlfriends."[85] However, the mask she wears allows her to reflect her listeners' experiences and feelings back to them as she acknowledges here: "A lot of times my fans don't come to see me be me. They come to see me be them. They come to hear me say what they want to hear, what they'd like to say themselves, or to say about them what they want to believe is true."[86]

Dolly's listeners also want some of that ecstasy (or heartbreak, joy, anger, desire, or happiness) Dolly expresses in her music, feelings her fans may be reluctant or unable to express themselves, afraid of their own loss of dignity. As Helen Morales put it, Dolly's lyrics "have a directness that acknowledges suffering, together with a wit that helps to alleviate it. . . . Songs package heightened emotions into manageable segments—three minutes of elation here, four minutes of anguish there—and in doing so, they make the emotions seem manageable too."[87] Through her songs, Dolly not only bears witness to people's untold stories, she acts a surrogate for people's emotions, opening up a space for their cathartic expression.

The restorative power that some feel in her music often attaches to Dolly herself, and for a number of people Dolly has a magical presence. Many celebrities, particularly popular musicians, have adoring fans who seek them out and study their every move and song. But Dolly has an additional effect on some who view her as a saintly, angelic figure, and it is no surprise that she has been cast as an angel in movies and televisions shows, including her made-for-television Christmas movies, *Unlikely Angel* and *Christmas on the Square*.[88] Dolly often appears as an angel through specially made outfits whose capacious sleeves become wings, like the one she wore for her acclaimed, ecstatic performance of "He's Alive" on the 1989 CMA Awards show.[89] In the cover photo for *I Believe in You*, she wore a costume that represented an iridescent blue butterfly, with added wings that could easily be those of an angel.

Remarkably, two people who wrote about Dolly's angelic, saintly aura are the late film critics Roger Ebert and Gene Siskel, neither of whom could be described as sentimental pushovers. Nonetheless, Ebert wrote this about their impressions of Dolly: "I had a one-on-one interview with Parton in a hotel suite. As we spoke, I found myself enveloped by her presence. This had nothing to do with sex appeal. Far from it. It was as if I were being mesmerized by a benevolent power. I left the room in a cloud of good feeling. Next day, Siskel and I were sitting next to each other on an airplane. 'This will sound crazy,' he said, 'but when I was interviewing Dolly Parton, I almost felt like she had healing powers.'"[90] Notably, beyond

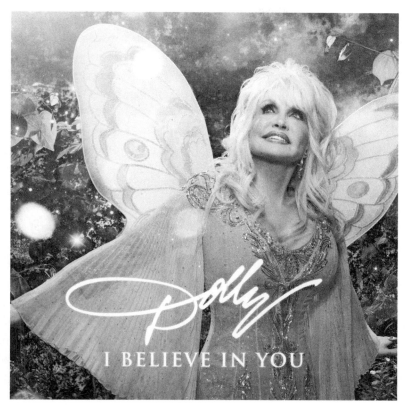

FIGURE 8.1. *I Believe in You* album front cover, 2017.

the effusive (perhaps undignified?) tone Ebert and Siskel use, neither of them was particularly stirred by Dolly as a sexual woman. Baffled by their response, they admit it was a bit daft to imbue her with such restorative powers.

Hal Crowther told a similar story. During his interview with Dolly, he witnessed fans in a restaurant interacting with her as if she were a religious persona, and Dolly responded accordingly. "Two hard-breathing autograph vultures hit her before we reach our table, and Dolly treats them like kin, like royalty. The waitress requests a laying on of hands, and Dolly indulges her, too. 'They love for me to touch them,' she tells us, without condescension."[91]

Actress Beth Grant spoke at length about Dolly's good mountain values in the documentary *Hollywood to Dollywood* and concluded, "So there's something just God-given. Sometimes I think the heavens just part and somebody's just born to do good in the world, and I think that's Dolly Parton."[92] In the same documentary, Manouschka Guerrier, a young African American woman, explained her connection to Dolly: "She speaks to your soul. She speaks about the human condition. We all go through what she has the cajones to sing about, honestly, and to write about it, to put that out there. You know, some people like to go to the Bible for an answer. I go to *Just Because I'm a Woman*. . . . She's as real as it gets. It's like, Stevie Wonder is the only person that can see, and Dolly's the only one that's real. . . . I just love her."[93]

Even more extreme versions of this phenomenon are illustrated in the documentary, *For the Love of Dolly* (2006). Filmmaker and director Tai Uhlmann interviewed dozens of hard-core Dolly fans and followed five of them at Dollywood and fan events. Several had devoted their homes to Dolly, either through their memorabilia collection (of commercial items and genuine Dolly relics) or replicating her "Tennessee Mountain Home" from Dollywood, sometimes rendering their own homes unlivable. Particularly moving is that these fans—either lonely, estranged from family, gay, abused, or disabled—spoke ardently about how Dolly's music gives them the strength to survive difficult times in their lives. Patric Parkey commented, "If you have something going on in your life, there's a Dolly song that will tell you how to get through it." Shelagh Ratner read from a letter she wrote to Dolly: "You are one of the most important people in my life that I have never met. I got through the fall of 1998 by listening to 'Light of a Clear Blue Morning' every morning. Sometimes the only reason I got out of bed was to put that song on."[94] Uhlmann, aware that viewers may find these Dolly fans ridiculous, undignified, and even pathetic, offered this kindhearted and astute explanation: "You can think whatever you want to about these people, but for them, Dolly is an occasion to express love and compassion and joy and honesty. They can experience these things with a lot of freedom, because they're focused on a kind of imaginary, mythic person."[95]

For many listeners, the restorative effect of Dolly's music seems to flow to them directly from Dolly herself, so they often experience her as a healer. This phenomenon recalls Lorde's notion of the erotic: it encompasses the circulation of joy between people and connects them though that sharing. Sometimes the healing comes from a particular song, as Dolly reports about "Coat of Many Colors": "I've had so many people tell me through the years that that song itself has had a healing effect on them."[96] Other times, Dolly herself is the embodied healer with pseudo-religious overtones. Uhlman commented about her subjects in the documentary, "The way they talk about her, she could be Our Lady of Guadalupe."[97] Andy Warhol created an image of Dolly in 1984, "in a halo of silvery locks," that Manuela Welloffman suggests was "perhaps inspired by the religious icons from his childhood Byzantine Catholic Church. By presenting

FIGURE 8.2. Saint Dolly.

her in an angelic look, Warhol elevated Dolly's Parton's status to that of an idol."[98] Ubiquitous online depictions of Dolly as a saint echo the commonplace iconography of the Sacred Heart of Jesus and the Immaculate Heart of Mary.

To her fans Dolly would say, "'You don't need to be worshiping me, because I don't believe in idol gods, false gods.' I'm always very careful not to lead people astray that don't really have that much strength of their own or know their own true identity, to where they just live through you."[99] But Dolly has occasionally described her music in religious terms. "Well, I'm saying my work itself is like—almost like my ministry. You know it's like—I feel like that you're out there trying to help people feel better about themselves, trying to give them some hope. And even when things are the hardest I try to write songs to lift people up."[100] But Dolly prefers to focus on the power her fans have in their own renewal: "I don't think anybody has the gift of healing unless you have such a gift of love that people can claim enough of that to heal themselves. Certainly I don't claim to be no healer."[101]

FIGURE 8.3. The Sacred Heart of Jesus.

FIGURE 8.4. The Immaculate Heart of Mary.

Dolly returns to her exuberant physical presentation when wondering what part she might play in helping anyone heal, and she believes her sparkling persona is a helpful distraction to people. While her fans focus on her artifice, mesmerized by her nails, hair, and bosom, they forget "about themselves and maybe have time to do a little healing then. . . . It has nothing to do with me. I'm distracting them, while they heal themselves."[102] Dolly also speculates that troubled fans who have something to look forward to—a new album or an upcoming concert—might live healthier lives than they might otherwise. "It might keep them from doing something bad to themselves or to somebody else. Like suicide. Or to keep 'em off the streets. Or give 'em something more to do than just dwelling on themselves so much."[103] Her theory here adds a twist to the notion of Dolly as a blank canvas who can reflect peoples' ideas back to them. In this case, she suggests her cartoonish look does the opposite and distracts fans from themselves, giving them time to heal. Both scenarios are likely happening simultaneously.

Dolly's feel-good and religious effect is not limited to her most unguarded fans. Frank Dycus, who worked closely with Dolly in the early 1970s, remarked, "Dolly was a magic person when she was born, and I think the magic has stayed with her through the years and I think the magic will stay with her right up to her last breath."[104] *Rolling Stone* music critic Chet Flippo referred to Dolly as a "purifier" who evokes "quasi religious experiences and cleansings of the soul" and who "was born with a natural gift for intense positive thinking."[105] Country star Marty Stuart remarked, "She's timeless, beautiful and spiritual. The Bible says 'many are called, but few are chosen.' I think we all agree that she is a chosen one."[106] Dolly counters these types of remarks in this way: "I just say who I am and how I am. If there's something you see in me that's got a light, then I like to think that's God's light—not my light. . . .That's why I want to ship that on up to God. I don't need nobody worshiping me. If I do shine and radiate, I'd like to think that is God's light and I'd like to pass that on. I want to direct people to Him, not me."[107]

In her account of her self-described pilgrimage to Dollywood, Helen Morales observed, "Listening to Dolly sing these songs is like administering to yourself an injection of empathy, a little burst of love."[108] For some, listening to Dolly is one path to happiness and an optimistic outlook. As a young African American woman, Jasmyn Payne, interviewed for the documentary *Hollywood to Dollywood* remarked: "You know, [Dolly is] where I'm gonna get my confidence from. And she motivated me. I always used to worry about, actually, just being myself. I always thought that I was getting judged. And one day when I saw her interview on the TV it really opened my eyes, and it made me realize that it's not about what anybody else thinks, you know. It's about how you feel within."[109] Dolly is mindful of this uplifting role she plays for people, particularly women. In a 2018 interview she commented, "It touches me to no end that I'm an inspiration. . . . And I look back and then I still see . . . that young women especially, which I love that: that they can look to me to say, Dolly had the strength to do it, or she got through it—that's really humbling, and it makes me feel proud, and I just thank God for it."[110]

One might listen to Dolly's songs about God, with their biblical language and hymn tunes and lyrics, and think she expresses only Christian beliefs. A non-Christian listener might tune out these songs, believing her inspirational messages lie for them only in her secular songs of hope and encouragement. But her overtly religious songs explore many philosophies and states of mind that are more all-embracing expressions of joy, doubt, humility, sorrow, and ecstasy and are not limited only to a sacred reading. Further, some of her secular, "tool kit for living"[111] songs such as "Light of a Clear Blue Morning" are saturated with the musical ecstasy that Dolly would have experienced in Pentecostal worship. As Dolly said in 2019 when commenting on three faith-based, "uplifting" songs she recorded in collaboration with other artists: "whether you believe in God

FIGURE 8.5. Dolly Parton glowing on stage (Tanglewood, Massachusetts, June 17, 2016). Photo: Lydia Hamessley.

or not, we need to believe in something bigger and better than what's going on because we're not doing too hot. We need to try to do a little better."[112]

According to one critic, Dolly's "particularly inclusive, distinctively feminine and sex-positive take on religion is sugarcoated enough to appeal to the old guard, but it is also strikingly rebellious in its fluid understanding of gender roles."[113] Once again Dolly is viewed in terms of dualities: she is a mixture of sweetness and rebellion in the way she mingles the sacred and secular in her inspirational songs. The pliancy of these songs—with their "strange mix of traditional and progressive values"[114]—accounts for why Dolly's fans are wide-ranging in their identities and beliefs.[115] At her concerts, audiences comprise conservatives and liberals; gay men and soccer moms; young and old; people of all gender and sexual identities in Dolly drag; lesbians and cowboys; people of all faiths, classes, races, and ethnicities; trans* people; and Christians, atheists, and agnostics all happily coexisting in their communal focus on Dolly who, in her sparkle and glow of rhinestones, becomes for each of them what they need to see and hear.

Chapter 9
"There'll Always Be Music"
Final Thoughts

"Music was just in my soul, and it still is."

In 1987, the community of Sevier County commissioned a statue of Dolly to be placed at the courthouse in Sevierville.[1] The vision of Dolly portrayed by the statue is intriguing. Although made during the time she was more known for her pop crossover music than her country songs, the statue depicts Dolly as a mountain singer, not a glamorous superstar. Casually posed on a large stone from the Smoky Mountains and holding a guitar with a butterfly perched on it, Dolly looks slightly upward with an open smile as if about to sing. One leg is easily crooked behind the other, and her arms embrace her guitar, which shields her breasts somewhat. This is no hyperfeminine image with extravagant hair, nails, makeup, and exaggerated figure. The artificiality is stripped away, and Dolly looks realistic. She is wearing clothing much plainer than she has ever worn publicly as a star. Her simple long-sleeve shirt is rolled up to the elbow, and her jeans are rolled up in cuffs to her mid-calf. Most surprisingly, she is barefoot—superstar Dolly always wears at least 5" heels—and her toes have the sheen of a venerated icon. Nothing about this image signifies Dolly the wealthy entertainer. Instead, she is represented as if she were still that mountain girl from Locust Ridge who dreamed of being a songwriter.

Dolly is gifted at juggling these contradictions. She embodies incongruous images that remind us of our own complex identities. Her songs capture and

FIGURE 9.1. The author with Dolly statue at the Sevier County
Courthouse (Sevierville, Tennessee, July 27, 2019).

balance seemingly paradoxical emotional states, deepening our understanding
of the human experience. The deep well of sorrow in many of her songs is
matched by unbounded joy in others. Through her songs and her image, she
models a compelling blend of strength and vulnerability, the eagle and the
sparrow. She is strong enough to be Dolly the superstar, and she is vulnerable
enough to be Dolly the songwriter who feels deeply and freely shares her
experiences.

Dolly has no plans to retire. In 2002 she said, "I'm a working girl. I really
love a challenge. I feel as energetic and as young as I did when I first left the

Smokies in 1964 to live in Nashville. I just really love to work. I have a lot of energy. I don't want to rest on my laurels. I don't want to set around and count my money. I'd rather count my blessings and count the songs I can write every day and all the good things I might could do for somebody else."[2] So this last chapter is not Dolly's last chapter.

Since I began writing this book, Dolly released three studio albums: *Blue Smoke* (2014), *Pure and Simple* (2016), and her first children's album, *I Believe in You* (2017). She toured extensively for these first two albums, performing in over 60 cities in the fall of 2016. Her 2014 performance at the U.K. Glastonbury Festival was highly acclaimed, and she produced and appeared in two made-for-television movies based on her life: *Coat of Many Colors* (2015) and *Christmas of Many Colors: Circle of Love* (2016). In 2018, she and Linda Perry cowrote five new songs for the film *Dumplin'* based on the best-selling novel by Julie Murphy. The following year, she launched her eight-part Netflix series, *Dolly Parton's Heartstrings*. Dolly appeared in select episodes, each inspired by one of her songs. Also in 2019, Dolly appeared in the Hallmark Channel movie, *Christmas at Dollywood*, premiered her musical *Dolly Parton's Smoky Mountain Christmas Carol*, and celebrated 50 years of membership in the Grand Ole Opry, performing in two sold-out concerts. In 2020, she won a Grammy Award for Best Contemporary Christian Music Performance/Song for "God Only Knows" with the Christian pop duo for King & Country, and she filmed another made-for-television movie *Christmas on the Square*.

Dolly's humanitarian and philanthropic efforts continue to garner awards. In 2016, she established a fund for the victims of the Tennessee wildfires, distributing $8.9 million. In 2018, Dolly dedicated the 100th million book from her Imagination Library to the Library of Congress, and she was named MusiCares Person of the Year in 2019. Her appeal as an entertainer is still widespread. In 2019, she cohosted the CMA Awards and was the subject of an in-depth documentary *Dolly Parton: Here I Am*.[3] In contemplating the reasons for her success and longevity in the music business Dolly made these remarks.

A lot of it has to do with personality, with character, your background, timing. There are so many elements. But I would just say that . . . I've been around a long time because I've never let my business slip. I've never lost motivation. Even at times when they weren't playing me on the radio because I was an older country artist. A lot of the artists like me just threw up their hands and gave up. . . . I didn't think like that. I thought, "How lucky have I been? I've won every award anybody could hope to win, I've had all these songs, I've had this wonderful career, so I'm grateful and thankful for that. But I'm not done!"[4]

Steve Buckingham observed that Dolly is always focused on future projects: "I don't think you'll ever walk in on Dolly and find her sitting around with a bunch of her albums reminiscing. That just isn't her. She always is looking forward and thinking up new ideas. She's a fountain of ideas. The most creative mind I've ever been around by far, and I've been around some pretty creative minds."[5]

Early in her career, Dolly wrote a song about music itself, "There'll Always Be Music." Although not well known, it is a statement of what she holds most dear about music as a boundless and abiding presence in our lives. Incorporating the modal sounds of her Appalachian heritage, Dolly fuses her reverence for nature with music: the wind whistles and sings tunes while rain beats out rhythms and birds join in song. The song's chorus encapsulates Dolly's affinity for story songs, her propensity to link music with the divine, and her belief that music will last long after we pass away:

> There'll always be music as long as there's a story to be told
> There'll always be music 'cause music is the voice of the soul

Music has defined Dolly's life. She began singing and writing songs as a small child and dreamed her way to Nashville and beyond while holding fast to her Appalachian mountain roots. People continue to ask her about retiring, and she is still not interested: "A lot of people my age are already, you know, like, they've already gone to seed. You know, they don't want to do anything. And I, for me though, I would rather wear out than rust out. I figure I'll be dead forever, and so I'm just gonna do everything I can while I'm living. I hope to drop dead right in the middle of something I love to do—like a song would be great. I'd love to just die in the middle of a great song—that I had written, hopefully."[6] Her grandfather Rev. Jake Owens once said about her, "That thing come here a singin'."[7] Apparently Dolly sang her way into this world, and she has every intention of singing her way out of it.

Appendix A

Song List

Song Title	Album Title	Date
A Better Place to Live	*Coat of Many Colors*	1971
A Gamble Either Way	*Burlap & Satin*	1983
A Good Understanding	*Once More*	1970
Appalachian Memories	*Burlap & Satin*	1983
Applejack	*New Harvest…First Gathering*	1977
Baby I'm Burnin'	*Heartbreaker*	1978
Back Home	*My Tennessee Mountain Home*	1973
Backwoods Barbie	*Backwoods Barbie*	2008
Banks of the Ohio[2]	*Blue Smoke*	2014
Barbara on Your Mind[3]		
Barbara on Your Mind	*Heartbreak Express*	1982
Bargain Store, The	*The Bargain Store*	1975
Berry Pie[4]	*Backwoods Barbie*	2008
Better Get to Livin'	*Backwoods Barbie*	2008
Better Part of Life, The	*My Tennessee Mountain Home*	1973
Between Us	*We Found It*	1973
Blackie, Kentucky	*Love Is Like a Butterfly*	1974
Bloody Bones (A Story for Kids)	*A Real Live Dolly*	1970
Bluer Pastures	*Little Sparrow*	2001
Blue Valley Songbird	*Hungry Again*	1998
Bobby's Arms	*Dolly: The Seeker/We Used to*	1975
Bridge, The	*Just Because I'm a Woman*	1968
Butterflies	*Rhinestone* soundtrack	1984

But You Loved Me Then	*The Fairest of Them All*	1970
Camel's Heart, The	*Hungry Again*	1998
Can't Be That Wrong	*Pure and Simple*	2016
Chas	*The Fairest of Them All*	1970
Coat of Many Colors	*Coat of Many Colors*	1971
Come to Me	*Love and Music*	1973
Crippled Bird	*Something Special*	1995
Daddy	*My Blue Ridge Mountain Boy*	1969
Daddy Come and Get Me	*The Fairest of Them All*	1970
Daddy's Moonshine Still	*Joshua*	1971
Daddy's Working Boots	*My Tennessee Mountain Home*	1973
Daddy Was an Old Time Preacher Man	*Once More*	1970
Dagger through the Heart	*Halos & Horns*	2002
Don't Let It Trouble Your Mind	*In the Good Old Days (When Times Were Bad)*	1969
Down from Dover	*The Fairest of Them All*	1970
Down from Dover	*Little Sparrow*	2001
Down on Music Row	*My Tennessee Mountain Home*	1973
Dr. Robert F. Thomas	*My Tennessee Mountain Home*	1973
Eagle When She Flies	*Eagle When She Flies*	1991
Early Morning Breeze	*Coat of Many Colors*	1971
Early Morning Breeze	*Jolene*	1974
Endless Stream of Tears	*The Grass Is Blue*	1999
Evening Shade	*My Blue Ridge Mountain Boy*	1969
Everything's Beautiful (In Its Own Way)[5]	*The Winning Hand*	1982
Everything's Beautiful (In Its Own Way)[6]	*Dolly* (4 CD set)	2009
Family	*Eagle When She Flies*	1991
Fight and Scratch	*Once More*	1970
Fighting Kind, The	*Two of a Kind*	1971
Fire That Keeps You Warm, The	*Porter 'n' Dolly*	1974
Fire That Keeps You Warm, The	*All I Can Do*	1976
Fuel to the Flame	*Hello, I'm Dolly*	1967
Get Out and Stay Out[7]	*Better Day*	2011
Girl Left Alone[8]		1959
God's Coloring Book	*Here You Come Again*	1977
Grass Is Blue, The	*The Grass Is Blue*	1999
Greatest Days of All, The	*Touch Your Woman*	1972
Gypsy, Joe and Me	*My Blue Ridge Mountain Boy*	1969

Hello God	*Halos & Horns*	2002
He Would Know	*The Bargain Store*	1975
High and Mighty	*Slow Dancing with the Moon*	1993
Hillbilly Willy	*As Long as I Love*	1970
Home	*Blue Smoke*	2014
Hungry Again	*Hungry Again*	1998
I Am Always Waiting	*We Found It*	1973
I Can	*Just the Two of Us*	1968
I Can't Be True	*Real Love*	1985
If I Had Wings	*Blue Smoke*	2014
If You Need Me	*Eagle When She Flies*	1991
I Get Lonesome By Myself	*Love and Music*	1973
I'm Doing This for Your Sake	*The Fairest of Them All*	1970
I'm Gone	*Halos & Horns*	2002
I'm in No Condition	*Hello, I'm Dolly*	1967
I'm Not Worth the Tears	*As Long as I Love*	1970
I'm Wasting Your Time and You're Wasting Mine	*Porter Wayne and Dolly Rebecca*	1970
In Each Love Some Pain Must Fall	*The Right Combination/ Burning the Midnight Oil*	1972
In the Good Old Days (When Times Were Bad)	*In the Good Old Days (When Times Were Bad)*	1969
In the Good Old Days (When Times Were Bad)	*My Tennessee Mountain Home*	1973
I Remember	*My Tennessee Mountain Home*	1973
Is It Real	*Two of a Kind*	1971
It Might as Well Be Me	*Porter Wayne and Dolly Rebecca*	1970
I Took Him for Granted[9]	*Dolly Parton: The Early Years*	2004
It's All Wrong, but It's All Right	*Here You Come Again*	1977
I've Been Married (Just as Long as You Have)	*We Found It*	1973
I've Been This Way Too Long	*The Right Combination/ Burning the Midnight Oil*	1972
I Will Always Love You	*Jolene*	1974
I Will Always Love You	*The Best Little Whorehouse in Texas* soundtrack	1982
I Will Always Love You (with Vince Gill)	*Something Special*	1995
Jeannie's Afraid of the Dark	*Just the Two of Us*	1968
J. J. Sneed	*Joshua*	1971
John Daniel	*Halos & Horns*	2002

Jolene	*Jolene*	1974
Jolene	*Something Special*	1995
Joshua	*Joshua*	1971
Just Because I'm a Woman	*Just Because I'm a Woman*	1968
Just the Way I Am	*The Fairest of Them All*	1970
Letter, The	*My Tennessee Mountain Home*	1973
Letter to Heaven[10]	*Joshua*	1971
Life Doesn't Mean Much to Me[11]		1954 or 1955
Light of a Clear Blue Morning	*New Harvest . . . First Gathering*	1977
Little Bird	*In the Good Old Days (When Times Were Bad)*	1969
Little David's Harp	*Porter & Dolly*	1980
Little Sparrow	*Little Sparrow*	2001
Little Tiny Tassletop[12]		1951
Lost Forever in Your Kiss	*Together Always*	1972
Love Have Mercy on Us	*We Found It*	1973
Love Is Like a Butterfly	*Love Is Like a Butterfly*	1974
Love Isn't Free	*Touch Your Woman*	1972
Makin' Fun Ain't Funny	*I Believe in You*	2017
Malena	*Always, Always*	1969
Mammie	*The Fairest of Them All*	1970
Man, The	*Heartbreaker*	1978
Marry Me	*Little Sparrow*	2001
Me and Little Andy	*Here You Come Again*	1977
Mendy Never Sleeps	*Porter Wayne and Dolly Rebecca*	1970
Miss You-Miss Me	*Blue Smoke*	2014
Mommie, Ain't That Daddy?	*Just Between You and Me*	1968
More than I Can Say	*Rainbow*	1987
More than Their Share	*The Fairest of Them All*	1970
More Where That Came From	*Slow Dancing with the Moon*	1993
Mountain Angel	*Little Sparrow*	2001
Muleskinner Blues[13]	*The Best of Dolly Parton*	1970
My Blue Ridge Mountain Boy	*My Blue Ridge Mountain Boy*	1969
My Blue Ridge Mountain Boy	*Heartbreak Express*	1982
My Blue Tears	*Coat of Many Colors*	1971
My Blue Tears	*Little Sparrow*	2001
My Hands Are Tied	*Always, Always*	1969
My Kind of Man	*Bubbling Over*	1973
My Tennessee Mountain Home	*My Tennessee Mountain Home*	1973

19th Amendment (A Woman's Right)	*27: The Most Perfect Album*[1]	2018
9 to 5	*9 to 5 and Odd Jobs*	1980
No Good Way of Saying Good-bye	*Something Special*	1995
No Reason to Hurry Home	*Always, Always*	1969
Not for Me	*Halos & Horns*	2002
Oh, the Pain of Loving You	*Two of a Kind*	1971
Old Black Kettle	*My Tennessee Mountain Home*	1973
Only Dreamin'	*Backwoods Barbie*	2008
Paradise Road	*Hungry Again*	1998
Party, The	*Just the Two of Us*	1968
Pleasant as May[14]	*Bubbling Over*	1973
Please Don't Stop Loving Me	*Porter 'n' Dolly*	1974
Puppy Love[15]		1959
Pure and Simple	*Pure and Simple*	2016
Put It Off Until Tomorrow (You've Hurt Me Enough for Today)	*Hello, I'm Dolly*	1967
Ragged Angel	*Once More*	1970
Raven Dove	*Halos & Horns*	2002
River of Happiness	*Jolene*	1974
Robert	*The Fairest of Them All*	1970
Romeo	*Slow Dancing with the Moon*	1993
Run That by Me One More Time	*Porter Wayne and Dolly Rebecca*	1970
Sacred Memories	*Love Is Like a Butterfly*	1974
Sacrifice, The	*Better Day*	2011
Salt in My Tears, The	*Hungry Again*	1998
Sandy's Song	*Great Balls of Fire*	1979
Seeker, The	*Dolly: The Seeker/We Used To*	1975
Shattered Image	*All I Can Do*	1976
Shattered Image	*Halos & Horns*	2002
Shine Like the Sun[16]	*Better Day*	2011
Shine On	*Hungry Again*	1998
Shinola	*Backwoods Barbie*	2008
Silver Dagger	*The Grass Is Blue*	1999
Smoky Mountain Memories	*Heartsongs: Live from Home*	1994
Something Fishy	*Hello, I'm Dolly*	1967
Something More[17]		2016
Something Special	*Something Special*	1995

Somewhere along the Way	*The Right Combination/* *Burning the Midnight Oil*	1972
Speakin' of the Devil	*Something Special*	1995
Star of the Show	*Great Balls of Fire*	1979
Steady as the Rain	*The Grass Is Blue*	1999
Sugar Hill	*Halos & Horns*	2002
Sweet Lovin' Friends	*Rhinestone* soundtrack	1984
Take Me Back	*Love Is Like a Butterfly*	1974
Teach Me to Trust	*Something Special*	1995
Tennessee Homesick Blues	*Rhinestone* soundtrack	1984
There'll Always Be Music	*Love and Music*	1973
There'll Be Love	*Two of a Kind*	1971
These Old Bones	*Halos & Horns*	2002
'Til Death Do Us Part	*My Blue Ridge Mountain Boy*	1969
Time and Tears	*Hungry Again*	1998
Together Always	*Together Always*	1972
Together You and I	*Porter 'n' Dolly*	1974
Together You and I[18]	*Better Day*	2011
Too Far Gone	*Porter 'n' Dolly*	1974
Touch Your Woman	*Touch Your Woman*	1972
Travelin' Thru	*Transamerica*	2006
Try	*Blue Smoke*	2014
Two Doors Down	*Here You Come Again*	1977
Two of a Kind	*Two of a Kind*	1971
Unlikely Angel	*Blue Smoke*	2014
Wait 'Til I Get You Home	*White Limozeen*	1989
Walls of My Mind	*Joshua*	1971
We'd Have to Be Crazy	*Porter 'n' Dolly*	1974
What a Heartache	*Halos & Horns*	2002
What Is It My Love?	*White Limozeen*	1989
What Will Baby Be?[19]	*Dolly* (4 CD set)	2009
What Will Baby Be?	*Slow Dancing with the Moon*	1993
When I'm Gone	*The Bargain Store*	1975
When Jesus Comes Calling for Me	*Hungry Again*	1998
When Love Is New	*Songcatcher: Music from &* *Inspired by the Motion Picture*	2001
When Possession Gets Too Strong	*The Fairest of Them All*	1970
When the Sun Goes down Tomorrow	*All I Can Do*	1976

Where Beauty Lives in Memory	*New Harvest . . . First Gathering*	1977
White Limozeen	*White Limozeen*	1989
Wildflowers	*Trio*	1987
Will He Be Waiting for Me	*Touch Your Woman*	1972
Will He Be Waiting for Me	*The Grass Is Blue*	1999
Wrong Direction Home	*My Tennessee Mountain Home*	1973
Yellow Roses	*White Limozeen*	1989
You	*Love and Music*	1973
You Are	*New Harvest . . . First Gathering*	1977
You're Gonna Be Sorry	*Just Because I'm a Woman*	1968

This table is not an exhaustive list of all of Dolly's songs. I list only those songs mentioned in the book.

Appendix B

Timeline

CHILDHOOD

1946   Born in Sevier County, Tennessee
1952   Begins singing solos in church
1953   Makes her homemade guitar around the age of 6 or 7
1954   Receives her first real guitar
1956   Appears on *The Cas Walker Farm and Home Hour* on radio and television
        Tree Music publishing gives Dolly and Bill Owens (Uncle Bill) a song-writing contract
1959   Records "Puppy Love" on Goldband Records (written with Uncle Bill)
        First appearance on the Grand Ole Opry
1963   Records six songs for *Hits Made Famous by Country Queens*

NASHVILLE—Early Years

1964   Moves to Nashville; signs with Combine Publishing
1966   Signs with Monument Records
        Dolly and Uncle Bill Owens start Owe-Par Publishing Company
1966   Her song (cowriter Bill Owens) "Put It Off until Tomorrow" is recorded
        by Bill Phillips, charts at #6, and wins the BMI Song of the Year Award
        Marries Carl Thomas Dean
1967   Her song (cowriter Bill Owens) "Fuel to the Flame" is recorded by Skeeter
        Davis and charts at #11
        Her first country music singles—"Dumb Blonde" (written by Curly Put-man) charts at #24 and "Something Fishy" charts at #17
        Hello, I'm Dolly, her first album

NASHVILLE—*The Porter Wagoner Years*

1967   Joins *The Porter Wagoner Show*
        Signs with RCA

1968   "Just Because I'm a Woman" charts at #17
        Porter Wagoner and Dolly Parton named Vocal Group of the Year by the
        Country Music Association

1969   *My Blue Ridge Mountain Boy* album

1970   Records Jimmie Rodgers's "Mule Skinner Blues," which charts at #3

1971   "Joshua" charts at #1—her first number one single
        "Coat of Many Colors" charts at #4

1973   *My Tennessee Mountain Home* album

1974   "Jolene" charts at #1
        "I Will Always Love You" charts at #1
        "Love Is Like a Butterfly" charts at #1
        Duet with Porter Wagoner "Please Don't Stop Loving Me" charts at #1;
        cowritten with Wagoner
        Her last appearance on *The Porter Wagoner Show*

1975   "The Bargain Store" charts at #1

THE POP CROSSOVER YEARS

1976   Hires Sandy Gallin of Katz, Gallin and Cleary as her manager
        Hosts a weekly variety TV show, *Dolly!*, for one season

1977   *New Harvest . . . First Gathering* released—her first self-produced album
        "Light of a Clear Blue Morning" charts at #11 on the country chart, but
        only #87 on the pop chart
        Here You Come Again album charts at #1 in country and #20 in pop
        "Here You Come Again" by Barry Mann and Cynthia Weil charts at #1 in
        country and pop
        Interviewed by Barbara Walters for her TV show

1978   Grammy for Best Female Country Vocal Performance for *Here You Come
        Again* album
        Appears on the cover of *Playboy*
        Entertainer of the Year, the Country Music Association

1979   Hosted *The Seventies: An Explosion of Country Music*, aired on NBC

1980   Appears in *9 to 5*, her first film role
        "9 to 5" charts at #1 in country, pop, and adult contemporary
        "9 to 5" nominated for an Academy Award for Best Original Song

1981   First woman, without a male cowriter, to receive a Grammy for Best Coun-
        try Song, for "9 to 5"

1982   Appears in the film *The Best Little Whorehouse in Texas*

1983   Duet with Kenny Rogers, "Islands in the Stream" written by the Bee Gees, charts at #1 in country, pop, and adult contemporary

1984   Appears in the film *Rhinestone*

1985   Andy Warhol creates *Dolly Parton*, synthetic polymer and screenprint on canvas

1986   Opens Dollywood Theme Park in Pigeon Forge, Tennessee

         Inducted into the Nashville Songwriters Hall of Fame

         Named one of thirteen Women of the Year by *Ms.* magazine

         A Smoky Mountain Christmas, a made-for-TV movie

RETURN TO COUNTRY

1987   Signs with Columbia Records after RCA does not renew her contract

         Trio album with Emmylou Harris and Linda Ronstadt; charts at #1 in country

         Hosts a second weekly variety TV show, *Dolly*, for one season

1989   *White Limozeen* album

         "Yellow Roses" charts at #1 in country

         Appears in *Steel Magnolias*

         Hosts *Saturday Night Live*

1992   Whitney Houston records "I Will Always Love You" for *The Bodyguard*

         Appears in *Straight Talk*

1993   *Slow Dancing with the Moon* album

         Honky Tonk Angels album with Loretta Lynn and Tammy Wynette

1994   *Heartsongs: Live from Home* album

1995   Records "I Will Always Love You" with Vince Gill

         Something Special album wins the CMA's Vocal Event of the Year award

1996   *Treasures* album, covers of 1960s and 1970s hits

         Unlikely Angel, a made-for-TV movie

         First cloned mammal, a sheep, named after Dolly

1998   *Hungry Again* album

1999   *Trio II* album with Emmylou Harris and Linda Ronstadt

         Inducted into the Country Music Hall of Fame

         Blue Valley Songbird, a made-for-TV movie

THE BLUEGRASS AND TRADITIONAL MUSIC YEARS

1999   *The Grass Is Blue* album wins the Grammy Award for Best Bluegrass Album

2001   *Little Sparrow* album

         Inducted into the Songwriters Hall of Fame

2002   *Halos & Horns* album; tours for the first time in 10 years

2003   Tribute album in her honor *Just Because I'm a Woman: Songs of Dolly Parton*

2004   Awarded the Living Legend Medal by the U.S. Library of Congress

2005   *Those Were the Days* album, covers of 1960s and 1970s folk rock hits
       "Travelin' Thru" nominated for an Academy Award for Best Original Song,
       written for the film *Transamerica*
       Awarded the National Medal of Arts

2006   Receives the Kennedy Center Honors

2007   Writes the score for the Broadway show *9 to 5: The Musical*; nominated for
       the Tony Award for Best Original Score
       Receives the Johnny Mercer Award from the Songwriters Hall of Fame

2008   *Backwoods Barbie* album

2009   Receives an honorary doctorate from the University of Tennessee

2011   *Better Day* album, which features four songs from *9 to 5: The Musical*
       Receives the Grammy Lifetime Achievement Award

2012   Appears in the film *Joyful Noise*

2013   *A Country Christmas Story*, a made-for-TV movie

2014   Performs at the Glastonbury (U.K.) Festival of Contemporary Performing
       Arts to a record crowd of over 180,000

2015   *Dolly Parton's Coat of Many Colors*, a made-for-TV movie

2016   *Pure and Simple* album and 64-city tour
       Receives the Willie Nelson Lifetime Achievement award from the Country
       Music Association
       Dolly Parton's Christmas of Many Colors: Circle of Love, a made-for-TV
       movie

2017   Receives the Gary Haber Lifting Lives Award from the Academy of
       Country Music
       I Believe in You, her first children's album

2018   Receives two Guinness Book Awards: Most Decades with a Top 20 Hit
       on Billboard's Hot Country Songs Chart; and Most Hits on Billboard's
       Hot Country Songs Chart by a Female Artist
       Receives two Regional Emmy Awards: Best Community Service Program
       for her Smoky Mountains Rise Telethon; and the Governor's Award for
       a Lifetime of Public Service
       Dedicates the 100th million book of her Imagination Library Program to
       the Library of Congress
       Receives the Bill Rosendahl Public Service Award for Contributions to
       the Public Good
       Writes and records several songs for the film *Dumplin'*

2019   *Dolly Parton's Heartstrings*, an eight-episode Netflix series, each based on
       one of her songs
       Christmas at Dollywood, a Hallmark Channel movie

Premieres the musical *Dolly Parton's Smoky Mountain Christmas Carol*
Named MusiCares Person of the Year
Celebrates her 50th Anniversary of membership in the Grand Ole Opry
2020   *Christmas on the Square*, a Netflix movie

All songs are by Dolly Parton unless otherwise noted.

Appendix C

On Modes

Most country songs are in major keys, and Dolly's are no exception. Sing do, re, mi, fa, sol, la, ti, do and you have sung a major scale. Pay particular attention to the way the 7th scale degree, ti, leads you to continue to the high do, or tonic pitch (stop briefly on ti to experience this pull to tonic). This 7th scale degree is called a leading tone because of its strong tendency to return, or lead, to tonic; it is just a half-step below the tonic note. "Coat of Many Colors" is an example of this major sonority with its use of three major chords (I, IV, V or C, F, G, for example). You can hear the tonic (I) chord through the opening lines with the subdominant (IV) chord punctuating the words *youth* and *to use*. The dominant (V) chord makes its first appearance on the words *way down in the fall*. Occasionally Dolly writes in a minor key (sing la, ti, do, re, mi, fa, sol, la), and "Jolene" is probably her most well-known example. Often people will hear the difference between major and minor as a contrast of happy and sad. Although there are many exceptions to this rule, it can be a useful rubric in quickly recognizing the different sounds of these scales.

In addition to songs that fall within this major/minor duality, Dolly writes songs that use different scales and chordal/harmonic structures—songs that are modal. One of the most common characteristics of the majority of modal songs is the alteration of the 7th scale degree (the ti of the major scale). In several modes, this note is flatted or lowered by a half step, resulting in a distinctive sound. In fact, technically "Jolene" can be considered modal, specifically the Aeolian mode, because, although its tonal center is a minor chord, it consistently uses a flatted 7th chord (♭VII) rather than a chord with a leading tone.[1] This moment is easily heard in "Jolene": after the opening iteration of the name "Jolene" that occurs over a variety of chords, the flatted 7th chord (♭VII) is extended over the words *begging of you please don't take my* and resolves back to the minor tonic on *man*. This harmonic move, italicized in the following example, is repeated in the next set of lines with the flatted 7th on *please don't take him just because you*, resolving back to the minor tonic on *can*:

> Jolene, Jolene, Jolene, Jolene
> I'm *begging of you please don't take my* man
> Jolene, Jolene, Jolene, Jolene
> *Please don't take him just because you* can

Two other modes that appear in Dolly's songs are the Mixolydian mode and, on rare occasions, the Dorian mode. The Mixolydian mode is simply the major scale with a flatted 7th scale degree (the syllable ti is lowered by a half step). To illustrate, we can use several well-known songs that use the ♭VII chord in a prominent way. In the following examples, the flatted 7th sonority[2] appears on the words that are italicized. In "Sweet Home Alabama" (Lynyrd Skynyrd), it is easy to hear the strong move down from the major tonic sonority to the flatted 7th chord (♭VII) at the beginning of the line:

> Sweet *home* Alabama
> Where the *skies are so* blue
> Sweet *home* Alabama
> Lord I'm *comin' home to* you

In "Ramblin' Man" (Allman Brothers Band), the first line of the chorus features the flatted 7th chord (♭VII):

> Lord I was *born a ramblin'* man

During the extended chorus repetition and the instrumental section that concludes this song, the major tonic (I) and the ♭VII chord rock back and forth in a classic Mixolydian sound.

Dolly rarely uses the Dorian mode, but its distinctive, bittersweet sound makes a powerful statement that she hears as old-world (her song "The Bargain Store" is in the Dorian mode). This mode is close to the minor (Aeolian) mode we heard earlier in "Jolene": the minor scale with the flatted 7th scale degree. However, there is one change that gives the Dorian mode its identity and brighter quality. The 6th scale degree is raised a half step from what it would be in the minor (Aeolian) mode. In the folk song, "Scarborough Fair," the flatted 7th scale degree in the melody appears on the words that are italicized, and the raised 6th scale degree is underlined:

Are you going to Scarborough Fair[3]
Par*sley*, sage, *rose*mar*y*, and thyme
Remember *me* to one who lives th*ere*
She once was a true love *of* mine.

Other examples are "Eleanor Rigby" (The Beatles) and the chorus of "Mad World" (Tears for Fears).

Often, songs mix modes by using both the flatted 7th scale degree (for a modal sound) and the raised 7th scale degree, the leading tone (for a major sound), in close proximity in different lines or sections, as in "Ramblin' Man." Dolly frequently mixes modes in this way in her songs, usually combining a major key with the Mixolydian mode. While some of her songs are completely within a single mode, many more feature this modal mixture.

Also relevant to Dolly's music are pentatonic scales, which comprise five notes. Play only the black keys on a piano to hear the distinctive folklike sound of this scale, which may also bring to mind the sound of some Asian musics that are pentatonic. Or sing these notes of the major scale: do, re, mi, sol, la. Because this scale leaves out two notes of the major scale (fa and ti), it is sometimes referred to as a *gapped scale*.

In folk music of the United States, this is the most common pentatonic scale, and it has a major sonority, such as the hymn "Amazing Grace," and the song "Cumberland Gap." But other pentatonic songs, such as the folk hymn "Wayfaring Stranger," will have a minor sound since they are built on the scale la, do, re, mi, sol (with la as the tonic). This scale sounds minor (because the interval between la and do is a minor third), and it also has a modal sound (because sol is a whole, not a half, step below la, the tonic, and thus has the flatted 7th sonority). While pentatonic melodies may sound major or minor, and they may or may not have a modal quality, they all have a distinctive sound that many recognize as folky.

Of course, not all modal or pentatonic melodies are folk music or Appalachian (much pop music uses the ♭VII chord in place of, or along with, the V chord). And people often associate modal music with Celtic music if the context is acoustic, country, folk, mountain, or bluegrass. In the context of Dolly's music, her songs that use modal chords usually suggest a mountain aesthetic for her listeners, and Dolly herself describes the ♭VII sonority as "that old mountain sound" and the "sorrow chord."[4] Old-time musician David Holt characterized major tunes as having "a wisdom about fun and just enjoyment of life," while modal tunes have a "dark kind of wisdom."[5] West Virginia old-time banjo-player Dwight Diller took it a step further when he said that his beloved modal tunes seemed to be saying one thing to him: "You're gonna *die!* You're gonna *die!*"[6]

For a more detailed description of modes in popular music, see Lloyd White-sell, *The Music of Joni Mitchell* (New York: Oxford University Press, 2008), 119, 126–127. For a study of modes in folk songs, see Bertrand H. Bronson, "Folksong and the Modes," *The Musical Quarterly* 32, no. 1 (January 1946): 37–49.

Appendix D

"Wayfaring Stranger" and Dolly's Compositional Voice—A Case Study

One of Dolly's approaches in her songwriting workshop is to take a tune, boil it down to its essence, and then rework the melodic elements into new songs. The tune of "Wayfaring Stranger" is one that Dolly draws on for four of her songs that sound, as she would say, old world. Through studying these songs, we have a window into Dolly's process as a songwriter. Dolly said the hymn "was important to me," and she has a vivid memory of hearing it as a child:

> One time when I was very small I remember going to this old wooden church up on Locust Ridge over in the holler, Tennessee Mountain Home area. And I remember this old man stood up at church right in the audience, he didn't go up front or anything, he just stood up in the middle of the service and started to sing "Wayfaring Stranger." And it was the saddest, most beautiful, most lonesome thing I'd ever heard, just seeing that old man there in his overalls and his old faded country shirt. And I think he just felt inspired, something must have touched him, and he just got up to sing it. And since then I think it just went so deep inside my soul that it just must be embedded. But I think it's a beautiful melody.[1]

Before exploring Dolly's songs inspired by this hymn, we should take a closer look at its melody and formal structure.

"Wayfaring Stranger" has a minor pentatonic melody that has a modal feel with its flatted 7th scale degree. The hymn has two sections, A and B, that form an AA'BA" structure for each verse. The A sections remain in the lower

EXAMPLE D.I. "Wayfaring Stranger"

half of the scale, spanning just the first five scale degrees, and they have two melodic phrases each, *a* and *b*. The first A has an open-ended cadence that ends on the 5th scale degree. A' has a fully-closed cadence that returns the melody to the tonic or 1st scale degree. The only difference between A" and A' is their opening melodic gesture. The B section also consists of two phrases, *c* and *c'*. This section quickly moves to the upper half of the scale with a leap to the upper tonic note from the 5th scale degree, which is a striking melodic opening to this section.[2]

   In the following four examples, Dolly shapes the melody of "Wayfaring Stranger" into new songs. When she creates songs inspired by "Wayfaring Stranger," she usually adheres most closely to the melody of the *a* phrase, while she usually riffs more freely on the *b* phrase, though she usually maintains the cadential note of this phrase. Further, she consistently uses the second *c'* phrase rather than the more melodically active *c* phrase. For Dolly, these *c* phrases merge—their initial melodic leap is the phrase's signature. Further, she often substitutes one of the *b* phrases for the second *c* phrase. The result is that in her reworkings of the "Wayfaring Stranger" tune, the beginnings of the sections are consistently similar to the original tune, but the second phrases are often more freely written.

Dolly's most recognizable use of "Wayfaring Stranger" is her song "If I Had Wings."

> *Chorus 1*
> A   a   If I had wings . . .
>   b   All of my . . .
> A'   a   I would fly . . .
>   b'   Heaven knows . . .
>   b'   Tag: If I had wings . . .
> *Verses 1 and 2 as above but no Tag, followed by:*
> *Chorus 2 & 3 (instrumental section between choruses)*
> B   c'   If I had wings . . .
>   b   All of my . . .
> B   c'   And I would fly . . .
>   b'   If I had wings . . .
>   b'   Tag: If I had wings . . .
> *Chorus 4 (free improvisation)*
> *Conclusion (original melody)*

Here, she sets the hymn melody to new words. But rather than retaining the AA'BA" form of the original, she uses only the AA' for the first chorus and two verses. Then in her return to the second and third chorus (with slightly altered words), she switches to the B melody, although she substitutes the *b'* phrase for the second *c'* phrase. However, she retains the characteristic leap up the octave at the beginning of the B section, which is what gives this section its particular identity. In the final chorus, she freely improvises with her backup singers. At the moment the song seems to be over, Dolly begins to hum and then wordlessly vocalize the hymn's original melody with no accompaniment, and she ends by singing the title line, "if I had wings," in a free rhythm. This improvisatory and unaccompanied ending recalls the sense of spontaneity she heard in the old man's performance from her childhood.

In 2001, Dolly reworked "Wayfaring Stranger" for her song "Little Sparrow." She uses the tune in a straightforward way in the opening lines of verse 1, and then she varies the melody throughout the rest of the song. (I use parentheses in the charts to suggest more substantial variations of the melodic phrases that are still related to the original).

> *Intro*
> B   (c)   Little Sparrow . . .
>   b   Precious fragile . . .

B	(c)	Little Sparrow . . .
	b'	Fly so high . . .

Verse 1

A	a	All ye maidens . . .
	b	Never trust . . .
A'	a'	They will crush you . . .
	b'	Leaving you . . .
B	c'	They will vow . . .
	b	Swear no love . . .
A"	(a)	Then they'll leave you . . .
	(b')	Break your little heart . . .

As she did in "If I Had Wings," Dolly substitutes the *b* phrase for the second *c* phrase in the B section of the verse. And Dolly once again includes an unaccompanied, rhythmically free section in "Little Sparrow"—this time in the introduction in which she highlights the leap to the upper tonic of the *c* phrase that is so characteristic of the hymn's tune. The intro's first and third phrases are sparse suggestions of this *c* melody; the second and fourth phrases reiterate the *b* melody. Thus, "Little Sparrow" is not simply the old hymn with new words (which one might say of "If I Had Wings"). Rather, it is a reimagining of the tune that Dolly writes in a way that feels improvisatory, as though she has fully absorbed the original melody and can now riff on it in a variety of ways.

Two other songs, "Crippled Bird" and "Only Dreamin'," both reminiscent of "Wayfaring Stranger," take this improvisatory quality even further. In "Crippled Bird," a song about grief, Dolly uses a major, rather than minor, pentatonic scale, giving the song a Mixolydian modal feel. Paradoxically, this major-sounding scale does not mitigate the sadness but gives the song more poignancy. The major third has a brighter, edgier sound than a minor third. That sharpness, combined with the flatted 7th scale degree and heart-wrenching lyrics, effectually torments the listener with the anguish of lost happiness. Also, Dolly more freely adapts the melodic gestures of "Wayfaring Stranger."

Verse 1

A	a	A broken heart . . .
	(c')	It must have . . .
A'	a	I am like . . .
	(b')	In hopes . . .

Verse 2 as above followed by:

B	c'	Oh to die . . .
	c'	Slow to heal . . .

A"   a'   Fragile . . .
       (b')   Crippled bird . . .

She opens "Crippled Bird" with a rhythmically flexible, unaccompanied first verse, evoking the same impromptu feeling she brought to her recordings of "Wayfaring Stranger" and "Little Sparrow." In the second phrase of the first A section, Dolly lingers more in the upper part of the scale, introducing the *c* phrase that she usually reserves for more climactic, anguished moments toward the end of her songs. For the *b* phrase of section A', she remains quite low in the range, dipping below the tonic.

Dolly's most complex reworking of the musical elements of "Wayfaring Stranger" is in "Only Dreamin'." Like "Crippled Bird," Dolly uses the major sounding Mixolydian pentatonic scale for "Only Dreamin'" for the same anguished emotional effect. Further, the opening melodic lines of both songs are identical. Again, Dolly does not adhere strictly to the AA'BA" structure of "Wayfaring Stranger" in "Only Dreamin'." In the songs discussed earlier, she retained the original duple structure of the hymn with phrases and sections coming in groups of two. But in "Only Dreamin'," Dolly constructs a different structure, with the chorus comprising three A parts subdivided into two phrases each.

Opening Chorus
A   a   Oh I know . . .
      (b)   'Cause I'll awake . . .
A   a   And my tears . . .
      (b)   As my broken heart . . .
A   a   Yes I know . . .
      (b)   But I'll just . . .
Intervening Verses, Chorus, Bridge
Final Chorus that moves up the octave
B   c'   Oh I know . . .
      (c')   'Cause I'll awake . . .
B'   c'   And my tears . . .
      (b)   And you will still . . .
A   a   Yes I know . . .
      (b)   But I'll just . . .

Following her usual practice, she substantially varies the *b* melody of "Way-faring Stranger," thus I use parentheses for these phrases. For the verses and the bridge of the song, she writes new melodic phrases in groups of two that are variants of the main melodies of the chorus. Moreover, she saves the B section of "Wayfaring Stranger" for the climax at the end of the song, which she extends with a repeat of the B section. As in the A section, the second phrases of the B section are different from the original phrases of "Wayfaring Stranger."

Dolly's manipulation of melody and form in "Only Dreamin'" is impressive and worthy of a closer examination. Like so many of her best songs, it is a study of musical economy. As shown in the Listening Outline, for most of the song Dolly uses, varies, and rearranges the *a* and *b* melodic phrases derived from "Wayfaring Stranger." Melody *a* has a rising contour: the leap of a 5th from scale degree 1 to 5. Melody (*b*) has a falling contour and usually comes to rest below the tonic. In the opening chorus of three couplets, this rise and fall is set out quite plainly, and it will be the only time in the song that it is so clearly declaimed in this form: *a* (*b*) *a* (*b*) *a* (*b*). For the verses, Dolly introduces two new melodies, *x* and *y*, both of which remain in the lower register of the mode. The opening chorus and verse are consistent and straightforward. But Dolly begins to develop this limited musical material—*a* and (*b*) with their variants *x* and *y*—in the subsequent choruses. As the song progresses, Dolly ventures further into melodic variations and substitutions, often ornamenting her lines and blurring the distinction between chorus and verse.

Dolly introduces other melodic or harmonic material in only two places. In a brief bridge section, she captures the expectant watchfulness of the singer's line about waiting for her lover's return by closing this section with a nonresolved, open-ended harmony. And in the first couplet of the final chorus, she replaces the *a* and (*b*) melodies with the *c'* melody from the B section of "Wayfaring Stranger." The distinctive melodic gesture of the *c'* melody, with its leap up the octave, reflects the desperation of the lyrics. It is the same move she used for the emotional outcry in the chorus of "Crippled Bird." For the second couplet of the last chorus, Dolly again pushes up the octave with the *c'* melody but then winds down the energy of the song by bringing back the lower melody *x*. She closes with a return to her original *a* and (*b*) for the last couplet and a final reiteration of the *a* melody for the tag. This line ends on the lower 5th scale degree, not the tonic—another open-ended gesture that signals the singer's unwillingness to give up hope.

Because every other line throughout "Only Dreamin'" (except the bridge) has the same harmonic progression—I ♭VII IV I—the song has a rocking motion with the constant recurrence of the modal harmony that feels relentless as it mirrors the singer's unquenchable desire for her lover. The repeated chord progression combined with the limited, but varying, melodic material give the

Listening Outline 6: "Only Dreamin'," *Backwoods Barbie*, 2008

Timing	Section	"Wayfaring Stranger" Form	Phrases (*a*, *b*, and *c* as in "WayfaringStranger")	Comments
0:00	Intro			Whistle, fiddle, wordless background vocals.
0:24	Chorus 1		Oh I know…	Unusual length: three couplets. The *a* is a tonic prolongation (I IV I); the *(b)* line moves through the ♭VII to the IV and back to I.
		A	*a (b)*	
		A	*a (b)*	
		A	*a (b)*	
1:13	Verse 1		I will dream…	Melody *x* uses the same harmonic progression as *a*. Melody *y* is a variant of *(b)* (same harmonic progression and related melody).
			x y	
			x y	
1:44	Chorus 2		And I will dream…	Lyrics changed. Melody varied slightly by using the *y* variant of *(b)*.
		A	*a y*	
		A	*a y*	
		A	*a (b)*	
2:35	Instrumental Interlude			Dolly sings wordlessly, then the pennywhistle enters. Same length and chord progression as verse.
3:07	Bridge		I'll be here…	Contrasting melody and harmony that is open-ended.
			z z′	
3:22	Verse 2		Some will say…	Variants of previous melodies. Melody *(a)* substitutes for *x*.
			(a) y′	
			x y	
3:55	Verse 3		But I will dream…	Further variant of melodies with more ornamented *y′* and the complete substitution of *a′* and *(a)* for *x*. Note melisma on "teardrops" at *y″*.
			a′ y′	
			(a) y″	
4:27	Chorus 3		Oh I know..	Slightly changed lyrics from chorus 1. Chord progression remains the same. First two couplets have a new melody: *c′ (c′)* becomes a high variant of *a (b)* and is the musical and emotional climax of the song. Note melisma on "tears" at *c′* in the second couplet. The reintroduction of *y′* moves the chorus back toward its original sound. Melodies *a* and *(b)* return for final closure.
		B	*c′ (c′)*	
		B	*c′ y′*	
		A	*a (b)*	
5:19	Tag		Yes I know…	Prolonged chord with whistle riff.
			a	

song an obsessive quality as the singer endlessly and deliberately keeps going over the same ground, pretending she is not alone: "Yes I know I'm only dreamin', but I must keep dreamin' on."

In this extended quote, Dolly talked about her process of writing the song and its connection to her memories of mountain music.

> I wrote "Only Dreamin'" on my birthday last year, and I always try to write something on my birthday, and I was in New York City working on the music for the *9 to 5* musical. I did not take a guitar because we'd already finished the music, and I was just there to work with the artists. So, all of a sudden I thought, "well, it's my birthday and I need to write a song and I don't have my guitar." . . . I just started humming 'cause usually when I don't have my instruments with me, I kinda go back to my mother singing all those old-world kinda songs that I grew up with. And I just started singing, "Oh I know, I'm only dreamin'" [sings the first line in minor like "Wayfaring Stranger"]. Before I got there I had it pretty much finished, and I walked in and this lady at the theater said, "Oh, you're writing a song. There's a piano upstairs." I said, "I believe I'm gonna need a dulcimer for this one."[3]

Her mention of the dulcimer, a traditional mountain instrument, also points strongly to the song's old-world character.

Dolly inadvertently revealed her reliance on the "Wayfaring Stranger" tune during this interview when she sang the opening line of "Only Dreamin'" to the minor melody of "Wayfaring Stranger."[4] Indeed, singing "Only Dreamin'" with its major, Mixolydian inflection is challenging without accompaniment to help with the major third. When I asked about her use of "Wayfaring Stranger" for several of her songs, Dolly said, "I do realize that so many of my songs, like 'If I Had Wings,' 'Little Sparrow,' 'Crippled Bird,' 'Only Dreamin','" are inspired by that folk hymn. She continued, saying they are old songs, "but they're also Dolly Parton songs too. But they're just kind of part of my being, really. And so, and it does come natural to me."[5]

The lyrics of "Wayfaring Stranger" embody a spiritual sense of alienation on earth and faith in a heavenly reward. So it is not surprising that Dolly limits her use of this tune to songs about heartbreak, loss, or sorrow. The hymn's lyrics encapsulate the image of the lost soul, the wanderer who is forever a stranger, abandoned, alone, and seeking solace. Dolly taps into this figure with these four songs that dwell on a deep sense of loss and loneliness, which she recalled was her first emotional response to hearing "Wayfaring Stranger."

Notes

Preface and Acknowledgments

1. Patrick King, "*9 to 5*: Comic, Clever, Classy" (January 11, 2017), http://theretroset .com/9-to-5-comic-clever-classy/.

2. Dolly Parton quoted in Michael Bane, "Hello Dolly, Again," *Country Music* 183 (1997): 34.

3. Dolly Parton quoted in Jerry Bailey, "Say Hello to the Real Miss Dolly," *The Tennessean Magazine* (October 20, 1974): 5.

4. Helen Morales, *Pilgrimage to Dollywood: A Country Music Road Trip Through Tennessee* (Chicago: University of Chicago Press, 2014), 69–70.

Introduction

1. Dolly Parton quoted in Toby Thompson, "Dolly Parton Is Such Sweet Sorrow," *Village Voice* 21, no. 16 (April 19, 1976): 12.

2. Lauren Collins, "Looking Swell," *New Yorker* 85, no. 12 (May 4, 2009): 19.

3. Fred Foster, liner notes, *Hello, I'm Dolly* (Monument: SLP18085, 1967). Ellipses in original.

4. Because I discuss duos by Dolly Parton and Porter Wagoner, I also use his first name for consistency. I also use first names for some of Dolly's family members. I use last names for other singers and musicians.

5. Dolly Parton quoted in Joyce Maynard, "What Dolly Wants Now," *McCall's* (May 1992): 144.

6. You will not find the house, but you will get a sense of the remoteness, the terrain, the darkness, and the beauty that surrounded her as a child.

7. Unless stated otherwise, all chart placement numbers refer to *Billboard's* Hot Country Songs or Top Country Albums charts.

8. Dolly Parton, *Shine On with Reese [Witherspoon]*, episode 1, "Interview," aired July 17, 2018, on Direct TV, http://start.att.net/exclusive/hello-sunshine/shine-on and http://start.att.net/exclusive/hello-sunshine/shine-on/episodes/dolly-parton.

9. Dolly Parton quoted in Bill Friskics-Warren, "The Other Dolly Parton, The Songwriting One," *New York Times* (July 21, 2002): A23.

10. Dolly Parton quoted in Joe Tennis, "Having Lunch with Dolly Parton," *Blue Ridge Country* (October 6, 2014), video, http://blueridgecountry.com/newsstand/online_exclusives/lunch-with-dolly-parton/.

11. Dolly Parton quoted in Connie Berman, *The Official Dolly Parton Scrapbook* (New York: Grosset and Dunlap, 1978), 67.

12. Bill DeMain, "Dolly Parton," *Behind the Muse: Pop and Rock's Greatest Songwriters Talk about Their Work and Inspiration* (Cranberry Township, Penn.: Tiny Ripple Books, 2001), 132.

13. Dolly Parton quoted in interview video, Jim Casey, "Dolly Parton Dishes on Her Admiration for Adele, the Secrets to a 50-Year Marriage and the Making of Her New Album, 'Pure and Simple,'" *Nash Country Daily* (August 26, 2016), http://www.nashcountrydaily.com/2016/08/26/dolly-parton-dishes-on-her-admiration-for-adele-the-secrets-to-a-50-year-marriage-the-making-of-her-new-album-pure-simple/.

14. DeMain, *Behind the Muse*, 132.

15. Mark Deming, "All Music Review: *Just Because I'm a Woman*, Dolly Parton," https://www.allmusic.com/album/just-because-im-a-woman-mw0000693334.

16. Dolly Parton, *Dolly: My Life and Other Unfinished Business* (New York: Harper-Collins, 1994), 10.

17. Foster, liner notes, *Hello, I'm Dolly*.

18. Dolly Parton quoted in Bill DeMain, "Dolly Parton," *In Their Own Words: Songwriters Talk about the Creative Process* (Westport, Conn.: Praeger, 2004), 29.

19. Michael Bane, "Hello Dolly, Again," *Country Music* 183 (1997): 34.

20. Parton, *Shine On with Reese*.

Chapter 1. Dolly's Musical Life

1. Parton quoted in Berman, *Official Dolly Parton Scrapbook*, 84.

2. The boyfriend lyrics are from the 1969 version. For the 1973 version, Dolly rewrote these lines. The later version also includes the title line at the end of the first chorus, unlike the 1969 version. The later recording has a more leisurely pace and is more effective at delivering its message about poverty.

3. Parton quoted in Berman, *Official Dolly Parton Scrapbook*, 18. Ellipses in original.

4. John Rockwell, "Dolly Parton, a Country Girl, Is Widening Her Scope," *New York Times* (August 2, 1975): 11.

5. Parton quoted in Berman, *Official Dolly Parton Scrapbook*, 19.

6. Dolly Parton, *Dream More: Celebrate the Dreamer in You* (New York: G. P. Putnam's Sons, 2012), 81.

7. Dolly Parton quoted in Lawrence Grobel, "Dolly Parton: A Candid Conversation with the Curvaceous Queen of Country Music," *Playboy* (October 1978): 110.

8. Dolly Parton, *Bravo Profiles*, "Dolly Parton: Diamond in a Rhinestone World," aired September 6, 1999, on Bravo.

9. Mary A. Bufwack and Robert K. Oermann, *Finding Her Voice: Women in Country Music, 1800–2000* (Nashville, Tenn.: Vanderbilt University, 2003), 312.

10. Alanna Nash, *Behind Closed Doors: Talking with the Legends of Country Music* (New York: Cooper Square Press, 2002), 377

11. Dolly Parton, personal communication, February 25, 2019.

12. Berman, *Official Dolly Parton Scrapbook*, 25.

13. Parton, *Dolly*, 83.

14. Ibid.

15. Ibid., 105–106.

16. Dolly wrote the song when she was eleven, but it was not recorded until 1959. This is not the "Puppy Love" that was a hit for Paul Anka (who wrote the song) in 1960 and Donny Osmond in 1972.

17. Dolly Parton, *Fresh Air*, "Dolly Parton: The Fresh Air Interview," interviewed by Terry Gross, aired September 6, 2010, originally broadcast January 23, 2001, on NPR, https://www.npr.org/2010/09/06/129611133/dolly-parton-singing-songs-from -the-heart-and-soul and http://www.npr.org/templates/transcript/transcript.php ?storyId=129611133.

18. Parton, *Dolly*, 125.

19. Parton quoted in Thompson, "Dolly Parton Is Such Sweet Sorrow,"13.

20. Willadeene Parton, "My Sister Dolly Parton," *McCall's* (July 1985): 125.

21. Dolly Parton quoted in Jack Hurst, "You've Come a Long Way, Dolly," *High Fidelity* (December 1977): 124.

22. Parton, *Dolly*, 164.

23. Porter Wagoner quoted in Thompson, "Dolly Parton Is Such Sweet Sorrow," 12.

24. Parton, *Dolly*, 170.

25. Parton quoted in Nash, *Behind Closed Doors*, 393.

26. Ibid., 383.

27. Dolly Parton quoted in Ralph Emery, with Patsi Bale Cox, *50 Years down a Country Road* (New York: William Morrow, 2000), 299.

28. Tom Rutledge quoted in Alanna Nash, *Dolly: The Biography*, updated ed. (New York: Cooper Square Press, 2002), 113. All subsequent citations refer to this edition.

29. Parton, *Shine On with Reese*.

30. Parton, *Dolly*, 175.

31. Ibid., 163–164.

32. Their 1980 album, *Porter & Dolly*, was mixed from tracks they had previously recorded while still a duo.

33. Parton quoted in Bufwack and Oermann, *Finding Her Voice*, 318.

34. Parton quoted in Nash, *Dolly: The Biography*, 181.

35. Ibid., 181–182.

36. Patrick Carr, "Dolly Parton: Hungry for the Real Thing," *Country Music* (September 1989): 31.

37. Parton quoted in Grobel, "A Candid Conversation," 91.

38. Parton quoted in Nash, *Dolly: The Biography*, 206.

39. Tom Carson, "Dolly Parton: *Heartbreaker*" (album review) *Rolling Stone* 276 (October 19, 1978): 92, http://www.rollingstone.com/music/albumreviews/heartbreaker -19781019.

40. Parton quoted in Nash, *Dolly: The Biography*, 185.

41. Dolly Parton quoted in Chet Flippo, "Dolly Parton," *Rolling Stone* 332 (December 11, 1980): 40, http://www.rollingstone.com/music/features/q-a-dolly-parton-19801211. On the album following *9 to 5*, Dolly wrote eight out of the ten songs.

42. For details on the contract and lawsuit, see Steve Eng, *A Satisfied Mind: The Country Music Life of Porter Wagoner* (Nashville: Rutledge Hill Press, 1992).

43. Parton, *Dolly*, 236, 242.

44. Ibid., 244–245.

45. Carr, "Dolly Parton," 30.

46. Elvis Mitchell, "Dolly Parton," *Interview* 38 (February 2008): 150.

47. Ken Tucker, "9 to 5: How Dolly Parton and Willie Nelson Qualified for 'Lifestyles of the Rich and Famous,'" *Country: From the Beginning to the 90s: The Music and the Musicians* (Nashville: Country Music Foundation, 1994), 275.

48. Carr, "Dolly Parton, " 32.

49. Ibid., 28.

50. Dolly Parton quoted in Paul Kingsbury, "Once More with Feeling: A Conversation with Dolly Parton," *Journal of Country Music* 19, no. 2 (1997): 37.

51. Ibid., 31.

52. Dolly Parton quoted in Chet Flippo, "Dolly Parton Returns to Country's Fore," *Billboard* 108, no. 36 (September 7, 1996): 13.

53. Ibid.

54. Parton, *Dream More*, 105.

55. Parton quoted in Flippo, "Dolly Parton Returns to Country's Fore," 13.

56. Carr, "Dolly Parton," 32.

57. Dolly Parton quoted in Jancee Dunn, "Dolly Parton," *Rolling Stone* 934 (October 30, 2003): 55–56.

58. Dolly Parton quoted in Ray Waddell, "The Importance of Being Dolly," *Billboard* 120, no. 17 (April 26, 2008), 32.

59. DeMain, *In Their Own Words*, 30.

60. Dolly Parton quoted in Thomas Goldsmith, "Dolly Parton: A Superstar's Song Journey Home," *Bluegrass Unlimited* 34, no. 6 (December 1999): 42.

61. Dolly Parton quoted in Fiona Ritchie and Doug Orr, *Wayfaring Strangers: The Musical Voyage from Scotland and Ulster to Appalachia* (Chapel Hill: University of North Carolina Press, 2014), ix.

62. Steve Buckingham, personal communication, October 11, 2018.

63. Parton quoted in Dunn, "Dolly Parton," 56.

64. Parton quoted in Goldsmith, "Dolly Parton," 43.

65. Edd Hurt, "Dolly Parton: Queen of the Backwoods," *American Songwriter* (January 1, 2008), https://americansongwriter.com/2008/01/dolly-parton-queen-of-the -backwoods/.

66. Parton quoted in Waddell, "Importance of Being Dolly," 32.

67. Carr, "Dolly Parton," 32.

68. Parton quoted in Nash, *Dolly: The Biography*, 278.

69. Parton quoted in Dunn, "Dolly Parton," 56.

70. Parton quoted in Nash, *Dolly: The Biography*, 168–169.

Chapter 2. Dolly's Songwriting Workshop

1. Dolly Parton quoted in Jennifer V. Cole, "Dolly Parton: The Southern Living Interview," *Southern Living* (October 2014): 109, http://thedailysouth.southern living.com/2014/09/11/dolly-parton-the-southern-living-interview/.

2. Robert Lee Parton quoted in Paul Soelberg, "An Indepth Look at Dolly Parton," *Country Song Roundup* (November 1971): 11.

3. Parton, *Dolly*, 81.

4. Parton, personal communication.

5. Ibid.

6. Dolly Parton quoted in Joshua Castle, "Dolly Parton: A Total Experience," *Country Song Roundup* (November 1969): 14.

7. Parton, personal communication.

8. Eng, *A Satisfied Mind*, 267.

9. Tony Maglio, "Dolly Parton's 'Coat of Many Colors' Lands Largest-Ever Delayed Viewing Gain for a Broadcast Movie," *The Wrap* (December 17, 2015), https://www.thewrap.com/dolly-parton-coat-of-many-colors-nbc-tv-ratings-delayed-viewing/.

10. Complete National Recording Registry Listing, https://www.loc.gov/programs/national-recording-preservation-board/recording-registry/complete-national-recording-registry-listing/. See also the essay on this honor by Cary O'Dell, "'Coat of Many Colors,'—Dolly Parton (1971)—Added to the National Registry: 2011," https://www.loc.gov/programs/static/national-recording-preservation-board/documents/Coatof ManyColors.pdf.

11. Parton, *Dream More*, 63.

12. Parton quoted in Cole, "Dolly Parton," 109.

13. Parton quoted in DeMain, *In Their Own Words*, 38.

14. Parton quoted in Waddell, "Importance of Being Dolly," 32.

15. Dolly Parton quoted in *Tell Me More*, "Dolly Parton on Faith, Politics and Hard Times," interviewed by Michel Martin, aired February 18, 2009, on NPR, https://www.npr.org/templates/transcript/transcript.php?storyId=100808732.

16. Parton quoted in DeMain, *In Their Own Words*, 38.

17. Emmylou Harris quoted in Berman, *Official Dolly Parton Scrapbook*, 81.

18. Porter Wagoner quoted in Soelberg, "An Indepth Look," 15.

19. Buckingham, personal communication.

20. Dolly Parton quoted in Joan Dew, *Singers and Sweethearts: The Women of Country Music* (Garden City, N.Y.: Dolphin Books, 1977), 120.

21. Parton quoted in Friskics-Warren, "The Other Dolly Parton," A23.

22. Parton quoted in Casey, "Dolly Parton Dishes."

23. Parton, *Dolly*, 206.

24. Dolly Parton, liner notes, *Hungry Again* (Decca: DRND-70041, 1998).

25. Parton quoted in Nash, *Behind Closed Doors*, 393–394.

26. Dolly Parton, "Dolly Parton, Interview by Deborah Evans Price, *American Songwriter*, March/April 1990," in *Song: The World's Best Songwriters on Creating the Music That Moves Us*, J. Douglas Waterman, ed. (Cincinnati: Writer's Digest Books, 2007), 264.

27. Parton quoted in DeMain, *Behind the Muse*, 132.

28. Parton quoted in Friskics-Warren, "The Other Dolly Parton," A23.

29. Parton quoted in Berman, *Official Dolly Parton Scrapbook*, 87.

30. Parton quoted in DeMain, *In Their Own Words*, 36.

31. Parton quoted in Price, "Song," 264.

32. Dolly Parton quoted in LaWayne Satterfield, "The Many Faces of Dolly Parton Reveal Beauty, Love, Compassion," *Music City News* (May 1972): 6.

33. Parton quoted in DeMain, *In Their Own Words*, 33.

34. Ibid., 38.

35. Parton, personal communication.

36. Steve Buckingham quoted in Nancy Cardwell, *The Words and Music of Dolly Parton: Getting to Know Country's "Iron Butterfly"* (Santa Barbara, Calif.: Praeger, 2011), 124.

37. Parton, personal communication.

38. Parton quoted in Grobel, "A Candid Conversation," 110.

39. Parton quoted in Dew, *Singers and Sweethearts*, 107.

40. Dolly Parton quoted in Mary-Ann Bendel, "A Different Dolly," *Ladies' Home Journal* (November 1987): 182.

41. Parton quoted in Eng, *A Satisfied Mind*, 253.

42. Pamela Wilson, "Mountains of Contradictions: Gender, Class, and Region in the Star Image of Dolly Parton." In Cecelia Tichi, ed. *Reading Country Music: Steel Guitars, Opry Stars, and Honky-Tonk Bars* (Durham: Duke University Press, 1998), 106.

43. Parton quoted in Grobel, "A Candid Conversation," 102.

44. Parton quoted in DeMain, *In Their Own Words*, 33.

45. Dolly Parton, liner notes, *Coat of Many Colors* (RCA: LSP 4603, 1971).

46. The photograph also appeared on the cover of *Porter Wayne and Dolly Rebecca* (1970).

47. Dolly Parton quoted in Chet Flippo, "What Would You Get if You Crossed Mae West with Norman Vincent Peale? Dolly Parton," *Rolling Stone* 246 (August 25, 1977): 38, http://www.rollingstone.com/music/features/dolly-parton-19770825. Ellipses in original indicating Dolly's hesitancy.

48. Parton, *Dolly*, 39.

49. Dolly Parton quoted in Bruce R. Miller, "Dolly Parton Relives a Piece of Her Life in 'Coat of Many Colors,'" *Sioux City Journal* (December 8, 2015), http://siouxcityjournal.com/entertainment/television/dolly-parton-relives-a-piece-of-her-life-with-coat/article_5a29eab2–6440–5b99-a453-fo3dcef8eca5.html.

50. See photo at http://dollyparton.com/tag/porter-wagoner.

51. Dolly Parton, *Coat of Many Colors*, illustrated by Judith Sutton (New York: Harper Collins, 1996).

52. "'Makin' Fun Ain't Funny' by Dolly Parton," http://dollyparton.com/life-and-career/makin-fun-aint-funny-by-dolly-parton/12846.

53. Parton, *Dolly*, 202.

54. The song was probably deemed too long for radio play with the additional verse: in its recorded version it clocks in at 3:02.

55. Parton, *Dream More*, 62.

56. Parton quoted in Berman, *Official Dolly Parton Scrapbook*, 80.

Chapter 3. Dolly's Appalachian Musical Heritage

1. Parton, personal communication.

2. Joseph V. Tirella, "Talking with ... Dolly Parton," *People* 55, no. 4 (January 29, 2001): 38.

3. Waddell, "The Importance of Being Dolly," 32.

4. Parton quoted in DeMain, *In Their Own Words*, 31.

5. Parton, *Dolly*, 97.

6. Parton, personal communication.

7. Ibid.

8. Ibid.

9. Parton quoted in Bufwack and Oermann, *Finding Her Voice*, 312.

10. Parton, personal communication.

11. Dorothy Jo Owens Parton (with Javetta Saunders and Dr. Jerry Horner), *Dolly's Hero Shares Mighty Mountain Voices* (Dothan, Ala: Royal Reflections Publishing, 2007), 8; Willadeene Parton, *Smoky Mountain Memories: Stories from the Hearts of Dolly Parton's Family* (Nashville: Rutledge Hill Press, 1996), 146.

12. Parton, personal communication.

13. *Kitty Wells and Johnny Wright Sing Heartwarming Gospel Songs* (Decca: DL7–5325, 1972).

14. Parton, personal communication.

15. Ronald D. Eller, foreword, in Dwight B. Billings, Gurney Norman, and Katherine Ledford, eds., *Confronting Appalachian Stereotypes: Back Talk from an American Region* (Lexington: University Press of Kentucky, 1999), ix.

16. Wilson, "Mountains of Contradictions," 108.

17. Ibid., 109.

18. Berman, *Official Dolly Parton Scrapbook*, 78.

19. Richard A. Peterson, *Creating Country Music: Fabricating Authenticity* (Chicago: University of Chicago Press, 1997), 5.

20. Berman, *Official Dolly Parton Scrapbook*, 85.

21. Jada Watson hears the steel guitar as a mountain instrument in "Region and Identity in Dolly Parton's Songwriting," in *The Cambridge Companion to the Singer-Songwriter* (Cambridge, U.K.: Cambridge University Press, 2016), 126.

22. Eng, *A Satisfied Mind*, 299.

23. Nash, *Dolly: The Biography*, 131–132.

24. Powel quoted in Eng, *A Satisfied Mind*, 299.

25. Carson, "Dolly Parton: *Heartbreaker*," 92.

26. Chet Flippo, "Dolly Parton," in *Encyclopedia of Country Music: The Ultimate Guide to the Music*, Paul Kingsbury, ed. (New York: Oxford University Press, 1998), 406.

27. Another of Dolly's childhood homes is on the cover of the album *My Blue Ridge Mountain Boy*.

28. Michael Ann Williams, "Pride and Prejudice: The Appalachian Boxed House in Southwestern North Carolina," *Winterthur Portfolio* 25, no. 4 (Winter, 1990): 223.

29. Parton quoted in Thompson, "Dolly Parton Is Such Sweet Sorrow," 12–13.

30. Pamela Fox, *Natural Acts: Gender, Race, and Rusticity in Country Music* (Ann Arbor: University of Michigan Press, 2009), 140.

31. Parton quoted in Scot Haller, "Come On Down to Dollywood," *People* 25, no. 18 (May 5, 1986): 134, http://people.com/archive/cover-story-dolly-parton-come-on-down-to-dollywood-vol-25-no-18/.

32. https://www.dollywood.com/themepark/Rides/Tennessee-Mountain-Home.

33. Parton, *Dolly*, 51.

34. Parton quoted in Nash, *Dolly: The Biography*, 278.

35. Parton, personal communication.

36. Bill C. Malone, "Music," in Richard A. Straw and H. Tyler Blethen, eds., *High Mountains Rising: Appalachia in Time and Place* (Urbana: University of Illinois Press, 2004), 115.

37. For a history of the connection between the music of Appalachia and Britain and Ireland, see Ritchie and Orr, *Wayfaring Strangers*. Dolly Parton wrote the Foreword of this book. For a history of these musical styles and their influences, see Robert Cantwell, "Ancient Tones: The Roots of Southern Songs," in his *Bluegrass Breakdown: The Making of the Old Southern Sound* (Urbana: University of Illinois Press, 1984), 115–142.

38. Parton, personal communication.

39. Dolly Parton quoted in Andrew Dansby, "Dolly Parton Shines Again," *Rolling Stone* (January 23, 2001), https://www.rollingstone.com/music/music-news/dolly-parton-shines-again-252734/.

40. Parton, personal communication.

41. For more details, see Ron Pen, "Ballads," in *Encyclopedia of Appalachia*, Rudy Abramson and Jean Haskell, eds. (Knoxville: University of Tennessee Press, 2006).

42. Parton, personal communication.

43. DeMain, *In Their Own Words*, 30–31.

44. Parke Puterbaugh, "Little Sparrow," *Rolling Stone* (February 20, 2001), https://www.rollingstone.com/music/music-country/little-sparrow-202984/.

45. Buckingham, personal communication.

46. Ibid.

47. Parton quoted in Sarah Liss, "Blond Ambition: Country Treasure Dolly Parton Comes Alive," *CBC News* (November 9, 2009), http://www.cbc.ca/news/entertainment/blond-ambition-1.829363.

48. Olive Dame Campbell and Cecil Sharp, *English Folk Songs from the Southern Appalachians* (New York: G. P. Putnam's Sons, 1917), 220–222. I am not suggesting that Dolly consulted Sharp or used the versions he collected. The song was common in the oral tradition in Appalachia, and Dolly recalled hearing it in her childhood.

49. Parton, personal communication.

50. Eng, *A Satisfied Mind*, 320.

51. The tune is actually a mixture of modal and tonal minor sonorities since it uses both the ♭VII (with the flatted 7th scale degree) and the V chord (with the raised 7th scale degree).

52. The song was presumably written for Sandy Gallin, her manager and close friend for 25 years. He was the driving force in her crossover into pop.

53. Jocelyn R. Neal, *Country Music: A Cultural and Stylistic History*, 2nd ed. (New York: Oxford University Press, 2019), 342.

54. Parton, *Dolly*, 77.

55. Nash, *Dolly: The Biography*, 152.

56. Zanaibar66, "This is exquisite—almost medieval," 2015, comment on "Dolly Parton 01—The Bargain Store," posted by littlesparrow185, https://www.youtube.com/watch?v=K94QvVXoHCY.

57. Mat Snow, "American Idol," *Mojo Music Magazine* 175 (June 2008): 64, http://www.mojo4music.com/2256/mojo-issue-175-may-2008/.

58. Parton quoted in Hurst, "You've Come a Long Way, Dolly," 123.

59. Buckingham, personal communication.

60. A well-known example is the soundtrack of *O Brother, Where Art Thou?* which includes little to no bluegrass music even though it is regularly labeled bluegrass.

61. For a comparison of old-time music and bluegrass, see Ritchie and Orr, *Wayfaring Strangers*, 268–269.

62. See Neil V. Rosenberg, *Bluegrass: A History*, 20th Anniversary ed. (Bloomington: University of Illinois Press, 2005).

63. Parton quoted in Goldsmith, "Dolly Parton," 41.

64. Teresa Goddu, "Bloody Daggers and Lonesome Graveyards: The Gothic and Country Music," in *Reading Country Music: Steel Guitars, Opry Stars, and Honky-Tonk Bars*, ed. Cecelia Tichi (Durham: Duke University Press, 1998), 57.

65. Ron Pen quoted in Ritchie and Orr, *Wayfaring Strangers*, 153.

66. *Sisters in Country: Dolly, Linda and Emmylou*, directed and produced by Dione Newton, aired November 4, 2016, on BBC4.

67. Parton, liner notes, *Hungry Again*.

68. Alanna Nash, editorial review for "Hungry Again," https://www.amazon.com/Hungry-Again-Dolly-Parton/dp/B00000ADG5/ref=sr_1_1?ie=UTF8&qid=1493920500&sr=8-1&keywords=hungry+again+dolly+parton+album.

69. Linda Ray, "Dolly Parton—*Hungry Again*," *No Depression: The Journal of Roots Music* (October 31, 1998), http://nodepression.com/album-review/dolly-parton-hungry-again.

70. Jocelyn R. Neal, *The Songs of Jimmie Rodgers: A Legacy in Country Music* (Bloomington: Indiana University Press, 2009), 32, 31.

71. Brian Carmody, "Questions for Dolly Parton: For God & Country," *New York Times Magazine* (November 21, 1999), https://partners.nytimes.com/library/magazine/home/19991121mag-qa-dolly.html.

72. Buckingham, personal communication.

73. Dolly Parton quoted in Jon Weisberger, "Dolly Goes Bluegrass," *Bluegrass Now Magazine* 9, no. 12 (1999), http://www.dollyon-line.com/archives/articles/bn_991200.shtml.

74. Buckingham, personal communication.

75. Buckingham believed ending with this deceptive cadence would make the song "more dramatic"; personal communication.

76. Buckingham, personal communication.

77. Dolly Parton, Interview, Special Features, *Songcatcher*, DVD, directed by Maggie Greenwald (Santa Monica, Calif.: Lionsgate Home Entertainment, 2001).

78. Charlotte Robinson, "Dolly Parton: *Little Sparrow*" review, *Pop Matters*, http://www.popmatters.com/review/partondolly-little/.

79. Jonathan Gregg, "The Bluegrass Just Keeps Growing," *Time Magazine* (February 1, 2001), http://content.time.com/time/arts/article/0,8599,97758,00.html.

80. Dolly Parton quoted in "Dolly Sings It Back Home," *Newsweek* 137, no. 5 (January 29, 2001): 63.

81. Buckingham, personal communication.

82. Friskics-Warren, "The Other Dolly Parton," A23.

83. Parton quoted in Dansby, "Dolly Parton Shines Again."

84. Steve Buckingham produced this song.

85. Parton, Interview, Special Features, *Songcatcher*.

86. Andy Argyrakis, "Dolly Parton: Blue Smoke (Sony Masterworks)," *CCM Magazine* (July 1, 2014): 38.

87. *On Top of Old Smoky: New Old-Time Smoky Mountain Music* (Great Smoky Mountains Association, 2016).

88. Parton, personal communication.

89. "Dolly Sings It Back Home," 63.

90. Joseph V. Tirella, "Talking with . . . Dolly Parton," *People* 55, no. 4 (January 29, 2001): 38.

91. Parton, personal communication.

92. Ibid.

Chapter 4. Dolly's Mountain Identity and Voice

1. Parton quoted in Tennis, "Having Lunch with Dolly Parton."

2. Dolly Parton, *Dolly Parton: Platinum Blonde*, directed by Jenny Ash, aired January 6, 2003, on BBC2.

3. William G. Frost, "Our Contemporary Ancestors in the Southern Mountains," *Atlantic Monthly* 83 (March 1899): 311–319.

4. Charles Morrow Wilson, "Elizabethan America," *Atlantic Monthly* 144 (August 1929): 238.

5. William Aspenwall Bradley, "In Shakespeare's America," *Harper's Weekly* (August 1915): 436.

6. Frost, "Our Contemporary Ancestors," 314.

7. Bruce Cook, "Dolly Parton Goes Pop," *New Leader* 61 (February 27, 1978): 29.

8. John Rockwell, "A Beguiling Dolly Parton Sings at Jersey Festival," *New York Times* (August 4, 1975): 14.

9. Thompson, "Dolly Parton Is Such Sweet Sorrow," 12.

10. Flippo, "What Would You Get?" 36.

11. Hurst, "You've Come a Long Way, Dolly," 123.

12. Otis James, *Dolly Parton* (New York: Quick Fox, 1978), 24. Berman, *Official Dolly Parton Scrapbook*, 20.

13. Nash, *Dolly: The Biography*, 134, 136.

14. Eng, *A Satisfied Mind*, 320, 242, and 240. One wonders if he was relying on Nash for his descriptions of "Jolene" and "Coat of Many Colors."

15. Flippo, "Dolly Parton," in *Encyclopedia of Country Music*, 406.

16. "Dolly Parton," on Country Music Hall of Fame and Museum's official website, http://countrymusichalloffame.org/artists/artist-detail/dolly-parton. "Dolly Parton," on Gospel Music Hall of Fame's official website, http://gospelmusichalloffame.org/dolly-parton/. As of December 2018, this site no longer uses *Elizabethan*.

17. Stephen Miller, *Smart Blonde: The Life of Dolly Parton* (London: Omnibus Press, 2007), 44. Jim Beviglia, "Lyric of The Week: Dolly Parton 'Jolene,'" *American Songwriter: The Craft of Music* (July 28, 2014), http://americansongwriter.com/2014/07/lyric-week-dolly-parton-jolene/?slide=undefined. Lauren Marino, *What Would Dolly Do? How to Be a Diamond in a Rhinestone World* (New York: Grand Central Publishing, 2018), 130.

18. Parton, *Dolly*, 196.

19. Buckingham, personal communication.

20. Flippo, "What Would You Get?" 36.

21. Cook, "Dolly Parton Goes Pop," 29.

22. Margo Jefferson, "Dolly Parton: Bewigged, Bespangled . . . and Proud," *Ms.* 7, no. 12 (June 1979): 20.

23. DeMain, *In Their Own Words*, 30.

24. Jean Ritchie does have a Dolly-like sound since she sings in a soprano range with a light tone laced with a tight vibrato.

25. Stephanie Vander Wel, "The Singing Voice in Country Music," in *The Oxford Book of Country Music*, Travis D. Stimeling, ed. (Oxford: Oxford University Press, 2017), 158.

26. Berman, *Official Dolly Parton Scrapbook*, 20.

27. *Dolly!* season 1, ep. 7, "The Family Show," aired March 7, 1976, on ABC, https://dollyparton.com/life-and-career/movies-television/dolly-1976-variety-abc-show/427.

28. Parton, personal communication.

29. Parton, *Dolly Parton Tour TV*, episode 1, Chugg Entertainment.

30. Parton, personal communication.

31. Dolly Parton quoted in Stephen L. Betts, "Old Treasures, New Voices, Borrowed Hearts and Blue Memories," *Country Music Today* (July 2002), http://www.dollyon-line.com/archives/articles/cm_020700.shtml.

32. Dolly Parton quoted in Jesse Green, "Dolly or Bust," *New York Magazine* (April 19, 2009), http://nymag.com/nymag/rss/artsculture/56148/.

33. *Sisters in Country*.

34. Sammie Anne Wicks, "A Belated Salute to the 'Old Way' of 'Snaking' the Voice on Its (ca) 345th Birthday," *Popular Music* 8, no. 1 (January 1989): 59, 60.

35. Joseph S. James, *Original Sacred Harp* (Atlanta, 1911), III.

36. Jean Ritchie quoted in Margalit Fox, "Jean Ritchie, Lyrical Voice of Appalachia, Dies at 92," *New York Times* (June 2, 2015): A19, https://www.nytimes.com/2015/06/03/arts/music/jean-ritchie-who-revived-appalachian-folk-songs-dies-at-92.html.

37. "No Hill Billies in Radio: Ballads Are Still Written, Says John Lair," *Prairie Farmer's New WLS Weekly* (March 16, 1935): 7; reprinted in Travis Stimeling, *The Country Music Reader* (Oxford: Oxford University Press, 2015), 72.

38. John Potter, *Vocal Authority: Singing Style and Ideology* (Cambridge, U.K.: Cambridge University Press, 2006), 134, quoted in Vander Wel, "The Singing Voice," 158.

39. Parton, personal communication.

40. Buckingham, personal communication.

41. Parton, personal communication.

42. Thompson, "Dolly Parton Is Such Sweet Sorrow," 12.

43. Parton quoted in Tennis, "Having Lunch."

44. Parton, *Live from London* (Dolly Records: 925-Butterfly 2AV, 2009).

45. Parton quoted in Ritchie and Orr, *Wayfaring Strangers*, x.

46. Buckingham, personal communication.

47. Dolly Parton quoted in Earle Hitchner, "Trad Beat Altan says 'Hello, Dolly' Again," *Irish Echo* (August 9–15, 2000), http://irishecho.com/2011/02/trad-beat-altan-says-hello-dolly-again-2/.

48. Dolly Parton quoted in Gary Graff, "Dolly Parton Makes Big Splash with Little Sparrow," ABC News (February 13, 2001), http://abcnews.go.com/Entertainment/story?id=109572&page=1.

49. Charlotte Robinson, "Dolly Parton: *Little Sparrow*," review, *Pop Matters*, http://web.archive.org/web/20131120012719/http://www.popmatters.com/review/partondolly-little/.

50. Shelley Marsden, "Dolly Parton: 'Ireland's in my Smokey Mountain DNA,'" *Irish World Newspaper* (November 7, 2013), http://www.theirishworld.com/dolly-parton-irelands-in-my-smokey-mountain-dna/.

51. Dolly Parton quoted in Robert Philpot, "Dolly Parton Talks about TV Movie, World Tour, Upcoming CD," *Star-Telegram*, Ft. Worth, DFW.com (November 9, 2013), http://www.dfw.com/2013/11/08/842558_dolly-parton-talks-about-tv-movie.html. Website discontinued; now available on http://www.freezepage.com/1385140522DMFXLRYPNV?url=http://www.star-telegram.com/2013/11/07/5315491/dolly-parton-talks-about-tv-movie.html.

52. Parton, personal communication.

53. Jean Ritchie quoted in Mairéid Sullivan, *Celtic Women in Music: A Celebration of Beauty and Sovereignty* (Kingston, Ontario: Quarry Music Press, 1999), 203.

54. Bill C. Malone complained, "It is amusing but irritating to learn that although the spurious doctrine of Anglo-Saxonism has been largely abandoned by students of mountain music, it is being replaced by the equally shadowy thesis of Celticism." Malone, "Music," 134, 47n.

55. Parton, *Dolly*, 319. Emphasis added.

56. Parton quoted in Dunn, "Dolly Parton," 54.

57. Carrie Havranek, *Women Icons of Popular Music* 2 (Westport, Conn.: Greenwood Press, 2009), 327.

58. Deborah Evans Price, "Parton Returns with 'Sparrow' On Blue Eye/Sugar Hill," *Billboard* (December 16, 2000): 36.

59. Dolly Parton quoted in Price, "Parton Returns," 36.

60. Goldsmith, "Dolly Parton." 42.

61. Parton quoted in Dansby, "Dolly Parton Shines Again."

62. Parton, personal communication.

63. Parton quoted in Price, "Parton Returns," 36. Ellipses in original.

64. Parton, personal communication.

Chapter 5. Songs about Love

1. Parton quoted in Maynard, "What Dolly Wants Now," 107.

2. Josh Klein, "Dolly Parton Was, as Always, an Entertainer at Ravinia," *Chicago Tribune* (August 8, 2016), https://www.chicagotribune.com/entertainment/music/ct-ent-0809-dolly-parton-review-20160805-story.html.

3. Parton quoted in DeMain, *In Their Own Words*, 36.

4. "Dolly leaves 'The Porter Wagoner Show'" (April 8, 1974; Updated August 23, 2015), http://dollyparton.com/life-and-career/movies-television/dolly-leaves-porter-wagoner-show/46.

5. Dolly Parton, "Dolly Parton and Porter Wagoner—'I Will Always Love You' | Live at the Grand Ole Opry | Opry," *Opry YouTube Channel* (October 29, 2007), https://youtu.be/wBLJIcaVC1w.

6. Dolly Parton, "Dolly Parton: 'You're Never Old unless You Choose to Be,'" CBC Radio show q, interviewed by Shadrach Kabango (August 16, 2016), http://www.cbc.ca/radio/q/schedule-for-tuesday-august-16-2016-1.3722655/dolly-parton-you-re-never-old-unless-you-choose-to-be-1.3722662.

7. Parton quoted in Snow, "American Idol," 63.

8. Parton quoted in DeMain, *In Their Own Words*, 36–37.

9. Their recording was simultaneously released on Vince Gill's album *Souvenirs*, (MCA: Nashville 11047, 1995).

10. Other songs that follow this same "Heart and Soul" symmetrical relationship between lines of lyric and chord progressions are "All I Have to Do Is Dream" and "Earth Angel." This progression is sometimes called the "ice cream changes," and there are several variants.

11. Dolly's is not the only song that operates in this way. "Blue Moon" and "Why Do Fools Fall in Love" are others. But these examples are not as plentiful as the "Heart and Soul" more symmetrical types.

12. Dolly Parton quoted in Lisa Butterworth, "All Dolled Up," *BUST* (June–July 2014), https://bust.com/entertainment/13573-the-bust-interview-dolly-parton.html.

13. Parton quoted in DeMain, *In Their Own Words*, 35.

14. Dolly Parton, *Dolly Parton Tour TV*, episode 7, "Dolly the Songwriter," released September 11, 2011, Chugg Entertainment.

15. Parton, *Dolly*, ix.

16. Parton quoted in Dew, *Singers and Sweethearts*, 99.

17. Parton quoted in Flippo, "What Would You Get?" 37.

18. Parton, *Dolly*, ix.

19. Parton quoted in Maynard, "What Dolly Wants Now," 142.

20. Parton, "Dolly Parton: 'You're Never Old,'" CBC Radio show q.

21. Dolly Parton, *Joan Rivers Show*, season 3, interviewed by Joan Rivers, aired March 1, 1993.

22. Parton, *Dolly*, 127.

23. Ibid., 128.

24. Ibid., 129.

25. Ibid.

26. Ibid., 201.

27. Parton quoted in Dew, *Singers and Sweethearts*, 114, 117.

28. Dolly Parton, *Nightline*, "Dolly Parton Unplugged," interviewed by Juju Chang, aired November 26, 2012, on ABC; article and video at Juju Chang and Victoria Thompson, "Dolly Parton on Gay Rumors, New Memoir," http://abcnews.go.com/Entertainment/dolly-parton-gay-rumors-losing-drag-queen-alike/story?id=17812138.

29. Dolly Parton quoted in Tom Lamont, "Dolly Parton: 'There's More to Me than the Big Hair and the Phoney Stuff,'" *Guardian* (December 6, 2014), https://www.theguardian.com/music/2014/dec/06/dolly-parton-more-to-me-than-big-hair-phoney-stuff.

30. Dolly Parton, *Joan Rivers Show*.

31. Dolly Parton quoted in Mary Murphy, "Dolly Parton: Interview," *TV Guide* (November 27, 1993): 14.

32. Dolly Parton quoted in Barbara Grizzuti Harrison, "The Other Dolly Parton," *McCall's* 108 (February 1981): 62.

33. Porter Wagoner with Glenn Hunter, "Hello, Dolly," *Journal of Country Music* 10, no. 1 (1985): 15.

34. Ibid.

35. Ibid., 14.

36. Parton quoted in Betts, "Old Treasures."

37. Nash, *Dolly: The Biography*, 137.

38. Dolly Parton quoted in Carol Botwin, "Dolly Parton Wants a New Image," *The Mercury* from Pottstown, Penn. (June 25, 1977): 64.

39. Parton, *Dolly*, 101.

40. Parton quoted in Dew, *Singers and Sweethearts*, 113.

41. This same gesture appears, though a bit shorter and in minor 3rds, in her recording of "Lonely Comin' Down" (*Jolene*, 1974) written by Porter Wagoner.

42. Dolly Parton, *Tonight Show*, episode 4.234, interviewed by Jay Leno, aired September 19, 1996, on NBC.

43. Parton, *Dolly*, 87–88.

44. The I⁷ and the II chords are secondary dominants (V⁷/IV and V/V respectively).

45. Parton quoted in Grobel, "A Candid Conversation," 106.

46. Dolly reused this melody for "What Is It My Love?" for a naive and disturbing effect.

47. Parton, personal communication.

48. Buckingham, personal communication.

49. Parton quoted in Hurt, "Dolly Parton."

50. Parton, personal communication.

51. Morales, *Pilgrimage to Dollywood*, 129–130. See her amusing taxonomy of Dolly's cheating songs.

52. Alanna Nash, "Sitting Pretty," *Journal of Country Music* 23, no. 3 (2004): 12.

53. Dolly Parton quoted in Tom Vitale, "Dolly Parton's 'Jolene' Still Haunts Singers," *All Things Considered*, NPR (October 9, 2008), http://www.npr.org/2008/10/09/95520570/dolly-partons-jolene-still-haunts-singers.

54. Ibid.

55. Dolly Parton quoted in Jean Vallely, "On the Rock Road with Dolly Parton," *Time* 109, no. 16 (April 18, 1977): 72.

56. Parton quoted in DeMain, *In Their Own Words*, 32.

57. Dolly Parton, *Dolly Parton: 50 Years at the Opry*, aired November 26, 2019, on NBC, https://www.nbc.com/dolly-parton-50-years-at-the-opry.

58. "500 Greatest Songs of All Time," *Rolling Stone* 963 (December 9, 2004): 130. It is listed at #219 in the 2010 update: "500 Greatest Songs of All Time," *Rolling Stone* (April 7, 2011), http://www.rollingstone.com/music/lists/the-500-greatest-songs-of-all-time-20110407/dolly-parton-jolene-20110527.

59. Parton quoted in Vitale, "Dolly Parton's 'Jolene.'"

60. Carson, "Dolly Parton: *Heartbreaker*," 92.

61. Eng, *A Satisfied Mind*, 320. "Jolene" projects an Aeolian mode throughout, though there is a momentary raised 6th scale degree in the harmony vocals of one of the choruses that subtly suggests the Dorian mode. Both modes have a minor feeling with their shared lowered 3rd scale degree.

62. Parton quoted in Nash, *Dolly: The Biography*, 137.

63. Parton quoted in Vitale, "Dolly Parton's 'Jolene.'"

64. Heidemann also links the song's asymmetric phrase structure to traditional Appalachian music (in addition to its modal quality). Kate Heidemann, "Remarkable Women and Ordinary Gals: Performance of Identity in Songs by Loretta Lynn and Dolly Parton." In *Country Boys and Redneck Women: New Essays in Gender and Country Music*, Diane Pecknold and Kristine M. McCusker, eds. (Jackson: University Press of Mississippi, 2016), 178–179.

65. Parton quoted in Hurst, "You've Come a Long Way, Dolly," 124.

66. Parton quoted in Vitale, "Dolly Parton's 'Jolene.'"

67. Nadine Hubbs, "'Jolene,' Genre, and the Everyday Homoerotics of Country Music: Dolly Parton's Loving Address of the Other Woman," *Women and Music: A Journal of Gender and Culture* 19 (2015): 75.

68. Morales, *Pilgrimage to Dollywood*, 129–130.

69. Elisabeth Vincentelli, "Parton's Musical Works," *New York Post* (May 1, 2009), http://nypost.com/2009/05/01/partons-musical-works/.

70. "Don't Let It Trouble Your Mind" was beautifully recorded by Rhiannon Giddens on her solo album, *Tomorrow Is My Turn* (2015).

71. Parton, *Fresh Air* Interview.

72. Chet Flippo, "Dolly Parton: Tennessee Mountain Home-Grown," *Rolling Stone* 193 (October 23, 1975): 24.

Chapter 6. Songs about Women's Lives

1. Dolly Parton, "Celebrating Women: Dolly Parton Marks 60 Years in Music," WATE-TV, interviewed by Josh Smith (March 16, 2019), https://www.wate.com/news/hidden-history/womens-history/celebrating-women-dolly-parton-marks-60-years-in-music/1854154522.

2. Parton quoted in Grobel, "A Candid Conversation," 110.

3. Robert Windeler, "Loretta Lynn's 'Pill' Is Hard for Some Fans to Swallow," *People* 3, no. 12 (March 31, 1975), https://people.com/archive/loretta-lynns-pill-is-hard-for-some-fans-to-swallow-vol-3-no-12/.

4. W. R. Morris, "Controversial Song Makes Money for Artist Despite Ban by Station" (The Country Sound column), *Florence Times and Tri-Cities Daily* (Alabama) 106, no. 47 (February 16, 1975): 36.

5. Loretta Lynn and George Vecsey, *Loretta Lynn: Coal Miner's Daughter* (Chicago: Henry Regnery Company, 1976), 56.

6. Parton quoted in Grobel, "A Candid Conversation," 110.

7. Parton quoted in Flippo, "Dolly Parton: Tennessee Mountain Home-Grown," 24.

8. Pete Axthelm, "Hello Dolly," *Newsweek* 89, no. 24 (June 13, 1977): 71.

9. Gloria Steinem, "Dolly Parton," *Ms.* 15, no. 7 (January 1987): 66.

10. Wilson, "Mountains of Contradictions," 115.

11. Butterworth, "All Dolled Up."

12. Dolly Parton, *Larry King Now*, "Dolly Parton on 'Pure & Simple,' Hillary, & '9 to 5' Reunion," interviewed by Larry King, aired September 10, 2016, on *Russia Today*, https://www.rt.com/shows/larry-king-now/358861-dolly-parton-on-pure-/.

13. Dolly Parton quoted in Susan McHenry, "Positively Parton," *Ms.* 15, no. 1 (July 1986): 14.

14. Jane Fonda quoted in Flippo, "Dolly Parton," *Rolling Stone*, 40.

15. Dolly Parton, *Dolly Parton Tour TV*, episode 8, "Biggest Hits," released September 18, 2011, Chugg Entertainment.

16. Parton quoted in Flippo, "Dolly Parton," *Rolling Stone*, 62.

17. Parton, *Larry King Now*, "Dolly Parton on 'Pure & Simple.'"

18. Parton quoted in Flippo, "What Would You Get?" 37.

19. Parton quoted in Nash, *Dolly: The Biography*, 82.

20. Wilson, "Mountains of Contradictions," 113.

21. Parton quoted in Dew, *Singers and Sweethearts*, 104, 106.

22. Parton quoted in Dunn, "Dolly Parton," 55.

23. Nash, *Dolly: The Biography*, 130–131.

24. Parton, *Sky News*, "'I've Been Hit on All My Life'—Dolly Parton Reflects on Her Career," aired February 18, 2019, https://news.sky.com/story/v3-final-dolly-vju-interview-signed-off-004mp4-11640973.

25. Steinem, "Dolly Parton," 66.

26. Dolly Parton quoted in "Love Secrets That Keep the Magic in Dolly's Marriage," *Star* (November 27, 1990): 12, cited in Wilson, "Mountains of Contradictions," 101, 11n.

27. Dolly Parton quoted in Cliff Jahr, "Golly, Dolly!" *Ladies' Home Journal* 99 (July 1982): 85, 139.

28. Jefferson, "Dolly Parton," 16.

29. Dolly Parton, *60 Minutes*, season 41, episode 28, Morley Safer, "Dolly Parton: The Real Queen of All Media," aired April 5, 2009, on CBS, https://www.cbsnews.com/news/dolly-parton-the-real-queen-of-all-media/.

30. Parton quoted in Friskics-Warren, "The Other Dolly Parton," A23.

31. Havranek, *Women Icons of Popular Music* 2, 316.

32. Wilson, "Mountains of Contradictions," 112.

33. Neal, *The Songs of Jimmie Rodgers*, 38.

34. Dolly Parton quoted in Barry Mazor, *Meeting Jimmie Rodgers: How America's Original Roots Music Hero Changed the Pop Sounds of a Century* (Oxford: Oxford University Press, 2009), 317.

35. Ibid., 316.

36. See Eng, *A Satisfied Mind*, 243–245; Mazor, *Meeting Jimmie Rodgers*, 303 and 317; Linda Ray, "Dolly Parton—The Smartest Working Woman in Show Business," *No Depression* 24 (November–December 1999), http://nodepression.com/article/dolly-parton-smartest-working-woman-show-business.

37. Dolly sang the song on *The Porter Wagoner Show*. Porter introduced the song as "a great number of hers." Dolly Parton, *The Porter Wagoner Show*, season 9, episode 48, aired September 12, 1970, https://vimeo.com/124297609.

38. Neal, *The Songs of Jimmie Rodgers*, 31.

39. See Lydia Hamessley, "A Resisting Performance of an Appalachian Traditional Murder Ballad: Giving Voice to 'Pretty Polly,'" *Women and Music: A Journal of Gender and Culture* 9 (2005): 13–36.

40. Dolly Parton quoted in Jewly Hight, "First Listen: Dolly Parton, 'Blue Smoke,'" http://www.npr.org/2014/04/27/306832152/first-listen-dolly-parton-blue-smoke.

41. Dolly Parton, spoken introduction to "Banks of the Ohio," "Dolly Parton—Track-by-track of her new Blue Smoke album," https://www.youtube.com/watch?v=Y_gi_Zt9WtM.

42. Fox, "Natural Acts," 244.

43. Ibid.

44. Parton, *Joan Rivers Show*. Emphasis added.

45. Dolly Parton quoted in Matt Yancey, "Country Singer Dolly Parton on Verge of Superstar Status," *Robesonian* (October 9, 1975): 17, https://newspaperarchive.com/robesonian-oct-09-1975-p-17/.

46. Parton quoted in Nash, *Dolly: The Biography*, 90.

47. The term *white trash* has a long history and numerous cultural resonances. I intentionally limit my use of the term to the context in which Dolly uses *trash*, as a description of her own image as well as some girls in mountain culture. For a study of white trash in the United States, see Nancy Isenberg, *White Trash: The 400-Year Untold History of Class in America* (New York: Penguin Books, 2016).

48. Parton quoted in Cole, "Dolly Parton," 109.

49. Parton quoted in Maynard, "What Dolly Wants Now," 107, 144. In the official music video for this song, images of Dolly as a child are juxtaposed with a grown-up Dolly looking both country in her sexy gingham and jeans and cosmopolitan as she walks the streets of Hollywood in a gauzy dress. See Leigh H. Edwards, *Dolly Parton, Gender, and Country Music* (Bloomington: Indiana University Press, 2018), 56–59, for an analysis of the video.

50. Dolly Parton quoted in Axthelm, "Hello Dolly," 71.

51. Parton quoted in James, *Dolly Parton*, 86.

52. Parton quoted in Carmody, "Questions for Dolly Parton."

53. Parton, *Dolly*, 58.

54. Parton quoted in DeMain, *In Their Own Words*, 31.

55. Parton quoted in Flippo, "What Would You Get?" 36–37.

56. When Dolly performed the song on *The Porter Wagoner Show* in 1968 or 1969, she took away the shock value of the ending by adding the final words *on the bridge*: "Here is where it started, and here is where I'll end it *on the bridge*." The song was edgy by mid-1960s standards, and this somewhat milder ending was likely viewed as more acceptable to a television audience than the more graphic depiction of suicide sung in the recorded version. For this performance, Dolly sang only to her own accompaniment on acoustic guitar, and the lack of insistent percussion or harmonic modulation also softened the song's effect.

57. Eng, *A Satisfied Mind*, 207.

58. "Ode to Billie Joe" spent eight weeks on the Hot Country Singles chart, peaking at #17, and four weeks at #1 out of a total of fourteen weeks on the Hot 100 chart. "The Bridge" did not chart.

59. For a lyrical reading of the song, see Eric Weisbard, "Love, Lore, Celebrity, and Dead Babies: Dolly Parton's 'Down from Dover,'" in *The Rose & the Briar: Death, Love and Liberty in the American Ballad*, Sean Wilentz and Greil Marcus, eds. (New York: W. W. Norton, 2005), 287–303.

60. This repeated, descending pattern is reminiscent of Renaissance ground bass patterns such as the passamezzo antico in which the bass line descends from 5 to 1 over the chords i♭VII i V, i♭VII i V i. The tune "Greensleeves" uses this pattern in the verses; the chorus uses a variant of this melodic formula, the romanesca.

61. Parton quoted in DeMain, *In Their Own Words*, 33–34.

62. Robinson, "Dolly Parton: Little Sparrow."

63. Parton quoted in Snow, "American Idol," 64.

64. Parton quoted in Jahr, "Golly, Dolly!" 85.

65. Dolly Parton, *Late Night with David Letterman*, episode no. 813: season 6, episode 28, interviewed by David Letterman, aired April 1, 1987, on NBC.

66. Parton quoted in Maynard, "What Dolly Wants Now," 107.

67. *Dolly Parton's Christmas of Many Colors: Circle of Love*, aired November 30, 2016, on NBC.

68. Parton, *Dolly*, 58–59.

69. Parton quoted in DeMain, *Behind the Muse*, 138.

70. Parton quoted in Miller, *Smart Blonde*, 59.

71. Parton quoted in Haller, "Come on Down to Dollywood," 140.

72. Parton, *Fresh Air* Interview.

73. Dolly Parton quoted in Lina Das, "Men Are My Weakness!" *Daily Mail Online* (January 8, 2014), http://www.dailymail.co.uk/femail/article-2024180/Dolly-Parton -rumoured-countless-lovers-45-year-marriage.html.

74. Cas Walker quoted in Nash, *Dolly: The Biography*, 38.

75. Parton, *Bravo Profiles*.

76. Wilson, "Mountains of Contradictions," 101.

77. Dolly Parton quoted in Jerry Bailey, "Say Hello to the Real Miss Dolly," *Tennessean Magazine* (October 20, 1974): 5–6.

78. Parton quoted in "Dolly Sings It Back Home," 63.

79. Parton quoted in DeMain, *Behind the Muse*, 138.

80. Linda Ronstadt quoted in Nash, *Dolly: The Biography*, 82.

81. Dolly Parton, *Big Interview*, season 1, episode 16, interviewed by Dan Rather, aired April 14, 2014, on AXS TV.

82. Samantha Christensen, "'Where It Counts I'm Real': The Complexities of Dolly Parton's Feminist Voice," in *Walking the Line: Country Music Lyricists and American Culture*, Thomas Alan Holmes and Roxanne Harde, eds. (Lanham, Md.: Lexington Books, 2013), 164–165.

83. Parton quoted in DeMain, *Behind the Muse*, 138.

84. Parton quoted in Berman, *Official Dolly Parton Scrapbook*, 42.

85. Parton quoted in Flippo, "What Would You Get?" 36.

86. Parton quoted in DeMain, *In Their Own Words*, 35.

87. Ibid.

88. Ibid.

89. Parton quoted in Axthelm, "Hello Dolly," 71.

90. Dolly Parton, "Celebrating Women: Dolly Parton Marks 60 Years in Music," WATE-TV, interviewed by Josh Smith (March 16, 2019), https://www.wate.com/news/ hidden-history/womens-history/celebrating-women-dolly-parton-marks-60-years -in-music/1854154522.

91. Yvonne Tasker, *Working Girls: Gender and Sexuality in Popular Cinema* (London: Routledge, 1998), 179.

Chapter 7. Songs of Tragedy

1. Dolly Parton quoted in Everett Corbin, "Interview: Music City News," 1967, in *Dolly on Dolly: Interviews and Encounters with Dolly Parton*, Randy L. Schmidt, ed. (Chicago: Chicago Review Press, 2017), 11.

2. Satterfield, "The Many Faces of Dolly Parton," 6.

3. Goddu, "Bloody Daggers," 51.

4. Jefferson, "Dolly Parton," 21.

5. Parton, *Fresh Air* Interview.

6. Parton quoted in Bufwack and Oermann, *Finding Her Voice*, 312.

7. Parton, personal communication. Dolly based her recitation, "Bloody Bones (A Story for Kids)," on this story.

8. Parton, *Fresh Air* Interview.

9. Ibid.

10. Parton quoted in Nash, *Dolly: The Biography*, 287–288.

11. Parton quoted in DeMain, *In Their Own Words*, 33.

12. Parton quoted in DeMain, *Behind the Muse*, 137.

13. Parton quoted in Friskics-Warren, "The Other Dolly Parton," A23.

14. *Blue Valley Songbird*, directed by Richard A. Colla, aired November 1, 1999, on Lifetime.

15. Dolly originally wrote the song for the film version of *The Best Little Whorehouse in Texas*, 1982, but it was cut from the final version.

16. *A Country Christmas Story*, directed by Eric Bross, aired November 9, 2013, on Lifetime.

17. Mitchell Morris, "Crossing Over with Dolly Parton," in his *The Persistence of Sentiment: Display and Feeling in Popular Music of the 1970s* (Berkeley: University of California Press, 2013), 198.

18. Cook, "Dolly Parton Goes Pop," 30.

19. Don Roth quoted in Nash, *Dolly: The Biography*, 228.

20. Laura Cunningham, "Dolly Parton: The Supersexy Superstar of Country Pop," *Cosmopolitan* 186 (January 1979): 134. Ellipses in original.

21. Rockwell, "A Beguiling Dolly Parton," 14.

22. Morris, "Crossing Over with Dolly Parton," 200.

23. Parton, *Dolly*, 5–6. Martha Williams, whom Dolly called Aunt Marth, owned the land that the Partons sharecropped until Dolly was five years old.

24. Parton, *Dolly*, 35.

25. Parton quoted in "Dolly Sings It Back Home," 63.

26. Parton quoted in Axthelm, "Hello Dolly," 71.

27. DeMain, *In Their Own Words*, 33.

28. Parton, *Dolly*, 65, 66.

29. Parton quoted in Eng, *A Satisfied Mind*, 209.

30. Will Carleton, "The Funeral," *Harper's Weekly* (August 28, 1886): 545, 550.

31. Lynette Carpenter and Wendy K. Kolmar, *Ghost Stories by British and American Women: A Selected, Annotated Bibliography* (New York: Routledge, 1998), xix.

32. "Put My Little Shoes Away," Samuel N. Mitchell (1846–1905); "Little Bessie," 19th century, origin unknown; "I Hear a Sweet Voice Calling," Bill Monroe; "There Was Nothing We Could Do," Chuck Carson.

33. Monroe copyrighted "The Little Girl and the Dreadful Snake" in 1953 using his pseudonym *Albert Price*. "The Water Lily" is by Australian poet Henry Lawson (1867–1922). Ralph Stanley recorded Tom T. Hall's setting on *Saturday Night & Sunday Morning* (Freeland Records: CD-9001, 1992).

34. "Little Rosewood Casket" was written by Goullaud and White in 1870.

35. *Hits Made Famous by Country Queens.* Bill Ellis, "'Little Blossom' Lyrics," https://groups.google.com/forum/#!topic/rec.music.country.old-time/HBSosS3WgiQ. The album also included another traditional weeper, "Two Little Orphans."

36. Parton quoted in Flippo, "What Would You Get?" 38.

37. Andrea DenHoed, "Slowed-Down Dolly Parton," *New Yorker* (August 27, 2013), https://www.newyorker.com/culture/culture-desk/slowed-down-dolly-parton.

38. Parton quoted in DeMain, *In Their Own Words*, 34.

39. Nash, *Dolly: The Biography*, 207.

40. Dolly Parton, *Dolly Live from London.* She made this comment to the audience after singing "Only Dreamin'."

41. Parton, *Dolly*, 36.

42. Zora Neale Hurston, *Dust Tracks on a Road: An Autobiography* (1942), 2nd ed., Robert Hemenway, ed. (Urbana: University of Illinois Press, 1984), 213.

43. Parton quoted in DeMain, *In Their Own Words*, 34.

44. Parton quoted in DeMain, *Behind the Muse*, 137.

Chapter 8. Songs of Inspiration

1. Dolly Parton quoted in Miriam Di Nunzio, "Dolly Parton Is Lovin' the 'Simple' Life," *Chicago Sun Times* (August 5, 2016), http://chicago.suntimes.com/entertainment/dolly-parton-is-lovin-the-simple-life/.

2. Dolly Parton quoted in Chris Chase, "The Country Girl," *New York Times Magazine* (May 9, 1976): 60, https://www.nytimes.com/1976/05/09/archives/the-country-girl-country-girl.html.

3. Parton, *Dolly*, 34.

4. Parton quoted in Flippo, "What Would You Get?" 37.

5. Dolly Parton quoted in Todd Aaron Jensen, *On Gratitude: Sheryl Crow, Jeff Bridges, Alicia Keys, Daryl Hall, Ray Bradbury, Anna Kendrick, B. B. King, Elmore Leonard, Deepak Chopra, and 42 More Celebrities Share What They're Most Thankful For* (Avon, Mass.: Adams Media, 2010), 165.

6. Parton, *Dolly*, 174–175.

7. Morales, *Pilgrimage to Dollywood*, 42.

8. Parton, *Dolly*, 72.

9. Parton quoted in Flippo, "What Would You Get?" 38.

10. Written by Sanford Fillmore Bennett, "In the Sweet By and By" (1868), http://www.hymnary.org/.

11. "I'm On My Way to Canaan's Land" comes from the African American spiritual tradition where it is also known as "I'm on My Way" and "If You Go Don't Hinder Me." The song entered white gospel culture with recordings by the Carter Family and other early hillbilly musicians in the 1930s.

12. The title alludes to the hymn "Precious Memories," written by John B. F. Wright, 1925.

13. Albert E. Brumley, "This World Is Not My Home" (1939); William J. Kirkpatrick, "Lord, I'm Coming Home" (1892); John Newton, "Amazing Grace" (1779); Albert E.

Brumley, "If We Never Meet Again" (1945); Lewis E. Jones, "Power in the Blood" (1899), http://www.hymnary.org/.

14. The tune most people know as "Amazing Grace" is the pentatonic melody "New Britain." This tune was joined with the lyrics of the hymn in the 19th century and disseminated through shape note hymnals, most notably *The Sacred Harp*, 1844, and *Southern Harmony*, 1847.

15. Parton, *Dream More*, 106.

16. Parton, *Dolly*, 301.

17. Dolly Parton, Commencement Address, University of Tennessee, 2009, "Dolly Parton Delivers Commencement Address at the University of Tennessee 2009," https://www.youtube.com/watch?time_continue=14&v=EuOm2lLIOoU.

18. Deborah Vansau McCauley, "Religion," in Richard A. Straw and H. Tyler Blethen, eds., *High Mountains Rising: Appalachian in Time and Place* (Urbana: University of Illinois Press, 2004), 183.

19. Parton quoted in Thompson, "Dolly Parton Is Such Sweet Sorrow," 12.

20. Parton quoted in Casey, "Dolly Parton Dishes."

21. Parton quoted in Flippo, "What Would You Get?" 37–38. Dolly also refers to "The Seeker" in her song "High and Mighty" with the line "Say God, I'm just a seeker."

22. Genesis 8:6–8.

23. Matthew 20:16.

24. Micah 4:3.

25. Isaiah 11:6. She also references Matthew 3:12/Luke 3:17 later in the verse with "and he'll separate all the chaff from the wheat."

26. Revelation 1:7.

27. Dolly Parton quoted in Bill DeMain, "Dolly Parton: River Deep, Mountain Soul," *Performing Songwriter* 10 (November 2002): 80.

28. Parton, *Dolly*, 70.

29. Parton quoted in Flippo, "What Would You Get?" 38.

30. Parton, *Dolly*, 71.

31. Ibid., 70–71.

32. Dolly typically just uses *gay*.

33. Parton, *Larry King Now*.

34. Dolly Parton quoted in Charles Gandee, "Good Golly, Miss Dolly," *Vogue* (January 1994): 166.

35. "Honoring Sandy Gallin" (April 22, 2017), https://dollyparton.com/life-and -career/honoring-sandy-gallin/13995.

36. Parton, *Larry King Now*.

37. Dolly Parton quoted in Stephen L. Betts, "Dolly Parton Gives Poignant Response to North Carolina 'Bathroom Bill,'" *Rolling Stone* (June 9, 2016), http://www.rolling stone.com/music/news/dolly-parton-gives-poignant-response-to-north-carolina -bathroom-bill-20160609.

38. Dolly Parton quoted in Peter Cooper, "Parton's Plea for Tolerance," *USA Today* (February 22, 2006), http://usatoday30.usatoday.com/life/people/2006-02-22-parton_x .htm.

39. Michael Foust, "Dolly Parton, Others Compile CD Benefiting Homosexual Group," *Baptist Press* (January 28, 2005), http://www.bpnews.net/20019/dolly-parton-others-compile-cd-benefiting-homosexual-group.

40. Parton, *Larry King Now.*

41. Jada Star Andersen quoted in Kim Severson, "Dollywood: A Little Bit Country, A Little Bit Gay," *New York Times* (August 22, 2014), https://www.nytimes.com/2014/08/24/travel/dollywood-a-little-bit-country-a-little-bit-gay.html?mcubz=3.

42. Parton, *Nightline.*

43. Dolly Parton quoted in Wayne Bledsoe, "Dolly Parton Responds to Dollywood Splash Country T-shirt Controversy," *Knoxville News Sentinel* (August 2, 2011), http://archive.knoxnews.com/news/local/dolly-parton-responds-to-dollywood-splash-country-t-shirt-controversy-ep-403504862–357637141.html.

44. Duncan Tucker quoted in Craig Shelburne, "Gender Identity and Country Music Merge in *Transamerica*," *CMT News* (March 3, 2006), http://www.cmt.com/news/1525363/gender-identity-and-country-music-merge-in-transamerica/.

45. The traditional hymn "I Am a Pilgrim" was likely on Dolly's mind as well.

46. Dolly Parton, *Larry King Live*, "Larry Discusses Transgender Individuals," aired February 15, 2006, on CNN, http://transcripts.cnn.com/TRANSCRIPTS/0602/15/lkl.01.html.

47. Parton quoted in Gandee, "Good Golly, Miss Dolly," 167.

48. Parton quoted in Cooper, "Parton's Plea for Tolerance."

49. *Larry King Live.*

50. Dolly Parton, *Dolly Parton's Heartstrings*, episode 2, "Two Doors Down," aired November 22, 2019, on Netflix.

51. Leslie Jordan, interview, *Hollywood to Dollywood*, DVD, directed by John Lavin (Philadelphia, Penn.: Breaking Glass Pictures, 2012). For more on Dolly and camp, see Morris, "Crossing Over with Dolly Parton."

52. Parton quoted in Cooper, "Parton's Plea for Tolerance." See also http://dollyparton.com/life-and-career/music/travelin-thru-transamerica-soundtrack/258.

53. Parton, "Dolly Parton: 'Never Old,'" CBC Radio show q.

54. Parton quoted in Di Nunzio, "Dolly Parton Is Lovin' the 'Simple' Life."

55. Ben Kaplan, "Dolly Parton Still Working 9 to 5 at 65," *National Post* (July 4, 2011), https://nationalpost.com/arts/dolly-parton-still-working-nine-to-five-at-65.

56. Dolly Parton quoted in Craig Wilson, "Dolly Parton Continues to Dream Her Dream," *USA Today* (November 27, 2012), http://www.usatoday.com/story/life/books/2012/11/26/dolly-parton-dream-more/1627505/.

57. Jac Chebatoris, "Dolly Parton: Back in the Saddle," *Newsweek* (February 23, 2008), http://www.newsweek.com/dolly-parton-back-saddle-93805?from=rss.

58. Parton quoted in Hurt, "Dolly Parton."

59. Dolly Parton quoted in Nancy Dunham, "Dolly Parton Has 'Better Day' Planned for June 28," *The Boot* (May 23, 2011), http://theboot.com/dolly-parton-better-day-new-album-2011/?trackback=tsmclip.

60. Dolly Parton quoted in Phil Gallo, "Dolly Parton Talks Worldwide Tour, New Record 'Better Day,'" *Billboard* (July 4, 2011), http://www.billboard.com/articles/news/469393/dolly-parton-talks-worldwide-tour-new-record-better-day.

61. Parton, personal communication.

62. Parton, *Dolly*, 21.

63. Castle, "Dolly Parton: A Total Experience," 14.

64. Wagoner quoted in Soelberg, "An Indepth Look," 13.

65. Parton quoted in Corbin, "Interview: Music City News," in Schmidt, *Dolly on Dolly*, 18.

66. Cook, "Dolly Parton Goes Pop," 30.

67. Parton, *Dolly*, 69.

68. Ibid., 73.

69. Ibid., 77–78.

70. Parton, "Dolly Parton: 'You're Never Old,'" CBC Radio show q.

71. Audre Lorde (1982) in *Conversations with Audre Lorde*, ed. Joan Wylie Hall (Jackson: University Press of Mississippi, 2004), 99. Reprinted from: "Audre Lorde," *Black Women Writers at Work*, Claudia Tate, ed. (New York: Continuum, 1983), 100–116.

72. Audre Lorde, "Uses of the Erotic: The Erotic as Power," *Sister Outsider: Essays and Speeches* (Freedom, Calif.: Crossing Press, 1984), 54.

73. Ibid., 57.

74. Parton, *Dolly*, 78.

75. Judith O. Becker, *Deep Listeners: Music, Emotion, and Trancing* (Bloomington: Indiana University Press 2004), 61, 79.

76. Parton, *Dolly*, 73.

77. The well-known writings of St. Teresa of Avila remind us that often the ecstasy of divine experiences can be sensual and sexual.

78. Parton quoted in Grobel, "A Candid Conversation," 106. Ellipses in original.

79. Howard Dorgan, *Giving Glory to God in Appalachia: Worship Practices of Six Baptist Subdenominations* (Knoxville: University of Tennessee Press, 1987), 59, 58.

80. Lorde, "Uses of the Erotic," 56.

81. Becker, *Deep Listeners*, 94.

82. Lorde, "Uses of the Erotic," 56.

83. Deborah Vansau McCauley, *Appalachian Mountain Religion: A History* (Urbana: University of Illinois Press, 1995), 218.

84. Dolly Parton, *Barbara Walters Special*, aired December 6, 1977, on ABC, https://www.youtube.com/watch?v=3Vj3Bb9aCvA.

85. Parton, *Dream More*, 93.

86. Michael Joseph Gross, *Starstruck: When a Fan Gets Close to Fame* (New York: Bloomsbury, 2005), 107.

87. Morales, *Pilgrimage to Dollywood*, 42.

88. "Dolly Makes a Guest Appearance on 'Designing Women,'" (January 1, 1990, updated August 23, 2015), https://dollyparton.com/life-and-career/movies-television/designing-women/1038. *Christmas on the Square* is reported to be released on Netflix at the end of 2020.

89. For a photograph of a similar dress also designed for this song, see Parton, *Dolly*, facing page 83.

90. Roger Ebert, "Dolly Parton: Gee, She's Really Nice," *Roger Ebert Interviews* (December 7, 1980), http://www.rogerebert.com/interviews/dolly-parton-gee-shes-really -nice.

91. Hal Crowther, *Gather at the River: Notes from the Post-Millennial South* (Baton Rouge: Louisiana State University Press, 2005), 63.

92. Beth Grant, interview, *Hollywood to Dollywood*.

93. Manouschka Guerrier, interview, *Hollywood to Dollywood*.

94. Tai Uhlmann, *For the Love of Dolly* (San Jose, Calif.: Wolfe Video, 2006). Patric Parkey and Shelagh Ratner, interviews, *For the Love of Dolly*, DVD, directed by Tai Uhlmann (San Jose, Calif.: Wolfe Video, 2008).

95. Uhlmann quoted in Gross, *Starstruck*, 104.

96. Parton quoted in Miller, "Dolly Parton Relives a Piece of Her Life."

97. Uhlmann quoted in Gross, *Starstruck*, 104.

98. Manuela Welloffman, "Andy Warhol's 85th Birthday Anniversary" (August 11, 2013), http://crystalbridges.org/blog/andy-warhols-85th-birthday-anniversary/.

99. Parton quoted in Gross, *Starstruck*, 112.

100. Dolly Parton, *Larry King Live*, "Interview with Dolly Parton," aired November 23, 2010 on CNN, http://transcripts.cnn.com/TRANSCRIPTS/1011/23/lkl.01.html.

101. Parton quoted in Gross, *Starstruck*, 107.

102. Ibid., 107–108.

103. Ibid., 113.

104. Frank Dycus quoted in Mike Kosser, *Hot Country Women* (New York: Avon Books, 1994), 54.

105. Flippo, "What Would You Get?" 33, 37.

106. Marty Stuart, liner notes, *Dolly Parton: Slow Dancing with the Moon* (Columbia: C.K. 53199, 1993), 14.

107. Parton quoted in Brianne Tracy, "Dolly Parton on Why She Started Making Christian Music: 'We Need to Believe in Something Bigger,'" *People* (November 22, 2019), https://people.com/country/dolly-parton-making-christian-music/.

108. Morales, *Pilgrimage to Dollywood*, 42–43.

109. Jasmyn Payne, interview, *Hollywood to Dollywood*.

110. Parton, *Shine On with Reese*.

111. Morales, *Pilgrimage to Dollywood*, 43.

112. Parton quoted in Tracy. "God Only Knows" with for King and Country; "There Was Jesus" with Zach Williams; "Faith" with Galantis.

113. Caitlin White, "Dolly Parton's Sex-Positive Gospel Will Make You a Believer," *Uproxx* (October 4, 2016), http://uproxx.com/music/dolly-parton-hollywood-bowl -show-review/.

114. Ibid.

115. As I was completing work on this book, Dolly was featured prominently in the media as a figure who bridges the stark divides in the United States: John Jurgensen, "Not Imagining It: Mister Rogers and Dolly Parton Are Everywhere: In These Polarized Times, a Quest to Find a New American Folk Hero," *Wall Street*

Journal (November 20, 2019), https://www.wsj.com/articles/youre-not-imagining -it-mister-rogers-and-dolly-parton-are-everywhere-11574271282; Lindsay Zoladz, "Is There Anything We Can All Agree On? Yes: Dolly Parton," *New York Times* (November 21, 2019), https://www.nytimes.com/2019/11/21/arts/music/dolly-parton.html. These articles were responding to the WNYC podcast "Dolly Parton's America," hosted by Radiolab's Jad Abumrad, that posited Dolly as a figure that everyone across the political landscape can admire, https://www.npr.org/podcasts/765024913/ dolly-parton-s-america.

Moreover, as this book was going to press, many turned to Dolly for inspiration during the COVID-19 pandemic. She offered these thoughts on her Facebook, Twitter, and Instagram accounts: "This virus has scared the H E double L out of us. I'm not making light of the situation. Well maybe I am, 'cause it's the light I believe that's going to dissolve the situation. I think God is in this, I really do. I think He's trying to hold us up to the light so we can see ourselves and see each other through the eyes of love. And I hope we learn that lesson. I think that when this passes we're going to all be better people." Dolly Parton, "Keep the Faith," https://twitter.com/i/ status/1243614161692745728, https://www.facebook.com/DollyParton, https://www .instagram.com/p/B-P4gsRIEKP/, March 27, 2020.

Chapter 9. Final Thoughts

1. Parton, personal communication.
2. Parton quoted in DeMain, "Dolly Parton: River Deep, Mountain Soul," 79.
3. *Dolly Parton: Here I Am*, directed and produced by Francis Whately, aired December 25, 2019, on BBC2. The U.S. version, titled *Biography: Dolly*, aired April 12, 2020, on A&E. It was also available on Netflix.
4. Parton quoted in DeMain, "Dolly Parton: River Deep, Mountain Soul," 79.
5. Buckingham, personal communication.
6. Parton in *Dolly Parton: Platinum Blonde*.
7. Berman, *The Official Dolly Parton Scrapbook*, 25.

Appendix A

1. This streamed album contains songs about the twenty-seven amendments to the U.S. Constitution, each written by different artists. Jad Abumrad, host, Radiolab & More Perfect (New York Public Radio, 2018).
2. This is a traditional song that Dolly added a few original lyrics to.
3. This recording, made during the *Jolene* sessions, remained unreleased until it was included as a bonus track on the 2007 CD rerelease of *Jolene*.
4. This song was not released on all versions of this recording. It appears only on the special Cracker Barrel version.
5. Dolly first recorded this song for Monument Records in 1965, though that solo version was not released at that time. Her recording was later released as a duet with Willie Nelson (*The Winning Hand*, 1982), in which Dolly's original version was over-

dubbed with Nelson's harmony. The two later sang the song together on a television special in 1983. Dolly's original solo version of the song was later released in Europe on the compilation album *Everything's Beautiful*, 1988.

6. Dolly had also recorded a second solo version of this song in 1969, but that was not released until 2009 with the 4-CD boxed set *Dolly* (RCA/Nashville Legacy: 88697 48086 2).

7. The song is also on *9 to 5: The Musical (Original Cast Recording)*, 2009.

8. Dolly wrote this song when she was around eleven, cowritten with her Aunt Dorothy Jo and Uncle Bill. It was released as the B side to her single "Puppy Love" on Goldband Records.

9. Dolly recorded the song in 1965 for Monument Records, but it was not released on an album at that time.

10. Dolly previously recorded the song in 1963 on *Hits Made Famous by Country Queens*.

11. This song is unreleased.

12. This song is unreleased.

13. Dolly added a few original lyrics to this song written by Jimmie Rodgers and George Vaughan.

14. The song was rerecorded on *The Complete Trio Collection*, 2016.

15. Dolly wrote this song when she was eleven, cowritten with her Uncle Bill. It was released as a single on Goldband Records.

16. This song is also on *9 to 5: The Musical (Original Cast Recording)*, 2009.

17. Dolly wrote this unreleased song for the 2016 show at Dolly Parton's Lumberjack Adventure Dinner & Show venue in Pigeon Forge, Tennessee.

18. The 2011 version has a new melody, though with the same lyrics of the 1974 recording.

19. This version was originally recorded in 1972, but it was not released.

Appendix C

1. The Aeolian mode is also called *natural minor*. Minor keys that are not modal have a raised 7th scale degree, creating the same goal-oriented leading tone heard in major keys. For a fleeting moment, the Dorian mode is also suggested in "Jolene." One of the harmony lines includes the raised 6th scale degree, along with the flatted 7th, which is characteristic of the Dorian mode. But in most places, that harmony line remains on the lowered 6th scale degree, so I hear "Jolene" as primarily Aeolian rather than Dorian.

2. By sonority I mean that the harmony at that point is built on the flatted 7th scale degree; the melody may or may not highlight this pitch prominently.

3. The word *Scarborough* is also harmonized with a flatted 7th sonority, but the melody notes do not use the 7th scale degree at this point.

4. Parton, personal communication.

5. David Holt quoted in Ritchie and Orr, *Wayfaring Strangers*, 208.

6. Dwight Diller, personal conversation with author, July 1999.

Appendix D

1. Parton, personal communication.
2. The melodic outline of "Wayfaring Stranger" is very similar to the traditional song "My Dear Companion," which omits the contrasting B section.
3. Parton, *Live from London*.
4. Ibid.
5. Parton, personal communication.

Further Reading

Cardwell, Nancy. *The Words and Music of Dolly Parton: Getting to Know Country's "Iron Butterfly."* Santa Barbara, Calif.: Praeger, 2011.

DeMain, Bill. "Dolly Parton." In *Behind the Muse: Pop and Rock's Greatest Songwriters Talk about Their Work and Inspiration.* Cranberry Township, Penn.: Tiny Ripple Books, 2001, 129–140.

————. "Dolly Parton." In *In Their Own Words: Songwriters Talk about the Creative Process.* Westport, Conn.: Praeger, 2004, 29–38.

Edwards, Leigh H. *Dolly Parton, Gender, and Country Music.* Bloomington: Indiana University Press, 2018.

Eng, Steve. *A Satisfied Mind: The Country Music Life of Porter Wagoner.* Nashville: Rutledge Hill Press, 1992.

Flippo, Chet. "What Would You Get if You Crossed Mae West with Norman Vincent Peale? Dolly Parton." *Rolling Stone* 246 (August 25, 1977): 32–39.

Fox, Pamela. *Natural Acts: Gender, Race, and Rusticity in Country Music.* Ann Arbor, University of Michigan Press, 2009, 138–142.

Grobel, Lawrence. "Dolly Parton: A Candid Conversation with the Curvaceous Queen of Country Music." *Playboy* (October, 1978): 82–110. Also in Golson, G. Barry, ed. "Dolly Parton October 1978, Interviewer: Lawrence Grobel." In *The Playboy Interview.* New York: Playboy Press, 1981, 578–606.

Havranek, Carrie. "Dolly Parton." In her *Women Icons of Popular Music: The Rebels, Rockers, and Renegades* 2. Westport, Conn.: Greenwood, 2009, 316–334.

Heidemann, Kate. "Remarkable Women and Ordinary Gals: Performance of Identity in Songs by Loretta Lynn and Dolly Parton." In *Country Boys and Redneck Women: New Essays in Gender and Country Music*, ed. Diane Pecknold and Kristine M. McCusker. Jackson: University Press of Mississippi, 2016, 166–188.

Hoppe, Graham. *Gone Dollywood: Dolly Parton's Mountain Dream.* Athens: Ohio University Press, 2018.

Miller, Stephen. *Smart Blonde.* London: Omnibus Press, 2007.

Morales, Helen. *Pilgrimage to Dollywood: A Country Music Road Trip through Tennessee.* Chicago: University of Chicago Press, 2014.

Morris, Mitchell. "Crossing Over with Dolly Parton." In his *The Persistence of Sentiment: Display and Feeling in Popular Music of the 1970s.* Berkeley: University of California Press, 2013, 173–208.

Nash, Alanna. *Dolly: The Biography,* updated ed., New York: Cooper Square Press, 2002.

Parton, Dolly. *My Life and Other Unfinished Business.* New York: HarperCollins, 1994.

Parton, Dolly, with Robert K. Oermann. *Dolly Parton, Songteller: My Life in Lyrics.* San Francisco: Chronicle Books, 2020.

Parton, Willadeene. *In the Shadow of a Song: The Story of the Parton Family.* New York: Bantam Books, 1985.

Ritchie, Fiona, and Doug Orr. *Wayfaring Strangers: The Musical Voyage from Scotland and Ulster to Appalachia.* Chapel Hill: University of North Carolina Press, 2014.

Schmidt, Randy L., ed. *Dolly on Dolly: Interviews and Encounters with Dolly Parton.* Chicago: Chicago Review Press, 2017.

Smarsh, Sarah. *She Come By It Natural: Dolly Parton and the Women Who Lived Her Songs.* New York: Scribner, 2020.

Watson, Jada. "Region and Identity in Dolly Parton's Songwriting." In *The Cambridge Companion to the Singer-Songwriter.* Cambridge, U.K: Cambridge University Press, 2016, 120–30.

Wilson, Pamela. "Mountains of Contradictions: Gender, Class, and Region in the Star Image of Dolly Parton." In Cecelia Tichi, ed. *Reading Country Music: Steel Guitars, Opry Stars, and Honky-Tonk Bars.* Durham, N.C.: Duke University Press, 1998, 98–120.

General Index

Song and Album Index

LYDIA R. HAMESSLEY is a professor of music at Hamilton College.

Women Composers

Kaija Saariaho *Pirkko Moisala*
Marga Richter *Sharon Mirchandani*
Hildegard of Bingen *Honey Meconi*
Chen Yi *Leta E. Miller and J. Michele Edwards*
Unlikely Angel: The Songs of Dolly Parton *Lydia R. Hamessley*

The University of Illinois Press
is a founding member of the
Association of University Presses.

————————————————————

Composed in 10.25/14 Adobe Caslon Pro
by Lisa Connery
at the University of Illinois Press
Cover designed by Jennifer S. Fisher
Cover illustration: Dolly Parton, song writing, 1960s.
(Courtesy Dolly Parton Enterprises)
Manufactured by Sheridan Books, Inc.

University of Illinois Press
1325 South Oak Street
Champaign, IL 61820-6903
www.press.uillinois.edu